W9-CIR-904

WELLBEING

WELLBEING

A Cultural History of Healthy Living

KLAUS BERGDOLT

TRANSLATED BY JANE DEWHURST

polity

First published in German in 1999 by Verlag C. H. Beck as Leib und Seele.
Eine Kulturgeschichte des gesunden Lebens and
© Verlag C. H. Beck, München 1999

This English translation © Polity Press, 2008

Polity Press
65 Bridge Street
Cambridge CB2 1UR, UK

Polity Press
350 Main Street
Malden, MA 02148, USA

ISBN-13: 978-07456-2913-1
ISBN-13: 978-07456-2914-8 (pb)

Typeset in 10.5 on 12 pt Sabon
by Servis Filmsetting Ltd, Manchester
Printed and bound in Great Britain by MPG Books Ltd, Bodmin, Cornwall

For further information on Polity, visit our website: www.polity.co.uk

The publication of this work was supported by a grant from the
Goethe-Institut.

For Doris

Similarly, the physical life of humanity could and should simply be considered as a whole, traced through all changes over time; its fortunes, the causes that determined them, the results that they produced, the way in which it reached its current state, should be presented adequately – which one could quite appropriately call a history of health.

Christoph Wilhelm Hufeland, 1812

Contents

Introduction

The fear of illness and suffering has dogged mankind since primeval times, and is documented in ancient Egyptian, Babylonian and ancient Persian sources.[1] We have evidence from as early as the second millennium BC of dietetic advice aimed at maintaining or restoring health. To be reminded of the historical dimension of concerns about health is not without appeal, especially now at the beginning of the twenty-first century, when environmental pollution, the risks inherent in technological developments, and the 'return of infectious diseases' are giving rise to the impression that human health and life are endangered today as never before.

The theme of this book is the history of both individual and collective health care. Inevitably, any account of theories and definitions of health, as well as of ways advocated in the past of improving and optimizing it, will not be without its problems. The discourse debate of recent years, which has also become fashionable among historians of medicine, demands that we use terms such as 'healthy' or 'sick' with circumspection,[2] and the often difficult distinction between 'literature and life'[3] assumes particular significance in this context. The definition of what constitutes health appears to be so difficult that many doctors, philosophers and literary scholars who have devoted themselves to the subject prefer to avoid giving one. It is easier to praise its advantages. The Alexandrian doctor Herophilus maintained around 300 BC that 'where it is absent, wisdom cannot flourish, art can find no expression, strength fails, riches are worthless, and astuteness is without consequence',[4] and twenty-two centuries later, to seize on a quotation from our own times, for the doctor and writer Arthur Schnitzler health belonged – alongside life and love – to the 'precious absolutes' of human existence.[5]

Beyond eulogies and invocations such as these, then, the essence of health has seemed hard to grasp. Since, at the latest with the Presocratics, it also became a *philosophical* topic,[6] any definition of it must take into account intellectual, religious and political considerations. It varies according to the cultural and historical context and, as a rule, takes its orientation from images of the ideal. In this, it constitutes something not only scientific and positivist, as present-day medical diagnosis suggests, but also something 'psychological and moral' (Gadamer)[7] with a strongly subjective component to it. In this connection, the concept of the 'silence of the organs' is useful insofar as healthiness – in contrast to sickness – is barely heeded, and even appears 'unobtrusive'.[8] In spite of the broad range of normative values used by patients and doctors, it is basically not measurable but rests on an 'inner appropriateness', in other words on the individual being in tune with himself.[9]

But of course, even the subjective experience of the 'silence of the organs' in no way excludes the possibility of illnesses; one thinks here of certain neuroses, psychoses or the early stages of infectious diseases. But even positivist definitions appear problematic, particularly since they frequently presuppose a transhistorical validity for the term. The writer Christoph Martin Wieland recognized in 1778 quite correctly that, 'as long as a man feels healthy, then he is also right to consider himself healthy'.[10] If, on the other hand, following Rothschuh,[11] one accords the concept 'pathos' a scientific notion of illness, and 'nosos' and 'aegritudo' a clinical and subjective notion respectively, then the 'silence of the organs' corresponds – in contrast to 'aegritudo' – to the subjective feeling of being healthy. In a debate about methods and theory adopted from Anglo-American models, and which increasingly influenced historians of medicine in the 1970s, particular emphasis was placed – throughout all the controversies – on the relativeness of medical terms. In fact, it is beyond dispute that the medical, technical or philosophical definition of health has changed many times. A quite different question, however, is the subjective response which is bound up with this concept. No one would seriously question that for most people – regardless of cultural differences – the idea of perfect health coincides with those notions assembled by Karl Jaspers (1883–1969) of 'life, long life, the ability to procreate, a body in productive order, strength, seldom tiring, lack of pain', a condition in which, 'apart from a feeling of joyous well-being', one is hardly aware of physical limitations.[12] In view of such 'fundamental desires' as these, the thesis proposed by sociologists of health as a 'construct'[13] has only limited application at the *subjective* or *existential* level. Not immediately visible, health manifests itself in the productive capacity of the individual personality as a whole, its visions for the future, its ability to plan and launch a variety of endeavours – a process, of course, clearly influenced by social systems, religion, educational ideals or scientific paradigms. In this, the *subjective* range of expectation – independent of cultural context or historical discourse – was for centuries confined within astonishingly narrow limits.[14] This situation is caught perfectly in Ludwig Börne's comment 'There are a thousand illnesses, but only one health'.[15] The thesis that the word health is nothing but an empty cliché, invested with a different meaning by each different culture, certainly has to be relativized, given Rothschuh's definition of the 'fundamental primary values which are essential for the conduct and maintenance of existence'.[16]

Although health is associated with the norm, it is anything but static. It is rather a fluid balance of uncertain delimitation, and subject to a multiplicity of influences and fluctuations. Like the puppets in Kleist's *Marionettentheater*, the healthy achieve a kind of weightlessness which can never be induced by force. The *steady state* of wellbeing is maintained without any particular effort, something for which the frail, the endangered and the sick strive in vain.[17] This physiological as well as subjective frailty is not only a problem when measuring health, it also makes it difficult to establish the point at which sickness begins.

It is well known that the definition of health of the World Health Organization, which is based on complete physical, mental and social wellbeing, has been frequently criticized. Only a minority of Europeans (one has only to think of the 'socio-cultural conditioning' brought about by degenerative illnesses or addiction) would be healthy by these criteria,[18] quite apart from the fact that it would be assumed that in many Third World countries almost *all* of the population are ill. The dictum of the WHO seems illusory, however, and not only in view of the rapidly escalating growth in the world's population and of mounting economic problems. It is also problematic in that it reflects the misconception (imported from the industrialized Western countries) that man knows only two physical states, either sickness *or* health.

This conception has been undoubtedly encouraged since the nineteenth century by the social legislation introduced in the West.[19] It is unsatisfactory by virtue of the fact that, as already indicated, every individual by nature lurches between, on the one hand, being free from infirmity and, on the other, having at least a subjective experience of it. The majority of cases which fall into this twilight zone – they would include most headaches or menstrual pains as well as insomnia or certain stress reactions – cannot, as both Herophilus and Galen observed, be classified as illnesses, but belong to man's day-to-day experience. Michelangelo's lament about going through life plagued by 'fever, piercing aches, and pains in teeth and eyes' is surely a much more appropriate description of what the average person experienced than the already mentioned 'silence of the organs' which so many longed for. Not until the increased use of means of easing pain and improving the circulation, but also the arrival of the fitness ideal propagated by the media and advertising, did the age-old experience that sickness was 'a necessary symptom of man's brief and care-worn existence', in other words that it was all a part of human experience, begin to fade.

Contrary to the World Health Organization's idealized image, a healthy life ebbs and flows; bad times contain the seed of better ones. The maxim on the theory of sport evolved at an early point in antiquity: 'melius est ad summum quam in summo' already assumes a dietetic significance.[20] For Goethe too, 'the eternal ups and downs of mood and bodily condition' resulted in 'constant new attempts, even impulses on the part of health, in order to achieve the optimum'.[21] The French medical theoretician Georges Canguilhem counts occasional illnesses as part of the 'norm of life' and emphasizes the possibility of intensified experience and hope which are bound up with the endurance of suffering: 'What constitutes health is the possibility to go beyond the norm which defines what is normal at any given moment, to accept breaches of the habitual norm, and in new situations to put new norms in force.'[22] Such abilities are also the prerequisite for that state of 'optimal efficiency required to fulfil those tasks and roles for which an individual has been socialized'. For large sections of industrial society – one needs only to think of the almost obligatory terms 'ability to work under pressure' or 'flexibility', found in job descriptions today – this represents an ethical challenge. In view of the *pressures on health* and the fiction of an easily achievable ideal physical condition, the ancient Western notion that sickness and suffering can also release *positive* forces belongs today very much in the realm of philosophical and misanthropic pedantry.[23]

What follows will attempt to give an introduction to doctrines of health from various centuries, but also to the manifold individual and collective efforts to benefit both body and soul. There will be no attempt to approach historical concepts of sickness systematically by reference to their inverse, that is to say, to abstract 'concepts of health'.[24] Apart from the heavily theoretical bias of such an endeavour, there would be the danger, which is an inevitable consequence of schematization, of overlooking numerous interdependent factors which influenced the quest for the nature of health. The longstanding convention in the history of medicine of according certain epochs dominant 'paradigms' or discourses – the common association of the seventeenth century, for instance, with 'Cartesianism' – cannot, as Schott demonstrated with the example of the eighteenth century, necessarily be sustained.[25] In reality, people in all ages use rational *and* irrational, fashionable *and* unfashionable methods of improving their wellbeing. The fact that society, religion, anthropology, philosophy, science, and the changing trends of school and 'orthodox' medicine have played an important role in this has been demonstrated by, among others, Rothschuh, Schipperges, Wöhrle, Canguilhem and Labisch.[26]

Repeatedly, in all of this, an important role has fallen to *dietetics*, that very diversely treated doctrine of healthy living which has accompanied us in the West at the very latest since Alcmaeon of Croton (*c.* 500 BC), and which is an exhortation to take personal responsibility for one's health.[27] The concern to achieve a vital 'balance' was for centuries the crux of Western 'ars vivendi'. It comes astonishingly close to modern theories of the *normal*, and was as a rule justified with a pointer to nature, which simultaneously controlled it. It is for this reason that the Hippocratic doctors regarded themselves as nature's servants.[28]

The contemporary reader can only wonder at the fact that, since ancient times, good health has been frequently viewed as testament to an orderly life and therefore regarded as a virtue. Goethe argued in this vein, as did Hufeland and Carus.[29] Setting aside the limitations imposed by genetic disposition, this notion of assuming responsibility for one's health could take on a new and unsuspected significance in the twenty-first century. Economic constraints give us once again cause to regret that the art of healthy living has lost its traditional importance, largely as a consequence of a change in the scientific paradigm in European medicine in the middle of the nineteenth century. Health at that time was degraded almost overnight to something of technical dimensions.

For the most diverse reasons publications on dietetics and health doctrine came into fashion at particular times – as in the eighteenth century, for instance. On the other hand, only very few of the ancient treatises on health can have been handed down, which makes generalization appear obsolete. The works of Kudlien for antiquity, Schipperges for the Middle Ages, Rothschuh, Canguilhem or Vigarello for the epochs since the Enlightenment, ease our access to these periods. The nineteenth century can, for reasons of space, be described only in outline, and would require a separate monograph. The literature dealing with the history of psychiatry in the eighteenth and nineteenth centuries has reached boundless proportions, and – not least due to the influence of the Foucauldian school – has become, for the time being, a modish topic for the history of medicine.[30] I hope that those readers who associate health and happiness predominantly with Eastern Asian doctrines will forgive me for the emphasis here on European cultural history – albeit that consideration is given to those ancient advanced civilizations as well as to the Islamic traditions, all of which were such a fruitful source of stimulus to it.

The author owes special thanks to Dr Ernst-Peter Wieckenberg of the C. H. Beck Verlag in Munich, whose encouragement accompanied the writing of this book, and also to Dr Christian Hick of the Institute for the History and Ethics of Medicine at the University of Cologne.

Prologue: The Ancient Advanced Civilizations – Egypt, Mesopotamia, Persia

The traditions of medicine in Egypt, Babylon and ancient Persia became significant for Europe because they influenced *Greek* doctrines of health which continued to have an effect down to modern times. Throughout its 3000-year history aspects of ancient Egyptian culture can be found which point the way ahead. On the Nile, health – as in all ancient advanced civilizations – was considered in the widest sense as a divine gift. Illnesses were interpreted 'ontologically' (Canguilhem): they were viewed as a threat from external forces – worms, for instance, the influence of evil spirits or of acts of magic, or as a punishment from the gods.[1] Life revolved around the river, the changing level of which imposed on people a cyclical image of time which also emphasized the transitory nature of health and life. The Nile, whose gift, according to the celebrated words of Herodotus, was Egypt,[2] was regarded as a vital giver of life.[3] It may well have been the annual existential challenge which prompted the creation of an advanced civilization and with it the conscious concern for physical and spiritual wellbeing.[4]

Egyptian doctors and priests considered the beating heart to be the centre of life. In the Middle Kingdom the image of 'heart-led man' even left its mark on officialdom and the structure of the court.[5] According to the ancient Egyptians, body and state had structural elements in common – a topos which played an important part in the history of European society and medicine into the nineteenth century.[6] The heart was given equal status to the soul (*ka*), but – on the physiological level – was the centre of a vascular system (*metu*) which served to transport mucus, water, blood, urine or excrement. Its harmonious functioning was a guarantee of life and health which, in contrast to age, sickness and death, manifested itself very clearly: 'You are given eyes to see, your two ears to hear what is spoken. Your mouth speaks, your legs run, your arms and shoulders twirl at your pleasure. Your flesh is plump, supple your muscles. You take pleasure in all your bodily parts. You find your body complete in that it is whole and well preserved.'[7]

One sought, through appeals to the gods, to bring about this condition. 'Give me health and a long life and ripe old age', as a prayer from the time of Ramses IV put it.[8] The Egyptian concept of health followed the principle of Ma'at, the 'divine order of life and the world', which embodied justice and security, balance and mean. Sickness, mishap or childlessness were explained as a rule by the loss of this god-granted harmony.

Demons and magicians, by contrast, stood suspected of wishing to inflict harm.[9] Thus it was that charms were legitimate weapons in the battle against disease. 'Yield, you who come as quick as arrows. May the gods who rule in Heliopolis keep you from us' was a characteristic incantation. A demon could also be frightened off by a demonstration of one's healthiness: 'I am of good health . . . How shall I be struck down when I am fit and well?' To impress the spirits, it was common to argue in the name of the gods: 'I am Horus who passed by the sick of Sachmet, Horus, Horus, healthy in spite of Sachmet . . . I shall not die because of you.' Since one was in almost daily contact with health-threatening demons, they were cursed, threatened, warned or invoked 'as if one were dealing with humans'. The gods, of course, were appealed to directly for health: 'Hail to you, Horus . . . I come to you and praise your beauty. Destroy the malady residing in my limbs.' Magical and religious traditions of healing did not, of course, exclude the introduction of 'rational' or causal therapies. With accidents in particular, doctors and healers administered in accordance with the rules of their art, and treated with ointments or drugs.

Despite their arduous working and living conditions, the health prophylaxis of the Egyptians was characterized by a standard of hygiene which drew the admiration of Herodotus (5 BC): 'They drink out of brazen cups, which they scour every day: there is no exception to this practice. They wear linen garments, which they are especially careful to have always fresh washed. They practise circumcision for the sake of cleanliness, considering it better to be cleanly than comely. The priests shave their whole body every other day, that no lice or other impure thing may adhere to them when they are engaged in the service of the gods.'[10] Such measures undoubtedly also served to conserve health. The practice of washing morning and evening, and before every meal, along with the use of ointments to prevent the skin from drying out, bordered on the ritualistic. The diet in Egypt consisted mainly of bread, milk, fish, vegetables and fruit (onions, melons, water melons, garlic, beans, cucumbers, dates, figs and grapes). People cooked, as a rule, with olive oil.[11] Children normally ran around without clothes; women who worked, or were servants or dancers, wore a loin cloth, or, like the men, a belt.[12] At night people protected themselves against the danger of insect bites with nets which, during the day, were used for fishing.[13]

The principal health-giving gods were Thoth, who had taught the art of healing, and Isis, in whose name the sick were treated by sleep cures and suggestion, but above all Imhotep, the legendary physician and architect at the court of King Zoser (c. 2600 BC), who was deified as the son of Ptah.[14] His cult as a healing god did not begin, however, until around 600 BC in Saqqara, where he was soon regarded as the equal of Aesculapius. In contrast to the other healing gods such as Horus, the doctor and magician Imhotep is a historical figure. In the *Hermetica* (attributed in late classical antiquity to Thoth, later known as Hermes Trismegistus) he was described as a doctor god.[15] In a papyrus preserved in Berlin every organ is entrusted to a specific divinity. The Church Father Origen (c. AD 185–254) also reports that the Egyptians had divided the body into thirty-six parts and dedicated each of them to the care of a specific god.[16]

Notwithstanding the exertion of any divine influence, health in Egypt remained a very pragmatic concept. Concretely it meant 'being able to eat, drink, and have sexual intercourse', or 'to eat with the mouth, and evacuate with the rear'.[17] For the faithful it culminated in 'the houses of eternity', where the dream of an existence free of pain promised to become reality.[18] The precepts of *Ma'at*, whose rhythms were present in Egyptian tombs in the representation of the daily course of the stars, and who was the divine incarnation of what was righteous, healthy and beautiful, was symbolized by the Pharaoh, who, as the 'renewer and increaser of births, nourisher of families, saviour of the infirm, rejuvenator of the aged, educator of the children, and liberator from pain', also became the guardian of health.[19]

In the cultural history of Mesopotamia, too, health and sickness were inseparably bound up with religion and magic.[20] In comparison to the Egyptians, however, the inhabitants of the land between the Tigris and the Euphrates took a rather more gloomy view of the afterlife, so that worries about health were accentuated by anxiety about death.[21] As on the Nile, attempts were made, by prayer or magical invocations, to influence the decisions of the gods, or the actions of demons.[22] No one was in any doubt that health and a long life were predestined by higher forces, with the king – at least in the Babylon of Hammurabi (*c*. 1700 BC) – considered to be the earthly representative of the health-bearing gods of healing: 'The great gods, they have called me. I am the redeeming shepherd whose staff is straight.' In response to Gilgamesh's despairing question about the path to immortality, Uta-napishti, the king of Shuruppak, declared that the gods 'draw the image of death . . . they have allotted death or life, but the day of death they do not disclose.' Thus the deadly god of plague was held to be Nergal, 'whose face was beautiful, whose mouth was feverishly hot, a raging fire'; he was the 'dragon who consumes the blood of living creatures'.[23]

In the face of dubious expectations of the life beyond, the dream of physical and mental wellbeing was pragmatic and firmly anchored in the here and now. 'May Shamash and Marduk grant you good health' was a popular greeting at the time of Hammurabi, and from Assyria has been preserved the stereotypical formulation of the royal letter writers: 'Ninib and Guyla shall confer happiness and health upon the king, my lord'. The résumé of an old man recorded on a late Babylonian cuneiform tablet would have been the wishful dream of many who lived on the Euphrates and Tigris around 1000 BC: 'The Moon God granted me many extra happy days and years and kept me alive to the age of one hundred and four. My sight was good until the end, my hearing excellent, my hands and feet were healthy, my speech coherent. I ate and drank what was beneficial, my health was good and my senses contented. In the fullness of health, I saw four generations of grandchildren and rejoiced in the enjoyment of my great age.'

If one honoured the gods as well as the ancestral spirits, if one respected taboos, amulets and incantations, then one could be relatively sure of the sympathy of the immortals, and of being protected from demons.[24] However, one had to exercise great caution in everyday life. Demons and the spirits of the dead, which lurked in ruins or behind trees, in meadows and at forks in the road, in lofts or behind rocks, could damage health in all manner of ways. It was not always a matter of crime and punishment – for instance, violation of a ritual. Even the decent and pious could fall ill and die prematurely. 'I thought only of prayer and pleading. Pleading and sacrifice ruled my life. The day for honouring the gods was the joy of my heart, the day of the discipleship of the goddess my riches and happiness', a patient lamented. 'There was searing pain, my illness grew worse. They broke and wrenched apart my neck, they laid low like a reed my lofty frame . . ., the house became my prison.' One might suspect that doubts were being nourished about divine justice from the following complaint from the Assyrian king Assurbanipal (seventh century): 'I have reintroduced the regulations which were no longer observed for offering sacrifices to the deceased and sacrifices by drowning to the spirits of the kings, my ancestors. I have done good to God and men, the dead and the living. Why have I been plagued with sickness, misery, and misfortune? I cannot contend with the discord in my land and the disputes within my family. I am beset on all sides by distressing scandals. I am brought down by afflictions of the spirit and the flesh. I spend my final days in lamentation.'

For the Babylonians the state of health also always had a metaphysical component to it. In a 'handbook of prognosis and diagnosis' which was compiled from older sources towards the end of the second millennium at the court of King Adad-apla-idinna, the unity of magic and empirical and rational concepts of healing is demonstrated particularly clearly.[25] Remarkable events, encounters with strange animals, meteorological phenomena or astrological conditions were used as much by the doctor in making his diagnosis as were lists giving head-to-toe symptoms of illness. The epileptic had been robbed of his health by the *utukku*-demon, puerperal fever was held to be the work of the female demon *Latastu*.[26] The misdeeds of spirits such as these are described on many cuneiform tablets which have been preserved. Sorcery, magic potions, the evil eye or secret incantations could also lead to loss of health, without the victim being able to fathom the causes. An important apotropaic role was ascribed to prophecy in this, above all to astronomy and hepatoscopy, which were characteristic of Babylonian culture.[27]

Great value was attached to traditional hygiene regulations. Anyone who touched a sick person became unclean and thereby exposed himself to evil spirits. An expiation ritual to restore health was necessary. The concept of contagion was initially to be understood as being 'purely spiritual and in no way medical'. Dangers could be conjured up merely 'by a glance at impure hands'. In the last millennium before Christ the loss of good health was also increasingly regarded as proof of a sinful life. As a consequence of perjury, adultery, a ritual or social misdemeanour, the sick person seemed to have lost the protection of the gods, whereupon society not infrequently reacted with reproaches and isolation.[28]

In Mesopotamia, the loss of health already had bureaucratic consequences. A patient by the name of Iratti was reported to King Asarhaddon by a fellow official as being sick: 'since he had not presented himself, it was necessary that the king be informed that he was suffering. Would the king, my lord, therefore not rebuke us on his account.'[29] As in all early advanced civilizations, it was important for hierarchical and cultic reasons to pay attention to health.

Finally, the Western tradition of health was also influenced by the history of religion and medicine in ancient Persia. The sixth book of the original version of the *Avesta* ('knowledge') which, according to Zarathustra (before 500 BC), was considered to be the revelation of the highest deity Ahura Mazda, deals in thirty-five chapters with illnesses, but also with ways of curing them. According to Mazdaistic lore, the history of humanity, wars and plagues reflected, as did illnesses and accidents, the constant battle between good and evil, between the god of life and light Ahura Mazda (or Ormuzd), 'who created happiness for mankind', and his adversary, the spirit of evil Ahriman, or Angra Mainyu.[30] In this confrontation, man was a plaything called upon to fight with Ahura Mazda against evil and demons by endeavouring, in keeping with the ethical law (*Asha*) handed down from Zarathustra, to make the correct moral decisions.[31] As in Egypt and Mesopotamia, health was closely bound up with religious concepts.

Ahura Mazda was considered a powerful, if not *all*-powerful, healing god, who, when requested to do so by the sick, sent out his angels, especially *Sraosha*, the helper in need, to assist them. The intoxicating juice *Haoma* used in libations induced a state of orgiastic arousal in the believer which brought him into contact with Ahura Mazda and eased both physical and mental pain.[32] It went without saying that, on the basis of demonistic nosology, body and soul, according to Mazdaistic thinking, could only be healed in tandem. In this, Ahura Mazda represented the principle of order (not only in relation to health matters), which was in competition with the pathogenous chaos of Ahriman. Perpetually embattled with traditional vices and habits, Mazdaism assumes a development for the good, at the end of which evil and sickness are conquered, with the fourth book of the present *Avesta* ('the law on evil spirits') showing the way.[33]

Logically, the status of physician in ancient Persia was, as in Babylon, closely connected to that of a priest.[34] Health and recovery rested on a positive mental state, as demanded by Zarathustra's moral law.[35] The goal of therapy was 'to win over every individual to health by securing a sound bodily constitution and the Asha-centredness of the soul.'[36] Since dirt also symbolized the ugly, the evil and the sick, purification and washing became an important component of ancient Persian dietetics. Pregnancy, birth, sexuality, excretion, breastfeeding, religious ceremonies, and so on were subject to rules whose observance preserved spiritual and physical wellbeing and fended off every form of misfortune.[37] Zoroastrian 'corpse repositories', the 'breeding grounds for all manner of evil', which were situated on mountains and towers, and where the dead were left rotting for the vultures, were regarded as threats to health. Here the danger of 'illnesses such as scabies and fever . . ., shivering fits, sleeping sickness, and infirmity' threatened. In ancient Iranian health lore can be detected for the first time the concept of a health-giving 'force for life or perception'. It could be strengthened by outstanding moral behaviour, that is, a life lived in accord with religious precepts. Insufficient attentiveness or breaches of ritual regulations, on the other hand, could give the demons of sickness an opportunity to enter the body.

Belief in demons, animistic tendencies, and the concept of sickness and health as either divine punishment or reward, along with the first manifestations of vitalism, characterize the early advanced civilizations of antiquity and accompany the history of doctrines of health up to our own time.

1

Greece

The ideal of health in ancient Greece

In the pre-classical period in Greece, too, concepts of health and sickness were closely bound up with religious traditions. It is significant that the Greek language has no word to describe health in a purely 'clinical' sense. Seers, bards and healers were often thought to have magic, sacerdotal powers; Empedocles considered doctors to be 'elevated even to the status of gods'. Health, healing and religious faith were regarded as one and the same; the condition of man was – as in Egypt and Babylon – determined by the will of the gods or of daemons.[1] Given that Homer himself describes surgeons acting in an entirely 'rational' manner, and that recent scholarship has at least relativized the notion of the 'priest-doctor',[2] it can be assumed that, even in ancient Hellas, the idea of illness as a punishment and of health as a gift from the gods did not preclude 'enlightened' forms of therapy. Nevertheless, Greek medicine claimed to be of divine origin: Apollo had, since time immemorial, been regarded as a redeeming god, as had Aesculapius, whose cult admittedly did not gain ground until the sixth century, when it replaced that of Apollo Kyparissios on Kos.[3] Aesculapius' teacher, the centaur Chiron, was, as his name suggests, considered a master surgeon. In certain lines of the *Iliupersis* (seventh century), which is attributed to the epic writer Arktinos, the Homeric doctors Machaon and Podalirius appear as the sons of Poseidon, who instructed them in the art of medicine,[4] and, although Hygieia was personified and worshipped as a goddess only from the fifth century onwards, she was very much in the tradition of the older divinities.[5] The Panhellenic Games were also accompanied by prayers and sacrifices. Health, bodily 'form' and victory were regarded in Olympia as gifts from Zeus.[6]

As in Mesopotamia and Persia, the view that illnesses were predetermined by the gods tended to stigmatize the loss of health and beauty.[7] Recovery was generally sought through prayer, but also by means of magical practices.[8] There was an astonishingly diverse range of healing professions: in the sixth and fifth centuries, in addition to philosopher doctors – Alcmaeon of Croton's dietetics comes to mind here – there were also healers who used magical practices, practical public physicians,[9] and seemingly sectarian faith healers such as the Aescleiads or the 'Iatromant' invoked by Aeschylus, for whom medical and religious wisdom were inseparable.[10] When Heraclitus (approximately 500 BC) attacks the 'disreputable' doctors, their painful treatments and their greed for money, he gives some indication of the extent to which, in his day, practical curative methods had already fallen into disrepute.[11]

The fact that no definition of health is found in early texts should not surprise us. As in the Egyptian and Babylonian cultures, the nature of health tends to be articulated in descriptions, wishes and accounts of subjective experiences. An example occurs in Solon's account of a man's journey through life (approximately 500 BC):

> When, in his seventh year, the boy loses his milk teeth, he is still completely immature, has scant command of language. But when God has completed a further seven years, one can already see that he is maturing into youth. In his third septennium he begins to sprout a beard, his blossoming skin begins to darken, and his body tautens with new strength. His manly strength develops especially in the fourth span of seven years. Now he performs great deeds. In the fifth septennium he seeks to marry to ensure the flourishing continuation of his lineage. In the sixth, his disposition matures and hardens; henceforth he has no truck with trivial affairs. For fourteen years, in the seventh and eighth septennia, his tongue and mind flourish and reach their peak. This lingers on into the ninth, but then at the height of his manly power and courage his wisdom and speech begin to fail. Whomever God then permits to reach the end of his tenth septennium is granted a timely and appropriate death.

The healthy Greek is characterized by norm, mean, temperance, social integration in family and state, progeny, contentedness, normal bodily functions and the greatest possible mental alertness. However, the idea of eternal freedom from illness or pain was already considered an illusion in Homer's age.[12] Hesiod consigned this state to the Golden Age, in which men lived 'like gods without sorrow of heart, remote and free from toil and grief'.[13]

The philosophical and pedagogical principle of *kalokagathia* is present from an early stage. This precept, which was to prove so influential in Greek intellectual history, holds that beauty is a prerequisite of health and that mental and moral superiority are manifested in physical perfection. In accordance with this principle, aristocratic education strove for the optimal maturation of body and soul. Solon's educational maxim of 'the mind of a sage in the body of an athlete' harkened back to earlier traditions. Greek intellectuals considered sport and mental activity to be equally important insofar as they *jointly* contributed to the moulding of the personality. It is significant that the verb *hygieinein* is used as late as the fifth century to refer to both physical *and* mental health!

This promotion of the ideal of the flawless human being is problematic, however, and not only from a modern perspective. As early as Homer, we see the heroes ridiculing dwarves and deformed people.[14] The equation of physical perfection and moral rectitude, although already disputed in antiquity,[15] frequently led to the ostracism of the ugly and sick; according to the testimony of Aelian, such individuals were even punished in Sparta on account of their physical shortcomings.[16] Taken to its logical conclusion, this aristocratic ideal of health could even be used in support of euthanasia. In the *Politeia*, Plato advocates that the incurably sick should receive no further treatment, and even that they should be killed.[17] According to Plutarch, this was the course of treatment administered by the town elders in ancient Sparta to weak or sickly new-born babies: 'They sent it to the so-called Apothetae, a chasm-like place at the foot of Mount Taÿgetus, in the conviction that the life of that which nature had not well equipped at the very beginning for health and strength, was of no advantage either to itself or the state.'[18] In the Hippocratic tract *The Sacred Disease*, whose author mounts an attack on demonological explanations for illnesses and magical therapeutic methods, we read that epileptics frequently withdrew from society because they were ashamed, and 'immediately hide their heads' in the company of others. For Empedocles, state of mind changed according to physical constitution. Conducted in accordance with this aesthetically determined doctrine of health and beauty, the care and inurement of the body promoted an aristocratic and no doubt idealized conception of the human being – particularly in Sparta, where it was hoped that the promotion of health by avoiding luxury and debauchery, as well as strict upbringing, would foster a society of warriors. Similar rules, such as simple food and regular physical activity, were propagated by numerous orators and pedagogues.

Even Thassilo von Scheffer considered Hippocratic medicine to be primarily an art aimed at 'restoring beauty'.[19] At the heart of the *kalokagathia* ideal lay the Greek maxim that maintaining *moderation* in all realms of life was the golden rule for mental and physical health.

The extent to which Greek sculpture with its ideal proportions, the harmony of Greek temples, the structure of the *polis* and the rules of the athletic *agon* mirrored this beneficial regime has, incidentally, long been a matter of contention.[20] In the middle of the fifth century, Polykleitos set down the ideal proportions of the body in his *Canon*, no doubt taking his cue from the model of health that was the permanent goal of *mímesis*.[21] The philosophy of moderation (*medén ágan*), propagated as early as Solon, influenced not only the protean ideal of health, but also the entire cultural history of the Greeks. It is worthy of note that the macrocosm of the *polis* had from an early stage been compared with the microcosm of the body, thus continuing the principle of *analogy* attested in Egyptian culture and defended by numerous Presocratic thinkers.[22]

The Olympic and Isthmic games, like the famous public games (*agones*) mentioned above, also served to promote physical and mental health.[23] The social esteem accorded to the victors also testified to the high premium placed on *physical*, 'external' perfection, which was traditionally regarded as evidence of internal equilibrium. This was the rationale behind the games, behind Greek gymnastics, and indeed behind the entire Greek enthusiasm for sport. Even in the 'heroic' age referred to by numerous later philosophers and doctors, physical exercise, bathing and anointing, for example after returning from battle, were indispensable rituals for restoring the lost harmony that was vital for the preservation of health.

In the works of Herodotus (fifth century), however, we see an early tendency towards the *dualism* which was to influence philosophy, theology and medicine – that is, towards the abandonment of the view that body and soul always fall ill or recover in tandem. The historian from Halikarnassos considers it 'not unlikely' that the mind can be affected by physical illness; however, mind and body are no longer presented as necessarily and inevitably linked.[24] The classical ideal of beauty continued to thrive in art and to fascinate aristocratic circles; however, it lost its therapeutic application. In *Eumenides*, the dramatist Aeschylus (525–456) talks of an independent 'health of the mind'; the Attic orator Isocrates (436–338) even refers antithetically to the 'health both of body and of soul'.[25] Plato's famous *soma-sema* formula, in particular, articulated a strict opposition.[26] The soul is not only superior to the body where dignity and health are concerned, it is also the prisoner of the body. If the fragmentary attestations from a later period are to be believed, the Pythagoreans held similar views. However, one of their most important exponents, Philolaos of Croton, describes health as 'love between the soul and the body', thus toning down the antithetical model.[27] Similarly contradictory arguments are put forward by the anonymous author of the Hippocratic treatise *Peri diaítes*, who states that the soul only serves the body when it is awake, and departs from it during sleep.[28]

During the Homeric age, the health of the individual was thought to be threatened by natural and supernatural processes. As mentioned above, plagues were believed to be punishments from the gods or the work of daemons. Apollo, for example, avenges Agamemnon's humiliation of his priest Chryses by striking the Greek camp with plague-infected arrows, while Ajax is stricken with insanity by Athena.[29] In the *Odyssey*, the protagonist is possessed by daemons.[30] Repeatedly, the *gods* inflict and cure illnesses, while magical incantations have the power to speed the process of recovery.[31] According to the Roman author Celsus (first century AD), the doctors in the *Iliad* preferred to treat battle wounds and injuries, accepting 'inner' illnesses as fate, the result of the will of the gods.[32] As the gods intervened persistently in the Trojan War, *all* illnesses, even life and death, as well as the health and emotional disposition of the Greeks and the Trojans, were considered dependent on their decisions. Medical assistance was provided almost incidentally by heroes such as Machaon and Podalirios, and, as pointed out by Kudlien, 'essentially in an empirical and rational way, and, therefore, with predominantly natural means'.[33] Such treatments were, as noted previously, mostly applied to wounds; however, the operations described in Homer also symbolize the restoration of the unity of body and soul, which had been disrupted by injury.[34]

The Homeric conviction that health is dependent on the benevolence of the gods was relativized as early as 700 BC by Hesiod. He describes how pathogenic evils have been afflicting human beings 'of themselves', or independently of the agency of the gods, since Pandora's famous box containing illness and misfortune was opened, even though this was in accordance with Zeus's will and due to the carelessness of the demigod Epimetheus.[35] Thereafter, illnesses are seen as spreading arbitrarily; however, their existence is still interpreted as a punishment for the human race, which had lived untroubled before Pandora's mistake. According to the 'Eunomia' elegy ascribed to Solon, every breach of law and order among the people creates a 'wound', which has damaging consequences for the social organism.[36] When this condition of *eunomía* is restored by means of a painful corrective process, generally in the form of the punishment of the wrongdoer, then individual and collective recovery is likely to follow.

Medicines or surgical interventions apart, from the beginning of the fifth century both doctors and laymen believed increasingly in the healing power of the individual lifestyle. If the afflicted could attain recovery by means of an appropriate diet, however, then it seemed fair to assume that the healthy risked contracting illnesses by adopting the wrong way of living. Such considerations were the starting point for the art of *dietetics*.[37]

The Presocratics

The example of Solon demonstrates the close connection between macrocosm and microcosm in Greek thought. The Ionian natural philosophers and other Presocratics of the sixth and fifth centuries were also of the opinion that cosmos, state and body were subject to one and the same laws. Questions concerning the *arché*, the source of all being, were crucial for politics as well as for health and the meaning of individual life. The injunction 'nothing to excess' alluded to above and attributed to Solon, the dietetic and philosophical character of which was obvious, served many philosophers and doctors as a crucial guideline.

Around 500 BC, Alcmaeon of Croton, a doctor schooled in philosophy, declared that health was nothing more than the equilibrium (*isonomia*) of the elementary 'qualities' of the body.[38] Like the later 'doxographer' or compiler of philosophers' opinions Aetius (AD 100), he taught that 'health is maintained by balancing wet and dry, cold and warm, bitter and sweet, whereas the supremacy (*monarchia*) of any one of them is the cause of disease'. This did not apply only to food. 'Illnesses sometimes have other causes: they are the consequence of the composition of the water or the soil, or of other things such as excessively strenuous activity or torture. Health, however, rests on a balanced mixture of the different qualities.' Thus Alcmaeon was able to develop a plausible theory of health, with the help of which bodily disorders and fluctuations could be explained without recourse to metaphysical arguments. The static and ontological concept of health disorders was confronted with a dynamic one which offered a ready explanation for fluid oscillations between sickness and health.[39] It also described, at an astonishingly early stage, the repercussions of environmental influences and excessive physical exertion for health.

Alcmaeon's theories were by no means unique. According to the (admittedly much later) testimony of Diogenes Laertius (AD 275), the philosopher Empedocles (fifth century) had two rivers close to the town of Selinunt drained, whereupon the number of cases of sicknesses, miscarriages and babies born deformed is said to have decreased considerably, and a plague was reportedly halted in its tracks.[40] Notwithstanding the religious tradition of such acts of purification, changing or improving the environment was considered an efficient means of guaranteeing the health of the population or of stemming the onset of plagues, and therefore became an important part of the duties of those in power. In the *Cyropaedia*, a pedagogic novel by Xenophon about Cyrus the Younger (423–401 BC), Cambyses urges his son to make good health provision. As army commander, the latter continues, he also bears responsibility in this respect for his troops: 'If you are going to stay for some time in the same neighbourhood, you must not neglect to find a sanitary location for your camp; and with proper attention you cannot fail in this.'[41] The great king also reminds his son of the danger to himself: 'It is not enough to have regard to the localities only, but tell me what means you adopt to keep well yourself.' Cyrus answers with an assurance that he does pay careful attention to his health: 'In the first place . . ., I try never to eat too much, for that is oppressive; and in the second place, I work off by exercise what I have eaten, for by so doing health seems more likely to endure and strength to accrue.' In the subsequent sentences, father and son also stress the necessity for physical education.[42] The passage demonstrates that the idea that the state of the environment has an effect on health had, at the time of Xenophon (430–355) – perhaps as a result of Hippocratic influence – long been common knowledge.

Although we should bear in mind that our knowledge about the Presocratics either comes from late sources[43] or has been handed down (by no means in a 'historical' sense) primarily by Plato and Aristotle,[44] the notion of *balance*, as well as of a harmony of body and soul, seems to have had an enduring impact on the Greek concept of health, at least by the fifth century. The problem remains, however, that, although Plato and Aristotle concerned themselves extensively with the Presocratics,[45] the oldest preserved text which draws 'in its entirety' on their thought is by a commentator on Aristotle, Simplicius, who was writing in Athens and Persia in the sixth century AD. On account of this temporal distance, we should be cautious in drawing conclusions about the school.[46]

According to Empedocles (fifth century), who dedicated a considerable portion of his writing to medical topics,[47] the four elements that constitute the cosmos – fire, water, air and earth – also form the basis of human physiology. The function and condition of the various parts of the body are also believed to be subject to the laws of harmony and proportion: 'Every individual is made up of the elements, not in an arbitrary way, but according to a particular relationship and structure.' Thus, he maintained, the fleshy parts of the body were composed 'of an equal mixture of the four elements, but the nerves of a double mixture of fire and earth'.[48] According to the philosophical doctrine of the Acragantian Empedocles, health is the consequence of an optimal distribution of the basic elements, which is determined by Aphrodite, but nonetheless entirely subject to the laws of nature.[49] Balance, harmony and inner peace are held to be the remedy for healing both body and soul, and the anti-dualist conception of the body as a microcosm requires, as with Alcmaeon, that therapy treat the person as a whole.

The concept that, in the final analysis, bodily harmony, health and beauty mirror the perfection and order of the universe has defined our image of the culture of the ancient Greeks up to the present day. It was central to their beliefs to explain bodily disorders in physical and cosmological terms. After Anaximander of Miletus had, as early as the sixth century, described the (invisible) normal condition of the air as the mid-point between condensation and rarefaction, the physician Diogenes of Apollonia, in the later half of the fifth century, also saw the cosmic constituents of the *pneuma* in the soul.[50] The process of undisturbed thought is only possible with the aid of pure and dry air; this is why the capacity for thought of those who are 'befuddled', for example by tiredness or drunkenness, is limited.[51] In the tradition of the Ionian natural philosophers, Diogenes, the doctor from Phrygia, traced all being – and therefore also the human organism – back to one single original source, since 'otherwise things could never mix with one another, or one thing benefit or harm another'.[52] According to Diogenes, the functioning of the body can be jeopardized in two ways: either by qualitative or quantitative changes to the air, or by disruptions (in a mechanical sense) of the vascular system which he regards as their mode of transportation. Holistic and mechanistic concepts complement one another to form an astonishingly differentiated physiology, whose perfection is understood as an expression of the divine order of things.[53]

According to Heraclitus (fifth century), the naturally divergent 'cosmic constituents' of being, that is, fire, water and earth, are forced into a harmonious relationship by the balancing effect of the *logos*.[54] The divergence of these elements as a result of the weakening of the *logos* is the cause of sickness in the body, or of death. Health disorders can be avoided by leading a life committed to the *logos* and to reason. Heraclitus' intellectually coloured dietetics is enhanced by physiological elements. As it is put in a fragment of his writings: 'The experience of sickness makes health pleasant and good; the same applies to hunger and repletion, exhaustion and rest.' The suggestion that upsets to health can have *positive* effects must, given the parallel traditions of *kalogathia*, have been regarded as revolutionary. Basing his assumptions on the concept of fire as the archetypal form of matter, Heraclitus postulates as life force a kind of individual living fire (*calor vitalis*). Just as a spider creeps towards a trapped fly from the centre of its web, 'pained, as it were, by the torn threads', so the soul speeds to the spot 'where the body has suffered injury'.[55] His reference to the dignity of man ('the most beautiful ape is, in comparison with the human race, repulsive') also has dietetic significance, as it urges respect for one's own body and relativizes the dualistic tendencies which are dismissive of it. That the power of the *logos* to prevent illness is by no means a foregone conclusion, particularly in the case of mental disorders, represents a pragmatic insight. As is stated in another fragment: 'Whatever path you take, you can never discover the limits of the soul, so inexhaustible is what it has to tell us.'

According to the atomist philosopher Democritus (fifth century), man's being and thought must be steered towards a positive state (*euthymía*) by means of 'moderation in pleasures and harmony in life', while the passions have to be bridled by means of self-control.[56] The philosopher from Abdera thus postulates personal responsibility for health, something that people all too readily left to the will of the gods. 'They do not know that they have power over it within themselves; by working against it in their lack of moderation, they become traitors to their own health.' For Democritus, mental health and physical health are inseparably linked. Maxims such as: 'A well-ordered inner being means a well-ordered life' or 'exceeding the right measure can turn what is most pleasant into what is most unpleasant' highlight the didactic and philosophical significance of this agnostic and early exponent of atomist theory, for whom – as for so many Presocratics, but in contrast to the majority of Hippocratics – the notion of *direct* therapeutic intervention by the gods was alien. According to Democritus, as a life force the soul is embedded between the atoms of the body. The partial weakening of the soul therefore results in the loss of health or local pains; its complete disappearance results in death.[57]

This is how Democritus propagates his technical and physical model of health. Yet his fellow citizens seem repeatedly to have advocated recourse to philosophy and the search for meaning. He was evidently the first to assign the care of the body to the art of medicine; the health of the soul, on the other hand, he viewed as the responsibility of philosophers.[58] He considered the sound condition of the soul more important than that of the body, however, 'for the excellence of the soul supports the weakness of the body; the strength of the body, however, without the power of intellect, does not improve the condition of the soul.' 'Correct moderation' (here the legacy of Alcmaeon is self-evident) is opposed to the ruinous extreme of want and excess. Mankind cannot hope for assistance from magic, religion or rituals, but only from self-control, philosophical insight and individual endeavour.

Heraclitus' and Democritus' contemporary Parmenides, on the other hand, considered health and beauty to be secured as long as the 'seeds of love' retained the correct composition after the act of reproduction. For the Eleate, fire and light constitute the masculine, formative and active principle, whereas night is associated with the cold, earthly, female principle. The relationship between these qualities determines the condition of the body and results in health or sickness.[59] Here, we see the beginnings of a genetic view of health and the constitution. A decrease in *vital warmth* results in sleep, sickness or accelerated aging; its complete extinguishment results in death.

The Presocratics took a primarily philosophical approach to questions concerning the physical and mental condition. There was a general conviction that man and world were subject to the same laws.[60] 'Just as the soul, which consists of air, holds us together, so breath and air surround the entire universe', as is stated in a rare fragment by Anaximander of Miletus. Gadamer considered Anaximander's *apeiron* to represent a recurrent, circular movement without limit and end, which highlights the temporality to which all life is subject.[61]

According to Pythagorean doctrine, on the other hand, physical and mental wellbeing were dependent on self-discipline and a way of life governed by mathematical regularity. For Pythagoras himself (sixth century), health signified the victory of soul and form over the divergent structures of the body.[62] Eating and drinking, rest and movement, diet and work, thoughts, and even one's choice of spoken words, all served this purpose. With the help of music, the initiates could cultivate an appropriate daily rhythm. The *rules* that are attributed to the master testify to the high value he places on magic. One should not eat any beans that have a ring around them; one should always put on the right shoe first; one should never tolerate a swallow in one's house, or cut one's nails during sacrifice; one should smooth away the imprint on the bedclothes after getting up, eat neither heart nor brain, not beget children with a woman who wears gold, nor look in a mirror in lamplight.[63] Of primary significance, however, is the fact that Pythagoras holds the individual responsible for the control of his passions and therefore for his health. As the Neoplatonist Iamblichus stated in the third century AD: 'He demonstrated that the gods are not to blame for suffering and that all illnesses and bodily pains are the result of excesses.'[64] Iamblichus' contemporary Porphyrios credited Pythagoras with being the first Greek who propagated the doctrine of metempsychosis, which naturally supposed the wellbeing of the body to be secondary to that of the soul.

For the Pythagoreans, mathematics was of crucial importance, not in the modern sense, but as a means of exemplifying physical and mental balance. Admittedly, recent research has proven that the 'Pythagorean way of life' praised by Plato was contested in antiquity.[65] Yet many ancient testimonies confirm that the master followed a particular *diaita*. According to Aristoxenos, a pupil of Aristotle, the latter nourished himself only with bread and honey, 'for those who eat only these at mealtimes always remain free from illnesses'.[66] Diodorus Siculus (first century AD) states that Pythagoras exhorted his followers 'to cultivate the simple life, since extravagance, he maintained, ruins not only the fortunes of men but their bodies as well.' He convinced many 'to live on uncooked vegetables and to drink water, striving their life long to attain true good'.[67]

Terms such as soul, nature, *logos*, *arché* or health assume an important role in the 'Presocratic' literature; however, their interpretation is often rendered difficult by fragmentary transmission.

The Hippocratic corpus

Well into the age of Pericles, most Greeks, whether they were philosophers, doctors or poets, were inclined to approach the question of living correctly and the essence of physical and spiritual health as a philosophical problem which also encompassed religious aspects. For most 'Presocratics', as well as for priests and doctors, the goal of harmony between body and soul took on the character of a kind of ethical imperative. The 'humoral doctrine' was still far from established, but it served, even at this point, as a point of departure for notions of a mechanical (*mixis*) or a chemical (*krasis*) mixture of elements and humours, to which the Hippocratics later ascribed particular qualities.[68] Established concepts such as *moderation*, *symmetry* or *kairós* were integrated into a highly heterogeneous system of health, sickness and therapy, with decisive importance imputed to the healthy way of living. The optimal mixture of humours (*eukrasia*) was opposed to the corresponding concept of *dykrasia*, which led to illness. Terms such as *grow* and *wilt*, or *wax* and *wane*, alluded to natural imagery; others such as *monarchia*, *isonomia*, *krisis* or *harmonia* invoked comparisons with the realms of society or the state. Of particular importance for the doctor fighting for the health of the patient was the concept of *kairós* attested in the first Hippocratic aphorism, which denotes the right moment for action and therapy as determined by the individual circumstances of each case.[69] For the Hippocratic doctor, health cannot be attained in every circumstance and at every point of time, but only at the appropriate individual moment.[70]

The *Corpus Hippocraticum* consists of fifty-two treatises by different authors, the earliest of which was written in 430 BC. The majority had been produced by the time of the death in 322 of Aristotle, who cites numerous treatises. The corpus, which was probably compiled definitively only in the second century BC, was attributed to Hippocrates of Kos (*c.* 460–370), and remained authoritative for almost two millennia. Its central theme is the description of a healthy way of living.[71] The majority of Hippocratics focus not on illness itself, but on the sick individual, a notion that influenced Western medicine into the nineteenth century. Plato alludes to this idea in *Phaedrus*, when, in answer to the question of whether one can understand the nature of the soul 'without taking it as a whole?', Socrates is told: 'If we are to believe Hippocrates the Asclepiad, we can't understand even the body without such a procedure.'[72] If books such as the *Prognostikon* [*Prognostic*] or the *Epidemiai* [*Epidemics*], which were regarded as 'authentic', contain interesting representations of illness, this is because they served primarily to promote understanding of *individual* sickness, in a genuinely Hippocratic sense.[73] Many of the fundamental ideas of the 'Presocratics' were modified by the Hippocratics and applied to medicine. Of all the (highly contradictory) physiological concepts, which are frequently preserved only in fragments, particular importance is attached to the doctrine of the four humours, or *humoral pathology*.[74]

In the tract *De natura hominis* [*Nature of Man*], ascribed to Polybos, the legendary son-in-law of Hippocrates, the idea that physical qualities determine the state of health appears for the first time.[75] Substances which are immanent within the body cause illness 'by heating, by cooling, by drying or wetting one another contrary to nature'.[76] The male sex is characterized by warmth and dryness, the female by coldness and moistness. An optimal mixture of these qualities was believed to guarantee the best possible state of health and could, it was generally believed, be cultivated by means of a particular way of living. Elsewhere in the text, the four 'cardinal humours', which were to define the Western 'humoral doctrine' for thousands of years, are identified: 'The body of man has in itself blood, phlegm, yellow bile and black bile; these make up the nature of his body, and through these he feels pain or enjoys health.'[77] The work also contains the oldest surviving alignment of humours, qualities and seasons:

these conditions of the year are most akin to the nature of blood, spring being moist and warm . . . And in summer blood is still strong, and bile rises in the body and extends until autumn. In autumn blood becomes small in quantity, as autumn is opposed to its nature, while bile prevails in the body during the summer season and during autumn . . . It is black bile which in autumn is greatest and strongest. When winter comes on, bile being chilled becomes small in quantity, and phlegm increases again because of the abundance of rain and the length of the nights.[78]

Hippocratic teachings on health were not, by any means, restricted to the four humours or elements; they encompassed a differentiated system of factors that act upon the human body. As in the case of Solon, the Presocratics and also Plato,[79] body and cosmos are subject to the same rational, inherent rules.

The author of the tract *Peri diaítes* claims to be the first to give a comprehensive and correct account of dietetic matters, although, as he concedes, others before him have written (inadequately) on the subject.[80] In his opinion, the condition of man is determined by the mixture of fire and water, which is influenced by age, sex, climate and the characteristics of the respective region, as well as by baths, unctions, vomiting, sleeping and waking, physical exertion and food and drink. 'For food and exercise, while possessing opposite qualities, yet work together to produce health.' Here he considers it important 'to discern the power of the various exercises'.[81] Seasons, weather conditions or star constellations also influence the state of health. The Hippocratic doctor thus develops an individual dietetic regime which takes all these factors into consideration; with a daily rhythm that is adapted to nature and a specific mental attitude, the patient should be able to defy all illnesses. Last but not least, dreams also give indications as to the correct, health-advancing way of living.[82] The fact that the practical implementation of this regime required a privileged social status and the resulting free time is surprising only from a modern perspective.[83] In the *Peri diaítes hygieines*, it is precisely the wealthy citizen or 'layman' (*idiótes*) who is exhorted to follow his personal regimen.[84] Only those with time and leisure could adapt their daily rhythm to accommodate ideally the required combination of physical exertion, nutrition and rest.

The author places particular emphasis on diet. The effects of individual foods are explained almost entirely with reference to humoral pathology, which results in a tendency to (sometimes rather rigid) systemization.

Wheat is stronger and more nourishing than barley, but both it and its gruel are less laxative . . . Oats, whether eaten or drunk as a decoction, moisten and cool . . . Beans afford an astringent and flatulent nourishment; flatulent because that the passages do not admit the abundant nourishment which is brought, astringent because that it has only a small residue from its nourishment . . . Beef is strong and binding, and hard of digestion, because this animal abounds with a gross thick blood . . . The flesh of asses passes by stool, and that of their foals, still better . . . Honey unmixed warms and dries; mixed with water it moistens, sends to stool those of bilious temperament, but binds those who are phlegmatic.[85]

Elsewhere, the author, entirely consistently with his defence of holistic medicine, criticizes the purported methods used by the neighbouring, older medical schools of Knidos to 'classify' illnesses, which Galen later claimed resulted in their identifying seven types of gall bladder complaint, four types of jaundice, twelve different bladder complaints, and so on.[86] Such a view of illness did not seem reconcilable with the integrated theory of the Hippocratic humoral doctrine. It was the individual, not the illness, that necessitated a dietetic regime. Questions such as whether a patient is fat or thin, 'whether the relationship between the substances is naturally evenly portioned or predetermined in some manner, whether he has a dry or a damp nature',[87] all have an effect on the entire personality.

Gymnastics and sport also play an important part in Hippocratic dietetics, 'because eating alone will not keep a man well; he must also take exercise. . . . For it is the nature of exercise to use up material, but of food and drink to make good deficiencies.' Many doctors therefore saw a real danger to health in the fact that men did not constantly have a doctor or trainer available for consultation.[88]

In addition to an appropriate diet and exercise regime, a mode of conduct *in harmony with nature* was believed to foster healthiness. 'I maintain that he who aspires to treat correctly of human regimen must first acquire knowledge and discernment of the nature of man in general', urged the anonymous author of the treatise *Peri diaítes*.[89] He considered health a synonym for harmony, which was itself thought to mirror the cosmos. A good doctor acts in accordance with the rules of nature and is not, therefore, dependent on 'supernatural' intervention. He uses symptoms to draw conclusions about the nature of the individual, which then reveals to him the cause of the illness.[90] Fever, diarrhoea, catarrh, bleeding from the mouth, nose and womb, abscesses, haemorrhoids and so on are, according to Hippocratic doctrine, nothing more than attempts at 'natural' self-healing, which should be encouraged.[91] As health was considered to be in conformity with the laws of nature, prophylactics, dietetics and therapy were also conducted in accordance with these laws. We learn little about folk belief, whose adherents, 'men, in need of a livelihood, contrive and devise many fictions of all sorts . . . putting the blame, for each form of the affection, upon a particular god.' Nor is much said about 'alternative' medical practices, although we are told a good deal about the duty of physicians to put a stop to such superstitions.[92]

Terms such as *eukrasia*, harmony or symmetry therefore give only an inadequate account of the Hippocratic concept of health. The condition of mankind appeared rather as 'a network of relations, linked together and attached to the environment with a thousand threads'.[93] There was a general conviction that a bad diet, overexertion, injury, an 'unnatural' way of living, an 'excess' or 'lack' in diverse situations could ruin both mind and body.

In the aforementioned tract *The Sacred Disease*, the view that epilepsy, apoplexies and madness have supernatural causes is criticized.[94] The author comments ironically on the 'fears and terrors, delirium, jumpings from the bed and rushings out of doors', often explained as night-time visitations by 'Hecates' or 'the heroes', which were associated in popular belief with pathogenesis.[95] 'My own view is that those who first attributed a sacred character to this malady were like the magicians, purifiers, charlatans and quacks of our own day, men who claim great piety and superior knowledge.'[96] The obscure forms of therapy practised by theurgists and magicians are also attacked: 'He who by purifications and magic can take away such an affection can also by similar means bring it on.' A deity cleanses and absolves, rather than afflicting with illnesses.[97] Hippocrates (the majority of scholars believe the tract to be authentic) thus accuses his opponents of insulting the gods. The use of religious arguments was, in fact, not unusual among the Hippocratic authors. They characteristically expounded a kind of pantheistic world view, whereby nature in its entirety, which determines the fate of man and cosmos, was deified. In the *Prognostikon* the reader is explicitly invited to consider whether particular patterns of diseases might not betray divine intentions.[98]

In the tract *Peri aeron, hydaton, topon* [*Airs, Waters, and Places*], we read:

> on arrival at a town with which he is unfamiliar, a physician should examine its position with respect to the winds and to the risings of the sun. For a northern, a southern, an eastern, and a western aspect has each its own individual property. He must consider with the greatest care both these things and how the natives are off for water, whether they use marshy, soft waters, or such as are hard and come from rocky heights, or brackish and harsh . . . The mode of life also of the inhabitants that is pleasing to them, whether they are heavy drinkers, taking lunch, and inactive, or athletic, industrious, eating much and drinking little.[99]

Such recommendations frequently led to obsessive behaviour. As contemporaries were quick to recognize, even when the dietetic prescriptions were observed religiously, health could prove fragile and uncertain. Failure was not always due to non-compliance with rules, but could, as was observed critically, be the consequence of uncontrollable, *external* influences, for example, professional commitments or a socially disadvantaged status. The Hippocratic doctrine on health only partially took such phenomena into account and was thus unable to provide an adequate answer to such criticisms.[100]

In *Epidimiai* [*Epidemics*], the author describes the state of health of the inhabitants of Thasos over the period of a year and analyses the relation between atmospheric conditions and illness.[101] He also attempts to classify the latter according to the sex, age, profession, etc., of the patient. The anonymous author was probably writing for miracle healers, who travelled from town to town, informed themselves on site about the health risks and then took therapeutic measures. One of his demands is that the physician should 'Declare the past, diagnose the present, foretell the future.'[102] With his thesis that health is also dependent on the environment and on provisions such as waste water facilities or street cleaning which can be 'steered' or controlled by the administration, the author appears as a precursor of modern epidemiologists. His descriptions do indeed represent the oldest preserved documentation of a European 'social medicine'.

The tract *Peri trophes* [*Nutriment*], which was also part of the Hippocratic corpus, was concerned with the correct choice of diet. An important aspect here is the notion of the *dynamis*, a spontaneous force located in the vegetative nervous system, which conserves health, and which was also postulated in a modified form by such philosophers as Heraclitus, Democritus and Aristotle.[103] It was, for example, assumed that the digestion of food (*pepsis*) was assisted by the heat of the body. The author claims that, in the course of this process, the nutriment is turned in the liver into blood, which is then transferred to the remaining organs. Meanwhile, breathing provides for the necessary reduction of the body temperature. It is interesting that the author imitates the style of Heraclitus, presumably in order to give his treatise greater intellectual weight, while partially adopting the latter's hypothesis concerning a vital force.[104]

Notwithstanding legitimate doubts about the unity of the works attributed to him, Hippocrates appears at the end of the fifth century as a historically tangible personality. Plato and Aristotle refer to him on numerous occasions.[105] Although the 'authentic' writings propagate only a 'doctrine of two or three humours' based on phlegm, bile and sometimes blood, with Polybos' *Nature of Man* we see the emergence of a doctrine of *four humours*. The number of humours may well have been increased to include 'black bile' in order to measure up to Empedocles' celebrated doctrine of the four elements.[106]

The individualizing, holistic character of the Hippocratic doctrine of health is only fully comprehensible when one considers the intellectual context of fifth-century Greek culture. The sculptor Polyclet was writing on the theory of human representation, the historian Thucydides was analysing the motives behind political actions with reference to psychological factors, whereas Aeschylus, Sophocles and Euripides were depicting human intrigue and guilt in their dramas. In the works of Democritus, Epicurus and Euripides, we find a code of behaviour that also encompasses the moral and dietetic aspects of daily life.[107] Although *The Plague* by Thucydides (430) presented disease and death of the masses as a part of daily life, intellectuals and artists were – perhaps as a direct result of such impressions – increasingly interested in the fortunes of the *individual*.[108] The whole man, psyche and body, was the focal point of their interest.

Diocles of Carystus, a fourth-century health pedagogue

Diocles of Carystus is the first Greek doctor to have left a comprehensive oeuvre, of which at least the titles are known today. The modern word 'hygiene' may well derive from his treatise *Hygieina*. The doctor from Euboea was, according to the testimony of Vindician, a staunch adherent of the doctrine of four humours, which he explained as transformations of food.[109] After Galen, he was classed as one of the foremost Hippocratic 'dogmatics', passing on the ideas of the master in a purportedly unchanged form.[110]

The doctrine of this 'doctor and rhetor', whom Pliny considered the greatest physician of all time after Hippocrates,[111] was closely connected with contemporary philosophy. The classical philologist Werner Jaeger believed it to be particularly indebted to Aristotelian ideas.[112] Today it is generally thought to be more closely related to Plato's *Timaeus* or, rather, to the Sicilian physician Philistion, who influenced the Platonic dialogue decisively.[113] In Diocles' work also, dietetics is only accorded legitimacy insofar as it focuses on the whole individual, and it is deemed the most important aspect of medicine altogether. A remedy is not effective 'because it is warm or cold or salty, for sweetness and spiciness and saltiness and everything else of this nature does not have the same effect in every case. One must rather see the entire nature (of the organism concerned) as the cause of the fact that a particular effect tends to occur.' Similar ideas can be found in the Hippocratic tracts *Peri aeron, hydaton, topon* and *Peri diaítes*: medicines, but also behavioural patterns, can sometimes have very different effects, just as health itself can be subject to the most diverse influences.

There are some rules that are generally valid, however. A fragment by Diocles passed down by the Byzantine doctor Oribasius (third century AD) contains a dietetic daily programme:

> Health care begins in the morning. When the individual awakes, the food should already have reached his intestine. The young man and the adolescent should awake shortly, approximately ten stages before sunrise, although in summer only five stages.[114] One should not rise immediately, however, but rather wait until the weariness and dizziness of sleep have departed. After getting up, one should massage thoroughly the neck and head, in order to banish the stiffness caused by the pillow. Then one should rub the entire body with oil.

Teeth cleaning after meals (with peppermint powder) is recommended, as are long walks beforehand. Sleeping on one's back is considered unhealthy. The nose and ears should be cleaned: 'Care of the head includes rubbing, anointing, washing, combing and trimming.' Those who have sufficient leisure time are again the privileged ones, and for them special walks are recommended. Before eating, 'evacuate the body and ensure that the food is absorbed better and the . . . meal digested more easily.' The main meal should be consumed in the evening:

> In summer it should be taken shortly before sunset and should consist of bread, vegetables and oat pastries. To begin with one should eat raw vegetables, with the exception of cucumbers and horseradish, which one should rather consume at the end of the meal. Cooked vegetables, however, should be eaten at the beginning. Other recommended fare includes cooked fish and meat, goat and sheep meat, mostly from young animals, and pork from older animals . . . Before eating one should drink water and somewhat later some more. Thin people should drink dark, viscous wine, but white wine after the meal. Fat people should always drink white wine; all should dilute their wine with water . . . Thin people with a tendency towards flatulence, who have bad indigestion, should lie down to sleep immediately after eating, while others should take a short, leisurely walk before sleep. Everyone will benefit from lying at first on their left side, until the food is within the region of the stomach. When the body is relaxed, however, one should turn onto the right side. It is not good for anyone to sleep on their back, however.

After eating, Diocles states, 'leisurely walks' are advisable. Subsequently, 'one should sit and see to personal affairs, until it is time to turn to body care. Young people, who require more training, should go to the gymnasium or take gymnastic exercise. Older and weaker people, however, should adjourn to the bathroom or to another sunny location in order to anoint themselves.' Dietetic discipline is also recommended after breakfast. 'One should not waste too much time on it and should (afterwards) lie down to sleep in a shady or cool and sheltered place.' However, Diocles does not deal only with the culture of eating and drinking. 'Frequent and lengthy sexual intercourse' is considered detrimental to health, although it can be beneficial to melancholics.

Diocles also regards nature as a force that acts according to ethical criteria, and whose healing properties evolve according to optimal rules. Natural dietetics can have no truck with, for example, artificially induced vomiting, which played an important part for the Hippocratics. Instead, nature spontaneously determines the appropriate moment for taking action to correct oneself, with the result that medical intervention is generally unnecessary.[115] Diocles' doctrine is based on a strictly teleological view of nature, which suggests that he was educated in close proximity to Aristotle.[116]

In a letter addressed to King Antigonus which was probably written in late antiquity, but was originally ascribed to Diocles,[117] an account is given of how to overcome illnesses which are already in an early phase. The unknown author confidently describes medicine and dietetics as royal disciplines which are 'appropriate to the person' of the ruler.[118] The patient is counselled on the basis of the doctrine of four humours; however, he must ultimately assume responsibility himself for the process of recovery, following the instructions of the doctor of his own free will. Mild remedies are recommended as a means of recovering health, for example hyssop or oregano against ailments affecting the head, as these herbs were believed to induce the excretion of the pathogenic phlegm (phlegma).[119] Particular emphasis is placed on the proper preparation of meals: 'For health as well as for enjoyment, the *cleaning* of raw, uncooked ingredients is essential.' This can be achieved by boiling or with the help of vinegar; 'that which tastes salty should be diluted, that which is dirty should be cleaned.' In this way, the unfavourable basic qualities of some meals could be corrected by means of side dishes with opposite effects. The choice of dish is therefore of similar importance to the choice of medication. Gymnastics, the frequency of sexual intercourse, drinking, sleeping, and so on should be modified in each case according to age, month of the year and climate.

Diocles of Carystus is probably representative of a fourth-century school of medicine which was known as 'western Greek'.[120] Relations between the leading Sicilian doctors,[121] classical Athenian philosophy and the school of Kos and Knidos must have been very close, however.

Numerous fragments have not, to this day, been ascribed to a particular region.[122] There are indications that Diocles also composed health regimens for professionals – for example, those who spent a lot of time at sea and soldiers who had to complete long marches.[123]

Around the middle of the fourth century, the Hippocratic author Mnesitheus, a 'dogmatic' like Diocles, explained that a doctor 'either preserves the health of the healthy or treats the sicknesses of the sick. He cultivates health with the aid of the same factors and dispels sickness with the opposite ones.'[124] The theory of the 'similia similibus' or 'contraria contrariis', to which he makes reference here, would feature in the history of European medicine right up to the eighteenth century. Mnesitheus also addresses the topic of intoxication from drinking wine, a popular vice among the Greeks, which was nothing less than a social obligation in Hellas. After some physiological arguments, he warns the carouser: 'Yet consider three things when you drink your fill: firstly, do not drink any bad and undiluted wine, and do not consume confectionery with it. Secondly, when you have had enough, do not lie down before vomiting more or less exhaustively. Thirdly, when you have vomited copiously, wash yourself briefly and lie down to sleep.' Wine, particularly when 'unmixed' and drunk to excess, was considered an ignoble means of destroying the harmony between the humours and qualities.

It should not be forgotten that the essential aspects of later European and Arabian dietetics first appear in programmatic form in the Hippocratic corpus as well as in the writings of 'dogmatics' such as Diocles or Mnesitheus: the absorption and evacuation of food and drink, climatic factors, the question of the environment, sleeping and waking, sexual intercourse, rest and activity, as well as optical and acoustic factors. Justification for the existence of medicine is found in the fact that the sick, as experience had established, do not benefit from the same diet and way of living (*diaita*) as the healthy. Although this notion appears in Pindar, Aeschylus and Herodotus, in Hippocratic writings it acquires a health-related inflection and simultaneously, thanks to its connection with the environment, society and religion, a philosophical and cultural-historical dimension.[125]

'Knidic' dietetics

Despite considerable competitiveness – Galen later reports that 'the doctors in Kos and Knidos strove to outdo each other with the amplitude of their discoveries'[126] – it seems fair to assume that the two most famous medical schools in Greece were not at all at variance as far as methodology was concerned. The Knidic authors were, after all, even involved in the composition of the *Corpus Hippocraticum*.[127] As on Kos, questions concerning the *preservation* of health assumed considerable importance in the town only a few kilometres away in Asia Minor, which was renowned as a centre for medicine. In his treatise *On Methods of Nutrition*, Galen even discusses the question of whether the Hippocratic tract *Peri diaítes* could not also have been composed by Knidic doctors such as Euryphon.[128] Insofar as we can judge from the remaining fragments, the latter apparently held the view that illnesses were caused by inadequate excretion. Euryphon therefore advocated a regular complete evacuation of the bowels as a prophylactic: 'When the stomach does not excrete the consumed food, a residuum develops which ascends to regions in the head and causes illnesses.'

For the physician Herodicus of Selymbria, who was probably also educated in Knidos and was of considerable renown in antiquity,[129] and who later organized gymnastics courses and walks outside the Athenian city walls, it was self-evident 'that illnesses are produced by an incorrect way of living. Life is conducted in accordance with nature when exertions and pains are present in an appropriate measure and when food is digested in this way.' Herodicus, who is believed to have been associated with the Pythagoreans, taught several decades before Hippocrates that health was given 'when the body, as far as the way of living is concerned, is in a natural state. Illness, however, results from the unnatural state of the body.'[130] Walks, gymnastics, breaks for rest, massages and baths, he argued, supported the healing power of nature. The claim that the sick could be cured by means of strenuous physical exercise was later fiercely criticized by Galen.[131] Plato also had little time for the rigorism of the Selymbrian, whose teachings are transmitted primarily in the *Anonymous Londinensis*, a papyrus from the second century AD: 'Herodicus was a trainer and became a valetudinarian, and blended gymnastics and medicine, for the torment first and chiefly of himself and then of many successors.'[132] To extend one's life by means of an exaggerated cult of the body and without any spiritual reasoning seemed to the philosopher to be a pointless and worthless endeavour. Herodicus' constant battle against ailments by means of gymnastics and dietetics was futile, he claimed, for, 'living in perpetual observance of his malady, which was incurable, he was not able to effect a cure, but lived through his days unfit for the business of life, suffering the tortures of the damned if he departed a whit from his fixed regimen. And struggling against death, by reason of his science he won the prize of a doting old age.'[133]

Plato's criticism, which was also adopted by Aristotle and Pliny,[134] demonstrates that rigid submission to fashionable doctrines on health was already regarded as ridiculous in ancient Athens. Herodicus' physical training in fact included a gymnastic marathon programme. In the senseless battling of sick people against death, Herodicus' critics saw only a prolonged death. A Hippocratic author even accused the controversial *paidotribes* (trainers of athletes) of causing the death of men ill with fever with their walking, wrestling, running and massaging,[135] and Galen claimed that they had renounced all logic and 'the factual observation of the empiricist'.[136]

The general condemnation of Herodicus certainly set the tone for subsequent developments. The traditional cult of the body met increasingly with disapproval, and not merely from doctors and philosophers. In Plato's day, many Greek intellectuals demonstratively rejected sport and physical training. Thus, in *The Clouds*, by Aristophanes (445–386), 'Right Logic' complains: 'if you practise what men nowadays do, | You will have, to begin, a pallid skin, | Arms small and chest weak, tongue practised to speak.'[137] And in *The Frogs*, by the same author, Aeschylus says to Dionysus: '. . . none | Has training enough in athletics to run | With the torch in his hand at the races.' Whereupon the latter answers resignedly: 'By the Powers, you are right! At the Panathenaea | I laughed till I felt like a potsherd to see a | Pale, paunchy young gentleman pounding along, | With his head butting forward, the last of the throng.'[138]

It was not Herodicus, but his contemporary Ikkus of Tarent, who was considered to be the first doctor to develop a dietetic method and apply 'gymnastics for medical purposes' *before* Hippocrates.[139] He is reported to have won the pentathlon in Olympia thanks to his prudence and sexual abstinence, and Plato mentions him with great admiration in the *Nomoi* [*Laws*].[140] It represents a problem, however, that later citations are our only source of information on the doctrines of such doctors, which renders attribution to a person or even allocation to a place impossible.[141]

It is therefore difficult to judge the veracity of claims made in some Hippocratic tracts that, rather than examining sick people, the 'Knidians' only investigated their illnesses ('although they wished to give the exact number of every illness, they were not even able to do this properly'). The same is true of the even more weighty reproach that they 'wrote nothing of any value about dietetics'. In reality, of course, illnesses were also explained in Knidos by reference to the incorrect composition of humours or elements and the corresponding varieties of prophylactics publicized.

Particular value seems also to have been placed on 'local' therapies, such as surgery with the knife or hot iron. The preferred prescriptions for chronic suffering were milk, whey or laxatives. *Time* was also seen as a healing, dynamic principle; patience was therefore considered an important *pharmakon*. Some scholars believe that Knidic medicine prepared the way for the school at Kos, and that the heyday of the former preceded that of the island school.[142] However, the assumption that the inconsistencies within the Hippocratic corpus 'reflects the battle between the two largest medical schools' remains disputed. It seems that the relationship was one of mutual stimulation rather than of opposition. This is particularly true of dietetics, which is of no small importance in the surviving fragments from Knidos.[143]

The doctor Chrysippos (*b. c.* 380 BC), who was also educated in Knidos, is believed to have developed blood-letting as a corrective technique because he regarded blood as the seat of the soul. In his view, health is guaranteed by the *pneuma*, which keeps the body alive, while the correct choice of diet sustains its 'nature' (*physis*). This quality is also supported by the prescription of emetics, enemas and plant extracts as well as the binding of arms and legs in order to hold back the blood. According to Pliny, Chrysippos also wrote a book about the healing powers of cabbage.[144]

In Knidos, as on Kos, magic notions of healing were also present. In the book *Concerning Women*, a female patient suffering from a discharge is given the following piece of advice:

On the days between the rinses, drink elderberries, hare's rennet, poppy seed husks, nettle seeds and the peel of the sweet pomegranate tree, and grind up equal parts of each. Add hulled barley and woman's hair . . . and black, spicy wine. Let her eat those dishes that are soft and neither salty nor spicy. Meat, particularly poultry or rabbit, is better than fish. Let her take warm baths, but not too frequently. If, however, the discharge does not cease and the womb becomes damp, one must perform fumigations with remedies prepared from pomegranate peel. Then let her go to her husband. And if she becomes pregnant, then she will become healthy.

Also worthy of mention in the history of dietetics is Philistion of Lokri, who, like Diocles of Carystus, was from the 'west Greek' school of medicine. As the medical attendant of the tyrant Dionysus II of Syracuse (fourth century), he considered health to be threatened in particular by three factors: by the excess or lack of an element, by physical dispositions towards an illness, and, finally, by the influence of the environment.[145] He also thought it to be jeopardized by wounds, excessive heat and cold, and spoiled food.[146] Philistion, who was also an adherent of the *pneuma* theory, considered the optimal respiration of the entire body to be the best form of health care. This involved air entering the body not only through the mouth and nose, but also through the pores of the skin. An improper mixture of the humours could, in classical Hippocratic manner, be overcome with a careful choice of diet and the customary corrective measures, such as blood-letting.[147] The assumption that physical and spiritual wellbeing could also be dependent on the individual disposition became increasingly prevalent in the course of the fourth century.

Health in Plato and Aristotle

Mention has already been made of the philosophical affinity that linked Diocles of Carystus and some Hippocratic authors with Plato and Aristotle. Plato's concept of health was indeed formative for many doctors and philosophers. The nature of medicine is discussed primarily in the *Timaeus*, where we are told that the first duty of the doctor is to advance health, which is based on the harmony of body and soul and enables unlimited physical exercise.[148] He considers sport and gymnastics to be particularly indispensable for 'intellectual workers': 'the mathematician, or anyone else whose thoughts are much absorbed in some intellectual pursuit, must allow his body also to have due exercise, and practise gymnastics.'[149] The largely aesthetic notion of the 'healthy mind in a healthy body', which had already been propagated in pre-classical Greece, is adopted and combined with the warning that mental and physical inactivity lead to death. Plato considered the most effective form of gymnastics to be a natural movement 'produced in a thing by itself', followed by a motion induced by an external movement (he had in mind passengers on ships being rocked backwards and forwards!). *Medical* therapy, however, is presented as legitimate only in an emergency, but otherwise 'will be adopted by no man of sense'.[150]

Plato also considered the art of medicine to be an appropriate model for illustrating ethical questions (while, conversely, doctors could find explanations of the essence and structure of illness and health in the Platonic dialogues). The purpose of ethics was to restore or protect virtue and spiritual health: 'for there is no proportion or disproportion more productive of health and disease, and virtue and vice, than that between soul and body.'[151] In the *Timaeus*, Plato uses the humoral pathological arguments that were customary in medicine, making panegyric reference to Hippocrates. 'Now everyone can see whence diseases arise. There are four natures out of which the body is compacted, earth and fire and water and air, and the unnatural excess or defect of these, or the change of any of them from its own natural place into another . . . produces disorders and diseases.'[152] He also adopts the doctrine of quantities: the body can become overheated and overcooled, dry and moist, thereby demonstrating the pathological behaviour described by Polybos and the other physicians of his day.

The idea of the harmonious balance of elements within the healthy body (which disintegrates into the individual elements after death) is, as a consequence of the age-old analogy, transposed onto the cosmos, where divine order also prevails. From the cognition of this interrelation emerges *thought*, which is regulated by the rational soul linking the human and divine realms.[153] Mental indolence weakens this soul and leads to the dominance of the appetitive soul that is located in the stomach. As the actual vital force, the rational soul controls not only the intellect, but also the respiration and other physiological processes. If it leaves the body, death occurs. The intestines serve to regulate the passage of food, in order to compensate for intemperance in eating and drinking, and so also counteract the feared *dyscrasia*.[154]

A balance of opposites is necessary not only in one's choice of diet, but also when planning to produce offspring. 'He who is conscious of being too headstrong, and carried away more than is fitting in all his actions, ought to desire to become the relation of orderly parents' – a recommendation that is reminiscent of similar exhortations by Hesiod to those preparing to marry, and that is also adopted by Aristotle.[155] Concern for public health, for Plato a prerequisite of a functioning polis, leads to the advocacy of eugenics and even, as mentioned previously, of euthanasia.[156] As wine disrupts the harmony between elements during intercourse, the bride and bridegroom should conduct themselves 'in moderation' during the wedding. In general, a parent should avoid everything that damages health: 'he cannot but imprint [his] colour and impress on the souls and bodies of the unborn.'[157]

In *The Republic*, the 'symmetria' of reciprocal governance and dependence is defined as the natural condition of a community.[158] In *Philebus*, Socrates asks: 'In cases of sickness, does not the right association of these factors bring about health?', and goes on to draw an analogy between medicine and the art of music, which was based on the doctrine of harmony.[159] In *The Republic*, Socrates also explains that 'to produce health is to establish the elements in a body in the natural relation of dominating and being dominated by one another, while to cause disease is to bring it about that one rules or is ruled by the other contrary to nature.'[160] As in *Timaeus*, virtue, beauty and spiritual health are considered to be in a relationship of mutual dependence, and opposed to disease, ugliness and weakness. They guarantee physical wellbeing: 'We should not move the body without the soul or the soul without the body, and thus they will be on their guard against each other, and be healthy and well balanced.'[161] Thus in the *Sophist* illness is represented as a rebellion and dissension of disruptive elements,[162] and, together with ugliness, even as a consequence of spiritual wickedness – in other words, of a lack of virtue. In the *Symposium*, Eryximachus sees the essence of every successful act of healing to consist in the support of nature, which strives for the restoration of harmony.[163] In the same tract, however, Socrates is compared with a Silenus or unusually ugly satyr that concealed images of gods, in a clear criticism of classical holistic ideals of beauty. By means of this comparison, Plato ranks 'inner' beauty, that is to say, the beauty of the soul, above that of the body, which provides a transition to the famous *soma–sema* antithesis ('the body is a grave').[164] This notion does not, however, imply a general contempt for the body. The basis for the philosophical concept of medicine is the idea of the perfect, harmonious human being.

For Plato, therapy should always apply to the entire man. In *Charmides*, Socrates explains that 'eminent physicians', when consulted by a patient with an eye complaint, 'cannot undertake to cure his eyes by themselves, but that if his eyes are to be cured, his head must be treated too.'[165] We find a similar passage in *Phaedrus*.[166]

It is important to Plato that the patient also contributes to the therapy. He therefore attacks 'men who are sick, yet from intemperance are unwilling to abandon their unwholesome regimen . . . they hate most in all the world him who tells them the truth, that until a man stops drinking and gorging and wenching and idling, neither drugs nor cautery nor the knife, no, nor spells nor periapts nor anything of that kind will be of any avail.'[167] A precondition for every act of healing, then, is catharsis, or the elimination of all evil from body and soul by means of a change in the way of living. The patient is himself partly responsible for the success of the therapy. Otherwise, 'for all their doctoring', their only achievement will be 'to complicate and augment their maladies'![168] All unilateral treatments or exercises represent a danger to physical harmony and disregard the holistic character of human existence.

For Plato, medicine is also *hygieínou epistéme*, the science of health, which at the same time is of programmatic significance: the goal of therapy is the individual as a harmonious entity. The ideal, philosophically trained physician attempts to guide the patient towards the fulfilment of this goal. In *Phaedrus*, medicine is therefore also compared with the art of rhetoric, which acts upon the soul 'to implant such convictions and virtues as we desire'.[169] Dietetics in the Platonic sense could never be reduced to medication, treatment or gymnastics.

The philosopher was well aware that doctors can also *create* illnesses by upgrading 'waters and winds' to medical complaints – here he alludes ironically to the humoral doctrine.[170] He also believed he could prove that certain professions foster specific attitudes towards health and sickness, that, for example, carpenters and other craftsmen generally do not have the time to fall ill.[171] The theoreticians of the fourth and third centuries BC were also in no doubt that health, experiences of illness, prophylactics and therapy differed according to social class.[172]

In many of his dialogues, Plato condemns debauchery and idleness as dangers to health. In a letter composed in 354, addressed to friends in Syracuse,[173] we read:

> One who advises a sick man, living in a way to injure his heath, must first effect a reform in his way of living, must he not? And if the patient consents to such a reform, then he may admonish him on other points? If, however, the patient refuses, in my opinion it would be the act of a real man and a good physician to keep clear of advising such a man – the act of a poltroon and a quack on the other hand to advise him further on these terms.[174]

The art of healing and ethics were intimately connected in the mid-fourth century, as were medicine and psychology.

The connection between medicine and *Aristotelian* ethics as an 'objective' science of ethical action based on experiences of real life was a matter of course for many Hippocratics.[175] Although his *medical* writings were hardly passed down, Aristotle had an even more enduring influence on the Western doctrine of health than Plato.[176] Like Polybos before him with the four humours, Aristotle assigns a pair of qualities to each of the Empedoclean elements: fire is classed as warm and dry, air as warm and damp, water as cold and damp, earth as cold and dry.[177] The arrangement of these qualities decides 'life and death, not to mention sleep and waking, prime and age, disease and health'.[178] Even though blood, phlegm and yellow and black bile are central to Aristotelian physiology, the doctrine of the four humours is described only vaguely in the surviving works (in the tract *Historia animalium* [*The History of Animals*]).[179] Ages and seasons can also be associated with particular qualities: old age is considered earthy (dry and cold), whereas children have the moistest heads, just as spring tends to be moist, summer dry, autumn moist again, and winter dry and cold.[180] In order to conserve health, the predominant qualities are to be reduced with the aid of particular nutrients or by means of vomiting and medication. Like Plato,

Aristotle relativizes the duties and influence of the physician by emphasizing individual responsibility. Medical knowledge is not enough to conserve health (just as the study of law does not make an individual just!) if it is not directed towards a proper way of living.[181]

Medicine, ethics and politics appear as *practical* arts. According to Aristotle, however, care for the body should precede the care for the soul.[182] He believes that 'to accustom . . . from early childhood to cold . . . is most useful both for health and with a view to military service.'[183] No one should be reproached on account of natural ugliness, but they should be upbraided for unsightliness that results from neglect of the body and a lack of physical exercise: 'though nobody would reproach, but rather pity, a person blind from birth, or owing to disease or accident, yet all would blame one who had lost his sight from tippling or debauchery.'[184] Pragmatic limits are therefore set to the exhortation to individual responsibility for health.[185] According to Aristotle, a natural, innate and individually varied state of health or beauty exists for each body, and the cultivation and preservation of this state determines the choice of gymnastic exercise.[186] Remaining healthy presents each man with a challenge of a different degree, depending on his individual disposition.

Physical exercise and exertion are considered conducive to health, because they eliminate 'harmful foreign substances'. 'It is healthy to reduce one's diet and subject oneself to great exertions, for illnesses are caused by the accumulation of matter for excretion, and this results from an excess of foods or a lack of exertion.' Aristotle believes a sedentary lifestyle to be more appropriate for women, although it does also account for numerous characteristic disorders.[187] One should constantly ascertain individually what is beneficial for the body, however, as 'presumably a professor of boxing does not impose the same style of fighting to all his pupils.'[188]

In the *Eudemian Ethics* the philosopher explains that health can be cultivated by diet, gymnastic exercises and with due attention to the appropriate moment in time, just as moral discipline results in the best acts and conditions of the soul.[189] The principle of *arête*, which is necessary for the conservation of health, is for Aristotle nothing other than the recognition of the mean between two possible excesses which cause disorders of the body and soul.[190] As in Plato, health care is elevated to the status of a virtue.

One of Aristotle's primary concerns was the *doctrine of temperaments*. According to this doctrine, a range of personality traits, but also health risks, could be explained by the improper mixture or improper temperature of the humours, a notion that – despite the entirely different physiological ideas – approaches the modern concept of a 'genetic disposition'. Once more, *balance* provides the best possible protection. Risk factors exist in the form of the treacherous affects: courage, for example, a sign of the health of the soul, is the desirable mean between cowardice and foolhardiness.[191] In the *Problemata*, for the first time in the history of medicine, we find a description of the typical 'melancholic', whose state of health, character and intelligence are determined by an excess of black bile (*mélaina cholé*). While drunkards adopt ostentatious patterns of behaviour only for short periods of time, this is the natural state of the melancholic. 'Now black bile, . . . if it is in excessive quantity in the body, produces apoplexy or torpor, or despondency or fear; but if it becomes overheated, it produces cheerfulness with song, and madness, and the breaking out of sores and so forth.'[192] Not only the quantity but also the quality of the black bile moulds the character. Only as long as the temperature of the *mélaina cholé* does not exceed its physiological limit can melancholics impress others with their genius, rather than appearing as 'spleenful' characters.[193] It goes without saying that well-tempered melancholy is always in danger of sliding into a pathological condition due to a change in temperature or quantitative changes.[194] Indeed, according to Aristotle, 'all excellent men, whether philosophers, statesmen, poets or artists, [were] evidently melancholics' – that is to say, highly gifted, but unstable as regards health.

Aristotle was convinced that the entirety of nature, mankind, animals and plants is governed by a divine principle and serves a predefined, rational purpose. Thus, for example, the form of the human body and its organs are adapted to this *télos*, and every effort towards health must make use of this tendency towards harmony. To become intoxicated, for example, is to act against the body's natural regulation of its absorption of food; the same applies to gourmands, gluttons and drunkards.[195] Physical exercise, games and recreation are also never an end in themselves, but rather routes to health, which, as is stated in the *Ars rhetorica*, in the first instance has advantages for everyday life.[196] Instruction in 'simple living', in balance and moderation, can be defended with teleological arguments: physical exercise can, for example, ease women's labour pains, as it improves the breathing, 'so that it can be stopped, and this decides whether the birth is easy or difficult'. Peasants' activities are recommended in this connection, as they not only strengthen the body, but also enable the individual to withstand weather conditions and exertions as well as – and this is one of the duties of the healthy – to confront the enemy.[197]

In the *Problemata*, Aristotle concerns himself at length with gymnastic exercise: long walks are more tiring on even than on uneven ground, while the opposite is true of short walks: 'for if there is a regular alternation of opposites, for example, standing and walking, this is tiring, as neither of the two becomes a habit, which alone can have a refreshing effect.'[198] It is, he claims, useless to wish to train the body and the mind at the same time, 'for it is the nature of the two different sorts of exertion to produce opposite effects, bodily toil impeding the development of the mind and mental toil that of the body.'[199] In addition, the goal of the cultivation of health is capability and not brute force; a muscleman devoid of mental maturity remained a ridiculous figure.[200] Of course, one could expect greater (and more specific) knowledge of dietetics from gymnasts or professional athletes than from laymen, just as every other expert has greater specialist knowledge of his own field.[201]

In his surviving works, Aristotle deals with numerous medical questions, such as house designs which are conducive to health and questions concerning clothing and diet or public health provisions. He urges the authorities to provide healthy drinking water as well as careful supervision of wells, and warns – on account of the risk of fevers and eye complaints – against damp houses.[202] To bathe in stagnant waters is presented, due to their vapours, as equally dangerous as wearing clothing that is too light or too warm. Leanness is a cause of less concern than obesity; cold baths are preferable to warm ones. If one wears a hat, one's hair will turn grey sooner.[203] Exposure to the east wind and shelter from the north wind – here we remember the Hippocratic tract *Airs, Waters, and Places* – represent favourable conditions for the health of the general public.[204] Social planning measures such as the ideal age for marriage or the optimal number of children are also representative of the Aristotelian conviction that individual health is only possible in a 'healthy', well-organized state system. In this regard, he defers to the experts, for 'the suitable bodily seasons are adequately discussed by the physicians, and the question of weather by the natural philosophers, who say that north winds are more favourable than south.'[205]

The Aristotelian concept of health was, last but not least, influenced by the philosopher's fundamental interest in biology. He believed that, wherever life manifests itself, it is always subject to the same principles or rules. The 'doctrine of the four causes', according to which every recognizable change or action, and therefore also the human physiology, is determined by a formal, material, efficient and final cause,[206] made possible an integrated, analogical approach to the entire cosmos.

Dietetics in Alexandria

By the fourth century dietetics had definitively established itself in Greece as a part of medicine. It 'had become a primary component of all philosophical educational systems.' Around 300 BC, the medical school in Alexandria took over from the traditional centres for the education of physicians. The leading doctor of the metropolis, which was founded in 331 BC by Alexander, was Herophilus (339–c. 260), who was influenced decisively by currents from the vicinity of Kos and Knidos.[207] In conformity with the Hippocratic tradition, he emphasized the importance of prophylactics and dietetics. For Herophilus, who was medical assistant to Ptolemy I, health care also included gymnastic exercise and ball games, as well as dietetic restrictions.[208] His complaint about the 'psychosocial' consequences that result from a loss of health, which was transmitted by Sextus Empiricus, a doctor and philosopher from the second century AD, was mentioned earlier. Herophilus is credited with having made a plethora of anatomical discoveries (according to Tertullian, he dissected more than 600 human corpses!), and treated illnesses according to an eclectic scheme of medication, which he based on the doctrine of the four humours and christened 'the hands of the gods'.[209] However, the doses of these divine presents had to be determined carefully and individually. The smooth functioning of the body was for Herophilus based on four factors (the number four had almost magical qualities in ancient dietetics): the power of the liver to convert food; the power of the heart to warm; the power of the nerves to feel; and the power of the brain to think. Here he distanced himself from Aristotle, who had identified the heart as the vital and sentient centre of the human being.

With regard to the question of whether health care is the domain of physicians or, as part of the 'art of gymnastics', of sports teachers, Herophilus held the view that the services of *both* were required.[210] As late as the twelfth century, a Byzantine monk by the name of Eustathius wrote that Herophilus had attached extreme importance to gymnastics, and particularly to ball games.[211] According to Galen, Herophilus assigned three main areas of responsibility to medicine: care for the healthy, care for the sick and care for the majority, who are typically in a condition of 'neither-nor' (*ne-utrum*), somewhere between the two.[212] Absolute freedom from all kinds of ills, from fears and worries, is, as in the case of illness, reserved for a minority. Sextus Empiricus reports that Herophilus was also the first to attempt to differentiate between healthy and unhealthy pulse rates for people of all ages; here he compared the movement of the arteries with *arsis* and *thesis*, the upbeat and downbeat in music or the metrical foot.[213] The beginnings of an interest in taking measurements were therefore already present in medical science in antiquity, although, admittedly, no theoretical or methodological link with modern medicine can be established.

The second great doctor in the Alexandrian school, Erasistratus (310–*c*. 250), inclined, according to the traditional view of historians of medicine, towards 'solidar pathology', which held that health disorders manifest themselves in the ailment of isolated parts of the body.[214] A particular catalyst of illness is the congestion of the arteries (plethora), which inhibits the normal functioning of the organs.[215] Fasting, purging, emetics, cauterization and cupping counteract plethora and fortify the body. According to Celsus, Herophilus and Erasistratus were the first to conduct dissections on people who had been condemned to death. The Roman encyclopaedist, who was active at a time of epochal change, defended this practice from charges of inhumanity, stating: 'Nor is it, as most people say, cruel that in the execution of criminals, and but a few of them, we should seek remedies for innocent people of future ages.'[216]

Erasistratus also reserved an important place for dietetics, or the art of healthy living: just as the helmsman of a ship prefers to reach his destination before a storm, rather than being carried backwards and forwards by it and then reaching the port after much peril, so the aim of the doctor is to avoid every illness a priori.[217] Like Herophilus, he assumed the existence of a state between health and sickness: 'There is another physical condition, which the school of Herophilus describes as "neither of the two", which affects those who have survived a severe fever at the time of their recovery, as well as those of an advanced age.'[218] This qualification presupposes an exalted ideal of health, which the renowned anatomist paraphrases as 'harmonious order and independence' (*eutaxía kai autárkeia*).

In Hellenism, as from time immemorial, specific medicinal herbs were thought to assist in protecting health. Nicander of Kolophon (second century BC) composed an important work about poisoning, particularly as a result of snake bites, and its treatment. Mithridates, the brutal king of Pontus (113–63), had a universally effective antidote prepared, the 'Antidotum Mithridaticum', which remained a popular and well-known panacea into the Middle Ages. The king is reputed to have taken it every day together with certain poisons and thus gradually to have built up an immunity. It was, in all likelihood, the magical associations rather than the therapeutic efficacy of such *pharmaka* that secured their popularity. In the superstitious world of antiquity, few would have been willing to dispense with such magic remedies, whose preparation was often a closely guarded secret.

The conquest of Alexandria by Caesar and the conflagration of the 'Museion' and the famous library (48 BC) put an abrupt end to the scientific ascendancy of the Alexandrine medical school.[219] However, important doctrines on health of Greek and Egyptian provenance reached the West at a later date via the cultural and scientific melting pot in Egypt.

Cures and miracles, Aesculapius and Hygieia

Alongside and largely in accordance with the teachings of the great medical schools, there persisted among the Greeks the age-old conviction (which had been articulated by Homer and Hesiod) that supernatural powers ultimately arbitrate over health and sickness. In particular, those patients who had been declared incurable and forsaken by the humoral medicine of the schools naturally pinned their hopes on these powers. The recommendation expressed in the Hippocratic tract *Ancient Medicine* that the physician should abstain from treatment in hopeless cases[220] had, when put into practice, the consequence that those facing death could not hope for help or comfort from physicians. It seems fair to assume that the rise of the cult of Aesculapius as well as the proliferation of diverse places of healing and cultic sites were related to this abdication of medical responsibility, which had been expressed as early as 1700 BC in the ancient Egyptian *Edwin Smith Papyrus*.[221] Healers who attempted to cure even hopeless cases were considered charlatans until the Middle Ages.

In a hymn from the sixth century, Aesculapius is celebrated as a 'healer of sicknesses' and as 'a great joy to men'. The god of healing, who was worshipped primarily in the Hellenistic and Roman periods, does not play any significant role in Homer's works, although he is named in the *Iliad* as the father of the heroes Machaon and Podalirius, who are skilled in the art of healing. However, he does feature in Pindar's third *Pythian Ode*, where his mythological birth is described. We are told that his father Apollo, after his mother Coronis had been killed at his command by Artemis on account of her infidelity, brought Aesculapius to the centaur Chiron mentioned previously, from whom he learned the basics of the art of medicine: the preparation of remedies, the use of the knife, but also the use of the right word at the right moment.[222] 'And those who came to him afflicted with congenital sores, or with their limbs wounded by grey bronze or by a far-hurled stone, or with their bodies wasting away from summer's fire or winter's cold, he released and delivered all of them from their different pains, tending some of them with gentle incantations, others with soothing potions, or by wrapping remedies all around their limbs.' When Aesculapius even brought a dead man back to life with his craft, he was killed by Zeus, as he had acted 'against nature as created by god'. According to Strabo, his earliest shrine was in the Thessalian Trikka.[223] The oracles and rites of incubation, as well as the worship of snakes, all of which were characteristic of his cult, were a good deal older, however.

Aesculapius, whose rise to fame was closely connected to that of his daughter Hygieia, the goddess of health, was attentive to the devout patient and, in contrast to the doctors, could help even when reason and experienced failed. The Greek *art* of healing was therefore supplemented in Epidaurus and other religious healing centres by the *cult* of healing. The shared rejection of charlatanism and magic on the part of doctors and priests led in practice to respectful mutual tolerance.[224] It is no coincidence that the heyday of the Aesculapius cult coincided with the zenith of Greek medicine. After all, none of the other ancient gods had tended to the afflictions of the individual with such intensity as the 'soother of painful ills', who thus had no difficulty taking the place of Apollo as *Alexikakós* in Epidaurus and on Kos.[225] Just as temples of his mythical father can be found at his cultic sites, so shrines to Aesculapius are always present in the vicinity of sites dedicated to Apollo. As far as the restoration of his health was concerned, the devout patient could be sure of the assistance of many gods.

According to an account by Pausanius (second century AD), the oracle of Delphi had identified Epidaurus as the first among the Greek places of healing and cultic sites.[226] In the fourth and third centuries, the shrine at Epidaurus was embellished on a grand scale. The suggestively religious approach to healing is evident in the inscription that, according to the testimony of the Neoplatonist Porphyrius, decorated the monumental gatehouse of the construction: 'Pure must be he who enters the fragrant temple; purity means to think holy thoughts.'[227] The temple should under no circumstances be 'contaminated', even in a metaphorical sense; neither birth nor death was to take place in its vicinity. This necessarily had consequences; those who were terminally ill were forbidden from entering the *temenos* – almost a prohibition of sympathy to the very end. The Roman senator Antoninus, however, again according to the witness of Pausanius, did have the 'Portico of Kotys' restored as 'a place in which without sin a human being could die and a woman be delivered'.[228] In late antiquity, the shrine was decorated with votive tablets, which decayed quickly, with the result that the priests had the accounts of healings (*iamata*) inscribed on stone steles.

The central component of the treatment was the therapeutic sleep. After the sacrifice, the priests led the sick to the rest areas. In the comedy *Plutus*, composed by Aristophanes, we read a description of everyday life in the *Enkoimeterion* on the island Aegina:

> Soon the Temple servitor | Put out the lights, and bade us fall asleep | Nor stir, nor speak, whatever noise we heard | So down we lay in orderly repose | . . . *he* [the God] went round, with calm and quiet tread, | To every patient, scanning each disease. | Then by his side a servant placed a stone | Pestle and mortar, and a medicine chest.[229]

Baths and springs were of particular importance. The aforementioned Portico of Kotys was extended in Roman times to include a large public bath, whose cultic character was emphasized by an incorporated temple. Restraint in eating and drinking, as well as sexual abstinence, were as much a part of the guests' duties as prayer and meditation.

Treatment was not 'a gift from the gods'; the patient paid a sum of money, the size of which was revealed to him in a dream by Aesculapius. A therapeutic sleep was not always necessary for the success of the treatment. As we read in an account from Epidaurus, 'A girl was dumb. As she was exploring the shrine, she saw a snake sliding down from one of the trees. Full of fear, she cried for her mother and father, and left healthy.' The 'psychosomatic' bases of many illnesses doubtless benefited the healing methods of the Aesculapius priests. The unconditional, devout willingness of the patient to follow the rules of the cult was a prerequisite; every doubt could prevent recovery, and even provoke the feared disfavour of the god, as the *iama* (healing) of a lame man demonstrates:

> As he was sleeping at the shrine, he had a vision. He dreamt that the god broke his staff and commanded him to fetch a ladder and climb as high as possible up the temple. He attempted this, but lost courage, rested on the cornice, gave up and climbed step by step back down the ladder. Aesculapius was at first angry about his behaviour, but then mocked him on account of his cowardice. But after daybreak he dared to perform the task, and went away unscathed in body.

Sceptics were not uncritical of such reports, however. According to Diogenes Laertius, the Cynic Diogenes said mockingly of the votive pillars: 'They would have been much more numerous if those who were lost had offered them rather than those who were saved.'[230]

In the visual arts, Aesculapius appears bearded, dressed in a cloak and leaning on a staff around which a snake is coiled. On a relief from the fourth century he is accompanied by his daughter Hygieia, the personification of 'health', with his sons Machaon and Podalirius, as well as the remaining daughters Aceso, Iaso ('the healing ones') and Panacea (the 'all-healing one'), who follow at a distance.[231] Hygieia, of whom there are numerous representations in classical art, had her own temples in Epidaurus and Pergamon and became a central figure of the Aesculapius cult. In Titane in the Peloponnese women offered her their hair, and as early as 400 BC the lyric poets Ariphon of Sicyon and Licymnius of Chios composed hymns to the popular goddess. In the cultic image of Aesculapius in Epidaurus, which was attributed to Thrasymedes and, according to Pausanius, was made of gold and ivory, the god sat on an ornate throne. His right hand was placed on a snake (a benign creature in the Aesculapius cult, which assisted the healing process by licking and touching), whereas the left grasped a staff.[232] A further figure frequently accompanies Aesculapius: Telesphorus, a gnome-like creature with a hooded cloak, who brings the healing process 'to a good end'. He is probably a personification of ancient earth gods, who also contributed to the recovery process.

In the course of the fifth and fourth centuries, numerous *Aesculapia* emerged, bringing with them a well-organized rhythm of pilgrimages and healings. In Corinth and Aegina, in the port of Piraeus and in Pergamon, there were soon flourishing centres of healing. The Attic mythological tradition recounts that in the year 420 BC, on the day of the mysteries of Eleusis, the god landed together with Hygieia and one of his snakes in Athens, where the tragedian Sophocles, who was also priest of the local healing god Amynos, received him in his temple. A cultic site was established there in 413.[233]

Although the earliest evidence of an Aesculapius cult on the island of Kos goes back to the sixth century, the famous *Aesculapion* was not established there until 400 BC. The island had won fame thanks to the Hippocratic medical fraternity and the cult of the healing god Apollo, who had been worshipped there since time immemorial in a grove of cypresses. The impressive terrace construction with its many steps, which was completed only in the second century BC and attracted pilgrims and those wishing to be healed from all over the Mediterranean, was originally made of wood and was not enlarged and embellished until some time later. It may have been on Kos that the 'scientific' faction of Greek physicians who practised humoral pathology first accommodated the flourishing Aesculapius cult, which also reached the coast of Asia Minor in the fourth century at the latest.[234] During the Roman period, the Aesculapius cult in Pergamon experienced a particular efflorescence. According to Livy and Ovid, the final significant site was founded on the Tiber island in Rome in 293 BC.[235]

Many other gods lent assistance in times of misfortune and illness. As early as the middle Minoic period (around 1600 BC), believers consecrated limbs to specific but unnamed *numena*, in the hope of an apotropaic effect in the broadest sense (for example, against plagues). Apollo's role as a healing deity probably originated with Paieon, the Homeric physician to the gods.[236] In Homer, Apollo spreads plagues as a punishment, but appears as a benevolent deity at the end. Here, illness is presented as a disruption of natural order, whether this is the harmony of the state, as in the case of a plague, or the harmony of the body, as in the case of individual illness. The parallels with later Presocratic and Hippocratic theories are self-evident here: it has already been mentioned that Hippocrates was considered a scion of Aesculapius. The latter became a particularly important institution in Attica as the *heros iatrós* (doctor hero). Many gods retained their roles thanks to rituals such as the laying on of hands, the interpretation of dreams and apparitions, sympathetic magic and incantations. As 'Eileithya', Artemis held her hands over women in childbirth. Hera (Hypercheiria) and Persephone also assumed this role, as did Epaphus, the son of Io and Zeus.[237] Even the father of the gods himself, who, thanks to his omnipotence, was invoked against many illnesses, is called upon in childbirth. Dionysius was already appealed to as healer by the Orphics, and was considered a 'doctor and fount of health' until well into late antiquity. The aforementioned Chiron proved himself to be a 'god with a palliative and skilled hand'. Priests and miracle healers such as the Neopythagorean itinerant preacher Apollonius of Tyana (first century AD) continued to work in late antiquity in the name of the gods.[238] Poseidon was worshipped for a long time as a doctor on Tenos; Athena was venerated in the Athenian acropolis as 'Athena Hygieia' or 'Paionia', and in Sparta – perhaps with a slight loss of status – as 'Athena Ophthalmitis', or protector of the eyes. In Eleusis it was Demeter and Helios, the sun god, who were considered the guarantors of healthy eyes. The deity or his or her chosen person could also bestow health by a kiss or placing a foot on someone. In late antiquity, the princes were believed to have similar powers: people wore amulets bearing pictures of Pyrrhus of Epirus, Alexander the Great, Vespasian and Hadrian.[239]

Dream healing and rites of incubation are also recorded in other cultural environments and, not least, play an important part in Christian thaumaturgy. The gods (or later, the saints) successfully performed those operations that 'normal' doctors failed to perform. Aesculapius drew spearheads from apparently incurable wounds, reinserted eyes, opened up stomachs in order to take out worms and leeches, and temporarily separated the head from the body, in order to allow harmful 'humores' to flow out.[240] Perhaps the sick also transposed their experiences with Hippocratic doctors onto their dreams so that, in practice, cooperation tended to be the rule in this respect as well. Somatic and psychosomatic treatment, reason and faith, ratio and irratio, all generally resulted in a holistic therapy which took both body and soul into consideration. The question of whether physicians and priests operated on drugged patients by night in the vicinity of the temple remains entirely speculative, however.[241]

It is therefore important to be aware that, parallel to Hippocratic medicine, which was based on 'physis', a religiously motivated art of healing remained popular in Greek cultural history, and evidently even grew in importance from the beginning of the fourth century. Its origins can be found in purification ceremonies (such as those described in classical mythology), in local cults of chthonic gods, in ancient literature (for example Hesiod), in the orgiastic cult of Dionysius and also in Orphic mysticism. Divine ecstasies, therapeutic incantations, the ancient Mantic art as well as the concept of a comprehensive, holistically understood *katharsis* played a by no means unimportant part.[242] The claim that, with the Presocratics, the transition 'from mythos to logos' was complete must also be relativized when applied to the history of medicine: the explanatory models for health and sickness were multifaceted and unthinkable without a religious backdrop. The erraticism of physical and spiritual disorders, the experience of natural disasters and accidents, the sudden death of many other men, but also the emotional involvement in religious festivals, all created a sense of integration in a divinely determined natural or world order, to whose workings seers or priests were more likely to have access than were doctors.[243]

A comment by Plato allows us to surmise why the 'Greek servants of Aesculapius' were revered by many patients as holistically oriented practitioners of 'somatics':

> this . . . is the reason why the cure of many diseases is unknown to the physicians of Hellas, because they are in disregard of the whole, which ought to be studied also; for the part can never be well unless the whole is well. For all good and evil, whether in the body or in the whole man, originates . . . in the soul.[244]

Likewise, this comment by a Thracian king, which is recorded in *Charmides*, recalls ancient psychosomatic notions; through the use of 'charms' and 'fair words' the soul is to reach a state that, for its part, promotes the *physical* healing process. 'And by [these means] temperance is implanted in the soul, and where temperance comes and stays, there health is speedily imparted, not only to the head, but to the whole body.'[245]

Notwithstanding their predilection for psychosomatics, the Greek physicians and healers recognized that every therapeutic method has its own specific indication. In Sophocles' *Ajax*, we read: "Tis not a skilful leech [doctor] | Who mumbles charms o'er ills that need the knife',[246] and Plato himself argues in his *Republic* that 'consultations' with physicians can only be successful when the sick person does not subject his 'physis' to an excessive (physical) 'diaita'.[247] The same can be said of mantics, the art of prophecy, which, in contrast to Hippocratic prognostication, also employed techniques that were not rationally intelligible. Ever since Kalchas and Tieresias (whose blindness strengthened his inner vision), mantics had played an important part in Greek mythology and religion. Apis, the mythical founder of Apia in the Argolis region, is described by Aeschylus as a *iatromantis* (doctor-prophet). Pausanius reports that the sick at an oracle site in Patras climbed down to a spring, from whose reflection their fortune would be prophesied:

> A very reliable oracle is situated there, not just for consultation, but also for healing. One ties a mirror to a very fine cord. Then one allows it to fall down over the spring, in such a way that only a part of the mirror is submerged, just enough for the water to touch its circular surface. Subsequently, one addresses prayers to the goddess Demeter and burns incense, and finally looks into the mirror, which now shows whether the sick person will live or die. So truthful is this water.

Finally, at least from Pythagoras' day, music played an important part in the healing process, as it was generally thought to advance the *katharsis* of the patient. According to Iamblichus, Pythagoras was

> of the opinion that music makes an essential contribution to health, if it is used correctly. And not only secondarily did he administer this form of 'purification' (for this is how he described healing by means of music). In the spring he carried out a melodic exercise of the following kind: in the middle he positioned one who played the lyre, and around this person sat singers and sang together certain paeans to this music, through which they, as they believed, became cheerful, and harmonically and rhythmically well marshalled. In the remaining time they also used music as a remedy.

Plato uses the example of the lyre in order to illustrate the 'musical' harmony of the individual with himself, the 'accord' of his own existence.[248] Just as the interplay of the high and the low, the fast and the slow, in the choral and instrumental arts is based on numbers, so health also rests upon a unification of opposites.[249] In *Cratylus*, Socrates stresses that the art of healing, like the related art of music, serves to purify. Medication, baths, consultations or scientific courses of treatment 'have all one and the same object, which is to make a man pure both in body and soul.'[250] Also in the Hippocratic corpus the interplay of the body parts is described with imagery taken from music: 'When it does not find harmony, however, and the deep notes are not in harmony with the high, whether in the fourth, the fifth or the octave, then, even if only a single note is omitted, the entire tune is flawed. For then there is no accord.'[251]

Music, therefore, acquired a special significance within Greek teachings on health, particularly as regards its philosophical theory. It was recognized at an early stage that the affects in particular could be controlled by means of this art. Under its influence, anger, despondency and mood swings could be harmonized with greater ease.[252]

Public health care and sport

Publicly appointed doctors existed in Greece as early as the Hippocratic age. The wellbeing of the *polis* was, in the opinion of politicians and philosophers, dependent on functional public health-care provisions. Herodotus reports that Democedes of Croton was employed as a remunerated public doctor in Aegina, in Athens and on Samos.[253] Diodorus Siculus later mentions that the constitution of Thurioi allowed doctors to be trained at the cost of the state thanks to the lawgiver Charondas, who had emended the older regulations, which had provided only for the free treatment of all citizens.[254] A doctor who was bound to the state in this manner – the majority were peripatetic healers who had taken up residence somewhere, and who were bound to a *polis* by means of annual contracts[255] – did not, admittedly, treat the citizens free of charge. Rather, the public salaries seem to have been calculated to cover just their 'basic costs'. It was common, then, for the patient to pay for the individual treatment or particular service separately.[256] That the financial situation of a 'public doctor' (*iatrós demosieúon*) was, in other respects, not particularly rosy is attested by an exclamation of a peasant in a comedy by Aristophanes (388 BC): 'Where is there another doctor in the town? The pay is bad, and so is the art.' For this reason, many public doctors were made to take both a professional *and* a civic exam before they were employed.[257]

The inhabitants of Gortys on Crete asked the priests of Aesculapius of Kos to find a good doctor. A certain Hermias responded to the 'job advertisement' and worked for five years, to the obvious satisfaction of the inhabitants, who honoured him with a memorial stone.[258] In 304 BC, the Athenians erected a stele to Pheidias of Rhodes, as he 'always acted for the good of the people of Athens and attended generously to those who needed him'. Smaller towns and localities in particular had difficulty in finding suitable candidates, who were therefore enticed with appropriate sums of money, houses or presents. The doctors who were brought into the locality from outside were often granted the privilege of citizenship, as in Cyrene for example, without the concomitant duties, such as electoral offices. On Lesbos, by contrast, a doctor was esteemed for assuming numerous public duties. The modes of payment were diverse: there were grain levies, 'medical taxes' (*iatriká*) or a regular revenue from private endowments. The Athenian municipal doctors enjoyed particular renown. According to Plato, they were elected by the public and required to have extensive professional experience.[259] The actual duties or the concrete status of the public physician probably differed from one locality to the next.

Indeed, in the Hellenic period people seem to have become aware of social problems of a previously unknown nature. At all events, doctors were praised with increasing frequency on account of their 'humanity'. It is extremely debatable whether we can assume that doctors administered at no charge to the *poor*, however.[260] There is just as little evidence, on the other hand, that 'public doctors' ingratiated themselves with the *polis* and feigned a social conscience with regard to such matters, in order to further their own interests, as has been claimed.[261] In general, there were both public and independent doctors working side by side in any Greek town. The main test of their mettle came in times of plague and war, where, Plato states, the primary, entirely utilitarian, concern was to care 'not only for the base and mechanical, but for those who claim to have been bred in the fashion of free men', in other words, to help the majority.[262] Public health care, then, served primarily the general welfare, or the well-being of the *entire* citizenry.

A comment by Sophocles suggests that the debate concerning health also encompassed social questions: 'It seems to me that no poor man is ever healthy, but rather always ill.'[263] If one also considers the description (second century BC) by Agatharchides of the wretchedness of the slaves in the Ptolemaic gold mines, one suspects (notwithstanding the exotic region and the despotism that predominated in Egypt) that treatment by a physician remained a utopian notion for the lower social classes of the Greek world. 'The sick, the cripple, the elderly and the weak woman received no clemency, no repose', Diodorus Siculus later commented.[264] Safety measures were, however, taken in some mines against lead poisoning. It was a matter of course throughout antiquity that working hours missed as a result of illness had to be made up afterwards or were subtracted from one's wages.[265]

The draining of swamps or alterations to road routes for reasons of hygiene – in accordance with the Hippocratic tract *Airs, Waters, and Places* – are attested from an early stage. Systematically constructed sewage networks probably first emerged under Hellenism, however. Such measures did not always result from a concern with sanitation or health; they sometimes, as is attested by Empedocles, were initiated for the purpose of symbolic purification or for aesthetic reasons. Even later authors such as Vitruvius were probably concerned with hygiene and climatology in part because of their place in the traditional encyclopaedic educational canon, and not exclusively for practical reasons. There is every reason to assume, however, that state provisions for public wells and the quality of drinking water, such as those mentioned by Plato and Aristotle,[266] were employed rigorously, particularly given that they tie in with ancient notions of water as potential centres of epidemic.

Even the eugenic policies of ancient Sparta aimed to promote public health. Plato and Aristotle likewise touched upon such matters. Plato's uncle Critias praised the legendary Spartan *diaita*: 'The way of life of the Lacedaemonians is governed by symmetry: eating and drinking in conformity with moderation, in order to be capable of thought and labour.' Such comments were also intended to have a public, didactic effect. Plato's views on eugenics, no less than Aristotle's pronouncements on this subject, advocated a comprehensive control of the individual by the authorities.[267] His suggestions on education were also pervaded by the idea of a rigorous health policy.

Public health care therefore also encompassed sport, whose 'infrastructure' was to be organized by the municipal government. As has been demonstrated by the example of Herodicus, however, Plato criticized (and here he was not alone) extreme forms of gymnastics and dietetics, which he suspected of 'cosseting illnesses'. In *The Republic*, every 'excessive care for the body, that goes beyond simple gymnastics' is rejected in part because it is 'incompatible with the management of a house, an army, or an office of state.'[268] It was, in the final analysis, the principle of moderation (*metrón*) that decided whether sporting activities were beneficial or detrimental to health. There was obviously a contrast between the views of a conservative circle, nostalgic for the ideal of 'kalokagathia', and those of diverse factions, inspired by the Stoa or by Platonism, which had a more suspicious attitude towards the cult of the body.

Sporting competitions doubtless have their origins in the ethical and religious sphere. Events such as the Olympic Games also promoted the identity of the nation.[269] It was not so much victory as a sort of physical and spiritual 'self-realization' that formed the focal point of the *agone*, at least at the beginning, although it was of course the gods who adjudicated on victory and defeat, despite all subjective efforts. Body and mind excelled beyond 'human' dimensions, which explains the veneration of top sportsmen, who were often elevated to the status of heroes. Numerous legends collected in their home towns around the figures of Milo of Croton and Theogenes of Thasos.[270] Training for the competitions was the responsibility of the *paidotribes*; however, doctors contributed almost as they do today to planning an optimal dietetic regime. Massages, diet, poultices, medicinal drinks and a sophisticated training regime figured almost daily, and the 'dosage' was determined in cooperation with sports and gymnastics teachers. However, as early as the third century BC we find a lament for the 'natural' training of the 'good old days' in a set of gymnastics instructions.[271] Competitive sport was probably no more or less beneficial to health in Greece than it is today.

Early Stoics and Cynics

According to Stoic doctrine, which was disseminated by Zeno of Kition (336–262) and enjoyed enormous popularity even in late antiquity, 'natural' living was the best way of attaining wisdom and health, which were crowned by bliss, assuredness and serenity. As with Plato, spiritual happiness is valued above that of the body. The Stoic devaluation of the body (for Zeno, questions concerning the physical condition comprised an entirely indifferent aspect of life) was, however, not as extreme as it is sometimes portrayed, and was probably largely a reaction to the aforementioned cult of the body which was widespread in Greece. Some schools of Stoic thought deliberately excepted illnesses from the *adiaphora*, the 'indifferent things' – in other words, concern for a healthy life was by all means a matter close to the heart of many Stoics.[272] For Chrysippus, the most important theoretician of the early Stoa (third century BC), it was even a sign of madness to 'deem health to be worthless'. Zeno himself seems not to have disregarded it entirely, as his pupil Ariston of Chios (around 250 BC) criticizes him with the argument that the sole goal of life is consonance between the self and the 'logos', in comparison to which one's physical condition pales into insignificance. With regard to the ideal of a natural way of living, however, health is accorded 'great value'. It is even considered, following Aristotle,[273] a prerequisite in order to effectuate 'the beautiful and good'. Epicurus (around 300 BC) also values health as a guarantor of spiritual tranquillity; even certain natural desires are considered permissible in order to 'rid [our body] of uneasiness'. In this desirable state, he writes in a letter to his pupil Menoeceus, 'the tempest of the soul subsides; seeing that the living creature has no need to go in search of something that is lacking, nor to look for anything else by which the good of the soul and of the body will be fulfilled.'[274] The philosopher, who was frequently confined to his sick bed, was of the opinion that body and soul disintegrate after death into those atoms of which they were formed. The goal of life was for him the *euthymia*, a serene, positive attitude towards the world, which was fulfilled by feelings of pleasure, spiritual joy and cheerful self-determination. It is only an apparent paradox that this joyful condition can only be attained by means of self-discipline, moderation and discernment, for even 'bread and water' can, according to Epicurus, give great pleasure. 'To habituate oneself therefore to a simple and inexpensive diet supplies all that is needful for health, and enables a person to meet the necessary requirements of life without shrinking . . . and renders us fearless of fortune.'[275]

The Stoic motto of a 'natural life' fell on fertile ground in Hellenism. Zeno, who taught in Athens from as early as 313, made a distinction between individual and cosmic nature: 'Hence the chief good is life according to nature, that is, according to one's own and to universal nature.'[276] This points towards a fundamental debate among the early Stoics concerning the nature of the 'physis': 'By nature, according to which one should live, Chrysippus understands both general nature and specific, human nature; Cleanthes, on the other hand, . . . only the general, but not the particular.'[277] As a life lived in accordance with nature was equated with virtue, its definition was also considered problematic. According to Diogenes Laertius, however, 'to take care of health and the sense organs' ranks without a doubt among man's 'fitting actions, and independent from the circumstances'.[278]

In the 'Middle Stoa', for example, in the works of Poseidonius of Apameia (*d.* 51 BC), the 'classic' four-part scheme was brought to bear to the extent that the four elements were once again related to particular mental and physical characteristics.[279] The definition of health as 'the highest among the goods of mankind' attributed to Poseidonius is hardly surprising, despite his affiliation to Stoicism. Care for the body and Stoic equanimity no longer appear in opposition around 100 BC: Athenaeus of Attaleia, a contemporary and pupil of Poseidonius, considered knowledge concerning the normal functions of the body (physiology) to be the most important medical discipline, followed by the science of disease (pathology), dietetics, the science of medication and therapeutics.[280] Athenaeus' dietetics, which, like the contributions of Diocles or Mnesitheus, reaches us through the transmission of the Byzantine doctor Oribasius (fourth century BC), were governed by the aforementioned Hippocratic axiom of *contraria contrariis*. Perhaps inspired by reading Solon, the doctor-philosopher described the normal, healthy development of a young person in a seven-year cycle, and then went on to outline the Hippocratic 'four seasons of life'.[281] The *pneuma* acquired the role of a life-giving principle within this scheme: as the stages of life were each presented as at risk due to specific illnesses, a primary concern was to reinforce the health-enhancing properties of the pneuma by means of a dietetic regime appropriate to the respective stage. By means of a careful selection of wet nurses, sports and games in early childhood, but also of a school education beginning late (at around seven years old) and governed by humane principles and not by the 'rod', a psychologizing mode of upbringing is defended, whose objective is to cultivate a zest for and competency in life.[282] The soul, which, as for the other Stoics, is the focus of concern, is presented as structured like the body, and must therefore be protected, almost like the body, from diverse dangers. Mental and physical exertion, interrupted by breaks, is believed to familiarize children with the rules concerning the correct way of living and dietetics. Athenaeus even becomes the first to declare dietetics an official school subject!

The culture of food, drink, gymnastics and bodily hygiene should, as with a healthy rhythm in daily life, be rehearsed by teachers. In the third septennium, that is to say, at the age of fourteen, the study of philosophy and systematic medicine begins. Again, for the well-to-do private citizen, who has the necessary time at his disposal, Athenaeus advocates a kind of lay medicine which goes beyond traditional prophylactics, and impressively highlights the socially determining role of dietetics during the final two centuries before the birth of Christ.[283] Advice is also offered to those in the later stages of life: the elderly should recognize that the highest point (*acme*) of their life has passed, but they can still excel in intellect and wisdom. The physical degeneration is considered to be *physiké anángke*, their fate as set down by nature, and should be dealt with philosophically. The suggestion that one should ensure that one has faithful friends for the eventuality that one will require nursing demonstrates that considerable pragmatism was invested in planning for the future.[284]

The route to *eudaimonia*, the spiritual state of happiness which relativizes all illnesses, was, as in Socrates' comments, but also in the works of the early Cynics, therefore considered as something that could be taught and learned. Man, it was thought, is capable of completely mastering his passions. Reason presents him with the necessary value scheme, and prevents him from becoming a slave to affects, feelings and daily impressions. The goal of this pedagogical strategy is rational action, as this imparts spiritual health and serenity.[285] The *objective* state of bodily health, on the other hand, was therefore logically considered by orthodox Stoics to be 'indifferent' (*adiáphoron*).[286]

To recapitulate, then, the everyday life of the Stoic physicians therefore bore little relation to the classic dualistic position. When Aretaeus (first century AD) considers the body in the traditional manner as 'slime and darkness' in which the soul is imprisoned, this assumption by no means implies an abandonment of the pursuit of health or the renunciation of doctors' assistance. Seneca later expresses similar views. There were doubtless diverse currents and schools of thought within the Stoa, although Kudlien is right to argue that the success and even the popularization of the doctrine whose original principle was contempt for physical needs and afflictions in the interests of the freedom and happiness of the soul would have been impossible without a corresponding prevailing mood, however diversified, extending from Zeno through to the Roman imperial age.[287] Among the 'adiaphora', the unessential things, Diogenes Laertius included 'life, health, pleasure, beauty, strength, riches, fame, nobility, as well as their opposites, death, illness, dislike, ugliness, weakness, poverty.' Health or beauty were, according to this later author, considered explicitly as a secondary good, 'for one can also be happy without these things'.

The *Cynics*' concept of health, on the other hand, was shaped by the notion of an autarchy of body and soul, which led to an ascetic contempt for the body. Plutarch reported that, according to the views of the Cynics, the 'joys of the flesh', which jeopardize self-discipline and ataraxy, are only encouraged by physical health; health is therefore opposed to the desirable state of Stoic indifference (*ataraxia*). Asceticism, on the other hand, was considered a promising *pharmakon* against affects such as fear, joy, sadness or desire. Socrates' pupil Antisthenes, founder of the Cynic school in Athens, was, after all, said to have called on the able man 'to train his body in the gymnasium and cultivate his soul through education'.[288] Even Diogenes, the most famous Cynic (fourth century BC), who, according to Diogenes Laertius, lived in a barrel, is full of praise for doctors, but, predictably, ranks responsibility for health over the art of healing: 'Men request health from the gods; yet most of them do entirely the opposite of that which is healthy.'[289] We should, of course, read in this light his statement 'The majority of people are decaying while still alive, as they cosset themselves with baths and melt away into the pleasures of love.'

In a speech by Diogenes, recorded by the rhetorician Dio Chrysostom (AD 40–120), the exemplary way of life of animals, which are 'strong and healthy' and require no doctors, is opposed to that of men:

> These lapse at every moment into illnesses that it is even difficult simply to name, and it does not satisfy them that the earth produces remedies for them; they also need iron and fire . . . No doctor, neither Chiron nor Aesculapius, nor his sons, can help them on account of their want of discipline and their wickedness, and similarly no soothsayer with his prophecies or priest with his tools of expiation.

According to Diogenes, man is first endangered on account of his way of life, 'for he avoids the sun just as he does the cold'. Moreover, slaves are less concerned with their health, 'partly due to a lack of self-discipline, partly in the assumption that, if something should happen to them, this is their masters' loss, but not their own.'[290] The Cynic sage is content in himself, which, indeed, also explains a certain social indifference. In order to attain one's ideal, one simply needs *judiciousness*. External activity, career or social involvement are all presented as irrelevant.

The knowledge of happiness and spiritual peace as a consequence of physical and spiritual harmony is defined by the majority of Cynics and Stoics as a virtue. It is uncontested that many did indeed put their teachings into practice. According to Diogenes Laertius, they were content with

> an unwasteful life, with frugal fare and a rough coat as clothing; they scorn riches, renown and noble birth. Some nourish themselves only from grasses and only ever drink cold water. They content themselves with the first suitable shelter available, even with a barrel, like Diogenes, who used to say that it is god-like not to have need of anything, and unlike the gods to need only little.[291]

However, this did not deter Stoic doctors such as Poseidonius and Athenaeus from also drawing on the traditional humoral doctrine. By means of analogies, correspondences and a relatively strict systematization, the humour blood, for example, was linked to the qualities 'warm and damp' and with the idea of spring, boyhood, morning and 'the first week of the month'; yellow bile, on the other hand, was linked with 'warm and dry', summer, youth, midday, the 'second week of the month' and the masculine principle, and black bile with 'cold and dry', as well as with autumn, manhood, afternoon and the 'third week of the month' and the feminine principle.[292] Health care meant maintaining these parameters, therapy aimed to correct deviations by means of the respective 'contraria'.

2

Rome

People and literati: dietetics in ancient Rome

In ancient Italic and Roman religion, life and death, health and sickness were in the power of numerous *numina*, which portioned out their power over mankind among themselves. Defence and protection were combined on the Palatine, for example, in the cult of Febris, who was originally a demon of disease. The god of war, Mars, could also protect one's health, while Juno offered assistance in childbirth. The Dioscures helped against the plague, and Livy confirms the worship of Apollo Medicus, who, however, was a deity of state and public, rather than private, character.[1] In the early ages of Rome, doctors were of little significance, although the word 'medicus' is Italic in origin, and the 'haruspex' of the monarchic period in all probability also employed his anatomical knowledge as a surgeon.[2] Like Pliny a good deal later, Cato the Censor was convinced that the Roman people had lived for centuries without doctors, and even that illnesses had first come to Rome with the emergence of the medical profession.[3] The worship of Salus and Valetudo played a part which is still not entirely clear today. Following the popularization of Greek gods such as Aesculapius and Hygieia in Italy, such cults were combined to form new ones.

In his work *De agricultura*, Cato (*d.* 149 BC) gave precedence to a peasant natural medicine, and advocated a dietetic regime based on a natural way of living. In doing so, the legendary historian, politician and conservative educator of the people was consciously harking back to traditions that had largely disappeared; he was, as Plutarch tells us

a man who wrought with his own hands as his fathers did, and was contented with a cold breakfast, a frugal dinner, simple raiment, and a humble dwelling . . . such a man was rare. The commonwealth had now grown too large to keep its primitive integrity; the sway over many realms and people had brought a large admixture of customs, and the adoption of examples set in modes of life of every sort. It was natural, therefore, that men should admire Cato, when they saw that, whereas other men were broken down by toils and enervated by pleasures, he was victor over both.[4]

The way of living in accordance with nature practised by the ancient Romans probably did indeed sustain their health and may have prevented many 'diseases of civilization'. Ancient Roman medicine was probably restricted to household remedies, surgical techniques and magical or religious procedures. Here, health was related to order, for which – within a household – the *pater familias*, but also the women and slaves of the house, were responsible.

With the exception of the Etruscan sacrificial priests, there was initially no such profession as the physician's. Health was protected by the gods – for example, the ancient Italic goddess Carna, who sustained the health of the intestines, but also protected children from demons carrying disease. Bona Dea, a mysterious goddess, to whom only women could offer sacrifices, was worshipped as guarantor of fertility, whereas Carmenta was the prominent protector of women in childbirth, and Mutunus Tutunus ensured fertility for women and potency for men. Around the years 293 to 291 the Aesculapius cult was introduced into the city. Ovid later gives an account of a pronouncement by the Delphic Oracle, which exhorted the Romans to entreat Aesculapius, and not Apollo, for deliverance during plagues. The former had then arrived in Rome from Epidaurus in the form of a snake, and a shrine was constructed to him on the Tiber island.[5] The entire institution of the Aesculapius cult was transferred from Greece, particularly the symbol of the snake, although the traditions of the therapeutic sleep and dream healing (incubation) cannot be observed with certainty in Rome before the first century BC.[6] Diverse votive offerings prove that Aesculapius became a true god of the people, to whom the state also appealed for help in an emergency; in around 180 BC the consul C. Calpurnius publicly appealed to him, together with Apollo and Hygieia, during an epidemic to bring the plague to an end.[7] Cicero, on the other hand, criticizes the fashion of incubation oriented towards Epidaurus, which was prevalent even in his day, and favours treatment by doctors,[8] whereas the author Lucian (second century AD), in his *Dialogus deorum* [*Dialogues of the Gods*], even mocks Aesculapius as a 'mixer of poison'. The opinions of the people and the intellectuals diverged as regards the healing power of the gods. The temple of Fortuna Primigenia in Palestrina, which was connected to an oracle's cave,[9] is reminiscent of Greek cultic sites such as the shrine of Aesculapius on Kos, which was also a terraced construction. We can assume that those in search of a cure as well as, for example, the childless, or those who considered themselves to be deserted by good fortune, sought assistance there in a manner similar to that in Greece. Significantly, when Sulla destroyed the town in 82 BC, he spared the temple area, at the centre of which was a statue of Fortuna (with Jupiter and Juno as her children) worshipped primarily by slaves and those of lesser standing; the statue is described by Cicero.[10]

Cato's rejection of physicians and Greek theories of health was part of a general aversion to the culture of the Greeks which was widespread among conservative Romans. 'When that race gives us its literature it will corrupt all things, and even all the more if it sends hither its physicians', he warned his compatriots in vain.[11] He was less opposed to traditional dietetics and 'conservative' therapies (which also played a part in Roman folk medicine), however, than to professionalized physicians who worked for remuneration. According to Plutarch, the Censor had in mind an oath allegedly made by Hippocrates (whom he considered suspect merely on account of his Greek provenance) that he would never treat barbarians – in other words, Romans. As he considered doctors less than trustworthy, Cato pleaded for self-help; Plutarch tells us: 'He himself, he said, had written a book of recipes, which he followed in the treatment and regimen of any who were sick in his family. He never required his patients to fast, but fed them on greens, or bits of duck, pigeon or hare. Such a diet, he said, was light and good for sick people . . . By following such treatment and regimen he said he had good health himself, and kept his family in good health.'[12] The philosopher Seneca (b. 55 BC) also confirms that ancient medicine comprised 'merely knowledge concerning some herbs which staunch the flow of blood from a wound and cause the wound to close'. The attitude of hostility towards physicians which was characteristic for conservative Romans can even be observed in an epigram by Martial (d. AD 102): 'I lay sick, but you, Symmachus, came to me accompanied by one hundred pupils. One hundred ice-cold hands felt my body. I had no fever, Symmachus, but now I am suffering from one!'[13]

The influence of the environment on health was, however, stressed repeatedly by the Roman theoreticians. In *On Farming*, by Varro (d. 27 BC), we find passages which comment on the construction of healthy country houses as well as other questions of hygiene and dietetics, passages that still fascinated authors in the Renaissance. The universal scholar even succeeded in halting a plague that threatened Pompey's army on Corfu by renovating the soldiers' quarters. In his epochal work *On Architecture*, which he dedicated to Augustus,

Vitruvius (first century BC) also discussed questions of hygiene. It is advantageous, he claimed, when a place of residence is situated high up, and is not exposed to mists, winds or great heat or cold. On the other hand, 'if the walls are along the coast and shall look to the south or west they will not be wholesome, because through the summer the southern sky is warmed by the rising sun and burns at midday.' A location facing west is similarly problematic: 'By the changes of heat and cold, bodies which are in these places will be infected.'[14] Heat, he claims, makes the inhabitants delicate and weak; however, on the other hand, care should also be taken that the streets do not turn into wind tunnels. Residential areas that are protected from the wind are, according to the Roman engineer, to be recommended not only for the healthy, but also for the sick, as, 'on account of the moderate climate . . . [they] will be still more quickly cured.'[15]

For the same reasons, the author and landowner Columella from Cadiz (first century AD), in his work *De re rustica* [*On Agriculture*], recommends paying particular attention to questions concerning health when buying a plot of land: 'Anyone who is preparing to construct a building must do this not merely in a healthy area, but in the *healthiest* location in this region.' An admirer of Virgil, Columella gives detailed instructions about the storage of wine in a cellar, the distribution of spring water or the use of different kinds of water. His description of an exemplary agricultural enterprise combines practical experience with a concern for the wellbeing of man and animal.[16] Authors such as Columella were doubtless influenced by the literature of Cato and Virgil, who had extolled the 'vita rustica' as a particularly auspicious and healthy way of life for body and soul. Indeed, in writing the *Georgics* it had been Virgil's intention to awaken love for the country life and respect for the work of the peasants within the educated classes. This was also the purpose of the pastoral poems collected in the *Bucolics*, notwithstanding, or precisely because of, their erotic connotations. 'Such a life the old Sabines once lived, such Remus and his brother. Thus, surely, Etruria waxed strong, thus Rome became of all things the fairest, and with a single city's wall enclosed her seven hills. Nay, before the Cretan king held sceptre, and before a godless race banqueted on slaughtered bullocks, such was the life golden Saturn lived on earth', Virgil enthused.[17] During Augustus' reign, the natural and simple nature of country life became famous and was contrasted with city life. The modesty of the women and the integrity of the families among the Germanic tribes also tally with the contemporary programme of enlightenment concerning public health, which had a strong moral and political flavour: 'In every household the children, naked and filthy, grow up with those stout frames and limbs which we so much admire. Every mother suckles her own off-spring and never entrusts it to servants and nurses. The master is not distinguished from the slave by being brought up with greater delicacy.'[18]

Cicero also concerned himself repeatedly with questions of health, exhibiting a Stoic attitude. In the tract *De natura deorum* [*On the Nature of the Gods*], he presents the organism as an elaborate, perfect construction of the gods. Every organ has its teleological purpose; the gods provide and plan for the entire species, as for the individual human being.[19] Cicero makes a careful distinction between old age and illness, as the elderly individual can by all means be in excellent health – like Cato himself. 'Yet, it may be urged, many old men are so feeble that they can perform no function that duty or indeed any position in life demands. True, but that is not peculiar to old age; generally it is a characteristic of ill health.'[20] If, for example, Publius Africanus had not fallen ill as an old man, he would, like his father, have become a second shining example to all. 'It is our duty, my young friends, to resist old age; to compensate for its defects by a watchful care; to fight against it as we would fight against disease; to adopt a regimen of health.'[21] Cicero developed a dietetic regime for the elderly, which combined the essential elements of Greek philosophy, in particular, of the Stoics. Elderly people should, according to this regime, take only light physical exercise, and consume 'just enough of food and drink to restore our strength and not to overburden it'. The mind and the soul should also be trained: 'For they, too, like lamps, grow dim with time, unless we keep them supplied with oil.'[22] The body, then, is burdened by excessive demands, whereas the mind is animated.

In a dialogue named after the much admired Cato, Cicero emphasizes the intellectual aspect of health. 'It is not by muscle, speed, or physical dexterity that great things are achieved, but by reflection, force of character, and judgement; in these qualities old age is usually not only not poorer, but is even richer.'[23] When he was writing the book *Cato Maior*, the 62-year-old had been politically disempowered and was seeking comfort in writing and intellectual edification. The work features an idealized Cato, although Livy also confirmed he was an individual whom 'not even old age that weakens everything could break'.[24]

The fear of losing one's health in old age appeared repeatedly as a theme in Roman literature. The comic writer Terence (second century BC) considered 'senectus' 'in itself a disease',[25] and not everyone could follow Virgil's dictum of the 'happy old man'.[26] In the *Tusculanae* [*Tusculan Disputations*], Cicero, like so many scholars before him, compares the imbalanced mixture of the humours (dyscrasy) with that of thoughts: 'Just as when the blood is in a bad state or there is an overflow of phlegm or bile, bodily disease and sickness begin, so the disturbing effect of corrupt beliefs warring against one another robs the soul of health and introduces the disorder of disease.' Philosophy can therefore be expected to provide a cure, particularly as a healthy soul is capable of judging the physical condition. 'There is an art of healing the soul . . . whose aid must be sought not, as in bodily disease, outside ourselves, and we must use our utmost endeavour, with all our resources and strength, to have the power to be ourselves our own physicians.' Spiritual health can be attained through virtue and intellectual endeavour, for 'physical aversions can occur without blame, while it is not so with aversions of the soul in which all diseases and disorders are the result of contempt of reason.'[27] Wisdom is regarded as health of the soul, foolishness is seen as an illness, and ailments such as avarice are corrected through reason and self-discipline, just as somatic disorders can be overcome by means of a course of therapy which balances out the humoral composition.

The poet and agnostic Lucretius, a contemporary of Cicero, concerns himself with health in his didactic poem *De rerum natura* [*On the Nature of Things*], although he also incorporates philosophical *and* physiological considerations. The body and soul of a human being, which are composed of atoms, constitute an inseparable unity. They fall ill together and recover to health in mutual dependence.[28] It is the power of the soul that sustains the body, whereas, on the other hand, 'when weakened by some cause or other [the mind] often appears to wish to depart and to be released from the whole body.'[29] Although, and even precisely because, the soul is mortal as well, and as it represents a force immanent in the body, it guarantees recovery, in the somatic as well as in the psychic realm. The individual is exhorted to curb his passions, but also to recognize the brief and constricted nature of life as well as the mortality of his soul, and is warned against overvaluing health.[30]

Many Roman intellectuals strove to lead a healthy life. Their role models were often Greek intellectuals or legendary characters from ancient Rome. The nephew of Pliny the Elder reports that his uncle took only a light breakfast 'in the old-fashioned way', and that he was careful during the day to alternate between physical exercise and mental relaxation. 'After his rest in the sun he generally took a cold bath, and then ate something and had a short sleep; after which he worked till dinner time as if he had started on a new day.' The author of the *Natural History* was, we are told, able to sleep at any time, although he had little need of repose.[31] However, Pliny, in this respect not dissimilar from Cicero, regarded all time as lost that was not devoted to studying. He found the 'vita rustica' alone too leisured, and after his daily bath 'he had a book read to him or dictated notes'.[32]

Seneca, the Stoic prophet of moderation, self-denial and balance, criticizes an excess of sport, bathing and exercise. He claims that country air is beneficial to health, while luxury and wealth are damaging. The real enemy of health, however, is agitation. Many people employ 'changes as remedies', he explains; they travel continually like vagrants, and 'wander over remote shores, and their fickleness, always discontented with the present, gives proof of itself now on land and now on sea.'[33] Yet in reality, as Lucretius recognized, everyone is merely fleeing from himself.[34] The 'vita rustica' was naturally particularly fascinating to town-dwellers; many nobles travelled regularly to the country, for example, to Baiae, to bathe or abandon themselves to idleness. Spa resorts and baths enjoyed a particular florescence in the later Roman period.

In the biographies of Plutarch (AD 46–120) and Suetonius, attention is also devoted to the state of health of the protagonists. Augustus, whose health was extremely frail, protected himself in winter 'with four tunics and a heavy toga, besides an undershirt, a woollen chest-protector, and wraps for his thighs and shins, while in summer he slept with the doors of his bedroom open, oftentimes in the open court near a fountain, besides having someone to fan him.' Summer and winter, he wore a broad-rimmed hat to protect himself against the glare of the sun.

> Yet in spite of all he made good his weakness by great care, especially by moderation in bathing; for as a rule he was anointed or took a sweat by a fire, after which he was doused with water either lukewarm or tepid from long exposure to the sun. When, however, he had to use hot salt water and sulphur baths for rheumatism, he contented himself with sitting on a wooden bath-seat, which he called by the Spanish name *dureta*, and plunging his hands and feet in the water one after the other.[35]

The emperor also loved games involving small and large balls, or to take walks, 'ending the latter by running and leaping, trapped in a mantle or a blanket'. Even as a boy, Augustus 'devoted himself eagerly and with the utmost diligence to oratory and liberal studies', albeit that sometimes 'because of weakness of the throat he addressed the people through a herald.'[36]

Suetonius attributes Caligula's mental confusion and epilepsy to an aphrodisiac, administered by his wife Caesonia, which 'had the effect of driving him mad'. Rational and magic concepts of dangers to health went hand in hand in Rome. That Caligula 'realized his mental infirmity' and 'thought at times of going into retirement and clearing his brain' seems equally remarkable.[37] An anecdote relating to Claudius demonstrates that court etiquette was also governed by health considerations: 'He is even said to have thought of an edict allowing the privilege of breaking wind quietly or noisily at table, having learned of a man who ran some risk by restraining himself through modesty.'[38] Almost all Roman rulers prized a successfully regulated diet, even when, like Claudius or Vespasian, they were bursting with health. Vespasian frequently had his throat and body massaged, and fasted one day a month. He attached particular importance to maintaining a regular daily routine.[39]

The cult of the Roman emperor, one of the pillars of the empire, also provided for the cure of illnesses. The people expected the almighty emperor to free them from affliction, whether this affected the commonweal or the individual. In political theory the analogy between the public and the individual organism was a common topos, probably thanks to Platonic influences.[40] We think, for example, of the legend related by Livy of the patrician Menenius Agrippa, who, in order to persuade the plebeians who had emigrated to Mons Sacer to return to the city, compared their social role with those of the organs of the human body.[41] The emperor, also the Pontifex Maximus, symbolized a sacral world order, possessed magic powers and, particularly in the east of the empire, was considered a new pharaoh and guarantor of *Ma'at*, as well as the personification of the combined deity of Serapis and Aesculapius.[42] Thus, according to Tacitus and Suetonius, Vespasian won fame in Egypt as a miracle healer (*thaumaturgos*).[43]

> A man of the people who was blind, and another who was lame, came to him together as he sat on the tribunal, begging for the help for their disorders which Serapis had promised in a dream; for the god declared that Vespasian would restore the eyes, if he would spit upon them, and give strength to the leg, if he would deign to touch it with his heel. Though he had hardly any faith that this could possibly succeed . . . he was at last prevailed upon by his friends and tried both things in public before a large crowd; and with success.[44]

As the highest priest, the emperor was subject to considerable regulations on cleansing, and, if he fell ill, it also presaged public catastrophes. When the emperors took office, it was expected that their personal vitality would bring about a 'rejuvenation' of the state. In the *Panegyricus* of Pliny the Younger, the people, represented by the four stages of life, hope that the sight of the emperor will bring them 'salvation and health' (*salutem sanitatemque*). The emperor played the role of an auxiliary in 'rebus fessis', in other words, 'for the fatigue-stricken state', comforted ill soldiers and showed consideration for the disabled when distributing alms. His prosperity, his fortune and his virtue appeared as 'remedium et salus' for the sick and the disadvantaged.[45]

The Roman theory of dietetics preached, as in the aforementioned example of Seneca, almost without exception the rejection of urban hustle and bustle, and of the *adiaphora* associated with 'negotium'.[46] Mythology and religion were also rediscovered in the imperial age, although it was often not so much religious as literary and aesthetic themes that awoke the interest of the educated public. A decisive factor here was that relaxation and the advancement or restoration of health were expected to compensate for the stress of public office and city life. Myth and literature taught that proximity to nature sustained health and pleased the gods. In Virgil's *Aeneid*, while Furies sit on Jupiter's throne 'and on the threshold of the grim monarch, and whet the fears of feeble mortals, where'er heaven's king deals diseases and awful death, or affrights guilty towns with war', Numanus, the brother-in-law of Turnus, praises the exemplary health of the ancient Latins.[47]

The literati also liked to popularize ancient magical, religious omens and advice. Thus, according to Virgil, the appearance of a blood-red comet sent by god in the night sky augured droughts and plagues: 'Or even as fiery Sirius, that bearer of drought and pestilence to feeble mortals, rises and saddens the sky with baleful light.'[48] The man who drank from the spring of Salmacis, we read in Ovid, would become a hermaphrodite; he who tasted the water of the Ethiopian lakes went mad or 'falls into a strange, deep lethargy'. Similar claims are made about the river that flows, 'between . . . green Cybele and high Celaenae . . . 'tis named the Gallus. Who drinks of it goes mad.'[49] The fear of infection was always a significant factor, whether one believed in miasmic theory or held the gods responsible. 'What timid man does not avoid contact with the sick, fearing lest he contract a disease so near', remarked Ovid,[50] who, in his *Tristia*, adopts the old thesis that the health of body and soul are mutually dependent. At all events, an ailing mind 'affects [the] limbs'.[51]

It is remarkable, particularly in comparison with the present day, how frequently the great Roman authors concern themselves with the theme of 'healthy living'. 'Lethargy and excessive sleep, undisturbed by anyone, games and a head reeling with copious amounts of wine deprive the mind of all its strength – without inflicting any wound', warned Ovid. The poet also informs us, however, about 'everyday' body and beauty care, about hygienic precautions such as washing before sexual intercourse, or the composition of beauty creams.[52] Pliny gives similar advice in the medical chapters of his *Natural*

History.[53] As was perhaps expected of court physicians, Trajan's doctor Kriton (around AD 100) composed a four-volume work about beauty care. In the *Amores* by pseudo-Lucian, the cosmetics collection of a Roman woman is scrutinized critically: 'There are silver dishes, jars, mirrors, dozens of pots as at a pharmacy, containers full of devilish stuff.'[54] Face masks, fragrant essences, ointments and perfumes, as well as hair colouring, were used frequently in the republican age. Propertius (50–15 BC), on the other hand, praised 'natural beauty'.[55] Cicero confirms that, in noble households, a bath was offered to guests before meals. Cato and Plautus also report that hands were washed before meals.[56] Meals in noble houses were followed by a one- to two-hour siesta, a practice that was observed even in Caesar's army.[57] Varro, one of the most intellectual among the Romans, emphasizes in *De re rustica* [*On Agriculture*]: 'If I could not break up a summer's day as a matter of course with my midday sleep, I could not live here' – an allusion to the southern climate, whose hot temperatures impair one's wellbeing.[58] Even after simple meals, fruits, pastries or sweets were offered as dessert, although Varro, with the digestion in mind, remarks: 'That dessert is particularly sweet which is not sweet.'[59] Ovid advocates daily dental and mouth care: 'Let your teeth be clear of rust . . . Let not the breath of your mouth be sour and unpleasing.' The practice of fumigating and sulphurating houses and bedrooms went on into the imperial age.[60] Lucretius recognized that every health measure and dietetic regime should be adapted for the individual, for what was correct for one could be poison for another.[61]

Philosophical and historical literature, even comedies and letters, therefore yield a colourful picture of everyday life in Rome. Pliny advised against taking rest after eating, as this leads to corpulence. In the *Mostellaria*, Plautus also observed: 'An after-luncheon snooze is no good.'[62] A passage in Tacitus' *Annales* even suggests that some Romans consulted doctors for regular examinations in the manner of a modern 'check-up'. Others evidently scoffed at 'men who, after thirty years of life, needed the counsel of a stranger in order to distinguish things salutary to their system from things deleterious.'[63]

Anyone who had reached this age in Rome had, at a conservative estimate, an average life expectancy of a further twenty-three years, although the overall average age in the city and among the slaves was considerably lower. Those who were older than forty constituted only 6 per cent of the population.[64] Alcoholism was widespread, although smoking was still unknown. It was well known that excesses, 'baths, wine and love', ruined one's health, but also, as one epitaph had it, 'constituted life', for 'hunting and bathing, playing and laughing:

that is really living.' The aristocratic ethos of the free citizens had, since the republican age, advocated an occupation in the political, legal or military spheres, whereby one satisfied one's own ambitions and increased the renown of the family. Accomplished men were pre-occupied, even harassed, by innumerable obligations.[65] Pliny the Younger recommended hunting and physical exercise as the ideal recreation for the 'homo politicus'. Walks in parks, on the beach or under a portico were also popular activities, although intellectuals such as Pliny the Elder wish to remain 'alone with myself and my books'.

For moral or satirical reasons rather than for reasons of public health, Seneca and Juvenal were concerned about the luxury of bathing resorts such as Baiae, where gormandizing was as common as idleness and sloth.[66] In a letter, Horace, who had his refuge in Tivoli, describes the dilemma of the sensitive poet who falls victim to urban bustle: 'Besides all else, do you think I can write verses at Rome amid all my cares and all my toils? One calls me to be surety, another, to leave my duties and listen to his writings. One lies sick on the Quirinal hill, another on the Aventine's far side; I must visit both.' The poet, with his aesthetic sensibilities, could not relax in Rome: 'In hot haste rushes a contractor with mules and porters; a huge crane is hoisting now a stone and now a beam; mournful funerals jostle massive wagons; this way runs a mad dog; that way rushes a mud-bespattered sow.'[67] Tibullus (*d.* 19 BC) also sings the praises of country life, which reinforces in him the old reverence for the gods. He claims that it shows the individual the unspoiled origins of civilization; however, it also represents an erotic magic garden.[68]

The Roman health doctrines and practices were tailored to suit the limited time at the disposal of the citizen subject to the demands of 'negotium', and demonstrated an impressive degree of tolerance and pluralism. From Hellenism, but particularly from the age of the Roman republic, the main concern was to adapt the elitist Greek '*diaita*', defined by the privileged status of the rich private citizen, to the daily life of the Roman patrician, which was subject to the requirements of the 'vita activa'. A daily routine governed by a dietetic regime, as formulated by Diocles, was as impracticable for the country landowner as it was for the town-dweller occupied with business or politics. As far as the Romans were concerned, the healthy individual had no need whatsoever of an inflexible pro-gramme for daily living. He needed advice, according to which he could structure his life in the country, in the town, or while travel-ling. Supplementary recreation *after* and not *instead of* daily labour was required.

New doctors, new theories

Around 219 BC, according to Pliny the Elder, a certain Archagathos appeared in Rome as the first doctor; his enigmatic character caused him to be associated less with healing or health than with the metaphor of a butcher (Carnifex).[69] In around AD 90, Asclepiades, another Greek doctor, arrived in the capital, where he also won renown as a rhetorician and intellectual. Asclepiades relativized humoral pathology and the Hippocratic notion of the power of 'nature'. Health for him signified a mechanically conceived interaction between body and soul, both of which consist of atoms, and whose movement is identical with 'life'. Body and soul constitute a 'network of pores', in which the atoms (or 'particles') of the *pneuma* circulate, as do the humours. According to this startlingly 'technical' notion, health disorders are caused by 'an unbalanced, hampered or increased flow of particles'.

The importance of nature as a healer is subject to doubt, according to Asclepiades: 'Not only is nature to no advantage, it is even sometimes damaging!' The ancient Roman dietetics of Cato was therefore deprived of its theoretical foundations. The duty of the doctor was rather to determine the *methods* that are conducive to normal movements of the particles or atoms. Massages, baths, physical exercises, gymnastics, fasting, but also wine, anaerobic exercises and spiritual tranquillity, all represented possible methods. In the case of mental illnesses, air, light and music also provided relaxation and recovery. It was logical that the doctors practising in Rome should defend their work *theoretically* and attempt to refute the tenet of the healing power of nature propagated by Cato. In addition to 'methodists' such as Asclepiades or his pupil Themison of Laodicea, who identified the condition of the pore walls as a criterion for health and defined health itself as a mid-state between the 'status laxus' (atony) and the 'status strictus' (contraction),[70] there were also 'pneumatics', 'dogmatics', 'eclectics', 'diagnosticians' and 'empiricists'. Despite, and even precisely because of, the demonstratively emphasized function of the physician as an arbitrator, for the majority of antiquity's influential doctors their own health represented proof positive of a successful dietetic regime. Asclepiades himself reportedly stated that he would not wish to be considered a doctor if he became ill himself![71]

The 'methodists' adopted a sceptical attitude towards the model of health known as 'eucrasy'. For them, evaluation of the pore walls and the stage of the illness, whereby one differentiated between intensification, an unchanging state and abatement, sufficed as therapeutic criteria. Thessalos of Tralles (first century AD) argued in the case of chronic ailments for a 'metasyncretic' course of therapy, which would fundamentally change the comportment of the body. A phase of invigoration by means of fortifying food, massages and gymnastics was followed by a succession of different diets, fasts, vomiting, baths and medication.[72]

Certain 'pneumatics' such as Agathinus of Sparta or the physicians Leonidas and Herodotus, who also practised in Rome, put together a composite, but apparently viable doctrine from a variety of medical and philosophical sources.[73] Active and passive movement, massages, purgatives, blood-letting, the consumption of and abstinence from wine, rocking in the sedan, walking, running, travelling by cart, sport and relaxation, bathing and fasting, could, depending on the case, all determine the dietetic regime of the healthy and the sick.[74] The intellectual eclecticism which characterized society in late Roman antiquity also influenced health care. As mere suggestions concerning dietetics or the Stoic maxim of a life ensuring health ('secundum naturam vivere') did not always find favour with the upper classes, many an enterprising doctor also prescribed pills guaranteeing beauty, health and potency. This explains the general increase in prescriptions – for example, the case of Antonius Musa, who recommended secret remedies for eye problems, nose abscesses and kidney pains in Augustan Rome, and even the emergence of theriac, which was developed by Andromachus, a physician in Nero's court, as a magical remedy for *every* illness or poison. It is entirely consistent with this that this doctor also composed a tract 'on the conservation of health'.[75] The description of all known medicinal herbs by Pedanius Dioscorides (AD 77), from Anazarbus in Cilicia, including detailed information on their habitat, preparation, preservation and use, is still worthy of our admiration today, but also demonstrates the enormous demand that there was for such information. Also of significance is the *Liber medicinalis* by Quintus Serenus Sammonicus (AD 200), which contained in verse form sixty-four suggestions for therapy, with particular emphasis placed on magical recipes – the most famous of which is the *Abracadabra*.[76]

Dietetics, prophylactics, gymnastics and sport were also in vogue, although the maladies of civilization such as obesity, alcoholism (which Pliny believed 'perverts men's minds and produces madness'),[77] prostitution, criminality, poverty, social deprivation and isolation, luxury and – among the slaves and the lower classes – hard working conditions also increasingly represented threats to health. The lack of an individual sense of responsibility for health and the tendency of many doctors to treat only symptoms, and not social or political causes, was criticized in the first century AD by Scribonius Largus, court physician to many emperors, who counted among the duties of the doctor humanity and compassion, as well as – entirely in the Platonic tradition – concern for the common weal.[78] For the author of the *Compositiones*, a change in living habits represented the precondition for every successful treatment.

One of the most important Roman scholars and authors was Cornelius Celsus, a contemporary of Tiberius (first century AD). Of his six-part *Encyclopaedia*, only the 'eight books on medicine' survive. At the beginning of the first volume we find the following advice:

> A man in health, who is both vigorous and his own master, should be under no obligatory rules, and have no need, either for a medical attendant, or for a rubber and anointer. His kind of life should afford him variety; he should be now in the country, now in the town, and more often about the farm; he should sail, hunt, rest sometimes, but more often take exercise; for whilst inaction weakens the body, work strengthens it; the former brings on premature old age; the latter prolongs youth. It is well also at times to go to the bath, at times to make use of cold waters; to undergo sometimes inunction, sometimes to neglect that same; to avoid no kind of food in common use.[79]

Celsus recommends a normal, balanced life, determined by everyday exigencies. One should eat now more, now less, but in any case no more than can be digested. The amount and type of food should be adjusted to suit one's profession and amount of physical exercise, for, whereas normal food and exercise are necessities, 'those of athletes are redundant' (for the normal individual).[80]

According to the scholar (who was probably not a physician himself, but merely compiling the medical knowledge of his day), moderation should also be practised in sexual intercourse, 'nor [is it] overmuch to be feared. Seldom used it braces the body, used frequently it relaxes.'[81] As licentiousness renders one weak, one should 'take care that whilst in health [one's] defences against ill-health are not used up' (according to ancient Hippocratic notions, coitus disturbed the balance of the humours). In general, those of a delicate nature, 'among whom are a large portion of townspeople, and almost all those fond of letters, need greater precaution, so their care may re-establish what the character of their constitution or of their residence or of their study detracts.'[82] They should protect themselves in particular from the midday sun and morning and evening chills, as well as from vapours exuding from rivers and swamps.[83] Celsus also recommends individually tailored breaks for rest before or after meals. Every extreme, as well as sudden change, should be avoided; every individual has his weaknesses and must make corresponding provisions for himself, although his goal should always be greater balance and harmony.[84] Celsus recommends a regular examination of one's own body, including an inspection of the colours of one's urine: 'He can tell that his body is sound if his morning urine is whitish, later reddish.'[85]

Physical or intellectual work immediately after meals is considered unhealthy. In summer, one may also work at night; 'in winter, it is best to rest in bed the whole night long.' Conversation, music and recitations are beneficial to the intellect and delight the soul, and for this reason often have a positive effect on the mentally ill.[86] Walks or gymnastics should be ceased when one sweats or a state of slight fatigue is reached. Celsus also recognized that a change of location can endanger one's health. 'The transition from a healthy area to an unhealthy one should preferably be carried out at the beginning of the winter, the transition from an unhealthy to a healthy one, on the other hand, at the beginning of the summer.'[87] Changes to one's way of living – from work to leisure, for example – should be carried out with moderation. The eclectic frequently reflected on the arguments that the Hippocratics had presented before him.[88] One keeps oneself slim by bathing in warm water (and in a sober condition), by consciously acquiring a sunburn (!), by worrying and losing sleep, by running and going for walks, and as a result of heat and tiring physical exercises and also of vomiting and diarrhoea. To those with a tendency to catch colds, Celsus recommends rinsing the mouth and dousing the head with cold water.[89] In Celsus' oeuvre, which only really became famous when it was printed in 1478, that is, in the Renaissance,[90] dietetics admittedly occupies only a small space in comparison with the comprehensive advice on surgery, the doctrine of disease and medication. Significantly, however, it appears at the beginning of the work.

Health-conscious behaviour should, as had been taught by Athenaeus of Attaleia, be adjusted to suit the time of year, as well as the stage of life. Thus, children and old people are less able to endure fasting than middle-aged people. Celsus, who compiled numerous works – from him we learn of no fewer than seventy-two otherwise unknown Greek authors – describes the optimal mode of behaviour in the case of a wide variety of illnesses and dispositions, thus giving us an excellent overview of the precautionary health measures taken by the educated Roman of his day. The modern reader may feel that one thing is lacking: the recommendation of recreational travel and 'holidays' in the modern sense. Rich Romans did travel to the country and to bathing resorts in order to enjoy the 'vita rustica' or 'contemplativa'. If the conditions there were more conducive to performing health-advancing exercises than in the town, then the doctors approved of such 'otium'. However, the advantages of such locations – particularly for the sick or the elderly – were always accompanied by the disadvantage of climate change and physical or mental adjustment. Galen was also reticent with regard to this matter.

Sport and baths

In Rome, as in ancient Greece, sport played an important part in social and public health matters. Swimming even became fashionable at times, although it remained largely insignificant at the thermal springs, where the swimming pools were small. Young men traditionally trained in athletic disciplines on the Fields of Mars in Rome, and even emperors or senators took part in ball games, or, like Augustus, regularly performed gymnastic exercise. Even Seneca, for whom philosophical exertion was the foundation of spiritual health, which, for its part, paved the way for the health of the body, advised intellectually active people to pursue sports as a means of compensation: 'There are exercises, light and short ones, which tire the body quickly and save time, and which are particularly worthy of consideration: running with a dumbbell, hand movements and jumping, either the high jump or the long jump.'[91] Ball games were also popular, and were cultivated in particular within the ambit of the thermal springs. The professionalization of certain sports, for example, gladiatorial fights and pugilism, admittedly seems to have fostered a more passive enjoyment among the masses, who participated as spectators in the arena.[92]

Of particular importance in Rome were the public baths, which, in the imperial age, acquired both dietetic and social significance, from the metropolis to the most distant provincial garrisons. They were certainly impressive as examples of architecture, whose functional complexity made ever greater demands of architects and engineers. The location, the climate and the arrangement of the rooms were of greater significance than in the case of private houses, as on account of certain relations and proportions functional buildings generally also met aesthetic requirements.[93] The Roman bathing culture was relatively undeveloped before the second century BC – people rarely washed, even in noble households! They were more likely to swim in rivers and lakes, like the Roman youth after the traditional training and sport on the Fields of Mars.[94] Bathrooms were still a rarity in houses and villas; they were generally situated next to the kitchen, were uncomfortable and cool and contained murky, used water. Slaves were invariably kept away from baths, as, in the opinion of Columella, too much water and moisture reduced physical strength, or rather manpower, and it had long been suspected that wet skin turned the pores in the body into entrances for disease. Theoretical health considerations of this kind were admittedly of less significance in later times, aside from the fact that the alternation between the 'frigidarium' (cold-water bath), 'tepidarium' (warm bath) and 'caldarium' (hot bath) in the public baths, as well as the use of sweat baths, was believed to have a beneficial effect on the circulation. Sweat baths ('laconica') were initially considered alien in Rome, and thought to have originated in Sparta.[95] Whereas the Greeks supplemented or concluded gymnastic exercises with baths, the latter were of central importance for the Romans. Sport was reduced to a marginal pastime, subordinate to the pleasures of bathing.

The public baths were primarily social and political institutions. In 33 BC there were around 170 bathing facilities in Rome alone. They were generally run by leaseholders and open in the afternoons. The entrance price was low, and entrance was free for children. One bathed naked; the bikini attire for women represented in the Piazza Armerina on Sicily was worn for sporting activities, but not for bathing. Those who wore loincloths could, as Martial attests, expect to be ridiculed.[96] In a letter, Seneca gives a vexed description of the noise and dimensions of the bathing establishment:

> I have lodgings right over a bathing establishment. So picture to yourself the assortment of sounds, which are strong enough to make me hate my very powers of hearing! When your strenuous gentleman, for example, is exercising himself by flourishing leaden weights; when he is working hard, or else pretends to be working hard, I can hear him grunt; and whenever he releases his imprisoned breath, I can hear him panting in wheezy and high-pitched tones. Or perhaps I notice some lazy fellow, content with a cheap rubdown, and hear the crack of the pummeling hand on his shoulder, varying in sound according as the hand is laid on flat or hollow. Then, perhaps, a professional comes along, shouting out the score; that is the finishing touch. Add to this the arresting of an occasional roysterer or pickpocket, the racket of the man who always likes to hear his own voice in the bathroom, or the enthusiast who plunges into the swimming-tank with unconscionable noise and splashing. . . . Then the cake-seller with his varied cries, the sausageman, the confectioner, and all the vendors of food hawking their wares, each with his own distinctive intonation.[97]

Bathing, particularly in the large thermal baths of the imperial period, included intensive body care, which encompassed gymnastics, rubbing with ointment, massage, shaving, and, for women, the application of make-up.[98] In late antiquity, the thermal baths were more amusement centres than places of physical regeneration; however, they did promote body care among the middle and lower classes. The bathing establishments often housed doctors' practices, particularly of surgeons and barbers. The Diocletian baths in Rome, according to the testament of Suetonius, even had an extensive library.[99] The entrance prices were often subsidized by public or private donors.[100]

The private villas of the imperial period also had at their disposal luxurious baths, as has been demonstrated by excavations in Pompeii and Stabiae, and even in estates north of the Alps. It goes without saying that the imperial palaces such as Tiberius' Villa Jovis on Capri or Hadrian's villa in Tivoli feature particularly sumptuous bathing facilities. In later antiquity, members of the imperial families probably suffered from a lack of exercise and from obesity, particularly given that bathing did not involve adequate physical exertion. The recreational programme of the well-to-do youth was determined increasingly by the refrain coined by the poet and social critic Martial (AD 40–102): 'promenades, chats, books, the Field of Mars, Porticus, shade, springs, baths'[101] and less and less by true sport or tournaments.

The sacred tales of Publius Aelius Aristides

The autobiographical medical history of the Greek sophist and rhetorician of the Roman Empire Publius Aelius Aristides (AD 117–181) represents an encomium to Aesculapius and introduces us to daily life at one of his cultic sites, Pergamon. The work demonstrates the fashionable status of magical and pagan religious healing practices, sometimes as an alternative, sometimes as a supplement to Hippocratic and Galenic humoral medicine, and demonstrates in particular their appeal to the well-to-do classes. The son of a priest of Zeus from Hadriani in the north-west of Asia Minor, Aristides corresponded with emperors and literati, won fame as a brilliant rhetorician and secured his renown and his legacy for posterity during his lifetime. According to his biographer Philostratus, his health was weak from his early youth. At the end of a trip to Rome in winter 144, he came down with a bad cold, as a result of which he visited the spas near Smyrna, which were famous in antiquity, in order to recuperate. It was here that Aesculapius commanded him in a dream to move to Pergamon, and Aristides indeed spent the subsequent years in the Asklepion, together with other worshippers of the deity. Short periods of recovery enabled him to leave the town temporarily; relapses and ailments meant a return to the 'health resort'. Aristides was in all probability suffering from malaria and tuberculosis, in addition to dropsy of an uncertain cause. But the patient, entirely 'addicted' to medical treatment with his fixations on illnesses and healing springs, showed primarily neurotic characteristics. The psychosomatic components of his numerous ailments are self-evident, however cautious we should be when making retrospective diagnoses. His days were filled with therapeutic fasts, enemas, induced vomiting, baths in ice-cold rivers during high fevers, and other similarly 'paradoxical' treatments. The course of therapy was determined by directions from the gods received in dreams, to whom Aristides entrusted himself devoutly. At the Asklepion, famous physicians such as Satyrus and his pupil Galen attended to the important patient, who, admittedly, was sceptical with regard to scientific medicine and had greater faith in incubation and the methods of the temple. Aristides worshipped the old healing deities, particularly Zeus and, in addition to Aesculapius, the Egyptian Serapis, who had saved him from peril at sea. On his estate at Laneion in Mysia, he composed from 170–71 onwards his 'sacred tales' (*Hierói lógoi*), which were based on diary entries. The content consisted, in his own words, of 'remedies of every kind, some discussions, extensive orations, all kinds of apparitions and prophecies'. Notwithstanding a degree of exaggeration, the tract serves to demonstrate once again how self-evident the concern with dietetics and health care was for the 'nobiles' of the Roman province. The claim made by Nicephorus Gregoras, a historian of the fourteenth century, that a fatal fever put an end to the author's career is likely to be a romantic elaboration, however.

Aristides decided 'to entrust myself to the god as to a physician' who gave him not only advice, but also a theoretical explanation for his complaints, by providing him, for example, with an insight into his own abdomen.[102] The treatment was generally accompanied by prayers delivered by the priests and discussed with other patients at the resort. It is not easy for the reader to separate the contents of dreams from real occurrences, as for Aristides the two merge together:

> I, however, asked the god to announce to me more clearly which of the two he meant: fasting or vomiting. I went to sleep on this, and it seemed to me as if I was at the shrine in Pergamon, and half the day had already been spent fasting. [The physician] Theodotus approached with several friends . . . I informed him that I was fasting; but he intimated that he knew this and said: after everything that these [friends] have done, I hesitate to use phlebotomy, for the pain comes from the kidneys.[103]

Even when fasting, the author did not forget to record his impressions:

I underwent the purgation of the upper digestive tract for two years and two months, in connection with enemas and blood-letting, in a quantity that no one has yet counted, and this with the most meagre nourishment . . . During all these periods of fasting, the earlier as the later, that we observed during this winter, we spent, contrary to expectation, the whole day writing, conversing and checking written texts . . . And when another fasting period began immediately after vomiting, it was precisely this that comforted me: the employment and preoccupation with such things.[104]

On occasions, Aristides, his physicians and his instructors all had the same dream, which naturally speeded the execution of the divine directions. His treatments, orations and votes of thanks were always public events: 'My friends, the notables of the Hellenic world at that time, visited constantly and were present at my recitals; although I delivered my disputations directly from my bed', he remarks proudly.[105]

In cases of doubt, Aristides insisted on carrying out the therapeutic suggestions seen in his visions against the will of the doctors. When the god prescribed an enema, the doctor treating Aristides hesitated, as he feared he would commit murder. 'However, I persuaded him with difficulty to do this, and immediately recovered.' Many of the therapeutic methods he tested appear more damaging than beneficial to health from a modern perspective – for example, the instruction to go rowing during a high swell in order to induce vomiting, or to go barefoot in winter.

Aristides' experiential world was dominated by prophecies, mysterious counsels, warnings and riddles. Naturally, only a member of the moneyed class was able to spend the year in the vicinity of temples and cultic spas. On one occasion, Aesculapius forewarned his charge that he would die within three days unless he took the preventative measures prescribed, such as presenting certain sacrifices.[106] For Aristides, the divinity determined who would lose his life, with the result that – all human efforts notwithstanding – the length of one's life was apparently predetermined. In his daily routine governed by dietetics and therapy, the author himself seems sometimes to forget this aspect, despite being in constant dialogue with Aesculapius. Aristides was also proud of the fact that, according to the testimony of the temple attendants, he had been bled the most frequently of all patients at the shrine, with the exception of a certain Ischyon.[107]

Aristides' dreams of instruction contain a metaphysically enhanced, extravagant concept of therapy, which was oriented less to religious needs than to the needs of a hypochondriac. The obsessive nature of the described forms of treatment perplexed even his contemporaries. The life of the human being is portrayed as part of divine providence, which can change at any moment, a phenomenon that the gods reveal to the devout, observant individual in more or less dramatic circumstances. The concept of health that formed the basis of this milieu was flamboyant and, in the final analysis, able to impress only pious health fanatics. Yet, throughout cultural history, individuals have seldom divulged their health problems and complaints in such detail as Aristides,[108] whose prodigious learning (he typically makes constant reference to Greek history and the world of the Homeric gods) afforded him additional forms of comfort and even psychotherapy, but also additional modes of self-representation.

The Roman Stoics: Plutarch, Seneca, Marcus Aurelius, Epictetus

In imperial Rome, teachings on healing, sects and philosophies of the most diverse persuasions burgeoned. The Stoics in particular experienced a renaissance and succeeded in inspiring many 'pneumatically' oriented physicians. Admittedly, the bathing culture, mass sports and combat games did conspire to trivialize dietetics to a certain degree; however, dietetic thought also acquired greater philosophical and ethical value within elite circles. Particularly influential was the tract *De tuenda sanitate praecepta* [*Rules for the Preservation of Health*] by the Stoic writer Plutarch (*b.* AD 45), an important figure in the Rome of Vespian and Trajan, and author of a comparative biography which remained part of the classical canon of literature for the educated until well into the nineteenth century. In a fictional dialogue, the reproach of the doctor Moschion that laymen commit a 'transgression' by concerning themselves with health care (*diaita hygieiná*), is refuted. In view of the diverse origins of Greek dietetics, comprising both philosophy and the sporting domain, for example, this argument was antiquated (particularly given that the point of controversy had already been resolved in a Solomonic manner by Herophilus). But this refutation does demonstrate how self-confident the medical profession in imperial Rome had become. Health care should be popularized, they concede; however, it should always be supervised by doctors. As was the case throughout antiquity, the term 'hygiene' was interpreted as 'the art of healthy living' in the broadest possible sense.

Plutarch's guidelines on health were of a practical and a moral nature: one should always keep one's hands and feet warm, so that one's body heat does not become concentrated in one area and cause a fever there. In addition, the healthy individual should eat the diet of a sick person now and again, so as to be better able to bear the deprivations of illness. The imperative of moderation in eating and drinking is emphasized sternly, in the manner of the ancient Stoics, although it is also stated that social difficulties, such as the wish not to offend hosts who have lovingly prepared an opulent meal, can be sidestepped by means of a clever excuse or joke. Submission to one's appetites is damaging in the culinary as in the sexual domain; even culinary experts are, according to the ascetically oriented author, no less vulnerable than women who are brewing love potions! As a good state of health is, he continues, the precondition for real enjoyment, the connoisseur in particular must pay attention to self-discipline, and even abstinence. Yet over-caution in matters of health, the author concludes, is just as inappropriate as disregard. Following exertions or excess, the body requires rest; after meals light entertainment is recommended rather than exercise. For the intellectually active, the healthiest form of gymnastics consists in regularly exercising the voice by declaiming, reading aloud and debating. Following this, however, a massage or gymnastic exercise is recommended by way of compensation.

Heavy food should be consumed only with the greatest caution, and meat, not at all, if possible. Milk is praised by Plutarch as a healthy, high-quality nutriment, created by nature itself. Music, literature or scholarly pursuits are considered an effective means of combating a gluttonous appetite. During meals, one should not discuss topics that are too difficult or distracting; exhausting luxuries should also be avoided. The greatest enemy of health for the Stoic, however, is idleness; the greatest tonic is a rational occupation 'for the good of the whole', which does not induce feverish agitation. The man who is calm within himself and who has mastered his affects is able to conserve his health and thus to work for the benefit of society.

In the remaining dialogues of Plutarch, the taming (but not the complete suppression) of the passions and the fight against vices such as avarice, irascibility, jealousy, curiosity, loquacity or excessive activity are popular topics, and encompass dietetic alongside ethical aspects. The route to ethical perfection and felicitousness is shown to lie in the age-old topos of 'moderate living', an inexhaustible topic in the imperial age. Guidebooks for young married couples or consolatory tracts for those suffering ill fortune have the same goal.

The philosophical and dietetic views of Seneca (AD 4–65), whose oeuvre, which has already been cited repeatedly, also influenced Christian ethics, were defined by his contempt for death. For the philosopher, this was the prerequisite for 'tranquillitas animi', for that condition in which 'the mind may always pursue a steady and favourable course, may be well disposed towards itself, and may view its condition with joy.'[109] If one fears neither death nor pain, then one is immune to the blows of fate and to illnesses.[110] The Greek tradition of 'eucrasy' and the golden mean is recalled when Seneca equates harmony with virtue, which manifests itself in 'a scheme of life that is consistent with itself throughout'.[111] 'Scorn pain; it will either be relieved or relieve you. Scorn death, which either ends you or transfers you', we read in the essay *On Providence*.[112] The route to peace of mind is based on understanding, the mastery of passions (such as anger), philosophy (for example, recognition of the brief and limited nature of life), and a dietetic theory of a thoroughly physical orientation. Concern for one's health should not be motivated by illness, pain and death; it should rather be rooted in the recognition of the inanity of these things.

The moralist considered luxury and immorality to represent the most important dangers to health. Like Cato, Cicero and Pliny, Seneca invokes the simple and healthy lifestyle of earlier generations: 'No wonder that in early days medicine had less to do! Men's bodies were still sound and strong; their food was light and not spoiled by art and luxury, whereas when they began to seek dishes not for the sake of removing, but of rousing, the appetite, and devised countless sauces to whet their gluttony, then what before was nourishment to a hungry man became a burden to the full stomach.'[113] In contrast to Cato and the Cynics, however, he defends the art of healing: 'The physician will prescribe your walks and your exercise; he will warn you not to become addicted to idleness, as is the tendency of the inactive invalid; he will order you to read in a louder voice and to exercise your lungs . . . or to sail and shake up your bowels by a little mild motion; he will recommend the proper food, and the suitable time for aiding your strength with wine', he writes to Lucilius.[114] Even if Hippocrates noted that women did not lose hair or suffer from gout, this unfortunately did not apply to contemporary Rome: 'Nowadays they run short of hair and are afflicted with gout. This does not mean that women's physique has changed, but that it has been conquered; in rivalling male indulgences they have also rivalled the ills to which men are heirs.' The tendency towards insobriety that is widespread among men and women is branded an 'overmastering and widespread madness'.[115] The philosopher considered mental illnesses to be the consequence of a lack of self-discipline – a modification of the Stoic tenet that health and virtue are closely related. In his book *On Anger* he recommends identifying one's own disposition and moderating angry outbursts, for example: 'for when [the passions] have established themselves in possession, they are stronger than their ruler and do not permit themselves to be restrained or reduced.'[116]

The Stoic ideal of health at this time was still influenced by Platonic dualism. A healthy body was, admittedly, a legitimate goal – as a result of spiritual perfection; however, there could be no question that it was precisely the experience of disease that motivated the individual to philosophical pursuits. In this regard, Marcus Aurelius (121–180) stated in his famous *Communings with Himself*: 'Listen to Epicurus where he says: *In my illness my talk was not of any bodily feelings, nor did I chatter about such things to those who came to see me, but I went on with my cardinal disquisitions on natural philosophy, dwelling especially on this point, how the mind, having perforce its share in such affections of the flesh, yet remains unperturbed, safeguarding its own proper good.*'[117] In sickness and adversity the wise man must, like Epicurus, meditate on philosophy, 'for it is a commonplace of every sect not to renounce philosophy whatever difficulties we encounter'.

The tendency towards contempt for the body, or at least towards the relativization of the corporeal, of health, sexuality and age, is self-evident: 'Whether the experience of these things lasts three hundred years or three, it is all one.'[118] The teachings of the philosopher emperor do not, however, culminate in an advocacy of self-mortification or suicide. True enough, he considers human existence to be 'streaming away', the senses 'dim' and the body 'prone to decay'; however, man is, insofar as he protects his soul from damage, ultimately 'lord of all pleasures and pains', and therefore able to anticipate death 'with a good grace'.[119] Medical efforts to secure physical wellbeing therefore seem to Marcus Aurelius – as with the early Stoics – to be superfluous and illusory. Even 'Hippocrates, who had cured many illnesses, himself became ill and died.' Death, though feared by many, was for him a natural occurrence, comparable with birth. 'A combination of the same elements, a breaking up into the same – and not at all a thing in fact for any to be ashamed of', he states, echoing Lucretius.[120] Spiritual tranquillity is important, physical health not, let alone sporting success or a beautiful body. Man is, as Epictetus had noted, only 'a little soul, carrying a corpse'. A cheerful, friendly superiority, which attaches little value to everything that plagues, disturbs and afflicts others, is the quintessence of a form of mentally controlled dietetics, which the emperor extrapolates in his meditations addressed 'to himself' and composed in a military camp. Yet proof that Marcus Aurelius did not employ exclusively philosophical arguments in his daily life can be found in his prayer to Aesculapius, whom he entreats to keep his teacher Fronto in good health. The popularity of diverse medical, religiously coloured, magical and philosophical recipes for attaining health and happiness was characteristic almost throughout antiquity and, generally speaking, represented the norm in the capital Rome – in the imperial age an ethnic and linguistic melting pot.

In his *Manual*, Epictetus (AD 50–130), a liberated slave who was later exiled to Epirus, and for whom Marcus Aurelius had great admiration, emphasized that illness was debilitating for the body but did not affect moral decisions: 'And say this to yourself at each thing that befalls you; for you will find the thing to be an impediment to something else, but not to yourself.'[121] The wise man should develop a philosophical plan for life which enables him to endure its vicissitudes, for life is shaped by unhappiness, suffering and hardship. This insight does not, however, free us from the obligation to arm ourselves against external adversity and to prevent afflictions of the body as of the soul, for 'he who finds himself in a good physical state of health can bear heat and cold. Thus can those who are healthy in their souls bear anger, pain, excessive joy and the other feelings.'[122] If one guards against becoming a slave to the body, then the fear of losing one's health becomes inconsequential. Such a fear is, insofar as the primary concern is physical wellbeing, entirely absurd. 'Is health a good?' we read in the *Discourses*; the answer: 'No, man, why would it be? The correct use of health is a good; the incorrect, an evil.'[123]

Like the Presocratics before him, Epictetus believes the human body to be bound to the laws of the cosmos. He does not, however, consider it to be the image of the cosmos, or the microscosm; it is rather, like animals and plants, a building block of the universe. 'Our body in sickness and health . . ., in youth and old age and notwithstanding all changes that it goes through,' is obedient to the cosmos. It is useless to rebel against this order, 'for it is powerful and stronger than we are, and has composed a better plan for our existence than we could.'[124] The integration of human existence within the cosmic order calms, comforts and liberates us. It therefore becomes clear why Epictetus advises us not to be alarmed by the diagnoses of doctors, for 'when you were healthy, what was good about it? Do not be downhearted when the doctor tells you that you are not well. What does this mean? That the soul is in the process of detaching itself from the body. What is bad about this . . .?' 'Sustine et abstine' ('endure and abstain') is his famous motto, as recorded by the poet Gellius.[125]

The dietetic theories expounded by the older Stoics are relativized by the late Stoics, in order to clear the stage for a philosophically coloured therapeutic approach. Seneca, Marcus Aurelius and Epictetus propagated their teachings in a society whose upper classes received the contemptuous devaluation of the body as an attractive and perhaps also fashionable option. It is not surprising, therefore, that Christian authors also eagerly adopted the idea of the 'vanitas' of the body and frequently invoked the Stoics.

Galen

Galen, the great physician of the second century (129–199), who came from Pergamon but practised in Rome, dealt extensively with teachings on health. Thanks to his posthumous fame, which is unique in the history of medicine, his dietetic guidelines also influenced the Arab, Persian and Western Middle Ages. Galen followed Hippocrates, arguing for a modified doctrine of the four humours.[126] His six-volume didactic work (*Hygieiná*), which could be described as a quintessence of ancient teachings on health, begins with the observation that medicine consists of two main areas: the preservation of health and the treatment of illnesses.[127] Galen examines, as had been advocated by Herophilus and Erasistratus before him, three human existential orientations: 'health, illness and the neutral condition in between',[128] the last of which is characteristic of, for example, the elderly, children and convalescents with their diverse complaints.[129] Similarly, the condition of the human being is determined by three 'causes': 'causae insalubres', 'causae neutrae' and 'causae salubres'. The second and third causes should be fostered carefully as guarantors of health, as they determine the functioning of the body in a complex manner. They consist of the more or less rhythmical processes of life, such as the air surrounding the individual, exercise and rest, sleeping and waking, eating and drinking, filling and evacuating, as well as the emotional processes.[130] These regulatory factors, which had been described in the Hippocratic tract *Peri diaítes* and were later characterized as the 'sex res non naturales' or 'six non-naturals',[131] occupied a central position in the Islamic dietetic canon of the subsequent 1600 years. The relationship between these factors has to be balanced, as they determine the condition of the body and can directly modify heat, cold, moisture and warmth as well as the interplay between the 'humores'. The individual should pay particular attention to cultivating them, as the organism cannot regenerate without their influence and as a result of 'nature' alone. Health and precautions against illness are once again subject to individual decision and regarded as virtues.[132] Galen's complex dietetics constitutes a compilation of the fundamental concepts of 'classic' Presocratic natural philosophy (cosmos, physis, nomos), together with the Hippocratic humoral doctrine and Aristotelian ethics.[133]

Galen was a pupil of the Hippocratic physician Stratonicus. In Pergamon, he had become familiar with the cult of Aesculapius, which had undergone a revival under Antoninus Pius, and had continued his education at the medical schools of Smyrna, Corinth and, in particular, Alexandria. He is likely to have gained practical experience in the areas of surgery and convalescence when working as a physician to gladiators and sportsmen in Pergamon (after 157). The practice of medicine taught there also influenced his teachings on health. 'I affirm that, of all physical exercises, the best are those that not only build up the body, but also bring recovery to the mind', was his judgement on the benefits of ball games, for example. He also emphasized the health-advancing, invigorating effects of gymnastics, which he considered subordinate to the art of the physician. This amounted to an affront to the 'gymnastics teachers' who were proliferating in Rome, profiting from the increasing concern with health; they were generally from the ranks of former professional athletes and, Galen reports in disgust, called the rhythm for the exercises 'with their unmelodic, barbaric voices', and even sometimes attempted 'to write about massage, correct behaviour (*euhexía*), health and physical exercise'. They 'presume', we read in the tract *Thrasybulus*, 'to act upon and discuss that which they have never learned'.[134] We can conclude from Galen's comments that the 'gymnasai', for their part, accused the physicians of insufficient practice, and even reproached their highest authority, Hippocrates, of being excessively theoretical ('When did Hippocrates venture onto the sports field or into the palaestra?'). The controversy between Hippocratic medicine and the lay healers – here we are reminded of Herophilus and Plutarch's Moschion – seems to have escalated in Rome in the second century. As the theory of dietetics based on the principle of balance seemed to them to be straightforward, increasing numbers of laymen felt compelled to compose health *regimina*, not only for themselves, but also for others. Galen differentiated between sporting exercises to be carried out in one's leisure time – such as wrestling, running, fist-fighting, swinging of the hands, hiking, shadow-boxing, finger-fighting, jumping, discus or javelin – and other kinds of physical activity that were routine within particular professions, but were also conducive to health – such as digging, rowing, ploughing, carrying loads, cutting vines, mowing, riding, fighting with heavy weapons, hunting, fishing and other things 'that craftsmen and unskilled workmen do for a living, such as carpenters, ore smiths, shipwrights, ploughmen, and those who carry out other works of war or peace.' Thanks to the humoral doctrine, therapeutic baths also appeared to make sense: the hard and tense parts of the body are softened by the water, the surplus humours distributed. For cold baths, however, Galen considered courage and cheerfulness to be prerequisites, as well as the absence of acute complaints and indicators of illness. Rubdowns with oil (using appropriate massage gloves) also invigorated the body, he claimed. A low body temperature and paleness after bathing were indicative of illness, or that the patient had spent too long in the water.[135]

Galen composed the most influential and comprehensive medical work that has reached us from antiquity. He supported the Hippocratic argument that health and healing are less gifts of fate than the consequences of one's own behaviour.[136] In the tract *De sanitate tuenda* [*Hygiene*], the multifaceted scholar becomes an eclectic, a proponent of Hippocratic and alternative medicine, a philosopher and a psychologist. Taking the Hippocratic tract *Peri diaítes* as his starting point, he at first highlights the influence and importance of the prophylactic: 'As in terms of both time and value health comes before sickness, we must first and foremost pay attention to how it can be preserved, and only in the second instance to how one . . . heals illnesses.'[137] For its part, health is considered a 'measured mixture of the warm, cold, dry and damp' as far as the 'equal parts' are concerned, as well as the correct arrangement, size, amount and form as far as the 'composite' parts of the body, in other words, the organs, are concerned. Health, sickness and the aforementioned mid-state between the two are in continual interplay – analogous with the constantly changing mixture between the humours, elements and their qualities. Galen sees – like the Greeks before him – the balance of health not as something static and momentary, but as something 'flexible, with a broad scope'.[138] In the tract *De temperamentis* [*On the Temperaments*] he designates it a characteristic of a 'healthy dyscrasy', that is to say, of a slight deviation from the ideal mean, 'if no function of the body has yet been significantly damaged'.[139] A further definition of health is as classical as it is pragmatic: it is described as a 'condition in which we neither suffer pain, nor are hindered in the use of our vital energies'.[140] This condition encourages these energies, which underpin the physiological processes, 'either to impede, curtail or completely dispel the illnesses'.[141] The dynamic equilibrium that underlies health is unsteady and barely measurable, an insight that the learned physician may have derived from Aristotle's ethics of moderation.[142]

Health, which safeguards the stability of body and soul, changes according to age. Like Solon and Athenaius of Attaleia, Galen discusses the education of the young in health matters according to the septennial scheme. Body and soul should be sensitized to the forces that jeopardize health and to unhealthy behaviour from a very early age.[143] The *pedagogy of health* acquires highly ethical dimensions, for 'food and drink and our daily undertakings' act upon the correct mixture 'and, as a result, contribute to the capability of the soul'.[144] The character of the soul is, logically, 'destroyed by bad habits in eating, in drinking, in taking [gymnastic] exercise, by theatre plays and plays for voices and the entire education of the mind'.[145] One should observe the dispositions of even small children and correct them by means of games and exercises. In the case of the best conceivable bodily constitution, which, however, is rare,

> the body, which sits entirely correctly in the flesh, conducts itself in such a manner that it . . . maintains the mean between meagreness and ample flesh . . . It maintains the mean between all excesses, so that one can call it neither shaggy nor bare, neither soft nor hard, neither pale nor dark, neither without [visible] nor with dilated veins, neither hot-tempered nor fainthearted, neither sleepy nor wakeful, neither lustful nor its opposite.[146]

Galen also developed logically consistent directions for the elderly. A prerequisite for health in old age, which 'is tormented by diverse sufferings as if by the hangman's helpers', is the adoption in youth of a way of life in accordance with the classic rules of dietetics. The topic had already been discussed by Hippocrates and Athenaius of Attaleia, who also devised a variety of gymnastics for older people. According to Athanaius, the sophist Gorgias of Leontinoi had attributed the perfect health that he still enjoyed at an age of over one hundred years to the fact that he had 'never [done] anything for the sake of pleasure'. In the *Macrobii*, which are attributed to Lucian, the poet lists famous personalities who also reached a very advanced age thanks to a consciously chosen way of living.

In the tract *Hygieiná*, Galen turns to the educated layman. Its pragmatism can be discerned in passages where he addresses those who, 'due to some circumstance or other, which their employment entails, are not able to eat, to drink and to perform exercises at the right time, and then those who – due to their nature – have a bodily constitution which is prone to illnesses.'[147] In such cases he recommends prophylactic *pharmaka* or, rather, prescribes specific remedies to correct an imbalance in the humoral mixture.

Galen also defends a holistic approach to health, as we would say today. For him, medicine therefore becomes an *encyclopaedic* discipline. He was acutely aware of the dependence of one's state of health on social factors, as well as on one's social status. The physician who attends to health must therefore concern himself with the 'whole' and, most importantly, be well versed in philosophy. He 'must master philosophy in all its parts: logics, physics and ethics.' The physician from Pergamon combines, to a greater degree even than the Stoics and the 'pneumatics', the Hippocratic system of the four cardinal humours – blood, mucus, and black and yellow bile – with the elemental qualities warm, cold, damp and dry, the cardinal organs, the main colours, the types of fever, the seasons, the stages of life and the times of the day.[148] In the classical tradition, he correlates the macrocosm and microcosm, and defines health as the complex and fragile harmony of the latter. Later Galenists also ascribed character traits to the four humours, and extended the doctrine of the four temperaments expounded by Aristotle (sanguine, choleric, melancholic and phlegmatic) to accommodate the theory of specific health risks.

Galen had no doubt that astrological knowledge and the mathematical skills necessary for the study of the stars were indispensable for a doctor when devising health plans. The Galenic concept of health manifests first and foremost a mysterious semantic affiliation to the 'mean', to 'balance', which was meant both somatically and psychologically. Health was classified as a *habitus*, which was not only oriented towards an optimal physical regime, but also aspired to the harmonization of all aspects of human life, and was in a lifelong interplay with the neutral mid-condition between 'ill' and 'healthy' ('neutrum').[149] It is not by chance that Galen reminds his reader of the Hippocratic phrase that the health of athletes who are just reaching their peak is particularly at risk. The soundest physical condition occurs, he argues, when this peak has not yet been reached and a further improvement is therefore possible.[150]

Galen explains genesis, nourishment, growth and health with the aid of the Aristotelian theory of efficiency, according to which nature avails itself of an extremely purposive, divinely ordained, 'teleological' physiology. As a dynamic force, nature ensures that every species, whether animal or human, survives and prospers.[151] The 'actus' and 'potentia' of all natural processes are determined by the aforementioned four different causes (*causae materiales, formales, efficientes* and *finales*).[152] Nature supports health by creating nothing unprofitable or superfluous and nothing 'that could be better in a different respect'. As in Hippocrates' works, the good physician considers himself nature's 'servant' (*minister naturae*).[153] However, the force of nature alone is not sufficient to guarantee a smooth functioning of the body. Routes of transport, regulatory centres, decomposition and so on cater, as nature's auxiliary instruments, for the correct humoral mixture.[154] The relationship between their qualities determines – within the limits prescribed by the individual 'nature' (*physis*) – the individual 'constituo' or 'dispositio' which is responsible for the medical profile, the *habitus* (*schesis*) of the individual human being.[155]

Whereas some ailments could be remedied by means of medical intervention or strong medication (whose effects were considered to be the result of support from the magnetic, constant, transforming and eliminating power of nature), other, mostly chronic illnesses could generally be cured only by means of a change in one's way of life. Galen advises convalescents to adopt employment in the fresh air; those afflicted by a lung complaint were told to embark on sea journeys or trips to the mountains. Admittedly, Galen, like many philosophers of his day, bemoans the general enfeeblement of Roman society; however, he condemns the 'ancient' practice of testing the vitality of the newborn by plunging them into ice-cold water.[156] The purpose of the art of healing is health; its ultimate goal is the conservation of health. The physician must recognize by what means the lost state of health can be regained, and offer the patient dietetic advice.

In the later imperial age, medical polypragmatism seems to have been the order of the day. The most diverse remedies were administered, not least because, as Galen himself admitted, 'the people demand medication'. Pliny and Dioscurides had already popularized the herbal remedies of Diocles of Carystus, Nicander (second century BC), Krataeus (70 BC) and Sextius Niger (*c.* AD 30) in medical compilations, and there can be no doubt that the number of known remedies multiplied with the expansion of the *Imperium Romanum*. Generally speaking, Galen repeated old didactic views, which were then canonized for centuries. Health care and prophylactics were – within the limitations of personal *dispositio* – elevated to the status of a virtue. The pursuit of a 'healthy' way of life, as the result of a personal decision, was a central concern of Galenic dietetics.[157] After Galen, the 'six non-naturals' were considered to constitute the 'golden way' to health.

Of particular cultural historical significance was the aforementioned insight, adopted from Herophilus, that there is a third condition between health and sickness, the *ne-utralitas*, 'being neither healthy nor ill'. This state provides information about the 'dispositio' of the individual, knowledge that is indispensable for the doctor and patient alike, as it can predetermine the destruction of health, as well as adumbrating a spiritual disaster independent of the state of health. Galen, comparable in this respect only to the great Greek philosophers, was aware of the diverse and subtle dependencies of the body on the soul, the structure of which he also sought to explain through humoral pathology. For him, medicine is anything but an esoteric discipline: its most important goals are attained precisely through the popularization of dietetic methods.

3

Jewish and Early Christian Traditions

Jewish doctrines of health

Concepts of health and dietetics in the biblical tradition are by no means uniform. Idealizing representations suggest a primarily static, aesthetic perception of the body and of health. The young David is described to Saul as 'a brave man and a warrior. He speaks well and is a fine-looking man.'[1] The young Jews assembled by Nebuchadnezzar were to be 'without any physical defect, handsome, showing aptitude for every kind of learning, well informed . . .'[2] When the Alexandrian Philon (first century AD) describes the body as 'inferior' and as 'the prison of the soul', he is merely showing his Stoic roots, which were not untypical of an educated, Hellenized Jew of late antiquity. There is no evidence in the Old Testament of a dualistic separation of body and soul after the Platonic and Stoic fashion; here we find rather the type of pragmatic views which show indulgence towards the body, and which are echoed in the second century BC by the book Jesus Sirach: 'Better off is a poor man who is well and strong in constitution than a rich man who is severely afflicted in body. Health and soundness are better than all gold, and a robust body than countless riches. There is no wealth better than health of body, and there is no gladness above joy of heart . . . Gladness of heart is the life of man, and the joyfulness of man is length of days.'[3] Despite the 'static' conception of health (Canguilhem) – the state of body and mind is ultimately determined by God – regulations relating to hygiene, that is to say, measures that served in a broad sense to promote and maintain health, were of considerable importance in ancient Israel. The rules for the construction

of toilets for the army may be explained by reference to the dignity of
the Lord, who 'moves about in your camp' (Deuteronomy 23: 13);
however, these rules could also serve to prevent the spread of plague.
As with all ancient cultures, it is difficult from our modern perspective
to differentiate between religious, purgative and practical, hygienic
motives. The prophet Elisha cured the Aramaic commander Naaman
of leprosy by instructing him to wash himself seven times in the River
Jordan. The biblical text ('your flesh will be restored and you will be
cleansed') does not make a clear distinction between bodily and spiritual restoration; however, Naaman's subsequent homage to Jahwe
indicates that Elisha also succeeded in healing the soul of the hostile
commander (2 Kings 5: 8–15).

Although the religious aspect cannot clearly be separated from the
elements relating to hygiene and contagion, it is clear that uncleanness
was considered a danger. This is substantiated by the instructions on
leprosy and its treatment, as well as on 'uncleanness' and menstruation and on contact with corpses contained in the books Leviticus and
Numbers.[4] The context is sufficient proof that the significance of the
ordinance 'You must not eat any fat or any blood' is less medical than
religious; it is followed in Leviticus 17: 11 by the sentence: 'For the life
of a creature is in the blood . . .'. The washing of hands and feet also
had primarily religious significance, and the same is true of the Mosaic
culinary distinction between 'clean' and 'unclean' animals. When
Daniel asks the chief official of the Babylonian king to give the young
Jewish men 'nothing but vegetables to eat and water to drink' instead
of the food and wine from the king's table, and the latter 'looked
healthier and better nourished' after ten days than the young
Babylonians, the religious and didactic grounding of this episode is
also clear. In Jewish literature, Maimonides was the first to discuss
the ancient dietary rules from an exclusively medical and hygienic
perspective.[5]

Gluttony and immoderate behaviour are presented as sinful vices in
the Old Testament. Nebuchadnezzar's revelries are condemned not, of
course, because they are detrimental to health, but for ethical or religious reasons.[6] The Ancient Hebraeans' strict directives concerning
meat were not originally motivated by hygienic, or even by 'scientific',
interests, even if they were in accord with contemporary standards of
knowledge.[7] The same is true of the sexual prescriptions aimed at the
prevention of incest laid down in Leviticus 18. No reference is made
to doctors in the Pentateuch; it is Jahwe who afflicts men with illness,
but it is also he who bestows health upon them.[8] However, there is no
reason to assume that the role of the doctor, or concerns relating to
health, are simply dismissed in the various manuscripts of the Old

Testament, which diverge considerably as regards date and author-ship. The ordinance in the Talmud which reads: 'It is forbidden to live in a city in which there is no physician' certainly derived from the tradition of ancient Israel.

The biblical view that health lies entirely in God's power predominated. Thus the king rejects Naaman's request to cure the commander of leprosy on the grounds that he is not a God who 'can . . . kill and bring back to life' (2 Kings 5: 7). Similarly, God commands the people on the way to Sinai: 'If you listen carefully to the voice of the Lord your God and do what is right in his eyes, if you pay attention to his commands and keep all his decrees, I will not bring on you any of the diseases I brought on the Egyptians, for I am the Lord, who heals you.'[9] Illnesses, particularly leprosy, are often presented as punishments or temptations, as in the case of Job (Job 2: 1–10). Thus sickness was perceived as a kind of 'trial', with recovery serving as the 'acquittal'. The role of Jahwe here is reminiscent of that of the sun gods of the ancient Orient.[10]

According to Proverbs 4: 22, the words of wisdom recorded in the book guarantee wellbeing, 'for they are life to those who find them and health to a man's whole body.' To consult other healing divinities, as King Ahaziah does (2 Kings 1: 1–17), was obviously commonplace in Israel. In the course of a cultic reform, King Hezekiah has the images of snake divinities removed from Jahwe's temple in Jerusalem (2 Kings 18: 4). As in the Greek and the ancient Italian cultures, the chthonic divinities and ancient domestic gods also continued to exercise some influence.[11] The expulsion of the scapegoat (Leviticus 16: 7–10) doubtless served to banish illness and to restore individual and collective health, as it had in Babylon.

The 'iatrotheological' foundation of ancient Jewish medicine did not entirely preclude a rational understanding of illness and evil, in spite of the metaphysical view of medical disorders.[12] Religion and hygiene, salvation and healing remain closely intertwined, however. The washing of hands and feet was part of the daily routine, but was also dictated by religious ordinances.[13] Toilets were generally located at a suitable distance from the dwellings.[14] Bathing places (and here we exclude the *mikva*) were numerous and even present in the temple.[15] Although considerable space is devoted in the Talmud to food restrictions, 'everyday' health care and dietetics, which were so important to the Greeks at that time, are not discussed in biblical writings.[16] Cultic fasting evidently took place rarely and initially only at festivals concerned with reconciliation. Later, however, public fasts were held after military defeats or plagues.[17] The attitude of the ancient Jews towards the deliberate renunciation of food was generally negative, which can probably be attributed to earlier nomadic experiences and traditions.

Although medical questions play only a minor role in biblical writings such as the Pentateuch, they are deliberately integrated into Talmudic teachings.[18] It should not surprise us that the ancient notion of 'moderate living' is also invoked here. 'Rabbi Chiya taught: those who wish to avoid bodily pain should accustom themselves to immersing themselves in winter and in summer. If you enjoyed your meal, then do not continue to help yourself; do not neglect to answer the call of nature when the time comes.'[19] The Talmudic sages even had faith in magical therapeutics. 'Rav Huna said: against three-day fever, one should take seven tips from seven date palms, seven splinters from seven logs, seven nails from seven bridges, seven motes from seven dustpans, seven pieces of pitch from seven boats, seven handfuls of caraway seed and seven hairs from the beard of an old dog, and then bind them with a light thread around the neck of one's garment . . .'

According to ancient Jewish lore, Noah had received a book of remedies from God that had been translated by ancient sages. In this book, an angel explained which herbs, roots and plants had curative effects; a similar book was also attributed to Solomon. The archangel Raphael was also presented as a healer, who had helped Tobias to heal his father Tobit (Tobit 3: 10). In the apocryphal book of Enoch, the 'angel of peace' describes a similar vision: 'This first is Michael . . ., the second, who is set over all the diseases and all the wounds of the children of men, is Raphael.' Hippocrates, Galen and Dioscurides were also recognized in Jewish tradition as medical authorities.[20] And according to Flavius Josephus, animist traditions, such as that of the mandrake, were commonplace. Roots, herbs, seeds and panaceas were used as medicines, no doubt influenced by models from the ancient Orient; King Hezekiah's boil, for example, is cured with a 'poultice of figs'.

In the Bible, macrobiotics, or the art of a healthy, long life, was of significance due to the fact that the patriarchs, those exemplary figures, reached an extremely advanced age. Between Noah and Abraham, however, lifespans decreased abruptly; the latter reached the age of 'only' 175. In Jesus Sirach's day, people lived a maximum of one hundred years, and the psalmist cites seventy as the average lifespan of the human, 'if he is strong'. In the Talmud, the rabbis answer questions relating to their longevity with various ethical answers, such as: 'I have never been angry in my house, I have never gone before someone who was more important than myself, I have never thought impure thoughts, I have never walked four cubits without thinking of the Torah, I have never slept in the schoolhouse.'

Elsewhere in the Talmud, charitable deeds are recommended as a means of prolonging life. 'Rabba, who only studied the Torah, lived only forty years; Abbai, on the other hand, who in addition to studying the Torah also performed charitable works, lived until he was sixty, although both men came from the same family.' It is evident that health and longevity were thought to be linked to the 'nature' of the individual.

Christus medicus

The Christian faith wrought lasting changes on the religious and philosophical situation in the West, despite the fact that the new doctrine also absorbed pagan traditions – for example, Stoic and, of course, Jewish elements. For several centuries, these traditions were in competition with each other – we need think only of the Aesculapius cult described by Aristides – although the doctrine of Christ prospered covertly, on account of persecutions. Leaving aside the religious and philosophical syncretism of late antiquity, the philosophical and dietetic views held by Seneca, Epictetus and Marcus Aurelius continued to dominate among the Roman and Greek upper classes for a considerable period of time.

Jesus frequently appears in the New Testament as a healer, as 'Christus medicus', whose help is invoked by the sick and afflicted, for: 'It is not the healthy who need a doctor, but the sick' (Luke 5: 31). Scenes involving the healing of the sick represent key passages in the four Gospels, as well as in the Acts of the Apostles. The promulgation of such scenes not only in early theology, but also in Christian art, which flourished from the third century onwards, established Christ as *the single* source of hope for those suffering from afflictions of the soul or body.[21] Luke's Gospel asserts that 'power was coming from him, and healing them all' (Luke 6: 19). Matthew cites Isaiah's prophecy: 'He took up our infirmities and carried our diseases' (Matthew 8: 17). Initially, the people followed Jesus more because they hoped to be healed than on account of his 'theological' sermons: 'A great number of people . . . had come to hear him and to be healed of their diseases' (Luke 6: 17–18). The kingdom of God, and, with it, deliverance from all evils, was also expected to come in the immediate future.

Jesus cast out demons and evil spirits, which in antiquity had almost unanimously been considered the cause of all types of affliction. It seemed reasonable to assume that God – and, for Christian believers, his son – could cure illnesses. The afflicted therefore served to demonstrate 'God's glory', because the divine nature of Christ was revealed in the act of healing (John 9: 1–3; 11: 3). Even though Christ warns a healed cripple to sin no more, 'or something worse may happen to you' (John 5: 14), in the New as in the Old Testament illness was no longer presented as a necessary consequence of guilt and sin. Instead, it represents a way of discovering God and consequently attaining a higher form of health. Despite the numerous parallels in the Gospels to the body–soul dualism of the Platonic and Gnostic traditions, this dualism is transcended. Christ explicitly states that he has '[healed] the whole man on the Sabbath' (John 7: 23).

The parable of the seven acts of mercy also resulted in the image of the 'Christus patiens': 'I was sick and you looked after me' (Matthew 25: 31–40), and the same parable also testifies to Christ's 'compassio': 'Whatever you did for one of the least of these brothers of mine, you did for me.' Believers therefore recognize Christ in their own suffering, and the act of combating illness is exalted as the Christian virtue of 'caritas'. Those who help others to attain health, such as doctors, are acting in accordance with Christ's doctrine. Like Aesculapius, who became a healing and redeeming God following his death from a lightning bolt, Jesus became the saviour of mankind despite, or rather because of, his death in a manner that would have been considered shameful by the ancients. This comparison was made quite deliberately by the apologist Justin in the second century.[22]

The example of the cult of Aesculapius is likely to have influenced the popular image of the Christus medicus.[23] Rengstorf argues for the significance of springs and water in St John's Gospel as a reflection of the central importance of the spring as a source of health in the cult of Aesculapius.[24] According to John (4: 14), the water offered by Jesus endows us with eternal life and ensures that we will never thirst. Three hundred years later, the church historian Eusebius (*b.* 262) describes in the *Vita Constantini* how the emperor opposed the cult of a competing god:

> Thousands regarded [him] with reverence as the possessor of saving and healing power, who sometimes appeared to those who passed the night in his temple, sometimes restored the diseased to health, though on the contrary he was a destroyer of souls, who drew his easily deluded worshippers from the true Saviour to involve them in impious error. The emperor, consistently with his practice and desire to advance the worship of him who is at once a jealous God and the true Saviour, gave directions that this temple also should be razed to the ground. In prompt obedience to this command, a band of soldiers laid this building, the admiration of noble philosophers, prostrate in the dust, together with its unseen inmate, neither demon nor god, but rather a

deceiver of souls, who had seduced mankind for so long a time through various ages.[25]

While it is generally recognized that Constantine's main concern was to abolish pagan cults in general, it is obvious that he was focusing in particular on this popular healing god (Soter).

Christ, who never referred to himself as a doctor, is presented as such for the first time by Ignatius of Antioch (AD 110): 'There is one Physician who is possessed both of flesh and spirit; both made and not made; God existing in flesh; true life in death; both of Mary and of God; first possible and then impossible, even Jesus Christ our Lord.'[26] In the Acts of John from the second century AD, the oldest apocryphal Acts of the Apostles, Jesus appears as 'the protector and healer of Thy people', in deliberate antithesis to pagan competitors and precursors. We should bear in mind that the epithet Soter ('saviour') had also been applied to Aesculapius. Clement of Alexandria (d. before 215) additionally propagated the image of the divine doctor:

> Therefore, the Word has been called also the Saviour, seeing He has found out for men those rational medicines which produce vigour of the senses and salvation; and devotes Himself to watching for the favourable moment, reproving evil, exposing the causes of evil affections, and striking at the roots of irrational lusts, pointing out what we ought to abstain from, and supplying all the antidotes of salvation to those who are diseased.[27]

The superiority, even the omnipotence, of Christus medicus vis-à-vis normal physicians is emphasized again and again. 'The doctor who cannot offer advice on health incurs the anger of the sick', whereas Jesus always offers effective assistance. According to the patristic interpretation, health signified first and foremost God's protection; however, as is demonstrated by the examples in the New Testament, it by no means excluded physical wellbeing.

Many other Church Fathers also regarded Christ as a superior teacher on health matters. 'Because the majority were ill, the doctor came', writes Jerome, and Augustine offers a similar explanation for the necessity of salvation: 'he found *not one* in good health.'[28] Those who have recognized their ailment, that is, those who know that they have sinned, should henceforth turn to the correct physician. Ambrose (d. 397) advises the sinner: 'Hurry to the doctor. Seek the remedy of repentance.' The divine doctor, he continues, requires 'confessio', which corresponds to anamnesis, but also brings about a spiritual 'catharsis'.

The patristic debate surrounding the medical role of Christ is intriguing. Jerome was probably familiar with Galen and Hippocrates, as well as the medical precepts of the Stoics. The pedagogical impetus behind the new, theologically oriented dietetics occasionally led to bold analogies. According to Augustine, Christ, the healthy physician, drank from the bitter cup 'so that the patient need not say: I cannot take the bitter medicine.' The Church Fathers devised a conception of illness that seems to incorporate all other images: illness is the result of distance from God, a spiritual ailment which leads to the loss of salvation. God alone can conquer death, by affording mankind true health, that is to say, eternal life. Ignatius of Antioch explicitly describes the Eucharist as a 'remedy for death' or an 'antidote that protects us from death'. Ephraim the Syrian refers to the 'medicine of life'.

'In the context of his theologia medicinalis, Augustine never tires of speaking of Christ as the medicus noster, medicus et salvator noster, omnipotens medicus, supernus medicus.'[29] His image of the saviour as medicus occasionally resembles that of the philosopher doctor.[30] The division of expertise in Stoic doctrine, whereby philosophers were considered responsible for afflictions of the soul and doctors for the health of the body, could have provided the foundation in early Christianity for certain tendencies towards contempt for the medical profession and the body. We need only remind ourselves of the endeavours of many to die as martyrs, and of the joyous anticipation of death as expressed in Dionysius of Alexandria's descriptions in the third century of life during the plague.[31]

Subsequent to Christ's mission, the power of healing, which in the eyes of the populace was restricted increasingly to physical restoration, was passed on to the apostles and disciples, and later to the bishops and priests (Luke 9: 1; 10: 9). In addition to acts of healing, assistance to the poor, the sick and the needy, for which supplications were made to Christ, became increasingly important. In the *Apostolic Constitutions* (*c.* 380), the largest collection of material on liturgy and ecclesiastical law produced in Christian antiquity, the bishop is called upon to heal 'all sinners, like a compassionate physician'. In addition, the methods and instruments of the surgeon are compared to the pastoral procedures used by the head of the community:

> Do not restrict yourself to cutting and burning and strewing powder, use bandages and charpie as well, administer mild and healing medicines, and bestow words of comfort as soothing dressings. However, if the wound . . . festers, then cleanse it with powder, that is to say, with chastisement; if it spreads over the raw skin, use a caustic ointment, or threats of divine judgement, to counteract it; if it begins to consume the area around it, however, burn the festering abscess with iron and cut it out, by imposing fasting.

Last but not least, Origen, no doubt thinking primarily of the Holy Spirit, but also using diction that was prevalent in contemporary medicine, describes the Christian as follows: 'The perfect Christian, the pneumatic, acts as a doctor towards his brothers and sisters . . . He serves the ignorant, weak and diseased members of the church in selfless and responsible love as spiritual teacher and shepherd, as a guide for souls and pastor, as a spiritual physician.'

In the third and fourth centuries, Christ grew in importance as the redeemer and source of hope for the seriously and hopelessly ill, who hoped that he would deliver them from their ailments, just as he had healed the blind and the lame. In patristic literature, we read of numerous miraculous acts of healing performed in Christ's name.[32] Basil the Great (330–379) distinguishes once again between ailments imposed by God as a consequence of sin, whether as punishment or purgation, and those that have physical causes. In the case of the first type, he prescribes abstention from treatment. However, he fundamentally disagrees with heretics such as Marcion or Tatian who rejected every concern for the body as unchristian, and instead defends the medicine practised by physicians, as opposed to (pagan) magic and invocations. 'For everyone, including those who are not physicians, knows that health is a necessity; however, only those who are experienced in the art of healing can state how health can be attained.' Eusebius of Caesaria attests that, around 200, many Christians greatly respected the works of Galen, or humoral medicine. It was considered beyond dispute, however, that the Redeemer and the healers authorized by him – the apostles and their successors – were superior to the most renowned medical authorities.

Tertullian defends Christus medicus, or, rather, the scandal that the healing and salvation of mankind were brought about by his *execution*, with an argument taken from the medical history of antiquity: 'You would probably admire the physician who administered remedies that have the *same* properties as plagues . . . yet you are moved to accuse God when he wishes to counter death with death, confound murder by means of murder, banish torments with torments, annul executions with executions.' Just as Origen imports the term 'Pneuma' into the theological debate, where it is used henceforth to refer to the Holy Spirit, Tertullian uses the precept of *similia similibus* championed by the Dogmatic school of the Hippocratic tradition and by Athenaeus of Attaleia as a justification for Christ's salvation of mankind.

Following the death of Augustine (*d.* 430) the significance of the Christus medicus motif in theological writings dwindled somewhat; however, the popular notion of Christ as a 'Soter' in every kind of adversity remained common currency. This may have been linked to the loss of significance of the cult of Aesculapius, who was regarded by Tertullius as a 'bastard' and a 'beast', by Lactantius as an 'arch-demon', and by Eusebius simply as the 'destroyer of souls'.[33] As the traditional pagan physician and god lost his influence, the Christian apologists no longer found it necessary to adorn the new saviour with his attributes.

Early Christian doctrines of health

It was by no means a matter of course that Christian doctors would consult the works of heathen scholars such as Hippocrates, Dioscurides, Galen or Soranus. The legitimacy of these sources was questioned constantly into the early Middle Ages, as, indeed, were the value and necessity of physical health.[34] 'If medicine is so beneficial to man, how can it be that we owe its invention to non-Christians?', asks an anonymous commentator in the fourth century. A contemporary supplies him with the comforting answer that holy men such as Solomon had also discovered remedies for physical ailments. However, he continues, the salvation of the soul would have been beyond the comprehension of heathens such as Galen.[35]

Early Christianity was influenced by many intellectual currents. For a long time, a particular brand of contempt for the body – influenced initially by the transcendence of the physical in martyrdom, subsequently by the *imitatio passionis* – was in favour. Asceticism was preached in particular by the Anchorites in the East. Basil the Great considered an extremely emaciated body 'with protruding ribs' and every sign of frailty as an entirely desirable condition.[36] Anthony the Hermit defended asceticism by reference to the words of St Paul: 'I beat my body and make it my slave' (1 Corinthians 9: 27). Temptations by demons and the devil could only be resisted by means of mortification of the flesh. Anthony consumed bread, salt and some water, never touched meat or wine, did without sleep almost entirely, abstained from every kind of care and cleaning of his body and yet, according to the legend, remained in the best of health. The objective of this type of conduct, which was at variance with every Hippocratic tradition, was the unification of body and soul in that primordial state that had been lost at the Fall of Man. According to reports by Palladius, the hermit Stephen felt no pain despite his terrible afflictions, 'while his limbs were falling like hairs'.

The Church Fathers and Apologists were also concerned that the old maxim of moderation, now interpreted according to Christian doctrine, should be enacted in the form of a life of piety and virtue. 'Lovely, then, is the virtue of modesty, and sweet is its grace! It is seen not only in actions, but even in our words, so that we may not go beyond due measure in speech, and that our words may not have an unbecoming sound', wrote St Ambrose, who about 391, in his tract *On the Duties of the Clergy* (the echo of Cicero in the title is deliberate), outlined a moral–ethical dietetics based on the four cardinal virtues.[37]

The heretic Marcion also denounced care for the human body as unchristian and omitted to mention the profession of Luke the Evangelist, as attested by Paul, in his commentary on the letters to the Corinthians.[38] Many even turned for support to Galen, who, in a contested passage, had shown sympathy for ascetic movements and was believed to have defended with philosophical arguments the sexual abstinence observed by some Christians.[39] The young Christian communities, however, placed increasing value on medical treatment; Christian doctors are therefore attested from an early stage (in addition to the example of Luke in Colossians 4: 14). Representatives of the healing profession are mentioned in many martyrologies dating from the third century, and even Septimius Severus had a Christian medical attendant. Aetius, a leading Arian, was just as well educated on medical matters as Aglaophon of Patara, who attempted to disprove the resurrection of the body by means of medical arguments.[40] The tradition of patron saints as defenders against illness began with the cult of the physicians and martyrs Cosmas and Damian. However, in early Christianity, medical assistance was only considered a charitable activity when it was offered – as in the case of the two *Anargyroi* – 'without money'.

Early Christian dietetics, as expounded by Justin the Martyr (second century) in his commentaries on the New Testament, was based on the conviction that the soul was immortal and could look forward to paradisiacal joys after death. Although this conviction did not necessarily entail the condemnation of the body, it did proscribe placing too great a value on *earthly* health. Justin was one of the first early Christian commentators to draw on heathen arguments.[41] Apologists such as Tatian (second century), however, had an entirely dualistic view of the health issue. 'Illnesses and conflicts' were, in his view, influenced by demons and affected matter only. Physicians and pharmacologists were tools of the Almighty: 'Even if you be healed by drugs . . ., yet it behoves you to give testimony of the cure to God.'[42] Nevertheless, in the Council of Nicaea (325) the early Apologists and Church Fathers almost unanimously rejected voluntary castration, which some (including Origen) considered the action most consistent with contempt for the body.[43]

Theoderic's chancellor Boethius (480–524), who was later executed, and was probably Christian, described the way to mental recovery in his *Consolatio philosophiae* [*The Consolations of Philosophy*]. It is based on humility and deeper insight and is shown to us by God. 'But let us thank the Giver of all health, that your nature has not altogether left you. We have yet the chief spark for your health's fire, for you have a true knowledge of the hand that guides the universe: you do believe that its government is not subject to random chance, but to divine reason', the personification *Philosophia* explains to her 'patient'.[44] God, who is the embodiment of wisdom, shows us the way to recovery. Recognition of God's divine plan is granted to the intellectual who practises meditation and reflection and – like Boethius – is committed to a dualism of a distinctly stoical tincture.

Theoretical considerations aside, from Justin onwards early Christian authorities had also been concerned with *practical* instructions on health. To this end, they drew on passages from the New Testament, such as Paul's recommendation to Timothy: 'Stop drinking only water, and use a little wine because of your stomach and your frequent illnesses' (1 Timothy 5: 23). There were indeed already communities where the Eucharist was celebrated with water – evidently not without reason, as Paul himself had found it necessary to reprimand those who got drunk and thought only of eating at the Lord's Supper (1 Corinthians 11: 21). In his letter to the Ephesians (5: 18) he commands: 'Do not get drunk on wine, which leads to debauchery.' Clement of Alexandria, in the second century, considered wine a '*pharmakon*', which, like every medicament, could be dangerous when consumed in excess: 'One Artorius, in his book On Long Life (for so I remember), thinks that drink should be taken only till the food be moistened, that we may attain to a longer life', warned the Church Father, whose concern was to synthesize heathen and Christian dietetics.[45]

In his *De cibis iudaicis* the Church Father Novatian (third century) criticizes the customs of some Christians: 'while fasting they drink in the early morning . . . What can they do after meat, whom meat finds intoxicated?'[46] Wine, however, was considered – no less than water – to be a gift from God; after all, had not Jesus himself turned water into wine (John 2: 1–12) and wine into his own blood at the Last Supper (Luke 22: 20)? The Gnostics, on the other hand, generally condemned alcoholic drinks, along with medicines and every type of physical therapy. Even bodily hygiene was suspected of being a heathen practice. The majority of Church Fathers, however, did condone baths for reasons of hygiene. According to Tertullian, 'there are four reasons for the use of baths: to cleanse, to warm, for health and for pleasure. Yet we should not bathe for pleasure.'[47] Going for walks, gymnastics and medicines were also recommended in the interests of preserving health. Julius Africanus praises, among other therapies, the effects of bathing in the Dead Sea. Frequent references are also made in early Christian writings to the divinely bestowed healing power of simple herbs, stones and animals. Jerome, like Galen, believed it was precisely in such simple substances (*simplicia*) as snake skins, bed bugs, stones, leeches or the droppings of various animals that a healing power resided.[48]

Clement of Alexandria penned 'the most famous philippics against gluttony and feasting in early Christian literature': 'For neither is food our business, nor is pleasure our aim', he argued. 'We must therefore reject different varieties [of food], which engender various mischiefs, such as a depraved habit of body and disorders of the stomach, the taste being vitiated by an unhappy art – that of cookery, and the useless art of making pastry. For people dare to call by the name of food their dabbling in luxuries, which glides into mischievous pleasures.' The Church Father also points out that even the most magnificent foods soon finish up in the sewers: 'But we who seek the heavenly bread must rule the belly, which is beneath heaven, and much more the things which are agreeable to it, which God shall destroy.'[49]

Jerome condemns gluttony in a similar way, although he uses medical arguments to underpin his moral concerns: 'Hippocrates in his Aphorisms teaches that stout, heavy persons, once they have attained their full growth, . . . develop tendencies to paralysis and other serious forms of disease.' The full dishes of meat, which 'make us their slaves' are rejected in favour of a meal of cabbage, vegetables and fruits, as had been taught by Cato. Moreover, he continues, Diogenes claimed that many wars had been waged due to costly food, but none for the sake of a simple diet.[50] The Church Father is concerned not only with the salvation of souls, but with a solid, sensible daily diet: 'The invalid only regains his health by diminishing and carefully selecting his food, i.e., in medical terms, by adopting a "slender diet". The same food that recovers health can preserve it, for no one can imagine vegetables to be the cause of disease.' The Christian has no need to become a product of meat dishes like Milo of Crotona, he continues – a reference to the cult of the body which was widespread among athletes.[51] The Church Fathers tended to associate sport with vanity rather than with health. Augustine claimed that the condemned man was put to sleep above all by pleasure. According to the moralist, the only cure comes from redemption through Christ, which is transformed into effective medicine in the form of the Eucharist.[52] Worldly distractions and desires, intoxication, lust for power and concupiscence were all thought to cause illness.

The emergence of Christian medicine and anthropology did not, however, bring about the end of 'worldly' medicine, owing in particular to the constant suppression and persecution of Christianity until Constantine's victory at the Melvian Bridge in 312. Particularly worthy of note in the fourth century are the dietetics devised by Oribasius, physician to Julian the Apostate, and who also won honours as philosopher in the court of the emperor and convert to the religion of ancient Rome. Oribasius had studied in Alexandria and was considered the last important heathen physician of the ancient world. In the learned circles of the court he defended an intellectual form of dietetics, which negated Christian traditions. Mysteries, gnosis, hermetics, astrology and Neoplatonism all played an important part; the tenet of metempsychosis stressed the primary importance of the health and liberation of the soul. It was primarily thanks to contact with the writings of the Neoplatonist philosopher Iamblichos (250–325) that Oribasius became an admirer of Pythagoras and of esoteric Egyptian cults. According to the Pythagorean model, 'the friendship . . . of the soul with the body' leads to satisfaction and the interplay of 'the opposite forces concealed in the mortal body'. A further desideratum is the state of balance (*insonomia*) already defined by Alcmaeon. The wise man strives for a harmony between all factors, fluids and elements which influence the body and the soul, with considerable importance attached to abstention, self-mortification, silence, periods of fasting and exercises to improve the concentration and memory. It remains unclear to what extent Julian's ascetic doctrine and refusal to remarry should be attributed to the influence of his physician. According to Oribasius, prayers to the gods also contributed to the perfection of the body and soul; he and the emperor continued to regard the locations of the Aesculapius cult as important and effective healing centres.

Oribasius' philosophical blend represents a unique model of dietetics, tailored to suit the intellectual requirements of Julian's court. Similar exercises to improve the concentration and memory were also known to the Christians, thanks to both patristic exegesis and diverse Stoic traditions. However, classical dietetics continued to be held in high regard for a long time. Caelius Aurelianus, a fifth-century medical writer from Sicca in Numidia, differentiated in his *Regulae ciborum regimina* between rules which were intended to advance the recovery of the sick and those which assisted in maintaining the body in an optimal condition. Like Asclepiades and Themison of Laodicea before him, Caelius called in his teachings on health for an individual remedy depending on the patient's condition, which oscillated between tension (status strictus) and atony (status laxus).[53] Based on the stage of the illness, he recommended abstention (at the beginning of the acute phase), simple nutrition, a varied diet and combinations of the three.[54] Caelius advised against the authoritarian imposition of dietary plans on the sick man against his will, advocated a diversified approach to nutrition and suggested that generosity should prevail after the *krisis* of the illness had passed.[55] Like Galen and some of the Hippocratics, he placed particular emphasis on active and passive movement: 'Thus it is advisable that the body should be exercised by means of intensive and constant passive movements, with a harnessed team of animals or the movement of a vehicle, by riding or in a boat.' Here we are reminded of Plato and Galen. Caelius continues: 'Also, by reading and voice exercises of great intensity, or in the form of a musical performance, as is customary at competitions . . .; also by means of running, dry massage with clean hands, with a rough linen cloth or with a sprinkling of sand, also by means of diverse types of activity in the sports' hall . . .; with a ball and by means of agile wrestling and dry massage.'[56] Such rules were extremely conservative and stood in stark contrast to the spiritual doctrines of health propagated by the Church Fathers and Oribasius.

Some time after 511, following his flight from Byzantium, the physician and diplomat Anthimos wrote a tract on dietetics at the court of the Frankish king Theodoric.[57] The objective of this tract was to relieve the king from stomach complaints and other ailments, 'according to the prescriptions of the medical authors . . . and because the first step towards good health . . . lies in a correct choice of diet.'[58] Anthimos was situated in the tradition of Galen and the ancient 'auctoritates'; however, he also stated that every recovery is only possible with Christ's help, 'through whose mercy we obtain a longer life, but, in particular, health'. Like Jerome, Anthimos advocates a frugal and simple diet, of the sort eaten by 'wild' but generally healthy peoples, as 'It is obviously precisely the small amount that is the cause of their health. However, we, who enjoy many delicacies and drinks throughout our lives, must moderate ourselves so that we do not contract health complaints due to excess, but rather preserve our health by our moderate behaviour.'[59] He favours cooked meals over uncooked; white bread is recommended as the basis of every healthy meal. Anthimos' *Letter concerning the diet of the Frankish King Theoderic* is an early example of the regimens which were popular in the Middle Ages, and which were to prove hugely influential, particularly following the reception of Arabic writings.

4

Medieval Traditions in the East and West

Healing and health in early monasticism

The foundation of the first Western monastery on Monte Cassino by Benedict of Nursia (529) represents a decisive development for Western medicine, as well as for the history of nursing and health care. Monastic communities are attested from the fourth century, for example, in Rome, Gaul and Germany; however, the Benedictines developed superior organizational structures and exercised considerable cultural influence. Augustine had encouraged 'coenobitic' movements in North Africa as early as the fourth century,[1] and the first 'rules', which were later attributed to him, were taken as a model by the early Christian communities (Acts 4: 32–5). In his binding *Regula* for the new orders, Benedict consulted in particular the *De institutis coenobiorum* by John Cassian (*b. c.* 360), who was probably inspired by the eastern Church Father Pachomius.[2]

The 'rule of St Benedict' constituted a comprehensive 'ars vivendi'. It was characterized less by ascetic requirements than by a daily programme of hygiene with strong psychological nuances, which made generous allowances for human needs and weaknesses and gave the inhabitants of the monastery directions on how to maintain their health.[3] It afforded the monks a happy medium between a hermitical existence and fulfilment within a community, and aimed to present a comprehensive preventative medicine, although particular emphasis is naturally placed on the relationship with God. Although the maxim 'Ora et labora' admittedly became well-known in this form only in the Middle Ages, it is a fitting motto for Benedictine pragmatism.

The abbot should lead the monks 'like a prudent physician'; the comparison with a form of 'therapy' is chosen deliberately here (chapter 28). Benedict is concerned with those who have transgressed, for 'they that are in health need not a physician, but they that are sick' (chapter 27). In the case of those who will not reform, the abbot should apply

> soothing lotions, ointments of admonitions, medicaments of the Holy Scriptures, and if, as a last resource, he hath employed the caustic of excommunication and the blows of the lash, and seeth that even then his pains are of no avail, let him apply for that brother also what is more potent than all these measures: his own prayer and that of the brethren, that the Lord who is all-powerful may work a cure in that brother. But if he is not healed even in this way, then finally let the Abbot dismiss him from the community. (chapter 28)

However, he should also take care that repentance and betterment do not cause the patient 'overmuch sorrow'; here Benedict's psychological gifts become apparent.[4]

The health of the soul is the primary therapeutic goal of the Benedictines, as it had been for the Church Fathers, and is dependent on the understanding of the individual monk, as well as on his environment and his monastic brothers and superiors. Benedict's pedagogic doctrine does not shield weaknesses, but it does protect weak *people*: the elderly, children, the poor and the sick.[5] Consideration and friendliness are recognized as factors which foster good health; the sensibilities and concerns of the individual are respected: 'For the Abbot must know that he has taken upon himself the care of infirm souls, not a despotism over the strong' (chapter 27). The healthy monk should not exercise rhetorical or therapeutic power over his fellow brother, but should show compassion: 'Above all things, let him be humble; and if he hath not the things to give, let him answer with a kind word' (chapter 31). If all men are to be treated equally, argues Benedict, then due consideration should be given to inequalities between them. Benedict warns the abbots not to build up walls of rules and regulations, which could be the downfall of the individual monk, but to adjust himself to the needs of each: 'To one gentleness of speech, to another by reproofs, and to still another by entreaties' (chapter 2). The 'father of monks' attempted to attain that comprehensive harmony of life about which the heathen physicians had also written. Terms such as justice, consideration, moderation, mean, modesty, wisdom and truth, but also piety and fasting, replace the gymnastic exercises suggested by Galen. The dignity of the individual is protected perceptively against collective ideas or moral pressure from the community.

In addition to prophylaxes and the considerate treatment of one another, care for the ailing brothers was ranked 'before and above all things' (chapter 36); the image of the 'Christus patiens' (Matthew 25: 40) immanent in each patient became a central precept. 'Works of charity' are recommended in the *Regula* as 'instruments of the spiritual art' (chapter 4).[6] A hospice for visitors and rules for care of the sick therefore became standard for Western (and also Eastern) monasteries. The ailing brothers were allowed frequent baths and meat dishes (which were generally only permitted to the monks in exceptional circumstances) and were instructed to be patient and 'not [to] grieve their brethren who serve them by unnecessary demands' (chapter 36). The elderly and children were given preferential treatment (chapter 37). Sleep, midday rests (for rest or reading), the nature and number of meals, meditation and, of course, the ritual of hourly prayer and worship were laid down precisely. The cyclical regularity of the Benedictine daily and yearly routine contributed to the internal harmony of the monastic community, as well as that of the inhabitants of the surrounding area and the congregations of the church services, who poured into the monastery from outside. In 818, the oldest surviving European *Monatsbilder* ('month paintings') were produced in St Peter's Abbey in Salzburg; these offer exemplary representations of the yearly cycle of activity within the neighbouring communities of peasants.

Since the Edict of Milan (319) there had also been Christian institutions for the care of the needy in the Latin West. The hospices (*Xenodocheia*) which were prescribed for each bishopric by the Council of Nicaea (325) became 'seed-beds of Christian institutional health care'. The foundation of these institutions certainly prevented the physical and spiritual impoverishment of many poor, ill and isolated individuals, as well as orphans and pilgrims (and therefore brought an end to a dark chapter of ancient, heathen cultural history, which is for the most part shrouded in ignorance), although care for the sick was only *one* of the functions of these asylums. Physicians had no influence in these institutions; as had been the case in the ancient world, they practised in ambulatories, which were progressively replaced by monastic institutions following the foundation of Benedictine monasteries. Within the Byzantian sphere, however, where there was evidently a desire to preserve heathen and ancient medical knowledge, an organized system of institutions was developed at an early stage. These institutions resembled later hospitals and were home to a remarkable synthesis of Greek medicine, Roman organizational forms and a Christian outlook.[7]

It was the monks, who, in the East and the West, collected the writings of ancient medical authors in order to expand on empirical medical knowledge and popular medical traditions. They also cared for the sick and needy, as prescribed by the precept of charity. In the thirty-first chapter of his *Institutiones* [*Institutions of Divine and Secular Learning*], Cassiodorus (*b.* 480), who was initially a high dignitary in the court of Theoderic and later founder of the model monastery Vivarium in southern Italy, listed those medical books which he considered indispensable to a monastery library, as well as describing the Christian notion of a beneficial healing process: 'Do not place your hope in grasses, or base the cure on human advice. For the art of healing is bestowed by God; without doubt, he, who gives men life, also gives them health . . .' However, the former senator does not hesitate to recommend to the monks 'the *Herbarium* of Dioscurides, who has described and drawn the field grasses with admirable precision', as well as Galen's *Therapeutica*, the tract *De medicina* by Caelius Aurelianus and a compilation of medicinal herbs attributed to Hippocrates. The *Institutiones* therefore effectively bridge the gap between Christian tenets and heathen medical writings.

Within the ambit of the monasteries there soon developed respectable schools of theoretical research, which were based on the seven 'artes liberales' and taught the monastic fathers' variety of dietetics to a wide circle of clerical and noble pupils. The patients were no longer tended by a professional doctor as they had been in heathen antiquity, neither were they treated at the gates of the monastery by an 'academically' trained physician acting as a representative of Christ, as in the high Middle Ages. Yet the reputation of monastic physicians often spread far and wide. As early as the tenth century, Notker, a monk in St Gallen, was described in the *Totenbuch* (register of deaths) as a *benignissimus doctor et medicus*; he was consulted by bishops, abbots and dukes and finally was summoned to the court of the Ottonian emperor to practise as medical expert 'pro remediis in aula regia'. He believed, perhaps not surprisingly for a monk, that some illnesses could only be cured with assistance from the saints.[8] The rapid development of interest in medicine necessitated an increased provision for health care. Following the Council of Aachen in 817, which consigned both medicine and nursing to monks and nuns, the plan of the St Gallen monastery after 820 includes a poorhouse, guest house, hospital wing, doctors' wing, blood-letting house, baths and herb garden.[9] In 842, the abbot Walahfrid Strabo praised the medicinal plants in this garden in Latin hexameters.[10]

Yet in addition to herbal remedies, dietetics, or the art of healthy living, became increasingly important in the monasteries, with the ascetic ideal assuming primary importance. Cassiodorus enjoined renunciation and contemplation upon the brothers, in order to avoid the 'sins of the flesh'.[11] John Cassian pointed to the vitae of oriental anchorites, who were famed for their humility and abstention.[12] A strict ascetic, Cassian even advises us to 'become the fools in this world, so that you become wise'. The monk's clothing should protect against dirt and cold and 'be free of excessive elaboration'; the hood should bring to mind the innocence of children. Cassian deliberately opposes the daily routine of the monk to that of the layperson; he considers the latter to represent a basic danger to health.

An early consequence of this propensity to spirituality and asceticism was that Augustine was obliged to mount an emphatic defence of manual and physical activity in his tract *Of the Works of Monks*.[13] Similarly, Cassian condemned the traditional concept of *acidia*, the sinful state of day-dreaming and destructive boredom, to which monks were particularly prone. Evagrius Ponticus (*d*. 399) included this health-endangering vice, which could lead to depression or to a 'distaste for life' (*taedium sive anxietas cordis* – Cassian), among the eight sinful thoughts (*logismoi*), which were based on the seven deadly sins as enumerated by Gregory the Great.[14] Evagrius considered melancholic idleness a health-endangering passion, which should be combated rather than suppressed: 'He who is always sad and feigns *apatheia* [freedom from passions] is like the invalid who feigns health.'[15] The ascetic considered it an incontestable fact that health can only be attained by means of religious endeavours: 'He who loves the Lord will be free from sorrow, for perfect love drives away grief.'[16] It should consequently not surprise us that the Cistercian Caesarius of Heisterbach portrays the health-endangering consequences of 'sadness' in his visions.[17]

However, asceticism represented only *one* variant of monastic life. The influence of the Benedictine rule, with its emphasis on cultural and academic achievements, as well as on the care of body and soul as a divinely ordained duty, grew steadily throughout the Western world.

The first German pharmacopoeia

It was in the Carolingian period that the European Benedictine monasteries experienced a period of cultural and scholarly efflorescence that proved to be one of the most significant in their history. In the West, doctors were recruited almost exclusively from the monastic orders, and attached particular importance to the preservation of health.

A further group, which is often overlooked, consisted of men and women who were well versed in herbal remedies, as well as magicians and individuals of both sexes who professed to administer God's grace. Magic symbols, which could soon be found on sculptures in Christian churches or on brooches, rings and other items of jewellery, were thought by laymen and clerics alike to have apotropaic powers against health-endangering spirits and evil.[18] The emperor himself, like all secular dignitaries, had clerical physicians, who also observed his diet and ensured a healthy lifestyle. His biographer Einhard does relate, however, that Charles, whose 'health was excellent', scorned their advice in his later years. He followed 'rather his own inclinations than the advice of physicians, who were almost hateful to him, because they wanted him to give up roasts, to which he was accustomed, and to eat boiled meat instead.'[19] The emperor rode and hunted, 'enjoyed the exhalations from natural warm springs, and often practiced swimming, in which he was such an adept that none could surpass him.' Frequently, 'a hundred or more persons' bathed with him. He dressed simply, and was 'temperate in eating, and . . . drinking'. He did, however, complain 'that fasts injured his health'. He drank little wine, ate a lot of fruit and slept regularly. The clerical panegyric also stresses the importance of the court of Charlemagne as a cradle of scholarship and intellectual education.[20]

Around 790 in the Carolingian imperial monastery of Lorsch, an unnamed monastic physician composed a pharmacopoeia, which is generally considered the oldest surviving work of its kind composed within German-speaking territory.[21] As has already been proved by Cassiodorus' directions, the influence of ancient dietetics had persisted, however rapid the proliferation of literature dispensing practical 'remedies'. The pharmacopoeia drew, among other sources, on the letter by the Byzantine doctor Anthimos (c. 500) mentioned in the previous chapter, whose central thesis was: 'The health of individuals rests primarily on the digestibility of the food consumed. If they are prepared correctly, they will be distributed well within the body. If this is not the case, they will burden the stomach and abdomen. They will then produce indigestible juices and cause stomach ulcers and eructations.' In the early morning, the anonymous author recommends the consumption of a herbal drink, whose composition varies according to the season. In January, wellbeing is ensured by ginger and rhubarb, in February by agrimony and parsley seeds, in March by solidago and lovage, in April by betony and burnet, in May by wormwood and fennel seeds, in June by sage and creeping juniper blossoms, in July by parsley blossoms and dropwort, in August by pennyroyal, in September by seaweed and mastic, in October by clove and pepper, in November by cinnamon and in December by lavender.[22] The author also lists rules governing general daily life, as well as blood-letting, purging, cupping and fomentation, eating and drinking. It is only in September that no restrictions are placed on food, as 'all foods are at the peak of maturity at this point in time'. Warnings are issued about the consumption of beef and white bread; drinks should only be consumed to the extent that they 'agree with the food'.

The author's apology at the beginning of the book demonstrates that 'secular' medicine was still under fire from theological authorities. Human health, he claims, is endangered in three ways: by illnesses sent by God as punishment, by those sent as a means of expiation or trial (as in the case of Job), and by a 'susceptibility to sickness' resulting from certain bodily dispositions or an unfortunate mixture of bodily juices. In such cases, he continues, charity and medical assistance are required, and even ordained by God himself. The religious aspect of diverse illnesses serves to legitimate the union of physician and cleric, which could also be found in the person of the monastic physician.[23]

As the anonymous author points out, Bishop Isidore of Seville (d. 636) had, in his *Origines sive etymologiae*, described medicine as a 'secunda philosophia'. Therefore the doctor, who is responsible for all aspects of his patient's health, requires a comprehensive, 'encyclopaedic' education (*enkyklios paideia*).[24] The task of medicine, he continues, is to 'preserve or restore the health of the body'. Isidore's strong dietetic bias and his debt to Galen are demonstrated by the fact that he traced the word 'medicine' back to *modus* (moderation).[25] The monastic author of the pharmacopoeia was also convinced, like Galen and the Church Father Jerome before him, of the power of home-grown herbs to restore health: 'We salute you, you holy hills and fields of the homeland; for your gifts are good for many kinds of therapy.'[26] In order to underline the importance of dietetics, the author consistently exculpates the doctor for any failures: 'If someone can in no way be restored to health, although he is nursed with a remedy, this is to be attributed to his own failing or to a [divine] trial, but not to the inexperience of the doctors.'[27]

It should not surprise us that the Lorsch pharmacopoeia advertises the benefits of medical substances and elements from the old 'filth pharmacies' as well as classical herbal remedies. Specially enriched parasites of elephants are recommended as a remedy for heart complaints. Such therapies continued the age-old tradition of domestic medical treatments, as had been recommended 400 years before by the imperial official Marcellus as a cure for pains in the hip:

You collect the dung of the ibex on the seventeenth day after the new moon, although it is of a similar potency if collected when the moon is waning and the medicament is prepared on the seventeenth day after the new moon. You then put as much of this dung as you can collect in the fist of one hand, as long as there is an odd number of pellets, into a mortar and add 25 carefully ground peppercorns. You then add a hemina of very good honey and two sextaries of very old and good wine, and, after the pellets have been ground, mix all the ingredients and preserve them in a glass container, so as to have the medicament ready to provide relief when required.

The Lorsch pharmacopoeia provides information about the development of doctrines of health from late antiquity through to the Carolingian period. It is likely to be entirely representative of standards of Western medicine and dietetics around 800.

Dietetics in Islam

In contrast to the West, where a new conception of health had been developing since the sixth century thanks in part to the influence of monastic and lay medicine, but particularly to faith in metaphysical aid,[28] Arab medicine had drawn on classical sources since its inception. It is therefore unsurprising that dietetics and prophylactics were also of central importance for Muslim doctors and philosophers. In accordance with the Hippocratic tradition, health in the early Islamic world was considered a chosen way of life rather than a physical condition. An anecdote about the Sultan Adud ad-Daula (936–983) recorded by Ibn-abi-Usaibia is significant here. When two doctors offered him their services one day, he rebuffed them, insisting on his strong constitution. When, however, the two men explained to him that they were concerned primarily with preserving health, and only secondarily with the treatment of illnesses, he appointed them his physicians.[29]

The loss of health was also considered in Islam to be first and foremost a divine punishment or trial. It is stated in the Qur'an that: 'Anything that happens to you . . . disease, fatigue, hurt, sorrow, distress, even the prick he receives from a thorn, comes from Allah, who expiates some of your sins for that.' Yet every recovery is also divinely ordained: 'The blessed and greatest God did not give man any illness without a remedy. You should therefore use the remedy.' Like the rule of Benedict, the Qur'an accords the sick privileges within society, but also in religious ceremonies.[30] Hygienic measures, ritual activities and strict nutritional prescriptions were of great importance to

Mohammed. Aside from the religious notion of 'impurity', one of the main reasons for the prohibition of pork may originally have been the danger of contracting trichinosis, just as the consumption of animals that had perished, rather than being slaughtered, was proscribed as a danger to health. As in the case of Old Testament directives, it is perhaps futile to speculate about whether the Islamic health laws were based primarily on religious, cathartic or medical concerns, particularly given that, in the East as in the West, there was not thought to be any contradiction between these concerns. The fruits of the respective lands were also considered in the Qur'an to bring health ('O Moses! . . . beseech thy Lord for us to produce for us of what the earth groweth – its pot-herbs, and cucumbers, its garlic, lentils, and onions').[31] The proscription of alcohol, considered to be a tool used by Satan to 'hinder you from the remembrance of Allah, and from prayer',[32] is well known. The use of alcohol as medicine was also condemned, as, according to the fatalistic view of the doctor Albukasis, 'if it is given to the sick man to recover, he will do so without wine'. Fasting, the diverse varieties of ritual purification, and even daily prayers, which were accompanied by physical exercises, were all of dietetic significance. Health denoted the wellbeing of body *and* soul and was considered impossible without religious affiliation. The old analogy with the microcosm and macrocosm was also adopted: 'The community of believers is like the human organism. When one part sickens, the entire rest of the body reacts with sleeplessness and fever.'

One of the earliest examples of ancient Arab dietetics can be found in the tract on hygiene by the physician Ali Abn Sahl Rabban at-Tabari (810–855). Drawing on Syrian, Indian, Persian and Greek influences, the author developed a compendium on the preservation of health based on the concept of the four humours *before* the wave of translations of Greek and ancient medical tracts had reached its peak. At-Tabari considered the presentation of methods of attaining and preserving health to be 'the most useful enterprise in this life'.[33] Scholars, he claimed, were agreed that 'God has created health for the continuation of life and not as a sweet, luxuriant condition.' Health did not therefore denote a painless and carefree existence in Arabic literature. As in Jewish and Christian doctrines, the Islamic conception of health combined medical notions with moral and religious precepts.

At-Tabari considered moderation to be 'one of the reasons' for physical and mental wellbeing.[34] Anyone who failed to maintain this mean in eating and fasting, in waking and sleeping, in movement and repose, as well as in purging, bleeding or sexual intercourse, was 'not safe from the appearance of illnesses and sudden harm'. Galen's tenet of 'six non-naturals', the harmonious alternation of waking and sleeping, eating and drinking, repose and movement, checks on excretion and the effects of as well as the care for the environment, was therefore present in the Arabic-speaking world as early as the ninth century. The scholar at-Tabari insists particularly on the importance of a healthy diet: 'I found that he who harnesses his eating habits and desires and restricts himself to the most necessary nutrition, has a healthy body, a longer life and stronger passions, requires fewer travel provisions and is more mobile than someone who carries these things to excess.' He also draws on the Galenic doctrine of degrees and complexions, by means of which the diverse varieties of dyscrasy (disproportionate mixture) within the organism could be diagnosed.[35]

The excess or lack of a quality should, according to this tenet, be corrected by the administration of its opposite: 'For he whose health is in a condition of warm temper, cooler things are appropriate. The same is true of damp and dry [complexions]. When the warmth increases and flares up, he benefits from cooling things.' Referring to Hippocrates, the author cites the old counsel that it is unhealthy to eat 'before one has worked a little'. At-Tabari's appeal for moderation developed into a popular moral precept, summarized as follows by the physician Hasan-al-Basri: 'Eat a third, drink a third, leave another third free for reflection.' At-Tabari also drew comparisons with other cultures: 'We have already set forth what the Greeks taught about health. The Indians say that he who wishes to preserve it must raise himself from sleep in the last seventh of the night, perform thoroughly the ritual ablution, put on his best clothes, begin with praise to God, pray to him humbly in difficulties, and clean his teeth with splinters from bitter or acerbic trees.'

As in Greek and Roman antiquity, Islam laid down specific rules for particular professions and ways of life. A *Medical Regime for the Pilgrims to Mecca [Risala fi tadbir safar al-hajj]* dealt with eight major topics: 1) resting, eating, drinking and sleeping; 2) the treatment of states of exhaustion; 3) illnesses caused by the wind or air; 4) prophylactics against and the treatment of insect bites; 5) questions relating to water quality and treatment; 6) ways of relieving thirst; 7) precautions against *Dracunculus medinensis* (an organism causing diarrhoea); and 8) precautionary measures against snakes and the treatment of snakebites. All these measures would only work 'if God so wishes', stressed the author, Qusta ibn Luqa, who was in all likelihood imitating Byzantian precursors.[36]

It was probably at the medical school of Gondishapur in Persia that Arab medicine (rustic and empirical in origin) was first melded with the Greek tradition. Here students could avail themselves of translations by Nestorian scholars, the most prominent of whom was

Hunain-Ibn-Ishaq, whom Western doctors later named Johannitus.[37] His *Isagoge* [Introduction] to medicine began with the famous words: 'Medicine is composed of two parts: theory and practice', and was an essential part of the *Articella*, a collection of Galenic and Hippocratic texts, whose influence in the West rapidly became established. Surprisingly, the field of dietetics was classified as medical practice. The tradition of the *Adab* [*Book of Etiquette*], which was widespread in Islam and, with its advocacy of a strict mental discipline, was considered a 'beacon to the body, a pillar to the soul and a light to the heart' for the wise, provided the foundation for the emergence in the twelfth century of the *Secretum secretorum* tradition. This work was originally thought to be a letter from Aristotle to Alexander and appeared in the West with the title *De regimine*.[38] Here, health is once again presented as a balance of qualities 'in the proper mixture'. Dietetics, moreover, implies the maintenance of the 'six non-naturals' and the awareness that life and health are a gift from God, a matter of course for the pious Muslim. It is interesting to note that medieval dietetics in East and West were largely in agreement as regards the classical humoral theory and the belief that God alone is able to cure.[39]

A typical example of 'Adab literature' can be found in an eleventh-century work by the physician Said B. Al-Hasan, from Rabbah on the Euphrates. In addition to such topics as the professional ethics of the physician and deontology, the work contains 'short pieces of advice, which will benefit the health of the person who follows and observes them, and will prevent him from falling into the hands of foolish doctors'. Once again, the 'classical' mean is advertised as the way to recovery:

> I maintain that healthy bodies generally receive their wellbeing from conditions suited to their nature, that the person concerned should therefore stay in temperate air, that is neither so hot as to oppress him and make him perspire, nor so cold as to give him goose flesh. Moreover, it should be a healthy and pure air that is pleasant to breathe. If the air is too warm at the respective point in time, let him balance it by cooling, if it is too hot, then by warming. He should be on his guard against infectious air and that which is mixed with damaging vapours and bad smells.

Al-Hasan stresses that baths are only advisable if the bath-water is at a pleasant temperature. The following piece of advice demonstrates psychosomatic awareness: 'One should not be intemperate and persist in anger, sorrow and lack of sleep.' Al-Hasan therefore advocates a regular *psychic* catharsis: 'One should have the following mental characteristics: enjoyment, judgement and [enthusiasm for] scrutiny of the intellect by means of moderate thoughts on learned questions.'

At-Tabari had emphasized that 'One should only live in countries that have four things: a just government, running water, usable medicaments and an educated doctor.'

In the twelfth century, Abd-al-Malik, a physician and philosopher from Cordoba, dedicated a book on dietetics to the caliph. The work contains an elaborate dietetic regime, based on the four seasons, in which various breads, meat and milk products, varieties of fish, fruits and vegetables, spices, drinks and oils are described and classified in Galenic mode on the basis of their essential qualities. There then follows advice on sleep, taking baths, sexuality, physical exercise and clothing, but also directions for pregnant women and on children's hygiene. The author claims that precious stones worn on rings will protect the ruling family against illness and misfortune.[40] Works focusing almost exclusively on nutrition were also composed by Ishaq Ibn Sulaiman al Isra'ili, Ibn Biklaris and other physicians.

As-Samarqandi set out a comprehensive diet for the sick, with recommendations on food, drink and rules of conduct specific to a variety of illnesses.[41] According to Schipperges, Arab dietetics drew on three main sources: 1) the Islamic culture of daily living, as recorded in the Qur'an and the histories of the prophets; 2) the Hellenistic tradition, which was associated with the authorities Hippocrates and Galen; and 3) sectarian directions concerning lifestyle, which were often circulated in mysterious 'missives'.[42]

In the eleventh century, Ibn-Butlan, physician to the caliph of Baghdad, organized various rules, translated from the Greek, on the subject of a healthy way of life into a tabular representation. This table was translated into Latin around the middle of the thirteenth century, probably in the court of King Manfred of Sicily. The Latin version of this work bore the title *Tacuinum sanitatis*, after the Arabic word 'taqwim'.[43] Such works also incorporated the 'Materia medica', a list of the herbal remedies necessary for the restoration and preservation of health, which also included magical components. The scene of the health-giving, anthropomorphic madrigal being torn from the ground by a dog and simultaneously killing the animal with a cry of pain, which illustrates both Arabic and European editions of the work, can be traced back to Ibn-Butlan.[44]

In addition to teachings on maintaining a balance and on mastering elemental affects, the author is particularly concerned to explain to *laymen* ('kings and great lords') how health can be preserved by means of a well-balanced way of life. This lifestyle should be based on the 'six non-naturals'. The Arab (and later, also the Western) reader is told that baths benefit the healthy, but not the sick, that ball games enliven the mind and exercise the body to a sensible degree, but damage 'weak joints', that sport is particularly beneficial when practised before meals but deleterious if practised afterwards, that sleep improves the memory and intellect and assists the digestion, that it is dangerous to swim when one is hot, that enjoyment makes one fat, and can even kill when it occurs very suddenly, that dwellings must be situated differently in the South and North due to the different light and wind conditions. Ibn-Butlan also considers health to be ultimately a gift from God, whose signals must be interpreted: 'Let the almighty God teach us, then, to strive for the good life and flee from the bad.' The mystic Gazzali, however, argued that therapeutic measures were only worthwhile if the sick man strove to attain a new, spiritual life through his recovery. Those who merely wished to be fit for work or to recover their unrestrained appetites for pleasure, were, according to Gazzali, narrow-minded, and would therefore remain ill. Naturally, such notions were also readily understood in the theologically oriented world of the Christian West.[45]

Health care and prophylactics against illness were considered by Arab physicians and philosophers to be individual duties, which were neither delegable nor subject to fate. According to Ibn-al-Gazzar's *Viaticum*, 'the duty of the physician is rather to prevent than to administer therapies.' Students from Cairo to Samarkand learned that, 'if you have a choice between a diet or medication as forms of treatment, always choose the dietetic lifestyle.' The exemplary doctor was expected to live temperately himself, and not to become a 'glutton or wastrel'. In Salerno it was even considered shameful for a physician to suffer from a protracted illness![46] It is not without reason, then, that Ali al-Ruhavi (ninth century) recommends a judicious regimen to physicians in his tract *Ethics of a Physician*: 'One should begin one's daily routine with a prayer and end it reading scholarly texts over a glass of wine' (which was not entirely unproblematic for a devout Muslim). Corresponding dietary prescriptions are given in Rhazes' *Liber continens* (tenth century). The work *Ad Almansorem* contains a 'summa' of contemporary doctrines of health, together with an explanation of the benefits and dangers of a wide variety of foods such as bread, meat, poultry, fruit and spices. All of these works, which were later translated into Latin, reiterate the classical imperative of self-discipline.[47]

The Arab bathing culture, which drew on the legacy of the ancient Romans, also contributed to the preservation of health. External cleanliness symbolized *internal* purification, a tenet that additionally drew on Indian and Persian traditions, as water is described in the Veda as the most effective form of medication.[48] According to the Qur'an, it is a duty of all believers to perform their daily ablutions (IV, 44; V, 7); the first bathhouses were situated close to mosques. It was from the Arab world, and not from ancient Rome, that medieval Europe took its bathing culture, and the social and hygienic importance of this culture persisted until the syphilis epidemic in the early sixteenth century. Together with schools and hospitals, bathhouses represented the most important institutions of Islamic medicine.[49]

The doctrines of health of Christianized Arabs such as the Nestorians represent a rather different phenomenon, with their emphasis on an early Christian dualism derived from the Stoa and the monastic tradition, and their aspiration to a spiritualization of life. A typical example can be found in the form of a letter by the ascetic bishop Elias of Nisibis (*d.* 1049), in which sexual abstinence is recommended as a panacea:

> Abstinence from sexual intercourse . . . increases natural warmth, which assists the natural functions; it conserves strength and increases the activity of the body, so that its movements become easier. The complexion becomes fresher; it preserves the powers of sight and fortifies the body, prolongs life, protects the sensory organs and hones the intellect; it conserves fortune and heightens esteem, engenders renown and increases rewards.

Avicenna (980–1037), the great Persian philosopher and physician, was also concerned with questions of health. His main, most renowned work, the *Canon medicinae* [*al-Qanun*], a sort of distillation of medical knowledge from Greek and oriental sources, was naturally concerned with hygiene and dietetics. The title alone evokes terms such as norm, standard, law, rule and code.[50] The comprehensive, didactically structured work exercised an unparalleled influence on Arab and Western medieval medicine, not least because the author subsequently summarized the voluminous subject matter for a student readership in a further work, the *al-Arjuzat fi'l-tibb*.[51]

It was in this didactic poem, which comprises 1326 verses, and was described by the philosopher Averroës as the best introduction to medicine, that the author presented a comprehensive lore for daily living. He took dietetics to mean the regulation, and even the stylization, of private and public life. The 'six non-naturals' appear once again as the foundation; however, Avicenna constantly shifts his attention from microcosm to the macrocosm, from body to environment. *Salus publica* and *salus privata* are both decisively influenced by light, air, water, climate, ground, and even politics and town planning. Strict self-discipline within the personal sphere is insisted upon; moderation in eating and drinking is presented as an imperative.[52] A further desideratum is the attainment of a rhythm in all areas of life, symbolized by the alternation of movement and repose as exemplified by the pulse. Avicenna draws on Herophilus' pulse theory, which can serve as a diagnostic aid: 'If the pulse has departed a long way from a steady metre, this suggests an unusually acute change in the condition [of the body].'

The body's excretions and secretions should also be monitored, according to Avicenna. Sexual intercourse is, in the first instance, a 'shock to an extremely delicately balanced system'; the balance is redressed by means of a sophisticated 'ars erotica'. Consideration should also be given to the 'affectus animi'; passions, joy, sorrow, despair, friendship, hatred and love, all have a strong influence on health. The human being, who according to Avicenna is not suited to solitude, should make judicious choices in the social sphere, in particular, for example, in the question of marriage (although the woman is considered a 'mas occasionatus', a 'not entirely perfected man'. All rules laid down by Avicenna for man and woman, old man and child, sick and healthy, scholar and craftsman, are valid only as part of a holistic mode of existence which encompasses the microcosm and the macrocosm, and in which the condition of body and soul cannot be separated from politics, ecology and social harmony, and, most importantly, religion.

Although the *Canon* differs from other ancient and medieval works in that metaphysical considerations are, for the most part, excluded, the conception of health espoused by Avicenna is far from materialist. Man is endowed with the ability to find the critical *mean* by God, along with the strength to avoid a deleterious loss of balance. It is not, therefore, the doctor who bestows health; health is dependent on a 'higher principle', which lends matter its form.[53] As was so often the case in the medicine of this age, the art of healing and the doctrine of salvation are intertwined; it is no accident that Mohammed was believed to have stated that there were essentially only two academic disciplines: medicine and theology (from which Islamic law also derives).[54]

Theodicy, or the question of how to interpret evil and illness in a world created by a benevolent and omniscient God, represents a central problem for Avicenna. He considers evil to be the price of free will, which appeals to man's moral responsibility and determines his dignity.[55] Illness could therefore also be considered part of a greater good. It is obvious, therefore, that concern for health should be considered a *moral* problem. While the *Canon* divides medicine into theory and practice, the *theorica* aim to guide the intellect towards an awareness of these moral aspects. It should come as no surprise, then, that Avicenna called his encyclopaedia of the sciences *Kitab al-Shifa*, the 'Book of the Healing of the Soul'. Knowledge alone was believed to give the power to cure.

Avicenna refers to the Prophet, who, he claims, has shown Muslims a rule which guarantees health and happiness. 'Follow thou that [way], and follow not the desires of those who know not.'[56] However, he stresses wisely that even the best health rules cannot override the disposition of the individual to illness laid down by nature:

> Each body has limited resistance to its own inevitable dehydration, a limit which is determined by its original composition, its original heat, and its original degree of moisture, and which the individual cannot exceed. Sometimes he reaches this limit prematurely, with the result that processes occur which particularly aggravate dehydration or are fatal in some other way. Many say that the death first described is natural and the latter type of death is only accidental. The task of medicine, then, is to allow the human body to reach that natural end which is known as natural death.

Medieval doctrines of health in the West

From the eleventh to the thirteenth century, the greater part of the aforementioned Arabic tracts were translated into Latin and thus made accessible to a Western readership. Directives for the best possible and healthiest lifestyle also became increasingly popular in the West. Here, the Hippocratic and Galenic traditions had not sunk entirely into oblivion, although their influence had dwindled in the course of the millennium following the birth of Christ owing to the spread of Christian and ascetic doctrines. Some time after 1075, Constantinus Africanus, a lay brother at the Abbey of Monte Cassino who converted to Christianity, translated the famous *Isagoge of Johannitius* (Hunain-Ibn-Isaaq), an 'introduction' to Galen's *Ars parva*, which was also known in the West as *Tegni*, *Microtegni* or the *Ars medica*. The *Isogoge* and *Ars parva* together formed the *Articella*, one of the most widespread and best-known writings in medieval medicine.[57] The *Corpus Constantinum* also encompassed works by the Persian doctor Haly Abbas, which Constantinus and his pupil Johannes Afflatius edited with the title *Liber Pantegni*, as well as Galen's *De methodo medendi* and numerous smaller treatises.[58] The *Liber Pantegni* classifies as healthy a body 'whose physiological and anatomical relations are in correct proportion and balance'.[59] In the twelfth century a further important school of translation grew up in Toledo, where the works of Aristotle, Rhazes, Alhazen and Avicenna, among others, were translated from the Arabic.[60] Under the influence of numerous works, including Galen's *Ars parva* (which, like Herophilus and Galen himself, defines medicine as 'the science of the healthy, the sick, and those who are *between* these two conditions'), as well as the *Isogoge of Johannitius*, the *Liber Pantegni* and the *Viaticum peregrinantis* by Ibn-al-Gazzar, but particularly Avicenna's *Canon medicinae* and the *Liber de medicina ad Almansorem*, both translated by Gerhard of Cremona, the notion of 'six non-naturals' became established as the guiding principle of all dietetic considerations.

Numerous physicians and philosophers were inspired to compose *regimina*.[61] Thomas Aquinas (thirteenth century), probably the most influential Western theologian, stresses in his *Summa theologia* the necessity of a law 'as a rule or measure of human acts'. It should be 'possible both according to nature, and according to the customs of the country'.[62] This *ordo vitalis* was adaptable to dietetic, as well as to political, ends.

The daily routine of the human being should, according to Aquinas, be governed by harmony and rhythm. Moderation is here defined as the cardinal virtue of 'Temperantia', which is also characterized by *verecundia* (shame) and *honestas* (moral conduct). The final aspect encompasses moderation in eating (*abstinentia*), drinking (*sobrietas*) and in sexual matters (*continentia*), modesty (*modestia*) and humility (*humilitas*).[63]

As ancient authorities had, at least since Cassiodorus and Isidore, been held in high regard in the West, their doctrines of health could be adopted fairly easily. Elementary everyday needs, checks on eating and drinking, on sleeping and sexual intercourse, on respiration and excretion, on clothing and habitation, on affects and emotions, all soon became matters of didactic concern in Italy, France and England, as in Arab universities. Professional and everyday life, private sphere, religion, life and death were integrated into a 'forma vitae', which made allowances for those areas of life that ensured mental and existential security.[64] On the foundation of the *regimina*, a Christian 'ars vivendi' emerged, which in the late Middle Ages typically also encompassed the 'ars moriendi'.[65] Thomas Aquinas, for his part, reaffirmed the 'classical' double role of the healing art: 'One role consists in leading the diseased back to health. This sick man needs this. The other task proceeds forwards, towards perfect health. This does not apply to the sick, but to the healthy man.'

Early health regimens, such as the aforementioned letter composed by Anthimos for the Frankish king Theoderic, or the *Diaeta Theodori*, whose provenance is still unknown but which was probably written by Theodorus Priscianus (AD 400), enjoyed increasing popularity in the West from the ninth and the eleventh centuries respectively.[66] However, like Ibn Butlan's *Tacuinum*, these works were surpassed in terms of influence and renown by the *Regimen sanitatis Salernitatem*. This work was probably composed within the ambit of the university of Salerno, the first medical school in medieval Europe, towards the end of the thirteenth century, and is considered the oldest 'native Western' regimen.[67]

Initially, Salerno benefited from the new translations. Indeed, the content of the tract, which professes to be dedicated to the English king and was also known as the *Flos medicinae* or *Lilium medicinae*, is drawn mostly from Eastern sources. The verse form and the ease with which it could be memorized may well have contributed to the popularity of the tract in many European countries. In one rule, for example, we read: 'I advise everyone to observe a diet. If we are afflicted by unpleasant illnesses, diet is half-way to a cure. He who does not heed this behaves unhealthily. If he were to fall ill he could be cured only with difficulty.' In contrast to the medicine of the first millennium, which was generally empirically structured, in the majority of the Salernitan rules authority is vested in the doctor, whose task it is to explain to the patient the 'how, what, when, how much and how often' of a therapy or exercise. Daily treatments are, according to the regimen, to be conducted carefully and responsibly; midday naps should be short; nutrition should be balanced and gymnastic exercise taken in moderation. Warnings concerning anger, alcohol and opulent meals occur in the very first rule, and the saying 'After eating [i.e., the evening meal] you should rest, or take one thousand steps' lives on as a proverb in German. The following verse exhibits both irony and wisdom: 'Baths, wine and love drain our strength; yet how invigorating are baths, wine and women.'

The *Regimen Salernitatem* also drew on the Aristotelian doctrine of temperance. Whereas in the *Philosophia mundi* by William of Conches (1080–1154) the terms 'cholericus, sanguinicus, phlegmaticus, melancholicus' are used purely physiologically, in the sense of an excess of one of the four humours, the scholastic Hugh of Folieto (*d.* 1172) associates them with particular characteristics: 'Doctors say that the sanguinarians are sweet, the cholerics bitter, the melancholics sad and the phlegmatics equanimous.' The *Regimen Salernitanum*, however, describes the melancholic as 'envious and sad, covetous in a persistent manner, not averse to deceit, timid and of a yellow complexion' (rule 93); the choleric, 'who desires to surpass all others', is described as 'magnanimous, generous, ambitious, unkempt, deceitful, irritable, lavish, bold, devious, slender, of dry nature, and of a white complexion' (rule 91).[68] According to the *Regimen*, melancholics are also prone to tachycardia and depression, cholerics to vomiting and insomnia (rules 96, 98). One of the tasks of health care was therefore to 'neutralize' the dominating 'humores' by means of a carefully monitored lifestyle, but also by means of treatment and medication.

Thanks to the regimen tradition and the flourishing medical school,[69] the mere name of Salerno became a synonym for healing and health. 'No one denies that Salerno is worthy of eternal praise', wrote the 'Archpoet' in the thirteenth century. 'There the entire world congregates due to illness, and I admit that the scholarship of Salerno should not be undervalued.' 'The Unfortunate Lord Henry', in Hartmann von Aue's narrative poem of the same name, also travels to Salerno, in what resembles a pilgrimage, to seek a cure for his leprosy.[70] The tracts that were written there, such as the *Articella*, were already prevalent in the twelfth century in Germany, and promoted the *fama Hippocratica* of their place of origin.

Aside from the Salernitan rules and the *Tacuinum sanitatis*, numerous other instruction manuals of 'healthy living' appeared from the twelfth century onwards; for example, the aforementioned letter to Alexander (twelfth century); from the thirteenth century the *Regimen sanitatis*, which was attributed to Maimonides; the *Régime du corps* by Aldobrandino da Sienna; the tract *De morte et vita* by the physician and, later, pope Petrus Hispanus, who practised in Italy; and from the fourteenth century the *Liber de sanitate* by the Bolognese professor of medicine Taddeo Alderotti; the *Liber de conservatione vitae humanae* by Bernard de Gordon, who taught at the University of Montpellier; the *Regimen sanitatis* by the physician Arnold of Villanova; the treatise *De sanitatis custodia* by Giacomo Albini, physician to the prince; the *Regimen sanitatis* by the physician Maino de Maineri; the *Regimen diaetae* by his Bolognese colleague Nicola Bertuccio; the *Libellus de conservanda sanitate* by Barnabas of Reggio; and the *Liber conservationis sanitatis senis* by the physician and anatomist Guido da Vigevano.[71]

By no means *all* doctrines of health were based on the *Regimen Salernitanum*. In this and other respects, the Middle Ages were a good deal less homogeneous than is often supposed. Individual Christian, Stoic, Gnostic, ascetic, empirical, humoral pathological, pagan philosophical and magical elements played a lesser or greater role, depending on the context. Indeed, there is no reason to doubt that the desire for freedom from physical discomfort and for harmonious integration into community and environment, in whatever role or capacity, was also a desideratum in those days. The Galenic tripartite division of the entire nosology into sickness, health and a neutral condition in between seems (aside from the reception history of the

Articella) to have been blurred from time to time by a theory of health and sickness that was more dualistic.[72] Yet people were very unlikely to go to a physician with daily complaints, for example insomnia; the wish for complete freedom from any discomfort was not yet well established. Healthy people doubtless also read the tracts listed above; however, they were particularly popular among the princes and senior clerics to whom they were often dedicated. Regimens and *consilia*, which were generally tailored to a particular addressee and therefore individually nuanced, became increasingly fashionable.[73]

A broader readership, however, was addressed by Konrad von Eichstätt (*d.* 1342) in his *Regimen sanitatis*, of which there were numerous adaptations. These include, for example, an *Ordnung der Gesundheit* (around 1400), a *Regimen vitae* (some time before 1400), a *Promptuarium medicinae* (1484) and a *Büchlein der Gesundheit* (some time after 1450), as well as the so-called *Albich Manuscript* (1425), which has been attributed to the royal physician and Prague professor Siegmund Albich.[74] 'Meister Chunrat' (Konrad) also refers to the 'six non-naturals', of which 'cibus' and 'potus' assume an important role. The rhythmicization and harmonization of daily life, it is suggested, promote physical and psychic wellbeing.[75] The 'arzet zu Eystet' (physician of Eichstadt) recommends urgently 'evaciatio', a well-regulated emptying of the bowels (in no other known tract on health is this point made with so much emphasis), which should be assisted by means of baths, as well as a particular sexual hygiene, blood-letting, dietetic regurgitation and enemas. The 'accidentia animi', those affects which could potentially be damaging to health, such as 'anger, joy, anxiety, sadness, fear and timidity' are given equally unique treatment.[76] Konrad, who obviously had the benefit of access to more recent translations completed in Toledo and Padua (in particular, *Colliget* by Averroës, which was translated in 1255 by Boncossa), included the wealth of dietetic and philosophical knowledge drawn from the Arabs, and also drew directly from the Greek versions of works by Aristotle and Galen (not from the Arabic).[77] His main source is Avicenna's *Canon*, which he frequently quotes verbatim, and whose structure he imitates.[78] The reader is informed in detail of the advantages and disadvantages of bread and meat dishes, of poultry and other meats, of individual organs, of fish, milk, cheese, eggs, fruit, cereal and spices. The emphasis is placed less on personal experience, as was the case in the greater part of the *regimina*, than on the author's faith in the revered authorities of the past.

Other *regimina*, such as the *Tractatus de regimine sanitatis* composed some time before 1317 by Arnold of Bamberg, or, to name a tract produced for clerics, the *Erfurter Kartäuserregimen* (a regimen for Carthusian monks, written in Erfurt around 1450), can only be mentioned briefly. Like the Anchorites before him, the anonymous author of the latter considered health disorders, pain and all worldly afflictions to be a consequence of sin, and medical science to be a gift from God.[79] It comes as no surprise when he cites not only medical authorities, but also the Bible, the Church Fathers and the rule of St Benedict. Belief in the power of the stars to influence the condition of man is also a matter of course for the clerical author. As in the case of the Benedictine monks, 'healing' is directed primarily towards the salvation of the brothers' souls. Solace in daily life, deliverance from pain and protection against illnesses can also be attained by observing beautiful things, for example, plants, precious jewels or the stars. The Carthusians, too, seem to have set great store by good, healthy air; before entering a monastery, the individual is exhorted to give due consideration to its climate and situation. For monks, as for Christ himself, recovery is never an end in itself. The brethren are instructed to arm themselves against illness 'so that they can serve God in health of spirit and body.'[80]

In Italy, the fifteenth century alone saw the appearance of the *Regimen sanitatis* by the Sienese professor Ugo Benzi, the *Libellus de sex rebus non naturalibus* by Michele Savonarola, personal physician to the Estes in Ferrara (and uncle of the revolutionary and Dominican Girolamo Savonarola, who was executed in Florence in 1498), the *Libellus de conservatione sanitatis* by Benedetto Reguardati, a *Libellus de sanitate conservanda* by Guido Parato, the *Tractatus de salute corporis* by (pseudo) William of Saliceto, the *Florida corona medicinae* by Antonio Gazio, and, finally, the tract *De vita triplici* by the important Florentine philosopher and physician Marsilio Ficino (1433–1499). Worthy of note in Germany were, in addition to the *Regimen vitae* by the Würzburg physician Ortolf von Baierland (fourteenth century), the health regimen composed by Bartholomäus Scherrenmüller for Count Eberhard im Bart, the founder of Tübingen University, and Johann Pfeiffelmann's translation of the *Carmen de ingenio sanitatis*, which Burkhard von Horneck dedicated to the archbishop of Mainz Berthold von Henneberg some time around 1500.[81] Around forty incunabula of the Salerno regimen were produced in Germany, France and Italy. There were regimens for infants and the elderly, for merchants and pilgrims, for members of religious or chivalric orders and for 'intellectuals', and, after the Black Death in 1348, of course, directives against the plague. The latter category includes the *Consilium* of the Umbrian physician Gentile da Foligno, and the so-called Prague missive, both of which were composed immediately after the outbreak of the Black Death.[82]

Among other, *specific* tracts are Bartholomäus Metlinger's *Regimen der jungen Kinder* [*Regimen for Young Children*] of 1473, and the *Frauenbüchlein* [*Book for Ladies*] of 1495, which was erroneously attributed to Ortolf.[83] Of particular importance were the 'Monatsregeln' (monthly regimens), which prescribed the patient's behaviour during specific months or seasons. These include, for example, the twelfth-century 'Graz Monatsregeln', the thirteenth-century manuscripts from Limburg and Wolfenbüttel, and the 'Monatsregel' devised by 'Meister Alexander', which were dominated by the precepts of 'moderatio' and 'abstentia', and available in German in the early fourteenth century. Some of these regimens can be traced back to pre-Salernitan works and cannot, therefore, be linked in an unqualified way to the flood of translations described above.[84]

A manuscript from the fifteenth century which can be found in Michelstadt also takes *macrobiotic*, or the art of growing old, as its central theme. 'A sorrowful heart, constant anger and a joyless mind waste the body away, [so] that the individual meets a fast end', we read in the third verse. We are then assured that 'a sorrowful heart drives us on to the destination of death, but a joyful mind makes every age blossom.' A further piece of advice is given: 'If there is a shortage of doctors, adhere to three kinds of medicine: a cheerful mind, peace and quiet, and moderate daily life.' The Michelstadt regimen regulated the everyday necessities of the layperson: 'Do not retain your urine, and do not rush your bowel motions. Do not hold back your stomach wind. All these things will make you ill.' The Lorsch author's belief that simple means often represent the most effective cures is referred to repeatedly: 'The heavenly father in his strength has made all things good; he has given the herbs the power to sustain life.' The exhortation to moderation recurs with similar frequency: 'If you wish to dispel your times of sickness and remain healthy, do not drink without thirst, and do not eat when you are full.'

The Kraków Dominican Nicholas of Poland preached that *simple* herbs (*simplicia*) and trivial things can preserve one's health. In his *Antipocras* (1270), he recommends the renowned 'filth pharmacies', which, he states, are not accountable to 'ratio', but only to 'experience'. For the cleric, who pursues a deliberately anti-intellectual line of argument (anything but self-evident in the 'scholastic' thirteenth century for a physician educated in Montpellier), every cure is dependent on the *virtus caelastica*, which is 'buried' in certain substances (*virtus sepulta*). Nicholas employed fetishes, prescribed amulets in rings and lockets, made medicines from ring snakes, crickets and frogs' hearts, used vipers' fat as an ointment, and recommended the consumption of snakes, 'for God loves lowly things'. He thought it arrogant and unchristian to wish to account for a cure. 'Why is this so?', he asks in the *Antipocras*. 'I do not know, and nor do you.'[85] It should be noted, however, that there is still some disagreement concerning the identity and authentic *oeuvre* of the Dominican author.

Asceticism and mysticism – feasts and beauty care

We should not be surprised by the popularity of *contemptus mundi* traditions and indifference to illness, which, following the emergence of the universities in the twelfth and thirteenth centuries, continued alongside a 'scientific' medicine derived from ancient natural philosophy and medicine.[86] If the phenomenon of illness was attributable to original sin and guilt, then there seemed to be grounds to question the legitimacy of every kind of therapy. Ascetics and mystics repeatedly demonstrated an inclination to tolerate, and even invoke, suffering as a test of character. Jacopone da Todi, the probable author of the apocalyptic hymn *Dies irae* (thirteenth century), prayed: 'Lord, visit me with an illness, a three- and two-day fever, and one that continues beyond this, as well as a great dropsy. Let toothache, head and stomach pains also come.' Health complaints were viewed positively as monitions from God; illness was thought to present an opportunity to follow Christ himself in his 'passio'. Illness, according to the doctrine of the Christian mystics, made man 'alert and sensitive', and liberated him from purely worldly preoccupations. Like Muslims, Christians considered the sick and suffering to be in the broadest sense the object of charity, to whom alms, assistance and support were due.

A mystic who gained particular renown was Meister Eckart, born in 1260 and educated in Erfurt and Cologne. The main assertion of this Dominican, who was famous even in the Middle Ages, was the Neoplatonic tenet that the human soul, thanks to its divine provenance, is constantly striving for fulfilment through unification with God and the 'unio mystica'.[87] According to Eckart, corporeal man, as God's creation, is increasingly drawn towards matter. Yet the innate wish to return to God remains with him throughout his life.[88] Illness and evil can be explained by man's distance from God, whereas the pursuit of health can be equated with man's longing for God, which is manifested in the soul's need for unification with the divine.

It is impossible to provide a full description of the 'unio mystica' at this stage, particularly given that it by no means constitutes a demonstrative withdrawal from the world for Meister Eckart. 'Only in the

darkness of suffering and adversity can light reach us.'[89] Worldly pleasures, claims Eckart, are likely to cause suffering, whereas suffering
always causes joy. Illness is a 'via aurea' that leads to true health 'in
God', as it distracts attention from the worldly. According to Eckart's
dualistic world view, every pain of body or soul should be considered
in relation to the salvation it serves to bring about. The 'imitatio
Christi' pursued through the 'passio' also signifies liberation in the
first instance. Illnesses, like poverty, serve for the author of the *Opus
tripartitum* as proof of God's mercy.

A prophylactic – in an exalted sense – against illness is for Meister
Eckart the 'vita contemplativa', which leads to rapt concentration, to
the contemplation of God. All faculties of the soul and body should
direct their energies towards this point, albeit at the right moment in
time and not to the detriment of everyday duties:[90] 'Those who wish
to lead a good life should act as someone who draws a circle [with a
pair of compasses]. If he has positioned the centre correctly and stands
steadily, the line of the circle will be good. The meaning of this is that
man should learn first to have his heart remain steady in God. Then
he will be constant in all his works.' Orientation towards the divine
simultaneously calms the body and soothes sensation, will and desire.
However, as man is a part of everyday life, absolute, radical and permanent meditation would prevent the performance of necessary good
works and contradict the biblical commandment of work. Absolute
recovery, without any disruption by physical and worldly grievances,
is therefore only possible *after* death, as, before it, 'time, corporality
and diversity' impede the 'unio mystica'.[91] It is easily understandable,
then, that attempts to restore or preserve health should be of secondary importance for the true mystic.

Female mysticism, however, was quite different in character. Here
the 'unio' was described using (sometimes quite bold) erotic imagery –
for example, in the work of Ida of Nivelles.[92] Sacralization of nature
and absolute internalization transform health complaints, illness and
pain into prerequisites for unification with God, and even part of the
aura accompanying this unification, which is experienced corporeally.
Physical flagellation and mortification are often considered prerequisites for an ecstatic transport, which for Beatrice of Nazareth constitutes an emotional process culminating in a 'storm of love',[93] and for
Luitgard of Aywières peaks in the state of 'agape', which is exalted
above any sexual experience.[94] Whatever the modern psychoanalyti-
cal interpretation of such experiences may be, they doubtless represent
variations on the traditional contempt for the body drawn from Stoic
and Neoplatonic doctrines. Here, a painful state of absorption is considered to be *imitatio* of Christ's passion. Mystic experiences often led

the mystics to the brink of physical destruction; yet this was by no means viewed negatively, as the visions were associated with hope and proximity to God. By means of asceticism, the mystics attempted more or less consciously to imitate the martyrdom of particular saints, or to participate in Christ's works of salvation.[95]

The nun Elisabeth of Schönau (twelfth century) wrote as a 23-year-old:

> I thank God . . . that I may carry his arrows in my body. My various illnesses have tormented not only me, but also all the sisters who are near me. May God grant them mercy, for they have borne the burden of my body with maternal compassion. They have often . . . given me medicine, but I merely grew weaker as a result, and one night in a vision heard a voice saying to me: 'Our God is in heaven, he may do as he wills'. I realized that I was being commanded to entrust my body not to human medicine, but to the will of the creator, and this I did.

For Elisabeth, suffering represents a direct route to God, and to spiritual health and freedom.

The most influential female mystic of the late Middle Ages in Europe was probably Catherine of Siena (1347–1380). She saw in the worship of Christ's blood ('exalt in blood, clothe yourselves in blood, suffer in blood, rejoice in blood') a way of partaking in the body of Christ: 'And so I will have peace in the time of battle and sweetness in bitterness.' She sought union with Christ in visions and contemplation. Like her contemporary Petrarch, Catherine exhorted all to strive for the health of the *soul*, considered far more important than that of the body. 'If the soul does not uplift itself, your eye does not open and take the immeasurable goodness and love of God towards his creation as an example', she wrote in 1374 to Fra Bartolomeo Dominici. The soul would remain so stinted 'that it could comprehend neither itself nor its neighbour'. Man's self-will, she instructed, should be cast off like a piece of clothing, and the will of God 'slipped on'.

Medieval mysticism worked a powerful fascination on innumerable people. The notion of death as the moment when the soul would be liberated from its corporeal prison circulated not only in the monasteries and nunneries, but also in noble circles and beyond. Health was often regarded as a purely spiritual state, as the liberating insight into the true nature of body and soul, which caused all other phenomena in life to assume secondary importance. Books of meditation and spiritual handbooks became popular. The *Speculum humanae salvationis*, the 'mirror of salvation', apparently of Italian provenance, offered spiritual assistance in everyday life. It was edited in 1324 in Strasbourg by the Dominican Ludolf of Saxony and became particularly popular with the Teutonic order of knights. The popularity of the *Speculum*, which survives in 300 medieval manuscripts and also existed in an extended, and a popular, abridged version, is due to a large extent to its typological illustrations. The work influenced stained-glass cycles in numerous churches (for example, Colmar, Strasbourg, Cologne, Esslingen), mural cycles (for example in Königsberg Cathedral) and tapestry cycles (Wienhausen) which depicted routes to salvation for the faithful.

The tendency to consider recovery to consist of more than mere *physical* restitution can also be observed outside the monasteries. Hartmann von Aue describes how the Unfortunate Lord Henry, leprous and despairing, travels in search of a cure to Montpellier and Salerno. There the wisest doctor assures him that he can be cured by the blood of a virgin who will voluntarily give her life for him. He succeeds in finding a girl who is prepared to do this, but, as he is watching the doctor sharpening the knife in order to open up her ribcage, Henry relents. He repents and becomes a new man, whose *soul* is in full health. In a cathartic development – from purgation through revelation to redemption – he finds God once more.[96] Similar sentiments are expressed by the baptized Jewish convert and court physician Petrus Alfonsi (1062–1140) in his book *Die Kunst, vernünftig zu leben* [*The Art of Prudent Living*]. Here, Alfonsi demonstrates by means of moralistic examples and narratives that the study of 'sacred philosophy', in addition to morality and piety, can endow the individual with the knowledge and ability 'to strive for a life of moderation and self-discipline, to obtain the prudence to avoid menacing ills and to pursue a way of life in this world that can lead to the kingdom of heaven.'

It is recounted in the *Fioretti* that Francis of Assisi, the unscholastic and unconventional thirteenth-century *poverello*, also restored the spiritual balance of the sick when he returned them to bodily health: 'He then undressed [the leper], and began to wash him with his own hands, whilst another brother threw the water upon him . . . Wherever St Francis touched him with his holy hands the leprosy disappeared, and his flesh was perfectly healed also . . . While his body was being purified externally of the leprosy through the cleansing of the water, so his soul internally was purified from sin.'[97] The saint, who himself suffered from a painful eye condition, considered this suffering 'a pledge' for the immortality that awaited him – a topos of the Christian experience of suffering.[98]

In the Middle High German sermon *Über fünf schädliche Sinne* [*On Five Damaging Senses*], written between 1250 and 1264, the Franciscan Berthold of Regensburg addresses the issue of meals. The major tenet of this philippic is that threats to one's health are a consequence of a sinful life:

> Now consider whether there is anything better and more precious for your body than health and long life. Those of you present who wish to live constantly in good health and to live long should be on your guard against two sins: one is called immoderation in eating and drinking, and the other immoderation of the flesh in unchaste things. They do so much damage to the health of the body that there is no way of describing it fully. Yet I wish to tell you something of this: immoderation in eating and drinking is called gluttony in the Bible and is one of the deadly sins.

In socio-critical mode, Berthold recognizes that his 'poor' listeners, in contrast to the rich gluttons, are unlikely to be susceptible to this sin. However, he warns against affluent living, to which, he argues, women are increasingly drawn. Many poor people indulge in this vice at the cost of their families, he claims, and adds that it is an error for a man to believe that 'the better that one eats and drinks, the stronger and healthier he will appear and the longer he will live', for 'the children of rich people are far less likely to reach old age or even adulthood than the children of poor people'. Berthold bases his argument on the warning in Romans (6: 23) that the price of sin is death; however, he uses medical arguments and therefore makes a contribution to his listeners' health education. Eating and drinking were continually regarded as evidence of prosperity and success, which people were anxious to flaunt, from the thirteenth through to the seventeenth century. Among the nobility it was even common to display inedible dishes and sumptuous table decorations, all merely for the sake of ostentation! It may seem surprising that collective meals comprising all members of an extended family, and certainly including representatives of different social classes, were the exception rather than the rule in the late Middle Ages.[99]

The devaluation of physical health as a worldly asset, and even as an 'adiophoron' in the Stoic sense, came under fire from prominent Christian doctors such as Arnold of Villanova (1240–1311). In the *Parabeln der Medizin*, he declares that the objective of medicine is not merely to preserve and restore health, but also to render life complete. Arnold, who was a scholar at Montpellier and personal physician to the pope, naturally also considered medicine to be responsible for *spiritual* healing, in other words, for salvation.[100] Physician and patient are appointed by God as 'socii naturae' to mobilize the natural forces of the microscosm and macrocosm. As Arnold was of the opinion 'that even medication which has only a weak effect is also dangerous if the body does not need it', he believed that the good physician relies initially on dietetics and consultation. Discipline in daily life is naturally preferable to all forms of medication: 'While trouble, noise and anger heat the blood, calm, silence and peace at heart cool it down.' Arnold also considers adherence to the cardinal virtues and a way of life in accordance with the laws of nature to be the optimal prophylactic. 'There is much inherent . . . in natural things from which the wise man can learn and that he can master, given true wisdom, justice, courage and moderation.'[101]

Yet the fascination that was inspired by the *regimina* or the 'six non-naturals' should not blind us to the fact that that the majority of the population were not affiliated to a spiritual 'ordo'; for most people everyday life was dominated by particular customs and cycles which emphasized the stability and rhythmical repetition of existence. Each year, spring signified a new beginning, hope and joy. People celebrated the fact that they had survived the winter; they feasted, sang and drank wine, danced and bathed in wooden tubs. The medieval May bathing ritual dates back to pre-Christian times; a new man, physically and spiritually cleansed from the filth of winter, emerged from the water.[102]

Public bathhouses soon became a compulsory facility in every town. Hostels and monasteries also offered bathing facilities in which travellers and the more noble pilgrims could cleanse themselves and relax. Numerous cookbooks, such as those which are extant from Würzburg (fourteenth century), Vienna and Mondsee (both fifteenth century) describe dishes which are as delicious as they are healthy, and which were also employed for medicinal purposes.[103] A book which originates from the monastery of St Dorothee in Vienna, for example, recommends a spicy sauce made from garlic, pepper and ginger to be consumed during cold weather.[104] Each housewife had her own 'house medicine', every family had its own members who were versed in healing, although they had rarely studied medicine. Lay healers, herbalists, faith healers and miracle healers all played an important part in the medical and dietetic aspects of everyday life.

As early as the eleventh century, the early medieval kinship structures were beginning to be replaced by the smaller unit of the immediate family. Advice was offered reciprocally on matters of health; 'everyday' complaints were treated with the aid of recipe books which were written for laymen and drew on knowledge from 'folk medicine'.[105] Even beauty care was included in dietetics. In the tract *De passionibus mulierum* [*On the Sufferings of Women*], which is attributed to the legendary Salernitan female physician Trotula (eleventh century), we find a chapter on the care of the skin. The professor of medicine William of Saliceto prescribed treatments for varicose veins and obesity, while his contemporary Gilbertus Anglicus wrote, among other tracts, a twelve-part cosmetic guide on the face and hair. Michele Savonarola, who is mentioned above, even gave advice on the reduction or enlargement of breasts: bandaging or diet, or mechanical exercises, when performed at an early age, were believed to be effective courses of treatment. Treatments were recommended to prevent the greying of the hair and balding. Teeth cleaning was common in Central Europe from the thirteenth century; the use of toothpicks was widespread. Very hot and very cold dishes were considered damaging to the teeth, as were citrus fruits. There was also a widespread assumption that coarse underwear and bedclothes harmed the skin. Bed rest and a sleeping position on one's back were believed to enhance beauty; bathing in warm water was considered deleterious by some authors, as it opened the pores and thus increased the susceptibility to infection. As beauty care was generally interpreted as part of health care, it was barely affected by the 'decrees against luxury' or religious prohibitions attested from the thirteenth century, for example those issued by Gregory X at the Council of Lyon in 1274. It is probable, however, that the majority of people in the Middle Ages were as ignorant of tracts on beauty care as they were of the aforementioned famous health *Regimina*.

Western and Eastern clerical scholars: Maimonides, Petrus Hispanus, Roger Bacon

One of the most original thinkers in the Arab cultural sphere was the Jewish doctor and philosopher Moses Maimonides (1138–1204). As a philosopher, he echoes Plato and some of the Stoics in lamenting the fact that man is rooted in the sinful world, which condemns him to death a priori. If one does not wish to imitate a whore who neglects her house and husband, he states, one should beware of matter, which is transient and desires the degeneration of the body. Just as God keeps the various divergent forces of the universe in check, he claims, so human reason works against the decomposition of the body. In Maimonides' writings, the struggle against the threat of illness and death becomes primarily an *intellectual* contest with the body. As animals are unaffected by health concerns and are unaware if their health is under threat – according to Aristotle, animals have no *animus intellectualis* – the human being is considered 'the most noble of all creatures of the lower world'.[106] In order to acquire a moral and spiritual education, which is indispensable for health care, it is not only individual effort that is required, but also a 'natural predisposition', the cultivation of which represents a particular challenge. In this respect, human will is free subjectively; however, considered objectively, it is subordinate to Providence. Wisdom, the teachings of the prophets and the anticipation of the Messiah all support this thesis: if the Messiah comes, the philosophical way of living and the deeper insight into these matters will become common knowledge.

The individual will not live long if he has a careless lifestyle (as Maimonides explained to his pupil Joseph Ben Jehuda in answer to the question of whether the time of one's death is appointed when one is still in the cradle) and does not learn to master the influences of his material body. 'However, if he takes counter-measures and arms himself to resist, he will survive and his life will be longer than . . . if he had not been careful.' The individual himself, therefore, holds the key to reaching the 'natural end' of his life. Maimonides' physiology bears the imprint of the old four-part scheme. The healthy man is the one who has attained a balanced combination of the elements, humours and qualities, is filled evenly with vital *pneuma* (believed by Aristotle to reside in the heart, which he considered superior to all other organs), and recognizes the superiority of reason over matter.

Maimonides divided the practice of medicine into three categories: prevention, therapy and rehabilitation. 'The first and most important is preventative medicine, the preservation of health.' 'Rehabilitation' designated the after-treatment or counselling of patients who could be described neither as healthy nor as sick, 'the treatment of cripples, for example, and of the elderly'.[107] Particular importance is attached to the healing powers of nature. It 'serves and protects us in all matters important to healthy living; accordingly it can also help us with illnesses. It knows . . . the constitution of our organs and looks after the distribution of nutriments within the body.' Medicine and nature together, according to Maimonides, bring about the healing process, which can be observed 'in all countries of the world and at all times'. He also considered health care important from a moral and philosophical perspective: 'A man should keep his soul in good health by means of the exercises that are described above, so that he can, by his deeds and failings, attain the greatest of all things, that is to say, perform works that are pleasing to God', and also 'so that the soul can avail of healthy and unflawed bodily organs in order to acquire wisdom . . ., virtue and spiritual accomplishments, all of which are identical with knowledge of God.' Healthy living is an extremely moral affair, as a body which is in good repair represents a kind of 'key to the attainment of the perfect state'. Yet, Maimonides observes, too few contemporaries attend to their health. 'If man were to bestow as much care on himself as he does on the animal that he rides, he would be spared many serious illnesses', he writes in the *Dietetics for Spirit and Body*.[108] Health can be assisted by means of carefully selected foods, fragrances, music and cheering anecdotes and stories, as well as ball games, wrestling or 'stretching one's hands or holding one's breath'.

Maimonides is strongly opposed to astrology and magic: 'Only a fool believes in the healing power of names and aphorisms, even if they do originate from saints.' He also argues that astrology is in contradiction to the basic tenet of free will. The universalist developed a 'prince's regimen' for the sultan:

> One should get up at sunrise or shortly before. Take two to three ounces of hydromel drink [made from sugar and wine] and rest a little longer. Then go for a ride at an easy pace and, as far as possible, without interruptions; afterwards perform a carefully escalating gymnastic routine, so that the limbs become warm and the mind fresh. Before breakfast one should pause for a short rest. For dessert, let there be pistachio nuts with raisins or dried sweet almonds. This should be followed by another short nap; this is particularly refreshing if accompanied by a slow, damped lute piece. Let the remainder of the day be devoted to reading, conversation, the cultivation of the intellect and the animation of the mind. Before dinner, [take] a sip of honey wine, and then a good evening meal.

Digestion plays an important part in this regimen. If it is unsatisfactory, 'this is the cause of most illnesses'. Following this, 'let singers be summoned as entertainment, retire . . . having given the singers directions to damp the music and recital gradually and to cease completely once a deep sleep is reached.'

Maimonides was convinced that the environment – air and climate, as well as food quality – had a strong effect on the health. 'The first thing to which we should turn our attention is the improvement of the air we breathe, then that of the water, as well as the quality of the food', he wrote. Poor climatic conditions in the towns, high buildings, narrow streets, waste and refuse, sewage and the constricted conditions of cohabitation change the pneuma 'without the individual becoming aware of the extent to which he is affected by this'. In case of doubt, he states, towns should be built on hills with winds from the north and the east – reminiscent of the Hippocratic tract *Airs, Waters, Places*. Yet individual self-discipline remains the basis of all dietetics:

> It is a well-known fact that the majority of people are immoderate in their eating and drinking habits and their sexual behaviour. They are incapable of recovery and disrupt the social order of the people as well as the family. [For] only to follow one's appetites like madmen has the result that the individual

loses his intellectual energy, mistreats his body and dies before reaching the term laid down by nature.

Maimonides' dietetics can be subsumed under three main rules: never eat without hunger, never drink without thirst, never delay defecation.[109] A healthy sleep results in healthy dreams, one in sixty of which are of a prophetic nature. Rest and leisure are imperative, for both medical and religious reasons. 'With the Sabbath we have been given . . . a twofold benefit: a corporeal, in that God shows us freedom from drudgery, a spiritual, in that He shows us, in peaceful tranquillity, the way to true knowledge.' Ablutions are only beneficial to one's health 'if the heart is free of base passion and habit'. 'All illnesses that can be cured through nutrition', warns the scholar from Cordoba, should never 'be treated otherwise'. Psychosomatic factors are also emphasized. In order to cure shortness of breath, the 'physical and psychic condition' of the patient should also be taken into account.[110] Healing is a holistic, spiritual matter and requires philosophical reflection on the part of the patient.

Petrus Hispanus (1210–1277), who was born in what is now Portugal six years after Maimonides' death, was one of the most important scholastic physicians, and also a philosopher of note. He was the only medical authority to be elected pope (John XXI, in 1276). For Petrus, the organism is, from a physiological as well as a philosophical and theological perspective, governed by the interaction of parts, forces, proportions, functions and actions, all of which are kept in check by the soul. This theological conception of order, which he adapted from Aristotle, also formed the basis of his writings on dietetics – for example, the *Summa magistri Petri de conservatione sanitatis*, the *Consulium de tuenda valitudine*, and the respectful *Epistula super regimen sanitatis*, which was addressed to Frederick II of Hohenstaufen.[111] He also produced a macrobiotic tract with the convoluted title *Translatio vetus libri 'De longitudine et brevitate vitae' vocata 'De morte et vita' in corpore vetustiori cum expositione Petri Hispani.*[112]

Petrus Hispanus believed medicine and philosophy to be closely related, although he did consider this relationship to be one of dialectical antithesis. He advocated the integration of Aristotelian thought in European philosophy, theology and medicine as strongly as his contemporaries Albertus Magnus, Thomas Aquinas or Roger Bacon. However, while Petrus Hispanus the philosopher, in accordance with Aristotelian thought, considers the heart as the *principium vitae*, Petrus the physician (he was equally proficient in both areas) identifies four *membra principalia*: heart, liver, brain and sexual organs.

Health is defined as the harmonious, undisturbed interaction of the vegetative, sensitive and intellectual energies specified by the Aristotelian tradition; intellectual properties are reserved for human beings only.[113] A balance between the opposite humours, elements and qualities is naturally also required, in accordance with ancient Galenic tradition. For the human being this condition is, sadly, attainable only in theory: man's transient condition, his very existence, which is regarded as *coagulatio levis*, tends inexorably towards *corruptio* and, finally, to *dissolutio* and *regressio*, i.e., to the dissolution of the life-giving nexus of these structures. Whereas the philosopher strives to heal the whole, the physician, as *minister naturae*, attends to the 'natura particularis' of the body. Of course, the two approaches overlap to some degree. With its complex layers and components, the microcosm is part of the *machina mundi*, of God's creation, and health is primarily an anthropological phenomenon. Disintegration and prophylactic are held in balance by an exemplary lifestyle. As life is, in the final analysis, only a prolonged process of dying, the theologian Petrus can find hope and comfort only in the Christian doctrine.

In his complex dietetics, Petrus Hispanus claims that the affects (*passiones animae*) form a necessary part of life as expressions of man's despair in his transient condition (*tempus est causa corruptionis*). 'Vanity, desire, anger, joy and whatever else affects the soul' therefore acquire existential significance.[114] Health is advanced not by the complete elimination of these passions (which is impossible anyway), but by exercising wise control over them. As the soul is 'motor et rector' of the body, the afflictions and inadequacies are also transferred to the latter. In order to combat physical as well as spiritual 'corruptio', the individual must act as a philosopher would act. Petrus Hispanus, who propagated Aristotelian teachings on the temperament, warns in particular against melancholy, which is also detrimental to health in that it prevents philosophical freedom.[115]

Petrus Hispanus distinguishes clearly between 'general' dietetics ('regula vivendi') and a 'special' regime of eating and drinking. Particular care should be bestowed on the spirit (*spiritus*) and warmth (*calores*) of life.[116] Health is also dependent on the 'harmony between the limbs, the strength of the actions', on age, colour of skin, *habitus* and gender.[117] The cultivation of the 'six non-naturals' is also advocated. Whereas a virtuous lifestyle that takes these factors into consideration is the responsibility of the patient, it is the task of the *physician* 'to conserve, or to restore health'. Healing and regimen cannot, therefore, prevent illness and death, the acceptance of which is part of the 'ars vivendi'; however, they can delay, alleviate, and even overcome them.

Petrus' maxim of 'Redeamus ad naturalia' does not relate so much to a 'return to natural life' in, for example, the Rousseauian sense, or to the scientific study of nature or Aristotelian nominalism; instead, it prescribes the cultivation of the 'res naturales' or 'res non naturales' ('naturals' or 'non-naturals').[118] By respecting the latter, it is possible to slow the 'corruptio' of life. Philosophical wisdom and the hope of salvation after death underpin the spiritual and anthropological dietetics of the scholar, who also wrote practical medical tracts, as well as the *Summulae logicales*, one of the most popular textbooks at European universities.

The art of 'extending life in health' (macrobiotics) was considered particularly important at the papal Curia, with which Petrus Hispanus was in close contact before his election as pope in 1276. The conviction that no pope, however young, would ever be able to exceed Petrus' legendary incumbency of twenty-five years had remained influential since the age of the reformer of religious orders, Peter Damiani (eleventh century).[119] As the lifespan of human beings was generally assumed to be decreasing, in comparison with the patriarchs of the Old Testament, some theologians resigned themselves to a presumed divine punishment. 'My few days will soon be at an end; hardly anyone reaches sixty nowadays, and very few seventy years', lamented Innocent III (1161–1216) in his tract *On the Misery of the Human Condition*. It is hardly surprising that in 1177 Alexander II should have sent his physician to India, the fabulous land of the Christian priest and king Prester John, where a mystical spring promised freedom from all illness and eternal youth (relative to the age of thirty-three reached by Jesus),[120] and a miraculous stone healed 'only Christians and those who wish to become Christians'.[121] It is no coincidence that the oldest medieval manuscript devoted exclusively to the extension of life (*De retardatione accidentum senectutis*) appeared in the thirteenth century in Rome. It is thought that copies were sent to Innocent IV and his political adversary Frederick II of Hohenstaufen. In the tract, emperor and pope are advised that, if they wish for a long incumbency, they require three sciences: 'The first teaches us to allow justice to prevail, as this ensures peace in the polity; the second, to conserve the health of the healthy and to heal the sick; the third, finally, to prolong one's own lifespan to the natural limit, that God in his might has fixed.' Law, medicine and macrobiotics are therefore the natural companions of the wise ruler.[122]

Petrus Hispanus' philosophical contemporary Roger Bacon (1219–1292) also deals with health and dietetics in his extensive *oeuvre*. His work *The Preservation of Youth* is complemented by the tract *General Regimen for the Elderly* as well as by a treatise with the related title *On Bathing the Elderly*. It is unsurprising that authorship of the treatise *De retardatione accidentum senectutis* [*The Cure of Old Age*], which was produced somewhere in the vicinity of Rome, was also attributed to the English Franciscan, whose *Opus maius* had been known to the Curia since 1265.[123] One of his principal pedagogical objectives was 'to protect young people from the aging process . . ., on the other hand, to rejuvenate the elderly in some way'.[124] Like Petrus Hispanus, the prominent universalist Bacon considered 'virtutes, spiritus and body heat' to be important guarantors of health. If they retain their vigour, 'the hair will not become white, nor will the skin wrinkle; one will remain young in appearance.' However, the loss of vitalizing body heat – as a result of old age or illness – impairs the digestion or other bodily functions. Such physiological laws notwithstanding, 'with wisdom, the aging process can be slowed'. Bacon defends with conviction the old topos that the individual is responsible for his own health.[125]

Magical remedies are also recommended: viper's meat, like gold compounds or pomegranate wine, was thought to have rejuvenating powers.[126] Cheerfulness was considered a particularly effective *pharmakon*, which invariably accelerated the healing process.[127] For the Aristotelians, the source of the heat (*calor*) thought to ensure health is the heart.[128] The premature dehydration and cooling of the body can, according to Bacon, be caused by two factors only: either it occurs involuntarily ('ex necessitatibus'), that is to say, as a result of physical disposition, or it occurs 'ex curis pessimis', or as the consequence of a bad regimen.[129] Aging and illness are advanced by the same destructive processes, and can therefore be combated with the same measures. In consideration of the close link between youth and health, the Franciscan Bacon regards physical beauty as a proof of health and its cultivation as a worthwhile pursuit. Extensive passages of *The Preservation of Youth* deal with skin, hair and body care.[130] Bacon describes how aging skin can be rejuvenated by means of oils, herbs, exfoliation or 'purification of the blood', the last of which can be achieved by consuming fruit wine.

Elderly people are advised to sleep well, defecate regularly, to be moderate in eating and drinking, and to avoid exertion and hard work. Bathing is permitted only in lukewarm water once a week or every ten days, and is even restricted to once a month in the case of the elderly and infirm.[131] As, according to Hippocratic doctrines, elderly people are susceptible to dehydration and chills, it is recommended that they seek out warm, humid climates, and avoid all tiring work.[132] Humoral pathological considerations should govern the choice of food and drink. The exhortative tone of the *Regimen for the*

Elderly is self-evident: the elderly individual is also first and foremost responsible for himself.

Like Petrus Hispanus and the author of *De retardatione accidentium senectutis*, Roger Bacon assumes a 'natural' lifespan, set down for every individual by 'God and nature'. Bacon's objective is to defer strokes of fate such as illnesses, 'to keep the five senses in good working order and to increase the heat bestowed by nature'. Medication can, of course, assist this process; however, an appropriate lifestyle is the most important factor. Specific regimens are, once again, and after the Arab example, assigned to the various professions, even to rulers and intellectuals.[133] A course of medication can only meet with success if an appropriate lifestyle is observed: 'The use of these remedies and medicines will not benefit those who neglect the teachings of the rules of health. They cannot protect the body of any man against changes if he does not pay attention to his regimen.' Bacon, who was sometimes forbidden by the Franciscan order from publishing his writings, recommended controlled vomiting as well as carrying health-preserving stones. As was often the case, magical and 'scientific' methods are employed side by side.

Recommendations such as those of Petrus Hispanus or Roger Bacon fell on fertile ground in the Middle Ages because they were part of the contemporary tradition of 'life skills'. Hugh of St Victor (1096–1141) had argued that a scholar's education comprised not only aptitude, practice, propriety, reading and reflection, but also the exercise of control in life. In his *Eruditio didascalica*, which was still being printed in 1470 in Strasbourg, he names six main dietetic rules, 'because they produce and preserve health, as long as . . . moderation is observed'. Air and nutrition, exercise and rest, sleep and alertness, defecation and changes in mood represent elements of life that should not be left to chance. The assurance of a divinely ordained *Ordo mundi* – and few scholars doubted in the twelfth century that reflection led necessarily to this insight – exercised a calming and health-sustaining influence, free of all doubts and questions.[134]

According to the health regimen of the Bolognese physician and philosopher Taddeo Alderotti, who served the pope as well as the doge of Venice, the psychic condition was of extreme importance for health. His *Regimen aegritudinis* corresponded to the *Regula* composed for the Florentine patrician Corso Donati, which was structured according to the seasons and placed particular emphasis on questions of personal hygiene such as dental or hair care.[135] However, first and foremost the sick should strive for a cheerful disposition, which could be achieved by remembering pleasant experiences or looking at beautiful things. Corso Donati was even advised to wear splendid clothes,

if this gladdened his soul. In the fourteenth century, then, a new sub-
jectivism begins to emerge, which heralds the beginning of the
Renaissance and subsequently has consequences for medicine.

Further proof that dietetic advice featured as a matter of course in
scholastic works can be found in the work *De regimine principium*
[*The Governance of Kings and Princes*] dedicated to Philip the Fair of
France by the Augustine hermit Aegidius Romanus (1243–1316), who
taught in Paris. This work was translated within a relatively short
period of time into German, French, Italian, Spanish, Catalan,
Portuguese, English and Hebrew.[136] Morality, religion, upbringing,
health, consciousness of one's status and scholarship are named as the
prerequisites of a 'salutary' life, which should also be marked by
piety and intellectual incisiveness. However, worldly topics are also
addressed: overly zealous, immodest, irregular, extravagant and excessive eating habits jeopardize, Aegidius claims, mental as well as physical wellbeing.[137] Even young boys should be accustomed to cold,
exercise and games (here he echoes the ancient authority Athenaios of
Attaleia), while older boys should be protected against overestimation
of their own capacities and sensuality. The environment should also
be appropriate; the palace of the king (and he is, after all, addressing
the future monarch) should be large, beautiful and practical, as every
house should be fashioned to suit the rank of its master. Misty and
damp areas are rejected.[138] Aegidius also combines moral and religious demands with traditional doctrines of health, although he does
not doubt that, as far as true salvation is concerned, strength, health
and beauty are of only secondary importance.[139]

The 'doctor christianissimus' Magister John Charlier of Gerson
(1363–1429), born one generation later, is also concerned with
'Christian health'. A 'good habituation' should introduce the child to
a fitting way of life; according to the theologian and admirer of
Boethius, priority should be given to education in the Christian faith.
The *consolatio theologiae* describes the route to *salus animae*, which
can be furthered pedagogically by means of acclimatization and per-
severance. For Gerson, who later became chancellor of the University
of Paris, the consequence of this ideal of health, which is centred on
contempt for the body, is that children should be schooled in the ten
commandments and the classical canon of virtues. However, pragmatism dictates that we should allow some human 'passiones', 'not
because they are pleasing or attractive, but in order that other, worse
passions do not spring up'. Perfect spiritual peace in the sense of
complete health is an unrealistic goal, and therefore inhumane.
Gerson's regimen is not, therefore, founded in Stoic maxims, but in the
Christian catechism, which he re-edited. Health care, once again,

signifies responsibility to oneself, a tenet that was also supported by Vincent of Beauvais (1184–1264). The author of the *Speculum maius* considers eating, drinking and sleeping to excess 'breeding grounds for impurity'; moderation in eating, drinking, sleeping, bathing and adorning oneself, on the other hand, is a precondition for chasteness.[140] The main ingredient for a balanced character and spiritual health, in comparison with which the body is of secondary importance, is the reading of the Holy Scriptures, as well as, more generally, the study of the 'artes liberales' and courtly literature, all of which were taught at medieval schools.

Hildegard of Bingen

A highly original conception of health, which takes the requirements of both body and soul into consideration, can be found in the works of the 'prophetissa teutonica' Hildegard of Bingen (1098–1179). A large number of works attributed to her deal with dietetics and health, and together constitute a comprehensive *Ars vivendi*. In these writings, the founder of several important convents does not restrict herself to classical humoral theory or to Arab-Aristotelian medicine.[141] Neither does she espouse the tendencies towards contempt for the body of mystic authors such as Elisabeth of Schönau or some of the Church Fathers. Hildegard records the routes to salvation imparted to her in numerous visions; she emphasizes that it is the act of writing itself, to which she is appointed by God, that conserves her health.[142] According to Hildegard, who was a visionary from Rupertsberg and corresponded with the pope, with bishops, with secular princes and with influential theologians such as Bernard of Clairvaux, health rests upon the individual's integration within the cosmos, which was created and is protected by God. To claim for oneself the status of an autonomous being would indeed have seemed highly presumptuous to medieval man, as this was considered a divine privilege, or, rather, as a burden of which God mercifully relieved mankind. Health complaints were believed to be caused by disregard for these factors, by a lack of orientation that is misunderstood as freedom. Health signifies integration in the divine order; illness is a stake in oblivion, in 'barrenness and emptiness'. Rather than an 'occurrence', illness is a failing, a type of disintegration, apostasy, self-destruction and self-castigation. Illness and evil are certainly closely related in Hildegard's world view; Lucifer succumbed to both of his own free will, and his choice between the alternatives of divine order and oblivion is made afresh by every individual. God guarantees health, he 'is life, and every breath and everything that lives is in his sway.' In her major works, *Scivias* [*Know the Ways*] and *Causae et curae* [*Causes and Cures*], Hildegard describes the world, which was constructed by God from four elements in addition to the winds and stars, and which is in the image of man. 'Just as body and soul are a unity and mutually sustain one another, so the planets and the firmament support and reinforce each other mutually.' As the macrocosm and the microcosm concord with one another, it is only logical that the visionary should begin her explanation of the nature of health and healing by praising the beauty and perfection of creation. A manuscript of the *Liber divinorum operum* [*Book of Divine Works*], which is located in Lucca, contains a magnificent representation of man enclosed in the macrocosm, the centre of which coincides with that of the world, but also with the creator who supports and enfolds it. The globe is encircled by air, water, ether and, finally, tongues of flame.[143] The health, beauty, hope and dignity of the individual depend on the extent to which he is anchored in God, while illness and evil are indicative of his disorientation. Thanks to the role delegated to him by God, man is able to 'set both the higher and the lower things in motion'. The emphasis on the corporeal is programmatic: matter is also essentially good, and part of God's work. 'It is the elements that have apportioned their structural distribution and their functional tasks within the whole of the human being in such a way that his condition is one of stable and balanced organization.'

The *temporal* order is of relevance: man organizes his life according to the rhythm of the calendar, and thus turns 'nature into culture'. Every breath and pulse beat, but also the alternation of day and night, the cycle of the feast days, of birth and death of man and animal, of the seasons, and of the germination, budding and blossoming of plants, all evoke the continuation of life, which is simultaneously a fragment of eternity. Without consciousness of the passage of time, health is inconceivable. The order of nature is contained within a system of stars, signs, relations and dependencies.[144] Hildegard refers frequently to *viriditas*, the verdant freshness of life, which maintains both the restorative processes of the bodily organism and the vitality of the mind. This verdancy is also dependent on the interplay between the four elements and, as a symbol of nature, provides for harmony between the body and the cosmos. Since Adam's fall 'into oblivion', the verdancy has faded, mankind has lapsed and become ill. Hildegard has experienced the burden of illnesses often enough herself; she merely emphasizes the value and the blessings of health ('And like a mother after the birth of a child, I can now speak again after my pain').

In Hildegard's writings, the aim of 'the art of healing' is to attain *integritas*, the conjunction of all parts within the whole. She has great regard for the traditional *materia medica*, is familiar with the *iuvamenta et nocimenta* (advantages and disadvantages) of the remedies, and recommends the discrete application of naturally occurring *simplicia*. She is, in all likelihood, indebted to the writings of older authorities such as Dioscurides for her descriptions of plants. Here we are told, to cite an example, that the blackberry is an effective remedy for chest complaints, abscesses, burns and inflammations; the roots, leaves, fruit and juice can be employed to cleanse the blood, as a styptic, and as a remedy for diarrhoea. The blackberry thorn can even be used instead of a knife to puncture abscesses, Hildegard states. Indeed, the blackberry does seem to have been well known within folk medicine for its astringent effects, which are due to the presence of large amounts of tannin.[145]

The watchword of moderation, which had been invoked since antiquity, also determines everyday dietetics in Hildegard's writings, although she can have had only partial knowledge of the works of the ancient authorities. Talking, remaining silent, sleeping, waking, praying and working, eating and fasting, sexual intercourse and abstinence, but also clothing, are said to influence the preservation of health; here the 'Regula Benedicti' is cited as an authority. Self-discipline is characterized not by the dogmatic observance of rules such as asceticism, sleep deprivation, permanent fasting or sexual abstinence, but by 'humble, moderate deportment'. As was so often the case in the Middle Ages, it is God himself who ultimately appears as healer and reveals himself to his prophetess: 'I am the great physician, and I act as a physician when he sees the sick man who wishes to regain his health.'[146] Hildegard interprets health in a holistic, even 'anthropological' manner. Instead of 'instabilitas' and 'incertitudo', equilibrium and security prevail; she warns against self-mortification, forcible repression and obsessive self-abasement as emphatically as against gluttony and drunkenness. Her humanity and her understanding for weaknesses and inculpatory failings enable Hildegard, like Benedict before her, to make allowances for everyday, banal sins; like her contemporary Bernard of Clairvaux, she refrains from excessive zeal and threats of punishment. Her cautions against retiring immediately after eating or against drinking immediately if thirsty in the night are formulated almost lovingly. The reader is impressed not so much by humoral and pathological explanations as by the sympathy and empathy she shows for the patient, who is never threatened or reproached.

With regard to sexuality, Hildegard appeals to the partners' sense of responsibility. As in Plato, parents are to exercise influence over the health of their offspring: 'If someone were to mix dirt or dung into pure clay, would he ever be able to make a solid vessel from it?' The image from pottery serves as a reminder that man is not only *opus dei*, but also *operans dei*, and, as such, responsible for subsequent generations. Although Hildegard devises a detailed sexual physiology, she also notes elsewhere: 'Abstinence preserves perfect health . . . and nourishes the whole human being, both body and soul, in sanctity.' She repeatedly draws a link between such ascetic, philosophical or cosmological considerations and everyday life: 'If an individual wishes to eat during the winter', she states in *Curae et causae*,

> he should find himself a room that is neither too warm nor too cold, but of a moderate temperature. He should choose neither too warm nor too cold, but moderate dishes, for only in this way can he sustain his health through food. He should not, however, sit in a cold room when eating, even if he wears warm clothing, as he will breathe in cold air when eating and come to harm. Yet the warmth that rises up a person's back when taking a meal by a coal fire is more beneficial than if the burning heat strikes him in the middle of his face.

Hildegard's writings on dietetics can be covered only briefly here. Enfolded within the cosmological scheme, as the image and even the centre of the divine order, man will, according to the visionary from Rupertsberg, find health as long as he conducts himself in accordance with the laws of this order and structures his life in full consciousness of his elect status and his responsibility. Hildegard's edifice of ideas is resonant of the theories of her contemporaries Bernard of Clairvaux, John of Salisbury, William of Conches and Hugh of St Victor, as well as of Boethius, Isidor and Benedict. Yet, with the exception of the works of the father of the Benedictine order and some Galenic theses, a clear debt, let alone direct dependence on these authorities, cannot be discerned anywhere in her writings. This fact makes Hildegard's role all the more unique.

Saints and miracle workers

The monastic author of the first German pharmacopoeia invoked the assistance and the example of divine miracle workers (thaumaturges) in order to justify man's endeavours to conserve health. To accord Galen and Hippocrates the same importance as the revered martyrs and patron saints of medicine Cosmas and Damian was certainly audacious within the intellectual climate of the eighth century. Like almost all of his contemporaries, the Benedictine monk believed that the miraculous powers of the saints surpassed all efforts of worldly physicians. The Acts of the Apostles contain a plethora of accounts of healings. Following the dominance of Christian medicine by the image of 'Christus medicus', some theologians, who were sceptical of 'heathen' medicine, recommended the invocation of intercessionary saints. The Frankish bishop Gregory of Tours (540–594), for example, alludes almost contemptuously to the 'Starstecher', who were responsible for the treatment of cataracts, when praising the patron saint of the diocese and surrounding area, Martin: 'Our dear saint has only one steel instrument, and that is his will, and only one ointment, and that is his supernal healing power.' Indeed, the cult of St Martin of Tours came to be regarded as exemplary for medieval intercessionary worship.

Many miracles also took place at the tomb of the local patron saint of Lorsch, Nazarius. 'For people often pour forth their prayers at the tombs of saints and receive the desired medicine', reported Gregory. The bishop of Patras, the town in which the grave of Andrew the apostle is located, admonished the local community as follows: 'How long, my dear brothers, . . . will you continue to seek medicine among men, when there is a heavenly healer who has often conquered the illnesses of weakened men?' Gregory said of Cosmas and Damian: 'Whenever a sick man who is full of faith approaches their grave, he immediately receives medicine'; he also considered a saintly abbot by the name of Abraham to be a 'potentissimus medicator'. For Gregory, 'sancti' are always simultaneously 'medici'. Thanks to their prior ascetic achievements and their pious conduct, they receive divine 'virtus' during their lifetimes, but particularly after death. This 'virtus' is then employed to the benefit of the sick. Naturally, these 'auxiliary saints' were not merely 'medici corporum', but were responsible for both body *and* soul. In Tours, a theriac mixed with earth 'from the sacrosanct tomb of the lord [Martin]' was venerated as the most effective panacea against all kinds of suffering. Gregory considered such remedies to be manifestations of God's omnipotence. The saints were honoured and invoked; God alone was worshipped.

Gregory tells of numerous intercessors who bestowed health by means of their divinely bestowed 'virtus'. On the tomb of St Marcellus hung a lamp whose oil was employed by the sick as medicine, a custom that was adopted in particular by pilgrims from the East. Gregory's concept of *sanatio* is closely related to that of *purgatio*, a notion that also occurs in the Old and the New Testaments (Leviticus 13: 47–59, Leviticus 14; Mark 1: 40; Matthew 8: 43). Yet sin was not necessarily the cause of a health complaint. The final judgement on such matters is passed by God, whose intentions are inscrutable even for the saint who requests mercy for the sick from his privileged position close to the Divinity. Thus 'the apostle Andrew begged God in Patras' to relieve the wife of a certain Gratianus of a haemorrhage on condition that she would lead a virtuous life in future.

Special healing powers were ascribed to martyrs and confessors, who were believed, in accordance with Jesus' words to the good robber, to enter paradise immediately after their death (Luke 23: 43). As patrons of the region and parish, the saints often took over the role of the pagan gods, whose temples and cultic sites were replaced with Christian churches following the Edict of Milan (313). One such example is St Sebastian, whose church in Rome (San Sebastiano al Palatino) was constructed on the site of the old temple of Apollo; thus prayers for health were offered at the same location in pagan and in Christian times.[147] Naturally, the saints were in competition with pagan healers. According to the vita of St Thecla, the saint was raped in Seleucia by men acting on behalf of pagan physicians who were jealous of her powers of healing.

The cult of St Sebastian, the patron saint who was most commonly invoked against the plague in the Middle Ages, was paradigmatic in many respects. The legend of the pagan officer who is martyred as a Christian with arrows, and then beaten to death with cudgels by the heathen militia, occurs for the first time in a sermon by Ambrosius from 388, and is subsequently amplified by a cleric in the fifth century and embellished in the thirteenth century in Jacob de Voragine's *Legenda Aurea*. The earliest representations of Sebastian in the Calixtus catacombs (from *c.* 400) show a clean-shaven martyr in a tunic.[148] The oldest *surviving* mural of the saint pierced with arrows, however, dates from the twelfth century (a fresco in the cathedral in Anagni).[149] The mention of the cult of St Sebastian in the litany of Gregory the Great (540–604), a 'liturgy for times of plague' composed by the pope himself, boosted the saint's popularity. He ultimately attained widespread popularity from the end of the fourteenth century. The image of St Sebastian, his body pierced with arrows, was still being reproduced in the visual arts as late as the eighteenth century, when the last major plague epidemic swept through Europe.[150]

As in the worship of the pagan divinities, springs, mountains or rivers were central to the cults of the Christian saints, as well as to the act of healing itself. As health complaints were also attributed to demons and diabolic intervention, saints were worshipped from an early stage as exorcists, to whom demonic beings were of course more obedient than to normal clerics. Belief in the healing power of saints was prevalent in Western society until well into modernity, and continues today in the Catholic and Orthodox faith. However, this did not deter the sick from placing their trust simultaneously in secular and spiritual physicians, charlatans, magicians, astrologers, occupational surgeons and specialists, lay healers, 'wise women', faith healers or herbalists.

According to popular opinion in the Middle Ages, life, death, health, sickness, accidents, storms, disasters and miracles were all subject to magical influences which could be curbed with ease by saints, stigmatics or visionaries, such as the sorcerer Simon reproached by Peter (Acts 8: 9–24). The church was opposed to pagan magic; however, certain incantations and benedictory gestures, as well as exorcisms and the so-called sacraments (such as holy water, sanctified candles, ashes and bells) which could be employed against magic powers, remained in widespread use.[151] The machinations of neighbours, the evil eye, hostile attacks, trials, unusual incidents while travelling and mysterious star constellations were also thought to represent a threat to one's health. The academic physicians who had been educated in Salerno, Padua or Montpellier probably treated only a fraction of the population, while the majority attempted to safeguard their health by means of formulae and rituals, incantations and assistance from exorcists, alongside prayer and intercessions. In addition to the canonized saints, there were very many popular saints, who were never officially recognized by the church, and were even suppressed.[152] 'Confessors', on the other hand, who avowed their faith on pain of death, and ascetics, whose aim was ultimately to attain martyrdom by means of penance and mortification, were accorded the same distinction as martyrs.

In the Middle Ages the ability to heal was ascribed to numerous 'viri dei' or 'famulae dei'. The following report is given of Bernard of Clairvaux's visit to Milan in 1135: 'Everyone kissed his feet . . ., threw themselves in adulation to the ground before him. They even plucked threads from his clothing wherever possible, tore strips from his garments in order to heal the sick with them. Whatever he touched was considered sacred, and they believed that touching or using such objects would have a healing effect.'[153] Bernard's everyday accoutrements became sought-after relics: 'The bishop treasured a bowl from which the saint had eaten, took food from it himself and was thus healed from an illness.' In the fourteenth century, the fourteen 'auxiliary saints' became popular, initially in South Germany. Each one of these saints, or 'Holy Helpers', was 'responsible' for a particular illness, organ or body part. Restorative powers were also, as in ancient Rome, ascribed to the emperor, who was regarded as God's 'anointed one', at least until the investiture controversy. Even in later times, the French king healed scrofula and other ailments, a testament to the enduring influence of the Old Testament topos of the 'rex et sacerdos'.[154]

The cult of relics had enjoyed a renewed and previously unforeseen increase in popularity from the early Middle Ages onwards. Whereas the liturgical worship of the saints had until the eighth century been confined to their respective memorial or burial sites, at least in Rome, in the course of the Middle Ages they came progressively to be worshipped ubiquitously as auxiliaries and intercessors.[155] The distribution of relics and fragments of relics enabled intercessory worship in different locations. However, pilgrimage to the grave of the saint remained the highest form of worship. The objects that the pilgrims brought home, such as lamp oil, candle wax, dust or rags that had come into contact with the grave or the relic, as well as spring water, images or pilgrims' insignia such as the scallop shell of St James, were all believed to have therapeutic powers. They were given to the sick and the dying in the hope that the 'power of God's mercy' would assist them.[156] The Siegburg book of miracles of 1183 describes over 200 healings:

> Thirty lame and as many blind, sixty bed-ridden or seriously ill . . . fifteen who were afflicted by dropsy and tumors, ten with diarrhoea and haemorrhaging, two with tooth complaints and five with burns, nine with heart complaints, five who were possessed by the devil, then 124 raised from the dead, nine who had fallen into water (mostly children), seven suffering from falling sickness, ten with fractures of which some were serious, three with diseases of the sexual organs, nine cases of deafness and assistance to two women who were giving birth.

As early as Carolingian times, healings of this kind had composed one quarter of all miracles. The faithful were prepared psychologically by descriptions of similar miracle healings in hagiographies.[157]

Images of Christ and the saints could also effect miracle healings. Effigies and sculptures gave preserved relics an almost human appearance. Despite the debate surrounding hypostasis (the tenet that Christ or the saint represented in an image is present in that image), which had led to the iconoclastic controversy in the Byzantine Empire, images were worshipped in the West primarily on account of their healing power. The 'miraculous image' was part of everyday life; the representations provided opportunities to beg the depicted saint for intercession.

From the fourteenth century onwards, the saints acquired medical 'specializations', beginning, as was demonstrated by the example of Sebastian, with the aforementioned 'fourteen Holy Helpers'. An account from as late as 1719 states:

St Sebastian and St Rochus are invoked for protection against, among other things, plagues; St Erasmus and Thiemo, martyr and archbishop of Salzburg, against stomach complaints; St Nicholas against water; St Florianus and Landericus, bishop of Paris, against fire; St Vitus for assistance with children who cry constantly; St Apollonia for assistance with toothache; St Ottilia for eye complaints; St Blasius for sore throats; St Wilgefortis or Uncumber in times of sorrow and great worries; St Saturninus and the bishop St Acacius for dizziness; St Donatus and St Isarnus for protection against storms and wildfire; St Dominus and St Urbanus for protection against hail and rain showers; the abbot St Magnus against crabs and worms; St Hubert, bishop of Liège, against dog bites; St Maturinus for assistance with those who are mad in the head; St Genoveva against 'all kinds of fever'; St Marculfus against deformities; St Patrick against hunchback; St Lupus, bishop of Sens, the blessed Amadeus, prince of Savoy, and St Valentine against falling sickness; St Liborius against stones and colic; St Theodosius against dizziness and loss of appetite; St Lidwina against dropsy; the abbot St Maurus against stitches in the side; the apostle saints John, Paul and Benedict against venom, viper- and snakebites; the Venerable Bede against breathlessness; St Bernard and St Thomas Aquinas against stomach upsets; St Ignatius against 'all kinds of unquiet spirits'. Finally, among the many saints invoked against incurable gout and arthritis were the city guardian St Chromatius, St Gregory the Great, St Martin, the first Roman pope, St Anno, archbishop of Cologne, St Otto, bishop of Bamberg, and so on.[158]

Faith in the healing power of the saints did not, by any means, rule out treatment by a physician. The Church Father Basilios explained as early as the fourth century that one should 'neither flee from medicine, nor invest all one's hopes in it', for, 'just as we entrust the helm to the steersman but beseech God that we may leave the sea safely, so we should consult a physician when rational consideration allows it, but we should not give up our hope in God while doing so.' The hope of assistance from the saints provided a lifeline for the vast majority of people in the medieval world.

The power of the stars

Few medieval doctors and clerics doubted that the stars exercised an influence on health. Pietro d'Abano, one of the leading European physicians at the beginning of the fourteenth century, ranked astrology among the most important medical disciplines, together with logic and scientific fields of study. Here he was able to draw for support on such authorities as Plato's *Timaeus* and the tract *Astronomia*, which was attributed to Hippocrates in the Middle Ages.[159] According to

Taddeo Alderotti, who was professor of medicine in Bologna in the fourteenth century, conclusions as to the humoral composition, character and constitution of an individual could be drawn from the mere date and time of his birth and used as a basis for a dietetic regime. It was also widely believed that the treatment of a patient could be tailored according to the star constellations. Astrological factors even played an important part in the 'plague consilia'.[160] In 1344, the physician Jacopo Dondi designed an astrological clock in Padua, as well as producing an astrological calendar intended for medical use and a summary of the *Alphonsine Tables*, which had been composed some time after 1275 in the court of Alphonso X of Castile and aided the mathematical decoding of the star constellations.[161] In the fourteenth century, astrology was dual in nature: whereas the theoretical branch attempted to investigate mathematically the laws governing the universe, in an everyday context astrology tended to take on a (pseudo-)religious character, dominated by the fear of demons and anxiety about what the future had in store.[162] Important philosophers such as Ibn Khaldun in the fourteenth and Piero Pomponazzi in the fifteenth century are credited with elucidating this dual character. Yet opposition to astrology came repeatedly from critical intellectuals, such as Dante, Petrarch, Salutati, Nicholas Oresme, Pico della Mirandola, Savonarola, Luther, Galilei or Kepler (the last of whom, like Galilei's pupil Cavalieri, was forced to produce horoscopes himself), who objected to a practice that they regarded not so much as a superstition, but rather as an attempt to erode man's free will.[163] Thomas Aquinas, like Vincent of Beauvais or Albertus Magnus, argues that the stars influence matter and the *anima sensitiva* or *anima vegitativa* of animals and plants, but not the *anima intellectualis*, which underpins man's dignity and responsibility. He also concedes, however, that astrologists are frequently successful in their assessment of men, because few are able to withstand their appetites (*appetitus*). Thomas also strongly disapproves of magical practices and amulets.

With the advent of the Renaissance, interest in the astral gods of the ancients increased, as antiquity came to dominate scholarship and daily life. Notwithstanding the debate on free will, which plays a significant role in the works of Petrarch and Pico della Mirandola,[164] the majority of people were convinced of the power of the stars, and believed that God had given man limited powers to look into the future. In general, the notion that the human body functioned independently of the stars conflicted with the view that man as the microcosm was not merely made in the image of the macrocosm, but was also subject to its rules. Astrological cycles and programmes could be found decorating houses of God, such as the baptistery in Parma or the church of Santa Maria del Castello in Mesocco,[165] and public buildings, such as the Palazzo della Ragione in Padua or the fifteenth-century Palazzo Schifanoia in Ferrera; *Monatsbilder* were incorporated within an astronomical context. As early as the twelfth century, Hugh of St Victor (*d*. 1141) had praised the 'natural aspect' of astrology, which was concerned with the 'temperamentum' of things, 'with health and sickness, with storm and calm'.[166]

A clear expression of the automatic link that was made between medicine and astrology can be found in a sermon by Bernardine of Siena from 1427: 'If medicine is administered to a sick person, one notes that the doctor says: this will only help if it is taken on a particular day . . . But if one administers it at another time, without paying heed to what day it is, it can have a harmful effect.'[167] However, Bernardine, like Thomas Aquinas, denies that the soul is dependent on astrological constellations.

Astrology also features in specialist texts and house books. The *Buch vom Menschen, Tier und Garten* [*Book of Man, Animal and Garden*] contains calendars, phlebotomy tables, details of the 'golden numbers', planetary text, prognoses for the life of a newly born baby based on details of his birth, and weather forecasts.[168] Whereas the monthly regimens laid down rules for healthy living throughout the year, and paid particular attention to dates for blood-letting and (seasonal) medicinal herbs, the 'Hebdomadare' and 'Lunare' generally provided prognostications for individual days of the lunar month. Here a distinction must be made between 'Speziallunare' (specialist guides to the lunar month, which focused on specific aspects such as prognoses or blood-letting) and 'Sammellunare' (comprehensive guides covering other aspects such as the interpretation of dreams).[169] Orthodox astrology went as far as to limit health care exclusively to the careful interpretation of the stars. Yet Thomas, Albertus Magnus, Vincent of Beauvais and other scholastics were of the opinion that an individual could never be coerced into acting in a certain way by their star constellation. The decision to lead a virtuous and healthy life remained a free one. Nicholas of Oresme (1320–1382) also argued that there were limits to the influence of the 'heavens' on health.[170] If astrological texts produced for laypersons were furnished with Bible citations, however, accusations of superstition were rapidly dropped.

Astrology was considered by most to be a serious science, which was conducted in accordance with the medieval criteria of *ratio*. Arnold of Villanova linked the star signs to the four-part scheme of humoral pathology, with the result that Taurus, Virgo and Capricorn were labelled cold and dry, and therefore predisposed to melancholy, whereas Gemini, Libra and Aquarius were considered hot and moist, and consequently susceptible to contagion. The organs were also assigned to particular star signs, stars and elements: the face was associated with Aries, the arm and the hand with Gemini, the stomach and intestine with Virgo, the genitals, womb, kidneys and liver with the planet Venus, and so on.[171] Such patterns were depicted in detail in numerous calendars and illustrations.

'Iatroastrology', identified by Rothschuh as the branch of astrology concerned with health and the healing process, reached a height of popularity in the Renaissance, or, more precisely, in the Neoplatonism propagated by Marsilio Ficino and Agrippa von Nettesheim.

5

Doctrines of Health in the Renaissance

Petrarch's conception of health

The first generation of humanists, of whom the leading lights were Petrarch, Boccaccio, Bruni and Salutati, were passionately opposed to what was, in their opinion, the excessively scientific orientation of medicine. The Florentine chancellor Leonardo Bruni considered the wish to investigate the secrets of the body 'not entirely honourable' (*non satis decorum*), particularly given that medicine was concerned exclusively with *worldly* health. His compatriot Coluccio Salutati believed that human intellect could never be adequate to comprehend the divinely ordained functions of the body.[1] The zenith of the famed *studia humanitatis* seemed to coincide with the 'silence' of the scientific disciplines and of medicine.[2] The desire for health was to be satisfied not by academic or scholastic but exclusively by 'spiritual' means. Whereas the scholastic authorities of the thirteenth century – for example, Bacon, Thomas Aquinas, Albertus Magnus, Petrus Hispanus or Vincent of Beauvais – regularly commented on medical and dietetic matters, Petrarch and the early humanists, at variance with contemporary popular opinion,[3] were initially interested in 'humanistic' subjects. Physicians and their Galenic, scientific conception of health were held in derision, as was astrology.[4] Petrarch propagated the notion of the health of the soul in his major writings, a condition that he equated with spiritual maturity, humanity, moral perfection and piety. He repeatedly criticized the health care practised by physicians, the treatment of numerous patients, the routine, the exclusive concern with the body, the supposed godlessness of the physicians, the technical nature of their profession as an *ars mechanica* and their 'overblown' language.[5] In his *Invecta contra medicum* (1352), which he directed at the medical attendants of Clemens VI, he opposed the 'garrulity' of physicians to the alternative conceptions of health and healing of Cato or Pliny and argued that a simple life, rather than elaborate prescriptions, offered the most promising route to health.[6] Petrarch's criticism pertains to the *quality* of contemporary medicine, the reputation of which reached a nadir during the years of the Black Death.[7]

Of decisive importance for Petrarch was the fact that the scientifically and scholastically schooled physicians of the fourteenth century were unable to answer newly emerging questions relating to the nature and the fortunes of the human being. Scientific and anatomical knowledge, the 'materia medica', number games or the consultation of authorities were, according to humanist views, of no value for a 'happy life'; they even encouraged us 'to disregard the character of man, his designation, his provenance and his destination'. The author believed that true health of the soul could only be attained within the 'vita solitaria' cultivated by monks and hermits, a lifestyle that was closed to physicians due to the very nature of their profession. This ideal way of life unified Stoic traditions with the Christian idea of asceticism: the intellectual was advised to pursue 'otium literatum', to retreat from society into the company of important authors such as Cicero, Varro or Cato, who had also pursued this goal.[8] The gurgling of the brooks, the beauty of the wood, the quiet of the countryside around Vaucluse or Arquá afforded him leisure, health, freedom, even the presence of God. Doctors, lawyers or merchants were, he argued, incapable of attaining real health, as they were unable to experience the 'vita contemplativa'. For Petrarch, health is endangered primarily by urban bustle, a state that in his opinion is particularly characteristic for physicians. The extent to which medieval Christian influences shaped his ideal of *solitude* can be discerned from the tenor of the tract *De otio religiosorum* (1347).[9] For the humanists, solitude did not denote the constriction of individual development after the fashion of monastic self-abnegation, but rather the regeneration of body and soul. The fundamental affirmation of worldly existence by the humanists led to a greater appreciation for aesthetics, the cultivation of certain ways of life, and a sensualized concern with literature, religion and culture. Solitary life led the 'solitarius' towards complete harmony with himself.[10] In Decembrio's famous dialogue, Lionello d'Este later identified St Jerome – both as a hermit and in the 'cell' – as his true model.[11] The 'homo activus' was to cure himself by means of meditation.

In his tract *De sui ipsius et multorum ignorantia* [*On his own Ignorance and that of Many Others*] (1367) Petrarch contrasts the 'Aristotelian' *scientia naturalis*,[12] popular among physicians, with Dante's vaunted *sapientia*, which is presented as a precondition for mental health. For Aristotle, then, so celebrated by Arab as well as by Christian physicians, 'true happiness [remained] hidden, however extensive his thoughts on the subject may have been in his "Ethics".' It is not surprising that Petrarch sees advantages in physical ailments. In his popular work *De remediis utriusque fortunae* [*Remedies for Fortune Fair and Foul*] (1366) he advocates the golden mean as a 'remedy' against all conceivable adversities in life and gives a meticulous account of the moral and pedagogical advantages of illnesses and misfortunes. Illness is conducive to meditation on the meaning of life and brings about *meditatio mortis*, whereas health frequently directs the senses towards worldly values. Petrarch even goes so far as to equate health with the Stoic state of 'adiaphora'. The notion of 'vanitas' thus becomes a theme of central concern for the author whom Renan describes as the 'founder of the modern spirit'.[13]

However, Petrarch does not always adopt such an inflexible moral position. In *Secretum*, a moral, philosophical tract composed in 1342–3 in Vaucluse, he also argues that physical health can only be relative ('What is it then that pleases you so about your body? Your strength? Your good health? Yet nothing is more precarious!'). However, he also defends the therapeutic value of 'talking therapy': in a fictional dialogue with Augustine, the 'internal applause' ('ipsius oratoris plausus interior') is embellished as the key element of a philo-sophical dietetics with a strong psychological component. Here, a bal-anced 'vita interior' which is agreeable to God is presented as more conducive to the health of body and soul 'than all the skills of phys-icians'. In the third book, 'Francis' the Church Father asks: 'Do you permit the sick person, who becomes conscious of his suffering, to say something now and again while you work?' Augustine answers: 'Why not? Many physicians have succeeded in finding the right cure thanks to what their patients said, as well as by analysing the symptoms.' He adds: 'As is the case with many, you will only admit that you were very ill when you are healthy again.'[14]

Petrarch and the humanists of the fourteenth century provided a comprehensive critique of medieval medicine. The medieval concep-tion of health and illness is dismissed as somatic. The reproach is not unfounded, given the strict adherence to Galenism; however, it is made in ignorance of Hippocratic writings.

Alberti and other intellectuals around 1500

The debate concerning the respective importance of the *vita activa* and the *vita contemplativa* persisted throughout the Renaissance until well into the sixteenth century. According to Lorenzo Valla (1405–1457), who attempted to achieve a synthesis between the epicurean and Christian 'ars vivendi', the self-knowledge necessary for the health of the soul could only be attained by means of interaction with other people.[15] In his dialogue *De voluptate et vero bono* [*On Pleasure or on the True Good*] (1431), he offers a revision of Petrarch in the form of his claim that the human pursuit of happiness is 'natural' and sanctioned by God. Every instinct and feeling of pleasure, as long as there is no evidence that it is harmful, can be satisfied, and promotes the stability of the body and the soul. Similarly, the Palermitan author Antonio Beccadelli defended sexual and moral liberality in his tract *Hermaphroditus* (1425), which he dedicated to Cosimo de' Medici.[16] The universalist and artist Leon Battista Alberti (1404–1472), by contrast, advocated the prudent alternation of public activity and private retreat, and inclined towards the moralism of the Petrarchan tradition. In his book *Della famiglia*, he recommended in his capacity as 'master and physician of health' regular physical gymnastics 'in the right proportion'. In a fictional dialogue between his father Lorenzo and family members, Alberti develops the 'summa of the humanistic savoir vivre': 'good counsel, sagacity, a courageous, firm, persevering mind, determination, orderliness, moderation, rectitude and discipline, equity, fairness, diligence and carefulness' are presented as guarantors against the vicissitudes of fate. Physical exercise, a selective diet and personal hygiene are presented as means of preserving health, a state that is associated with beauty, youth and the ancient ideal of 'kalokagathia'. A further sign of healthy living is perfect time management, which is opposed to the agitation of city dwellers; a hard-working person always walks slowly.

Within the family sphere, the father is responsible for the health of the family members (including the servants, and even the animals). Climate, air, location, degree of shelter from the wind, and so on, also influence man's wellbeing, according to the tenor of the *Ten Books of Architecture* (1449). The surrounding area of inhabited houses should be 'temperate'; animals should also feel comfortable there. Enough food should be produced, many people should retain their health in old age, the young generation should be comely, births should run smoothly and no deformities should issue forth. (Alberti reports that, in an Italian town situated at a high altitude, many such children, along with others with hunches and strabismus, were born, and consequently advises his reader to avoid it!) Extreme cold and heat are considered harmful, as are westerly locations, where fog is prone to collect, as well as strong draughts ('intermittent winds') and insufficient light.[17] The 'good household', a fundamental concern for the individual who longs for security, is dependent on the location, although it is also influenced by familial, political, social and religious factors. The town is a large house, the house, a tiny town.[18]

Alberti's humanistic panegyric to the city of Florence combines aesthetic aspects with those relating to public health. 'Many villas are situated around Florence', he enthuses, 'in crystal-clear air, in pleasant countryside, with magnificent views. There is little fog, no deleterious wind, everything is good, including the pure, healthy water, and among the numerous buildings are some which can be compared with palaces of princes, some with castles.' The architect Alberti considered hygiene provisions to be particularly important, and recommended flushing with water from a cistern for private residences, as this 'causes the least offence to the eyes and the nose'.[19] 'However, if the sewers cannot be channelled into the sea or a river, one should dig as far as the ground water in a suitable location and fill the pit with stones. If this is not possible, one should excavate pits and pour in coal; then one should fill them up with sand. All sewage that is conducted into the pit is digested by the earth and disappears without producing any fumes or malodour.' Aside from chemical and bacteriological analyses, Alberti's guidelines for waste disposal omitted barely a single modern consideration.[20]

Of particular importance for the history of architecture were the *Four Books on Architecture* composed approximately a century after Alberti by the Vicentine architect Andrea Palladio. For the Venetian villa it was necessary, to single out one theme, to find 'a cheerful, comely, practical and healthy location'. Even the construction plan was expected to meet dietetic requirements. Palladio's instructions concerning the height of the rooms or the arrangement of cellars, roads, gardens, squares and towns are highly reminiscent of the Hippocratic tract *Airs, Waters and Places*, whose central ideas were well known in the Italian *cinquecento*. Sunlight (and certainly rain) should never be allowed to penetrate the interior of a house. Stables should be situated apart from housing on account of their smell. Cellars should be dry and lit only by emergency windows, in order to protect food and wines from heat. The same prescriptions are made for storehouses.[21]

Marsilio Ficino (1433–1499), philosopher, doctor and intellectual spokesman for the coterie around Lorenzo de' Medici, also addressed dietetic matters in his major work *De vita libri tres* [*Three Books on Life*]. The first book is concerned with 'healthy living or health care among those who devote themselves to study or scholarship', the second with 'long life'. As detailed above, the influential Neoplatonist vehemently defended the medical importance of astrology. His specialist dietetics for intellectuals can, *in nuce*, be traced back to the Middle Ages; however, it was amplified extensively in 1489 within the sphere of the Florentine Medicis.[22] The *Regimen studiosorum* by the Basel theologian Johann Ulrich Surgant, which deals with the same topic, appeared soon after (1502), and in 1549 Vesalius' teacher Jacques Dubois edited a work on healthy living for intellectuals, in which social aspects such as the unhealthy living conditions of many students were also taken into consideration.[23] Ficino located thought processes in *spiritus*, which were formed 'from blood'; for this reason, he argued, one should give due consideration to 'blood-forming' organs such as the stomach, liver and heart.

According to Ficino, three activities endanger the health of the intellectual: excessively frequent sexual intercourse, which exhausts the 'spiritus'; excessive consumption of wine and food, which fills the head with deleterious juices and gasses; and, finally, working at night, which is contrary to the nature of the body and impairs intellectual productivity, which is at its highest in the mornings.[24] A further three factors explain why the majority of intellectuals are prone to melancholy: firstly, because of the astrological constellation that dominates at the moment of their birth; secondly, because black gall (which, according to the doctrine of temperaments, admittedly makes possible the greatest intellectual and artistic achievements) collects in the brain in the course of difficult thought processes; and, finally, because of their lack of movement, which slows the metabolism. Ficino recommends regular refreshment of the senses as a means of correcting the 'black' temperament: walks, the sight of beauty and gardens, water, music, travelling, the society of pleasant people, games and gymnastics. One should take two meals a day, refrain from sleeping after the midday meal and only stay awake for an hour after the evening meal. The observation and careful interpretation of the stars remained both an intellectual and a legitimate matter for the circle around Ficino and constituted a part of the daily dietetic schedule.

For the Platonist Ficino, philosophy and theology were identical. Man could partake of the divine idea by virtue of his intellect, but also through the medium of love, a notion closely related to the concept of the 'unio mystica' which had already been anticipated by Bernard of Clairvaux and Jacopone da Todi.[25] In 1556 the Swiss doctor Konrad

Gesner also addressed those 'qui minus exercentur', and warned philosophers and authors against physical inactivity.[26]

In his *Asolani* (1530), which he dedicated to Lucrezia Borgia, the cardinal and humanist Pietro Bembo argued that an ailing body 'strives by nature for health'. In the ancient Hippocratic tradition, he praises the 'healing power of nature', which must of necessity be supported. Pain is merely nature's way of exhorting us to reflect and change. However, Bembo also emphasizes the ambivalence of worldly health, happiness and love. In accordance with the Neoplatonic tradition, he even considers the body a prison of the soul: 'That we happily and voluntarily give in to the powerful enticements of sensuality, which lead our soul into temptation at every time and in every place, and degenerate into stupid animals due to our appetites – that is in accordance with the will of nature?' By means of a unification with the divine – here the parallel with German mysticism is striking! – true health, 'the symmetry of the limbs, the harmony of the human shell', can be attained. Through his perception of the elementary and astral order, man enters the spiritual world. His body remains imprisoned in the material realm, 'there, on the other hand, reigns eternal perfection, unimpaired by flaws, by age, by death.' Bembo's conception of nature, which is placed in the mouth of Lavinello in the *Asolani*, is close to Ficino's notion, according to which health, beauty and piety flow together. Simultaneously, it is reminiscent of Pico della Mirandola's emphasis on man's obligation to decide of his own free will between God, happiness, (spiritual) health and virtue, on the one hand, and material ensnarements, sin and suffering, on the other.

Baldassare Castiglione's book *Il cortegiano* [*The Courtier*] (1528), which refers, among other works, to Xenophon's *Cyropaedia*, also casts a significant light on the humanistic 'ars vivendi'.[27] Ways of living in court constitute the main topic of conversation in the palace of the duke of Urbino. The ideal *cortegiano* is a noble whose behaviour is defined by etiquette, who is skilful with words, and who has a perfect command of courtly conventions such as dance and table manners, as well as superficial chat. Spiritual anguish, despair or melancholic moods are well-nigh suffocated by deportment and etiquette; the experience of illness is suppressed by stylization. Rather refined topics, such as the question of whether women are capable of divine love, ensure the intellectual and aesthetic pleasures of the courtier. The idea of illness disturbs his view of the world (and, after all, those who are seriously ill have the option of withdrawing from court life in order to meditate) to the same degree as social problems or even revolutionary thoughts.[28] For Castiglione, even the prince's court is part of nature; etiquette and artificiality can thus be embraced as 'regimen vitae'. Health is, admittedly, threatened by 'fortune', which, 'an enemie to vertue', punishes the young duke Guidobaldo with gout; however, it can also be kept at bay with harmony and music, as in the case of those bitten by tarantulas.[29]

In a letter entitled *On the Miseries Endured by Courtiers* (1444), Enea Silvio de Piccolomini, who would later become Pope Pius II, laments the unhealthy life of the *cortegiani*, for whom he expresses something akin to compassion. Their entire daily routine, he recounts, is determined by etiquette: 'One can never eat at the right time, and therefore often meets a sudden death, and that is the reason for premature aging, for digestive complaints, nausea, pains caused by stones, powder and all kinds of illness.' In the code of good conduct entitled *Galateo*, on the other hand, Giovanni della Casa (1503–1556) also introduces table manners founded in dietetics. Last but not least, the four elements, humours and qualities also featured in palace iconography, for example in the sixteenth-century 'Studiolo' of Francesco I de' Medici in the Palazzo Vecchio in Florence.[30]

The artificiality of the lifestyle in the Renaissance courts was opposed to coarse everyday habits such as those described north of the Alps by, for example, the Lüneberg clergyman Friedrich Dedekind in the satire *Grobianus* (1549). The 'six non-naturals' met only with derision here: nose-blowing, sneezing, coughing, dental care, eating, drinking, belching, passing wind and other excretions, sexual intercourse and similar basic needs were caricatured radically. Such an 'anti-education' is also depicted in Rabelais' *Gargantua*, and opposed to the humanist cultivation of soul and body.[31] Topics such as 'the art of living' or 'dietetics' were doubtless congenial to the humanistic elite, who were obsessed with self-adulation, but met with little response among the general populace around 1500.

In 1499 a further 'bestseller' appeared in Venice in the form of Francesco Colonna's *Hypnerotomachia poliphili* [*The Strife of Love in a Dream*], which lauded the art of gardening, country life and an erotically transfigured pastoral idyll, and thus chimed with the mood of the day. The banal contents recede far behind the artificiality and symbolism of the representation.[32] Similar to the *Arcadia* (1503) of the Neoplatonic humanist Giacomo Sannazaro, which appeared at almost the same time, the work publicized a new, ideal way of life, and relativizes the *virtuous* character of health emphasized by Alberti. *Joie de vivre*, games, elegiac atmospheres and the return to nature obviously had an irresistible attraction for the Italian humanists. The *Arcadia* therefore begins with the description of the wood and of nature, with the 'free birds that sing above the green branches', which are contrasted with their relatives in the 'enchanting and ornate cages' of the towns. Tasso's *Aminta* and Guarini's *Pastor fido* can also be traced back to Sannazaro, in whose works, as in the *Hypnerotomachia*, water assumes a special role as a source of life and health.[33]

Choreography and dance were also beneficial to health, according to the views of the humanists. The dance master and instructor Guglielmo Ebreo argued that the harmonious consonance of step and music tended towards the golden mean between retardation and acceleration and therefore contributed to the equilibrium of the mind.[34] The age-old notion of 'harmony' also appeared in many instruction manuals on games, sport or gymnastics. In the tradition of the arcadian ideal, the physician Agnolo Pandolfini (1565) argued for 'moderate and enjoyable physical exercises', which must 'take place in an open and beautiful location, so that they cheer the mind in the correct manner, which indeed is their most noble purpose.'[35] The doctor and historian Paolo Giovio reported in the vita of Jacopo Sforza (1542) that the latter had such a strong constitution 'that he easily overcame illnesses in their early stages by means of physical exercise'. His colleague Cardano recommended gymnastics as the surest remedy for gout, 'taken with an empty stomach until sweating strongly'.[36]

Medics such as Valescus de Tarenta (*d.* 1418) also praised physical exercise as a prophylactic against the plague, as he believed exercise to reduce the decay-inducing hot moisture in the body. In order to prevent the inhalation of damaging miasma, the Umbrian physician Gentile da Foligno (1348) had already advocated sport practised in an *enclosed* space; many Renaissance tracts on plague emphasized that one should not perform any exercises out of doors! Ficino also considered the heating effect on the body produced by sport to increase the danger of infection. The Tübingen doctor Leonard Fuchs (*d.* 1566), however, who won fame as a botanist and was the author of an epoch-making herbal book, recommended moderate exercise 'in a temperate location, whose air has previously been purified with medicaments and fumigation'.

In the Renaissance, tournaments, regattas, ball games, football, running races, horse sports, wrestling and fencing all played a major role, although physical exercises were supplemented by mental relaxation. Even war games were included in the programme of many folk festivals.[37] Skittles and throwing games had a tradition in Italy that reached back into antiquity. These games were also valued on account of their benefits for health: for young people, the reduction of moisture was paramount; for the elderly, however, most important was the increase of the *calor vitae*.[38] Finally, the idea was sometimes propagated that merely refusing to think of an illness was an efficient prophylactic. Affected by his experiences of the plague, the Florentine

Giovanni Morelli extolled in the fourteenth century the pleasures of riding, which provided a distraction and put one in an optimistic frame of mind; Siegmund Albich (*d.* 1427), professor at the University of Prague, urged readers of his plague regimen 'neither to speak of the plague, nor to think of it, as merely fear of the pestilence, the mere thought or mention of it, makes man ill.'[39]

Against syphilis, which had been rife in Europe since the siege of Naples by the French army (1498), the Paduan physician Gabriele Falloppio (*d.* 1561) recommended extensive gymnastic exercise:

> It is particularly effective for strong youths, who, as a consequence of the sweat they work up and of the resulting purification of the body, are restored to health; for wrestling, throwing the javelin, jumping or playing ball games cause the body heat to increase and the body's damaging waste products are broken down; the vital spirits are renewed, they become pure and can therefore . . . mount opposition to death.

Similar sentiments to those of Falloppio, who advocated the use of a linen condom as a prophylactic during intercourse, are expressed by his colleagues Niccolò Massa and Bernadino Tomitano. In the third book of his tract *De contagionibus e contagiosis morbis et eorum curatione* (1546), the physician and poet Fracastoro, whose verse epic *Syphilis sive morbus Gallicus* gave the disease its name, states: 'It is incumbent on you to summon up all zeal and all effort; work and sweat! I say this, exhort and command you: run, jump, hunt, play the ball game of the gladiators! With these means you will turn the heavy matter into liquid, dilute it and expel with it the seeds of contagion.' A balanced, sporting way of life is the best prophylactic: 'All sorrow and grievance is to be held at a distance; no study, no arduous work should oppress the mind.'

As in the Middle Ages, clergymen played sports in order to counteract the dangers of *otium* or *acidia*. Gymnastic exercises were sometimes even subjected to ascetic interpretation. They were, in any case, considered a pious activity in Giovanni Dominici's *Regola del governo di cura familiare* (fifteenth century), and many educators of the day, such as Guarino da Verona or Vittorino da Feltre, also gave this argument to substantiate the benefits derived from sport.[40] In his work *On Celibacy*, written in 1538, Bernardinus Scardaeonius advised the monk to perform *Gymnastica ascetica*, 'so that you hoodwink the devil himself in this manner or by means of some other respectable physical exercise and labour.'[41] Sporting exercises should not, naturally, involve any kind of gambling; they should serve only to promote relaxation. Even the strict Savonarola, incidentally, advocated 'introducing children to disports and sporting games under the supervision of older people'.

House books and manuals – health and literature

The late medieval and ancient philosophical tracts on health that were rediscovered in the Renaissance (or suddenly made available by the printing press) dealt with moderation, balance, eucrasy, and the harmony of body and soul requisite for physical health. In the aforementioned *Eruditio didascalica* by Hugh of St Victor, which was written in the twelfth century and printed in 1470 in Strasbourg, health-care provisions played an important role. In addition to the neglect of dietetic rules, the scholastic considers the emotions to represent a particular danger, as, like anger, they tempestuously stoke up the vital warmth or, like sadness, 'irritate internally and externally' the vital forces.[42] In his influential *Adagia* (1508), Erasmus of Rotterdam reflects on maxims such as 'too much is unhealthy', 'more haste, less speed', 'know thyself' or 'prevention is better than cure'. In his *Oration in Praise of the Art of Medicine*, the great humanist also praises the doctors' profession: 'Let us suppose that there were no illness and everyone enjoyed complete health, how should we be able to preserve this if the physician did not educate us about the difference between beneficial and harmful foods and about the organization of our entire way of life or diet, as the Greeks said?' According to Erasmus, the *fifth essence* in particular sustains health, 'for it is not a fable, but rather attested by a number of witnesses that by means of the fifth essence man can shed decrepitude like a snakeskin and rejuvenate himself.' Of equal importance, however, is a 'holistic' dietetics, 'for as a consequence of the close interplay between body and soul the afflictions of the soul affect the body just as the ailments of the body suppress the vital force of the soul.' Even if the doctors have difficulty in surveying medical scholarship, the humanist resident in Basel states, half in sympathy, half disapproving, one should 'at least be familiar with the part that deals with the preservation of health'.

The 'fifth essence' (*Quinta essentia*) mentioned by Erasmus had already been described in the fourteenth century by the Franciscan John of Rupescissa, whose *Treatise on the Quintessence of All Things* was translated into numerous languages. According to John, but also to the philosopher Raymundus Lullus (thirteenth century) and the previously mentioned doctor Arnald of Villanova, this essence could be produced as an 'aqua ardens', 'anima vini' and 'aqua vitae' in a process of distillation, and had the same relationship to the four humours as 'the heavens to the four elements'. The production of this fluid was, in addition to that of gold, a major goal of alchemists for centuries. As it was generally thought to guarantee health, famous Renaissance physicians, such as the Zurich doctor Konrad Gessner (1555), Hieronymus Brunschwig (c. 1500) from Strasbourg, Philipp Ulstad (1525) from Nuremberg, Walther Hermann Ryff (1545), who taught in Frankfurt, Mainz, Nuremberg and Würzburg, and Paracelsus, wrote about its properties.

Numerous chapters of Sebastian Brant's *Narrenschiff* [*Ship of Fools*] (Basel, 1494) also deal with the pedagogy of health. It is not so much the illness of folly that is castigated, as a 'foolish', unhealthy, useless, senseless, uncontrolled life, which leads to illness and ruin. Humoral medicine is not condemned here either; the care for physical health is legitimate and important: 'He is a fool who does not understand what a doctor counsels him when in difficulty, and who does not wish to live correctly according to the diet that the doctor has given to him.' Elsewhere in the text we read: 'He who wishes to escape an illness quickly should withstand the beginning.' Brant strongly condemns magical practices: 'He is a fool who consults the doctor and does not consider what he says, yet holds fast to the advice of old wives and has his last benediction performed with amulet and fools' parsley.' As in the Middle Ages, health is presented as impossible without metaphysical assistance. Anyone who does not seek it from God and the physicians is, according to the author of the *Ship of Fools*, 'completely lost in folly, madness and blindness'. For Brant, health disorders are ultimately connected with a lack of self-control, with devotion to worldly things and with estrangement from God. Gluttony and drunkenness are only outward signs of the internal decay. Wine in particular, he continues, destroys reason and the senses, and shortens one's life, for which history and the Bible provide countless examples.

Inspired by Marsilio Ficino, the physician Agrippa von Nettesheim, author of the mysterious tract *De occulta philosophia* [*Of Occult Philosophy*] (1533), composed a 'cosmically' systematized dietetics. The notion that the 'anima mundi' had transferred itself onto the sublunar world via the celestial bodies in a process of emanation was a Neoplatonic one. The world soul brought about the eucrasy of the humours by means of the 'spiritus animales', while dyscrasy could be caused by unhealthy conduct or the wrong diet, by miasma in the air, or by sin. The external proportions emphasized by contemporary artists such as Dürer or Leonardo are transposed by Agrippa onto the internal order of the body. The healthy body should comprise eight parts blood, four parts mucus, two parts yellow bile and one part black bile; music, it is stated, represents an appropriate means of retaining these proportions (8: 4: 2: 1).[43] The regulatory 'virtutes' of the organs is ultimately activated by cosmic influences; plants and medicine also have healing powers. Like Ficino, Agrippa, who was himself educated in Italy, is convinced of the influence of the stars on man's state of health. The 'insane science which attached itself to the stars' pointed in Italy, as north of the Alps, less to superstition than 'to the acute desire to know the future'.

In his tract *The Uncertainty and Vanity of the Sciences and Arts* (1531), Agrippa accused the representatives of classical dietetics of unsettling patients by making unrealistic demands. They

> lay down rules for the diet to which no man can adhere. At the same time, they gorge themselves on precisely those foods that they forbid or restrict for others, as greedily as pigs devour acorns, and are the first to transgress the prohibitions that they impose on others, and, indeed, not through inadvertency, but completely intentionally. If doctors had to live according to their own dietary rules, they would sustain not inconsiderable damage to their health.

An old reproach from patristic literature is also taken up: 'Ambrosius says of these dietary rules: "They are against God's commandments, for they advise against fasting, prohibit the holding of vigils at night, thereby impeding intensive meditation, and thus, finally, do harm to the individual because he concerns himself with doctors instead of with more important things." ' Good dietetics may not, according to Agrippa, be divorced from reality; it consists rather in a healthy mixture of foods, in an 'appropriate preparation of food' and 'moderation in drinking'. The culinary art also plays an important part, he continues, being 'in no way dishonourable, if it does not exceed the limits laid down for it'.

Surprisingly, even the astronomer Copernicus concerned himself with herbal therapy and botany. In his *Regulation of Health*, the canon of Frauenburg Cathedral stressed that dietetics represented a school of life as self-evident as it was necessary. The cathedral physician – Copernicus had studied medicine – prescribed bloodletting for important persons, among them the bishop of Ermland, adjusting the course for each individual.[44] In his tract *Nützliche Reformation zu guter Gesundheit und christlicher Ordnung* (Frankfurt, 1573), the Gelnhausen physician Joachim Struppius also demanded 'that we should honour bodies not as our own, but as God's image'. The fact that man was modelled on his creator obligated him to take particular care of his physical and spiritual wellbeing, which was also, in the Lutheran sense, considered desirable as a prerequisite for all social activity.[45]

The invention of the printing press led to the increasing popularization of dietetics. Medical *house books* became fashionable, particularly in Italy and Germany. The reader learned how to bring up children correctly, how to delight body and soul, how one should nourish and clothe oneself and how to ensure reproduction. The 'contents page' of a tract on health published in 1490 by Hans Schoposser in Augsburg included a representative summary of the common subject areas: '1) provide for every individual in his own state of health; 2) attend to and care for the sick and their needs; 3) arrange a blessed departure from this world; 4) assist with admonitions in the last hour; see to the administration of goods and belongings.'[46] The knowledge imparted by house books also concerned the practical questions of everyday life, including medical topics, cooking and baking, the production and storage of wine, weather proverbs or gardening (including medicinal herbs).[47] The 'master of the house' consulted certain medical texts, mostly written for laypersons, such as short prescriptions, which 'oscillated between speech and writing' (Keil), and 'consilia', which offered herbal remedies alongside dietetic advice. Sleeping patterns and the related 'healthy' daily rhythm were also considered a crucial part of a comprehensive set of rules for the house and for health, whose enforcement lay in the remit of the master of the house as well as of the physician.[48]

More encyclopaedic in character was a *Hausbuch* which appeared around 1480 and was kept from the seventeenth century in Schloss Wolfegg. The book was probably written and illustrated by a gunsmith from the Rhineland.[49] The illnesses of man and animal, but also love potions, astrological questions, prescriptions for the home economy, and technical military problems are all dealt with briefly, in addition to the care of wounds, the cure of bone breakages and dysentery as well as the treatment of kidney stones, constipation, impotence and obesity. Discussions on the philosophy of health and the 'six non-naturals' are avoided in favour of the 'practice' of tough, everyday life in war. This type of book is thought to be descended from the 'Feuerwerksbücher' [*Fire-work Books*], which also contained technical and military topics and were in evidence as early as the beginning of the fifteenth century.[50]

Since the late Middle Ages, *secreta* books, which also dealt with domestic remedies and questions of domestic hygiene, had been consulted in lay circles.[51] These were 'folk encyclopaedias' with comprehensive chapters on dietetics. In these 'books of secrets', which were often written by those outside the medical profession, alchemy had frequently left its mark, as had astrology, pharmacy, metallurgy or magic. Leonardo Fioravanti (1518–1588) published eight *Libri de' secreti* between 1562 and 1582; Alessio Piemontese[52] composed a similar work as early as 1555, which was translated into Latin, French, English, German, Spanish, Danish, Polish and Dutch![53] The contents extended from the conservation of foodstuffs through to the manufacture of perfume, cosmetics, dyes and textiles. Some authors, such as the physician and humanist Giovanni Battista della Porta (1535–1615), were members of the *Accademia secreta*, which was founded in Naples and made this kind of medical literature respectable, among both doctors and humanists. An early example of the '*secreta* literature' can be found in the form of the fifteenth-century *Esperimenti* by Caterina Sforza. The *Secreti* of Isabella Cortese (also fifteenth century) contained information about, among other things, plague remedies and antidotes, in addition to measures to be taken against fistulas, haemorrhoids and gynaecological complaints. Significantly, the delicate chapter dealing with diseases of the penis is written in Latin.[54] From the *Secreti* a good deal can be inferred about the ideal of beauty of sixteenth-century Italian women. 'Light, soft and depilated skin, white teeth, thick and preferably dark hair, a youthful radiance, and a firm body' were the characteristics of the handsome, healthy ideal woman.[55]

The authors of the house and *secreta* books recommended herbs, 'folk remedies' and magical techniques, which played an important part in daily life, and found an open market for them. In the nineteenth canto of Ariosto's *Orlando Furioso*, Angelica, assisted by a shepherd, tends the injured Medoro with magical herbs:

> Angelica alights upon the ground, | And he her rustic comrade, at her hest. | She hastened 'twixt two stones the herb to pound, | Then took it, and the healing juice exprest: | With this did she foment the stripling's wound, | And, even to the hips, his waist and breast; | And (with such virtue was the salve endued) | It stanched his life-blood, and his strength renewed.[56]

Even in a town as cultured as Ferrara, with its ducal residence and university, where Tasso's works were first read, Angelica's behaviour may have borne a closer relation to therapeutic reality than did learned tracts. In the case of memory loss or impotence, when afflicted by anxiety states and inexplicable symptoms, people still had recourse to incantations of the devil or magic spells, and touching relics doubtless raised more hope for many than school and alternative medicine together. The apothecaries also offered curative jewels to rich customers and stocked mysterious substances and magic remedies. Last but not least, 'simple' remedies, as well as herbal therapies, chimed with Renaissance man's irrational dream of the 'vita rustica'.

Further humanists – Platina, More, Luther

None of the Renaissance humanists applied themselves – within the framework of general teachings on health – more exclusively to the *food*-related aspects of dietetics than Bartolomeo Platina (1421–1481), the prefect of the Vatican library, whose appointment by Sixtus IV was recorded in the famous fresco by Melozzo da Forlí. This author of numerous historical works invokes the *Libro de arte coquinaria* by Martino da Como, cook to the patriarch of Aquileia. He also consults, in the manner of contemporary scholars, numerous authors from antiquity and from his own age; among his medical authorities are Arnald of Villanova and Barnaba da Reggio. In the dedication to Cardinal Bartolomeo Roverella he indicates that the topic (*Il piacere onesto e la buona salute*) is not a self-evident one for a humanist of distinction; he even expresses the fear that 'some adherents of Stoicism' could frown at the subject of 'eating and drinking'. 'It is my concern precisely to identify that healthy type of nourishment which the Greeks named dietetics, to define the nature of nutrition and foodstuffs and, finally, to give some advice on the treatment of illnesses. For it is not true that this topic . . . is not suitable for a cultured man.' He lists the advantages for society of such a book and alludes to the example of ancient authorities such as Cato, Columella or Varro.

A wealthy and intelligent man should, in accordance with the example set by Vitruvius, 'choose a healthy, quiet, cheering, friendly location, where he can devote himself to husbandry, the arts and the muse'. In summer, high altitudes are preferable, where the air is clear and pure. The windows should face north-east, so that the first rays of sunshine in the mornings can purify the spent air of the night; however, the room should not become overheated in the evening sun. This is particularly important for houses on the coast, as those in a southern location 'become so heated during the day that our body, which is already aglow from the summer heat, is vulnerable to serious and dangerous illnesses if given no opportunity to cool down.' In the spring or autumn, on the other hand, one can also live on low-lying lands, for example by the sea, as long as the region is not marshy. As with heat, one should also avoid icy cold and winds, as they are damaging to the nerves and are responsible for coughs, catarrh and eye inflammations.

Platina sets great store by gymnastic exercises, 'in order to cleanse the blood, which becomes poisoned when insufficient exercise is taken.' The warmth that results stimulates the appetite, but also the mind and the sense organs, leading to a better apprehension of the secrets of nature, which is necessary for the cultivation of a healthy life. One should only participate in sport *after* digestion, however. 'Walks constitute effective exercises, as does daily work and the ascent and descent of inclines.' Ball games are recommended for young people, as are tournaments on horseback or on foot, and even gladiator fights, which are admittedly not considered very decorous. Even jumping exercises, which had obviously rather gone out of fashion, in addition to throwing lances, archery, wrestling, hunting and, if the fatherland requires it, armed combat, improve physical wellbeing, according to Platina. Also beneficial to health is – here the author invokes the authority of Celsus – everything that induces sweating and causes exhaustion.[57] The author advises his reader to 'eat with moderation' and, after eating, to avoid both physical and mental work for around two hours. Coitus should – according to the individual nature – be performed neither too frequently nor too rarely, preferably in the winter or spring and at night, as long as one does not have to work the next morning. Those who carry out intellectual work should take frequent walks in the sun without covering their heads. Farming activities are particularly beneficial to health, Platina argues, for example, working with a rake, hunting birds with a falcon, sowing, harvesting, bee-keeping or, in general, the observation of the annual cycle of nature. Platina intends to develop a 'regimen', the observance of which will, despite its regulatory character, pave the way for a pleasant lifestyle. However, he argues, everyone should gather their own experiences, although, in case of doubt, Socrates' words hold good: one does not live to eat, one eats to live.

Even careful chewing is important as it facilitates, as Platina emphasizes, the digestion of food in the stomach. The choice of healthy foodstuffs, for example, fruit, vegetables or spices, is dependent on the season, as the 'humores' also vary according to the time of year. In accordance with the example set by Martino, particular responsibility is placed here on the good cook, who decides the menu. In his German tract *Von der erlichen zimichen auch erlaubten Wolust des Leibs*, from 1542, the Augsburg physician Pacimontanus cites the benefits listed by Platina that gymnastics brings to representatives of different professions.[58]

In his famous *Utopia*, written in 1516, Thomas More describes health as the 'greatest of pleasures': 'Almost all the Utopians regard it as great and as practically the foundation and basis of all pleasures.

Even by itself it can make the state of life peaceful and desirable.'[59] More gives a negative answer to the question of whether health consists in the absence of pain alone; this is only true when one is joyfully aware of one's state of health. Illness is associated with pain, but health with pleasure, and the latter alone completes the joy of wellbeing.

> The assertion that health cannot be felt [the Utopians] think to be far wide of the truth. Who in a waking state, ask they, does not feel that he is in good health – except the man who is not? Who is bound fast by such insensibility or lethargy that he does not confess that health is agreeable and delightful to him? And what is delight except pleasure under another name?

Of all pleasures of the body, then, the Utopians 'give the palm to health'.[60] The mere tenet that meals yield considerably less pleasure than health is, according to More, sufficient grounds for a reduction in one's diet: 'Just as a wise man should pray that he may escape disease rather than crave a remedy for it and that he may drive pain off rather than seek relief from it, so it would be better not to need this kind of pleasure rather than to be soothed by it.'[61] Health, strength and beauty are mutually interdependent.

Aside from More's *Utopia*, the demand for the provision of state health care was voiced by many in the sixteenth century. Indeed, contrary to an old legend concerning the history of medicine, numerous doctors also worked in public hospitals, although their principal duty had been to care for the needy, rather than to heal the sick. In the Ospedale degli Incurabili (founded in 1522) in Venice, numerous doctors attended to those afflicted by syphilis;[62] in Luther's *Table Talk* we read the following comments on this topic:

> In Italy, the hospitals are very well equipped, attractively built, offer good food and drink, have hard-working attendants and learned physicians. The beds and clothing are nice and clean and the houses are nicely painted. As soon as a sick person is brought in, his clothes are removed in the presence of a notary, who faithfully records and describes them . . . Soon two physicians are brought to him and attendants bring his food and drink in clean dishes.

On the whole, Luther considered concern for physical health almost as important as the care of the soul: for the reformer, medicine and theology shared the same legitimation. It was for him beyond dispute that health was related to the psychic condition: 'Heavy thoughts bring on physical maladies; when the soul is oppressed, so is the body. . . . But when the heart is at rest, and quiet, then it takes care of the body, and gives it what pertains thereunto.'[63] The interdependence of health and heart is also underlined in his tract *Vom ehelichen Leben* [*On Married Life*]: 'Therefore one also sees how weak and unhealthy unfertile women are; those who are fertile, however, are more healthy, purer and gayer.' Sadness therefore appeared to him to be a 'preferred death' (*praestatissima mors*); he considered melancholy to be the work of the devil. The true Christian 'should and must be a cheerful person', just as Christ is praised as a 'God of joy' (*deus laetitiae*). Luther considers it a self-evident fact that illnesses can be sent by the devil and therefore calls for severe punishments for magicians, 'so that others are deterred from such devilish conduct'.

The reformer is also convinced – and here comparisons with Athenaeus of Attaleia and Galen suggest themselves – that mysterious forces regularly regenerate the body; at the age of seven, fourteen, twenty-one, and so on, a new period of life begins. As far as health is concerned, particular junctures can be anticipated – for example, the fiftieth year, the 'annus climacterius'. Like the anonymous monk from Lorsch in the eighth century, Luther is of the opinion that the native herbs are adequate to cure basic illnesses. With respect to therapy, one should pay attention to the correct moment in time: 'In January, medicine does not do any good. Purge the bowels and conserve your blood. Eat warm foods and do not bathe, although good wine and spices are not bad.'[64]

Luther also advocated the sterilization of anyone with a hereditary illness: 'He is a burden for the land, fills the land with beggars, one should excise him.'[65] An observation in *Vom ehelichen Leben* about the innumerable women who died in childbirth in the sixteenth century is offensively insensitive to our ears: 'If they bear children until they are exhausted and, finally, die, that does not matter. Let them bear children until they perish – that is what they are there for. It is better to live for a short time in good health than to live for a long time in ill health.' It is impossible to judge the extent to which the doctrine of predestination influenced such statements.

Yet, according to the doctrine of God's mercy, health signified a gift from God. 'My health, my happiness, my life, misfortune, sickness, death' are, according to Luther, in God's hands.[66] 'Oh, dear Lord God', he prayed in 1538 during a serious illness, 'like a precious jewel is a healthy body that can eat and drink, sleep, pass water and shit. How little one thanks God for it.' Luther believed that an individual 'regimen' was necessary for every limb or organ, and when he was himself suffering from diarrhoea, he conceded: 'One should not curse and swear at the arse; it just wants its own regimen.'[67] Luther's pithy observations do not yet give any indication that 'Protestant ethics' would later insist on the responsibility of every individual for the

health of his body, because 'civic' and economic success and the capacity for social involvement are dependent on mental and physical
productivity. 'Health' and 'wealth' are linked together in the logic not
only of Puritanism.[68] Anyone who wished to be successful first had to
be healthy.

A close connection between illness and immorality was, however,
affirmed by Luther's contemporary Ulrich von Hutten (1488–1523),
who, like the Venetian Alvise Cornaro, surmised that decadence and
gluttony were the cause of declines in health. In his tract *Über die
wunderbare Heilkraft des Guajakholzes und die Heilung der
Franzosenkrankheit* (1519) he condemns 'daily feasts, dripping with
fat'. The 'goal of life' for his German compatriots, he claims, consists
in the 'pleasures of the stomach'. Whereas in fact Sallust's observation
holds true, that 'many people wander through life, uneducated and
immoral, completely abandoned to gorging themselves and sleeping',
many men accuse God of making them ill, 'after we have recklessly
assailed our health and wasted our paternal inheritance'. They behave,
he continues, like 'Juvenal's drunkards', who, 'when they sense illness
in their body, believe themselves to be under attack from the gods'.
Following Cato's example, he praises the simple life of the forefathers:
'Alas, if we would just return to our oatmeal and to our woollen clothing that we so loved, and that lies close to the limbs. If we, weary of
silk, would only pursue the full garments with infinite hatred! For
what are they other than destroyers of all that we have inherited and
carriers of illnesses?' Hutten calls for a comprehensive social and
health reform, taking the ancient Germans and even the emperors
from the early Middle Ages as his models:

> Our ancestors . . . clothed and fed themselves in the way described. Their
> bodies were strong and . . . hardened by the experience of exertions to hunger
> and thirst, frost and heat, while we draw in our hands and feet at the first
> snow . . ., with the consequence that in Germany, I tell you, hardly one noble
> can be found among ten nowadays who is not suffering from gout, rheuma-
> tism, dropsy, sciatica and leprosy, or from the serious consequences of the
> French disease.

The knight and man of letters, who was tormented by syphilis, and
whose works were also translated a short time later into English and
French, laments the 'immoderateness of life, from which all plagues
and illnesses stem'. It should be clear to everyone, he stresses, 'that
those who flavour their food with native herbs . . . remain healthy and
will reach a ripe old age, whereas those whose fingers are stained with
saffron, who taste cinnamon when they belch, who exhale cloves and

delight in luxurious clothing, are susceptible to all kinds of illnesses.' Like the eighth-century Lorsch author, but also Luther, Hutten has faith in the health-preserving strength of 'native herbs'. His aversion to competitive sportsmen, 'whose entire art consists in fattening themselves up', is reminiscent of Plato. As their minds 'lie buried in blood and fat as if in a dung heap . . ., incapable of higher things', they cannot 'expect a long life or health'.

The notion of assuming individual responsibility for one's health acquired extremely fashionable traits in the sixteenth century. Innumerable tracts on hygiene were printed, among them, still, the *Regimen Salernitanum* (Lyon, 1519).[69] It was not by chance that Rabelais (1494–1553), himself a physician in Lyon and Metz, coupled Gargantua's upbringing with comprehensive schooling in dietetic and literary matters (1534). Moderation, gymnastics, rubdowns, a rhythmical alternation between rest and recreation, music and singing, all protect the health of the bookman,[70] for whom health is a prerequisite for his literary pursuits (a problem to which Marsilio Ficino but also medieval scholastics such as Hugh of St Victor had already applied themselves). Not without its dangers, in this respect, was the isolation of the intellectual in a *studiolo*, about which the monastic father Cassian had already expressed his suspicions. It is no coincidence that Rabelais devised a corresponding educational model for the Abbey of Thélème, while Juan Luis Vives (1492–1540), the philosopher and friend of Erasmus and More, recommended the construction of public gymnasiums; physical 'fitness' was recognized as a prerequisite for optimal intellectual activity.[71]

From the fifteenth century onwards, however, many seem to have dreamt of not only a healthy but also a *long* life. The appointed term was no longer considered to be *only* determined by divine arbitration, death was no longer *exclusively* a passage to eternal life. This does not mean that people no longer believed in an afterlife in the next world; it rather corresponds to the combination, typical for the Renaissance, of faith in God with an enthusiasm for art, literature and all the beautiful things in *this* world. The new attitude can therefore be attributed not so much to a 'demystification' of death as to the planning of personal goals in this life, for which time was required.[72] The new cultural scene in the towns doubtless also offered previously unimagined opportunities to undertake such activities on an intellectual, a political, an artistic or a literary level. It was soon recognized that a healthy body represented a decisive precondition for assuming public roles.

A further motivation for aspiring to physical and spiritual health was the mental agitation that was characteristic of the age of mannerism. Although 'mannerist' tendencies marked the art and literature of the Renaissance from an early stage, and can ultimately be detected in almost all artistic periods, certain themes enjoyed particular popularity in European cultural life between 1520 and 1600.[73] Ornamentation, morbid elegance and artificiality were accompanied by an interest in the abnormal, delight in cruelties, the fashion for melancholy, dreams and the art of their interpretation, exaggerated fancies, games with symbols, occultism, a longing for death and the representation of the macabre.[74] This devotion to ugliness simultaneously fostered a predilection for beauty and purity, for the female body, for paradise and the ideal world of Platonism. The fear of fires and storms, of sorcery, magic, superstition, mantic and a strangely cultivated culture of menace nurtured the ideal of the healthy, invulnerable, strong and long-lived body.

Philosophy of health and prophylaxis in Venice – Mercuriale, Rangone, Cornaro

Italian society in the Renaissance was particularly attracted to questions concerning dietetics and teachings on health. The bathing culture had reached a zenith in Veneto, but also elsewhere in Italy, as early as the fifteenth century. The concern of the upper classes with physical wellbeing was fostered by numerous incunabula on this topic, for example, Michele Savonarola's *De balneis et thermis* (1485) or the *Tractatus de balneis Patavinis* (1440) by Bartolomeo Montagnana. However, a practical application of the theory was required.

Thus in 1522 the aforementioned Ospedale degli Incurabili, the largest and most important syphilis hospital of its day in Europe, was opened. It was directed by St Gaetano of Thiene, the founder of the Theatine order.[75] Responsibility for the 'organization' of health care was placed on the orders, but also on the municipal administration. Despite a worsening recession and growing religious insecurity – books by Luther and Erasmus were traded under the counter[76] – the town on the lagoon constituted an ideal seedbed for eccentrics, hypochondriacs, disbelievers and zealots. Withdrawal from responsibility, as well as the criticism and even mockery of society, to an extent took on fashionable characteristics. In the town's *palazzo* as in the villas of the mainland, people conversed not only about business, but also about the prevention of illnesses and remaining healthy into old age. Convinced of having been born under the sign of Saturn, artists and scholars loved melancholic moods, which were generally of a spleenful nature rather than indicative of real illnesses.[77]

In his tract *Dialogo sulla pittura*, which appeared in 1548 in Venice, the theoretician of art Paolo Pino suggested that painters were particularly vulnerable given their quiet occupation, which could be conducive to daydreaming and melancholy. He therefore advised them to seek a counterbalance in sports such as riding, ball games and other activities that were advisable for town-dwellers who took little exercise. Sannazaro's *Arcadia* had been in circulation in the town since 1505, and its effusive veneration of nature chimed exactly with the mood of the day. The famous Giorgionesque landscape also seemed to encapsulate the town-dwellers' longing for nature, for relaxation, for health and the 'vita contemplativa'. Many intellectuals were concerned with the idea of fleeing the town, with the 'vita contemplativa' and with the pastoral idyll. The comic playwright Ruzzante, whose play *La pastoral* was performed in the Venetian or, rather, Paduan dialect, is one example.[78]

The patrician Alvise Cornaro (1484–1566), who had been exiled to Padua, publicized the aesthetic and public-health aspects of the 'vita rustica', or, more precisely, of its classical interaction with the 'vita activa', which had already been extolled by Petrarch and Marsilio Ficino. It would certainly be misrepresentation to attribute the regulation of rivers on the mainland, which he carried out at high financial cost, as well as his efforts to drain the Venetian hinterland, to a mere 'capitalist' pursuit of profit.[79] 'I have drained away water, at which point the earth became dry and the air healthy', he wrote proudly, and invoked Fra Giocondo from Verona, who had re-routed the Brenta and the Piave half a century previously, to prevent the harbour at Rialto from sanding up.[80] Such technical enterprises naturally served a purpose as regards trade policy; however, they also helped to prevent epidemics. The expanding marshes in the lagoon, the mixture of fresh and sea water, and the enormous fly-infested pools on its edge were, correctly, considered a dangerous breeding-ground for disease. Whenever individual or private prophylaxis proved insufficient, the Venetian state consistently intervened. Changes to the landscape were undertaken relatively frequently in the Renaissance; one need think only of the draining of swamplands around Mantua, in the Tuscan Maremma or in the Campagnia region south of Rome.[81]

Like Palladio, Cornaro's friend Falconetto designed villas and houses. The villas were more than just buildings; they also served the purpose of physical and mental recreation and imitated arcadia. In his *studiolo*, the master of the house devoted himself to the 'vita solitaria', surrounded by books, artefacts, portraits of the countryside with bucolic motifs, and views on the surrounding nature. Here one could also enjoy oneself on weekdays free of engagements (Italian: *ferie*) and recover, in a very holistic sense. From here, as the example of Cornaro's villa in Luvigliano illustrates, the better part of the properties, vineyards and fields could be surveyed, as well as the houses of the administrators and labourers.[82] It is hardly surprising, then, that Colonna's *Hyperotomachia*, printed in Rialto in 1499, was received by a grateful readership in this environment. 'Town air makes you ill, country air, free', was the motto.

It was in this context that Petrarch was rediscovered in Venice – a prime example is Cornaro. The literary 'Petrarchismo' doubtless resulted in a philosophical variant, which also touched on questions of public health policy. Although the trecentist author's escapism only took the form of a literary appeal, it was imitated in diverse ways. Once again, villas and country life were presented as prerequisites for the 'vita contemplativa'. Bembo, the aforementioned author of the *Asolani*, published Petrarch's works in printed form at the end of the fifteenth century. One example for the new 'anti-medicine' can be found in the figure of the architect and sculptor Jacopo Sansovino, the builder of the Biblioteca Marciana, who had migrated from Florence to Venice. Vasari reports that Sansovino abstained from consulting doctors and scorned medication all his life, even after suffering a stroke. When afflicted by illness, he simply took to his bed, and yet lived to the age of eighty-four. 'In summer he lived virtually only on fruits, often eating four cucumbers at once, as well as citrus fruits . . . He had a brilliant memory well into old age.'[83] Of course, the same could have been said of Petrarch or Cornaro, who both had a similar preference for 'simple' foods.

A consciously 'healthy' way of living is also attested by Cornaro's friend and portraitist Tintoretto. The poet Andrea Calmo wrote to the painter in 1549:

> You are an enemy of idleness, as you spend the hours in part increasing your fame, in part replenishing your physical strength and in part edifying your mind. Working, in order to obtain fame and advantage, eating, in order to live and not lose the flesh from your bones, making music, laughing and singing, so as not to go mad, as happens to many who become so deeply engrossed in the production of a work of art that they then suddenly lose their mind together with their brains, keeps you young and healthy.

The health consciousness of the patriciate and their enthusiasm for nature and country life are manifested last but not least in the Venetian fashion for gardens. If one had no villa on the mainland, then one cultivated a garden in the town. On Murano or the Guidecca island (the island location reinforced the association with Elysium) humanists such as Bembo or Daniele Barbaro met in the marvellous gardens of the nobility, which were lauded by poets such as Calmo or Castaldi da Feltre.[84] Here one conversed with artists such as Aretino and Tintoretto, Trissino and Speroni, Gaspare Contarini and Giovanni della Casa, the aforementioned author of the *Galateo*, about Petrarch, literature, dietetics, politics and the beauty of women. In the garden paradise of the Trevisans, one read the *Agricultura* of Crescentius, a fourteenth-century author, who, however, only achieved fame when his works were printed in Venice in 1495. Crescentius' work was, once more, a bestseller which exalted farming and country life.[85] The works of Alberti, who reported that the renowned master builders of antiquity also applied themselves to the construction of gardens, or, rather, to a 'healthy' method of construction, were also circulated.

It is hardly surprising that, in Venice, a large number of pieces of writing were produced on the subject of the care and preservation of the body. At the state university in Padua, which in the mid-sixteenth century housed the most respected medical faculty in Europe, the professor Girolamo Mercuriale wrote a tract called *On the Art of Gymnastics*, a 'useful work for all those who are interested in old texts and are concerned to preserve their health', which he dedicated to Emperor Maximilian II. The humanist Lorenzo Gambara considered the famous doctor, whose misdiagnosis was admittedly to blame for the catastrophe of an initially unrecognized plague epidemic in Venice in 1576, to 'shine like new stars among the Greek and Latin authors'. Mercuriale's book constituted a kind of cultural history of gymnastics and sport: long jump, discus and javelin throwing, riding, hunting, swimming and other sports are discussed in detail. The fourth book, however, instructs on the art of healthy gymnastics. According to Mercuriale, not all people should take sporting exercise, and the exercises should be modified individually. The sick, old and healthy have to observe entirely different rules. Conversing, public speaking, laughing and crying all have an effect on health, he continues. Joyous events advance health; sorrow and anxiety endanger body and soul. The somewhat disorderly book constituted a kind of encyclopaedia of classical dietetics, without presenting new ideas, which, admittedly, can be said of many Renaissance authors on health. Still impressive are the numerous woodcuts by an anonymous artist, which enable us to gain a comprehensive impression of the practice of contemporary gymnastics.

Mercuriale of course knew the physician and philosopher Tommaso Rangone of Ravenna, who had taken up residence in Venice and won fame there as a patron of the arts and commissioner of works by Tintoretto. Rangone's tomb on the façade of San Giuliano is indicative of the medical profession's bombastic self-conception.[86] In the 'jubilee year' 1550 Rangone published the tract *How One Can Lengthen the Life of Man beyond 120 Years*, which he dedicated to Pope Julius III. Merely the title of the first chapter raised hope: 'Why men believe erroneously that their life could last for only 120 years'. As previously in works by the Lorsch author and the clerics of the thirteenth century, the long lives of the patriarchs in the Old Testament and of many Church Fathers are presented as examples.

In the tradition of the doctrine of the four humours, Rangone recommended a quiet lifestyle and careful selection of diet, in addition to artificial adjustments such as vomiting and blood-letting. For him, as for Ficino and Rabelais, health was prerequisite for creative thought and a humanist way of life. Suggestions on the cure of syphilis, on measures to combat the plague, on cosmetics and gymnastics could not be omitted, in accordance with the comprehensive nature of the work. The author became a well-known consultant and publicist in questions of health whose fame extended far beyond Venice, although his 'manner, which was presumably bigoted and supercilious, his self-assurance, based on the conviction of his own superior knowledge and mastery of everything . . . may have deceived simple minds, although not responsible heads.'[87] Rangone presented himself as a member of the upper class, in complete contrast to the manifold non-academic 'healers', who doubtless attended to the majority of the people in the sixteenth century.[88]

Characteristic of the Venetian philosophy of health in the sixteenth century was the part played by the humanist, agronomist and social critic Alvise Cornaro, who between 1558 and 1563, when already in his eighties, composed the *Discorsi intorno alla vita sobria* [*Discourses on the Sober Life*], which also dealt with the topic of the preservation of health and prolongation of life.[89] The 'six non-naturals', which had been developed in the Corpus Hippocraticum, extended in Hellenism and standardized by the Arabs, are correlated by Cornaro with writings on health from his own age, for example Gaspare Torella's *De regimine seu praeservatione sanitatis* (1506), Antonio Basi's *Florida corona* (1519), the *Praeservatio sanitatis* by Francesco Bernardini (1539), as well as Leonardo Lessio's *L'arte di godere sanità perfetta*. According to the tenor of the Discorsi, everyone must identify his own specific disposition towards illness by means of self-observation (the author, for example, considered himself to be a choleric, in other words, afflicted by an excess of yellow bile). 'Man cannot be a perfect physician for others, only for himself', was his logical conclusion.[90] Cornaro was, perhaps due to Platina's influence, so convinced of the power of the diet to influence health that he ventured to claim that an appropriate degree of moderation, combined with composure of the mind, would, in principle, preclude all illnesses and lead to a gentle, painless death at an advanced age. He based his rules for the construction of the 'villas' on Vitruvius and Palladio: of primary importance was not the architectonic regularity, he explained to his beauty-crazed compatriots, but rather the health of the inhabitants. A short time later his tract *La fabbrica del duomo di Padova* was published, in which the house constructed in accordance with health requirements is extolled as a guarantee that an advanced age will be reached. His own villa contained both dry and warm and fresh and cold rooms, 'without stoves, with only a little heating and without dampness and draughts', the author describes proudly, 'because I had them built with consideration and have learned the art of architecture, which is capable of extending human life.'[91]

Venetian man was particularly enamoured of country life. He took care of the welfare and health of his servants, visited friends, worked as a man of letters, and patronized builders, painters, sculptors and musicians. He organized great feasts, enjoyed the company of his family, and his success nourished his health. He rejected the notion of illness as a punishment from God and believed that 'the wise man is also master over astrology'.[92] His dietary suggestions – he developed a particular preference for bread – are reminiscent of monastic fasting diets; 'healthy hunger' is considered a 'constant and natural companion of a moderate lifestyle'.[93] Cornaro's assertions seem to be not so much academic as human. He teaches in a friendly, even fatherly manner, drawing more on experience than on literature, although the allusions to humoral pathology attest to the role of medicine as an educational discipline at the height of the Italian Renaissance.

It was also precisely in the everyday routine that moderate living manifested itself. Art, music, villa and family admittedly contributed to the harmony of life, but table manners remained the most decisive elements. 'Oh miserable, unhappy Italy', Cornaro exclaims, 'do you not notice how debauchery snatches more men from you every year than the terrible plague or the fire and the sword in many battles could achieve?'[94] That which Hutten had bemoaned in Germany, Cornaro now castigated in Italy. Both assumed that foreign influences on morals had destroyed the simple way of life and the virtue of moderation. Notwithstanding the significance he places on individual responsibility for health, however, the Venetian does not contest the competency and good will of physicians, particularly in acute cases of illness:

> I do not wish to deny that one needs doctors and should heed them in order to recognize and cure illnesses, to which those people are prone who live a life

without moderation and order. For if a friend who visits you when you are ill and comforts you only with words and sympathy is performing a pleasant service, how much more should you esteem the physician, who visits you in order to help you and promises you health?

With enthusiasm, Cornaro cites Galen, who had asserted that moderation in eating and drinking prevents damage to health resulting from non-culinary excesses.[95] 'He who wishes to eat a lot, should eat little', he concludes logically. Those who eat less, live longer, and therefore consume more than every glutton!

In the nineteenth century, perhaps thanks to a remark by Hufeland, Cornaro became one of the best-known Renaissance authors on health. His argument that a 'natural' way of life advanced or conserved health played, thanks to the influence of Rousseau, a prominent role in the 'Goethezeit'.

Gabriele Zerbi and the *Gerontocomia*

There were certainly precursors to Cornaro's bestseller on the art of growing old in good health, as well as to Rangone's macrobiotics. Works giving advice on preserving one's health into old age had existed as early as the thirteenth century. The aforementioned *Libellus de retardandis senectutis accidentibus* [*The Cure of Old Age*] attributed to Roger Bacon was paraphrased around 1330 by Arnald of Villanova in a work entitled *De conservanda inventute et retardanda senectute*. In 1335 the physician Guido da Vigevano, who taught in Paris, wrote the *Liber conservacionis sanitatis senis* for elderly pilgrims to the Holy Land. In 1440, the aforementioned doctor Michele Savonarola from Ferrara argued that many famous men had extended their life by consuming wine in moderation every day.[96] However, the first high point of the genre came in 1489 with Gabriele Zerbi's *Gerontocomia*, which was printed in Rome on the press of Eucharius Silber, a man of German origins, and was dedicated to Innocent VIII. Zerbi (1445–1505) taught as an anatomist and practitioner in Padua, Bologna, Venice and Rome, and at the court of the Bosnian sultan; he secured his place in this history of medicine by authoring significant anatomical works, as well as tracts on medical ethics (*De cautelis medicorum*, 1495). He postulated the existence of a natural vital force ('whether one calls it God or something else'), which optimized the quality of life for every individual and was the cause of the natural wish to continue to live. 'Thus it is that most men wish to grow old in spite of the fact that they curse old age when they have reached it.' The 'breath of life' appears to Zerbi to be 'so sweet for each man that no one is so old but that the hope of another year of life at least survives in him.'

Zerbi considers philosophical encomia to the shortness of life, such as those expressed by Pliny,[97] or the contempt for the body and for health in the theories of the Stoics and Ascetics, to be contrary to nature. Longevity is, he claims, a basic human goal, 'which each individual is able to attain'. Only those measures should be employed 'by which hastening age and its causes are halted and life is extended'.[98] Zerbi moves between philosophy and practice, between reflection on the advantages and disadvantages of old age and the concrete description of life-prolonging foods and herbs. He lists causes of aging, reads prognoses for the life of elderly people from their appearance, identifies characteristics which enable young people to anticipate a long life, and compares the astrological disposition (he had no doubt that the stars of an individual determine his life 'from leaving the womb until the end of his life') with the benefits derived from individual efforts. The *Gerontocomia* modifies the 'six non-naturals' for the everyday life of the elderly, emphasizes the tasks and duties of the physician (*gerontocomus*) in this regard, and advocates accommodation that is suitable for old age (it must be warm and sunny, in order to compensate for the insufficient 'calor vitae' of the geriatric) as well as daily hygiene (from the correct clothing through to the ideal bed). The work includes a gentle gymnastics programme and gives information about bathing and periods of rest. The advantages and disadvantages of vigils and sleep are discussed, along with the life-prolonging effects of particular moods and emotions. The reader is also enlightened on the subjects of sexual intercourse in old age and means of preventing hair from greying. Zerbi's work represented the summa of the authoritative information known to that date on dietetics for the elderly.[99] The author concedes that there is a natural death, which is 'neither to be lamented nor feared'. Nor does he forget to mention the physical disposition, or 'nature of the individual', which also determines length of life, despite all regimens. As the embryo is formed from blood and mucus in the process of its creation, man remains during his entire lifetime in the congenital state of insecurity.

According to Zerbi, each limb or organ can be influenced by a particular diet. Internal heat, complexions, limbs, 'spiritus', the interaction between the humours and parts are so diversely apportioned by nature that no two prognoses are identical. 'We grow old by a cold mixture of fluids or temperament, some more swiftly, others more slowly.'[100] By means of a healthy way of life which is adapted to suit the individual complexion, however, the aging process and death, which is 'its close neighbour', can assuredly be delayed. Zerbi even pleads for a new profession, a sort of health consultant for the elderly, and gives a detailed description of the characteristics and duties of this individual. The *gerontocomus* must be familiar with the family circumstances of his charges as well as being a competent physician, particularly given that his duties include the inspection of urine (uroscopy). His assistants can be male or female, but should manifest exemplary modesty and politeness.[101]

Zerbi's book doubtless flattered the vanity of many contemporaries. Efforts to delay hair greying or the aging of the skin could also be accounted for by the Renaissance desire for beauty. The 'refinement of life', which Jakob Burkhardt identified as typical for the age, indeed led towards the end of the fifteenth century to a greater sophistication of the toilet, of the cult of the body and of personal style – even mules were treated with salves and fragrant substances at festivals – that had been unheard of previously.[102]

In the course of the sixteenth century, macrobiotics became an indispensable topic in writings on health, comprising, with the exception of the paradigm of the humoral doctrine, extremely diverse pieces of advice. The English author Thomas Elyot, for instance, followed the example of Democritus and the Roman Pollio Romulus in his work *The Castell of Helth* (1540), recommending honey wine and oil as guarantees of long life. Girolamo Cardano also subjected this topic to a detailed discussion in his treatises *De sanitate tuenda* and *Theonoston*. In almost all works on macrobiotics, elderly individuals from history, myth and the Bible were presented as ultimate proof that a life lasting well over one hundred years was possible. Only in the works of seventeenth-century medical authors, such as the *Via recta ad vitam longam* by the English physician Tobias Venner, did professional, 'scientific' arguments come increasingly to the fore.

Paracelsus' teachings on health

Theophrastus Bombastus von Hohenheim (1493–1541), who, under the name of Paracelsus, became one of the most famous doctors in the West, had probably encountered Galenic dietetics as a student in Ferrara. The 'Luther of the art of healing' considered philosophy, astronomy, alchemy and ethics to be indispensable resources for attaining good health. The physician, he stated, must learn to interpret and understand the patient in all his complexity, 'for it is *one* science, how the man is healthy and how he is or becomes ill. Just as sickness emerges out of health, so health also comes from sickness.'[103] This tendency towards a 'holistic' perspective doubtless had its origins in humoral pathology, of which Paracelsus is critical elsewhere.

The physician from Hohenheim's model of health relativized the scheme of the doctrine of four humours, however. He postulated in reality a modified analogy between the microcosm and the macrocosm, according to which the elements of the human body, which he subdivided into an 'elemental' and a 'sidereal' (spiritual), are subject to the same laws as those of the external world.[104] Paracelsus thereby once again ascribed particular importance to astrology: every form of existence, whether man, animal, plant or healing herb, receives its powers from the stars. Every being or element has its own individual 'science', which must be investigated and which is conducive to the restoration of health, 'for in the same way that there is no illness against which no medication has been created or employed in order to drive it out or heal it, so there always exists one means against the other.'[105] In his theory of the consubstantiality of body and stars, Paracelsus differentiates his position from the ancient and medieval doctrine of the microcosm and macrocosm. It is not the analogy between the body and the cosmos that is at the centre of his anthropological theory, as it is, for example, in the case of Hildegard of Bingen, but rather the idea that, in man, the 'elemental' and 'spiritual' (sidereal) vital principles encounter and battle against each other. Medication is created by God; however, the practitioner of medicine must, as it is put in the *Labyrinthus medicorum errantium*, free it from its 'waste products' by means of alchemy.[106] Through this discipline Paracelsus pointed the way to the iatrochemistry of the seventeenth century, which gave 'chemical' explanations for bodily processes as well as for illnesses and modes of therapy, and became particularly influential thanks to Johann Baptist van Helmont (1577–1644).

According to Paracelsus, health is related to an understanding of these interrelations. It is the physician's duty – and here he follows the ancient Galenic teachings – 'to preserve the body in good health and return the sick man to his former health'. This assistance can only be given by the philosophically trained doctor, whose function is divided by Paracelsus into three stages: he should proceed from dietetic advice (*diaita*) to 'materia medica' (pharmacy) and finally to 'ultima ratio', surgery.[107] Paracelsus particularly prized folk remedies: 'The old *philosophi* nursed themselves to excellent health, in order to attain a long life in cheerful health. In order to attain this same end, they employed this remedy made from the black hellebore but, alongside this, also adhered to a regulated and a moderate regimen or bodily order.'[108] That Paracelsus, like Luther and Hutten, here prizes 'the remedies of the German nations' over all other herbs is a reference back to ancient folk traditions, but must also be seen in the context of nationalist comments by Italian physicians and humanists.[109] The physician from Hohenheim recommends mysterious elixirs 'against all forms of decay of the living, and also of the dead, body', the effectiveness of which he attributes to chemical processes.[110] It is important that everyone follows a regimen of health: 'He should know what he is eating and drinking, how he labours and what may arise from this to prolong his life . . . Thus the individual is his own doctor; for insofar as he helps nature, so nature answers his needs and thus gives him a garden for his own cultivation. If we reflect thoroughly enough on these things and strive for them, then our own nature itself is our doctor.'[111] No man can attain health without the assistance of nature. He should never forget 'that he is born of nature and not in Leipzig or in Vienna'.[112]

In the *Liber de longa vita*, Paracelsus concerns himself with drugs that extend life. Firstly, all carry the power of good *and* bad within them and must therefore be cleansed, purified and changed, for 'the dose alone decides that a poison is no poison'. The art of macrobiotics becomes an individual test of character: 'For when one man eats for his health and avoids that which shortens his life, that is the real faster. For all our things should serve to bring us a long life.'[113] It is necessary, in the various stages of life, to make use of the respective 'conservationes' and mobilize the natural forces against death, 'for every natural illness hates death and flees from it, no limb on the body loves it.' The regimen must be adapted to the three ages of life,[114] although one should take into consideration that also, 'of the regions, lands, towns and valleys, one is more healthy and of more benefit for a long life than the other, and one gives life more joy, more delight, more *humores* than the other.'[115] That the environment affects health was a central argument for Paracelsus, who, in *Bad Pfäfers*, also reminds us of the old importance of healing baths. A course of treatment must be well considered and carefully planned, however. The bath supplements the everyday regimen, 'so that it squares itself against illness and with health and not to the exoneration of the doctors'.[116]

Paracelsus' complex medical philosophy was probably influenced by Johannes Trithemius (1462–1516), the 'pansophist' abbot of Sponheim monastery, who also counted Agrippa von Nettesheim among his pupils.[117] For those in this circle, health was not only a consequence of the 'ordo vitae', but also a human achievement. The body can, advanced by its own endeavours, even in a kind of mystical enhancement, achieve spiritual and, secondarily, physical health.

Particular importance is again ascribed to nutrition, from which we receive our own body of grace or mercy: 'See then, what the body is: we are eating ourselves.' The body can be kept in good health by means of a diet bestowed by God. 'For this reason, we should not let it degenerate, that is, indulge in revelry, but practise day and night to set the natural and eternal in motion.' According to Paracelsus, man lives in a state of constant tension between the pull of his *higher* body and the appetites of his *lower*, food-driven body, the *spiritual* and the *elemental* vital principles. Both are dependent on moderation and order. Man should 'drag and guide his body in his sweat and not let it indulge in revelry.'[118]

Paracelsus also refers to the 'things of which there are six', to which numerous references have already been made, although he modifies their meaning considerably. In at times cryptic language he describes food and drink as 'corpora of the astra', thus recalling their affinity with the stars. Paracelsus considers the neglect of the 'six non-naturals' to be a sin; intemperance in eating is for him tantamount to a kind of suicide: 'Thus let everyone eat and drink so that he is able to answer for his gluttony and what arises from it for him on Judgement Day.'[119] Even the traditional criteria of physiology, 'which grow out of the ens: complexiones, qualitates, membra', can be supported with magical powers 'such as incantations, that is magic, imaginationes, that is images, and aestimationes, that is fancies', and thus contribute to the recovery of health.[120]

In the *Paragranum* the author applies himself to the 'bestial' elemental and 'sidereal' spiritual body, the latter of which allows man to partake in the 'external firmament'. Overexertion of the intellect can obstruct the route to God, for which reason Paracelsus develops a weakness for the 'fools' and 'stulti', who are untroubled by astral reason and therefore 'not spurned by God'. Throughout the work, he repeatedly stresses the individual orientation of man. Everyone must seek his *own* means of relaxation. 'So man takes pleasure in things, one in the element of earth and seeks his delight in the minerals, another in the element of water and seeks his pleasure in the same, the third in the element of fire, he is gladdened by the stars and their works, the fourth in the element air and seeks his manna in the air, that is the fruit of the air.' Concerning the age-old art of arranging *otium* and *negotium* sensibly, Paracelsus comments wisely: 'Peace is better than agitation, yet agitation is more useful than peace.'[121]

In addition to the classical doctrine of regimens, in his early work *Volumen Paramirum* (1520) Paracelsus developed (but did not resume in his later works) the famous doctrine of the *entia*, according to which health can be impaired by the 'ens astrale, venenale, naturale, spirituale and deanale', in other words, by the stars, by unfavourable environmental influences, by disposition, by spiritual processes or disturbances and finally by God, who wishes to test or punish man by means of illnesses.[122] It makes sense that the individual has to meet these dangers or, rather, challenges from God *actively*. The spectrum of prophylaxes stretches from astrological advice through care for the environment to a kind of 'positive' mental attitude, as well as prayers for the preservation or recovery of health.

In the work *Volumen Paramirum*, which was printed posthumously in around 1550, the pathophysiology of illnesses is linked to the 'tria prima': with 'sulphur', the fiery, 'mercurius', the quick, and 'sal', the firm principle. In the same book Paracelsus writes on the subject of the 'tartaric' illnesses, which jeopardize health on account of pathological residues in the body ('tartarus' or tartar).[123] Theoretically, then, there are numerous dangers and disruptions to health; humoral pathology, on the other hand, was based on one *single* theory of illness.

In view of the complexity of this doctrine of pathology, it is hardly surprising that the author also deals in detail with theological questions, such as teachings on the healing of the soul, although the majority of his writings on this subject have never been edited. He argues that metaphysics is not qualitatively different from philosophy, that is, the cognition of nature and the pursuit of physical health; it is merely a question of degree. In the final analysis, Paracelsus thinks deterministically: 'God alone keeps the body alive; he wants us to have a long life, and, to this end, provides us with all kinds of assistance and support . . . And if the devil himself were to tell us that silver and gold can bring us health and medicine, then be sure of this, everything happens at God's behest.' Elsewhere we read, in the same vein: 'There, where illnesses arise, the root of health can also be acquired.'[124]

Paracelsus' teachings on health were as extensive as they were abstruse, complicated and contradictory. Today, it is beyond dispute that, for the distinguished doctor, medicine consists less in treating and operating than in precautions and prevention. Paracelsus' target readership consisted of ordinary people, the 'man on the street', who knew enough about the traditional regimens from hearsay.

Herbal books

From the end of the fifteenth century onwards, printed herbal books were a genre apart in literature on health. They were, of course, part of a tradition that went back to the medieval herbaria and compendia – for example, the famous ninth-century *Hortulus* by the Reichenau monk Walahfried Strabo, in which twenty-five healing plants are praised in poetry. 'Practice and scholarship, utility and poetry, nature and culture, academe and life, gardening and the art of healing' all came together in this epochal work, which, alongside architecture, literature and book illuminations, attests to the cultural florescence within the Carolingian monasteries.[125]

Hildegard of Bingen had mentioned sixty-eight wild plants, twenty-six imported plants and forty-three that were cultivated in the garden, and in the thirteenth century the work *Circa instans*, attributed to the Salernitan physician Mattheus Platearius, became the most prevalent and comprehensive book on remedies in western Europe.[126] From late antiquity, all experiences gained were passed from generation to generation; at the end of the fifteenth century medical interest in plants increased rapidly.[127] Enthusiasts examined them curiously, compared the conclusions of authorities and ventured to criticize them. Dioscurides and Pliny were placed in the dock, but were also defended passionately. This 'critical revival of botany'[128]contributed to a general upturn in medicine around 1500. Excellent physicians such as Fracastoro (1478–1553) favoured 'mild plants' over operations and blood-letting. Last but not least, the Europeans were overwhelmed by the 'materia medica' of the Indians. According to Hernandez, court physician to the king of Spain, the Aztecs had at their disposal more than 3000 medicinal plants. Europe did not take only the potato or luxury foodstuffs such as cocoa from America's natives, but also many medicinal herbs.[129]

Until the end of the seventeenth century, herbal books played a significant role in medical faculties, at royal courts and in monasteries, but also in medical practice and among wealthy laypersons.[130] The book composed by the Palatinate physician Tabernaemontanus (1520–1554), to name one example, assisted in the identification of particular herbs and gave instruction on the most favourable time for collecting them, on their preparation and on their therapeutic effects.[131] Many authors and editors attempted to identify the plants mentioned by Galen and Dioscurides (that the 'auctoritates' could have been mistaken was a bitter realization for authors, who had frequently been educated at scholastic universities). A parallel development was the increasing fashion for herbaria, collections of dried plants, which probably went back to the Italian botanist Luca Ghini and his pupils Cesare Aldovrandini and Andrea Cesalpino.[132] The first systematically organized botanical gardens appeared in Padua (1545), Pisa (1547) and Bologna (1567).

According to the *Kräuterbuch* [*Herbal Book*] of Adam Lonitzer (1528–1586), the divinely bestowed 'fruits of the earth' included not only herbs and trees, but also metals, minerals and animals, as well as the component parts of the animal and human bodies.[133] The Frankfurt municipal doctor Lonitzer defends the popularization of the science of medicaments by alluding to the divine authorship of the *Materia medica*, an argument that had already been put forward in 1485 by the physician Johann Wonnecke from Kaub, author of the *Hortus sanitatis Germaniae*. Lonitzer described the effects of herbal mixtures, native fruits, the resin of rubber plants, simple minerals, the bodies of creatures such as earthworms, snails, ants, birds, toads or their excrement, spices, types of cereals and herbal essences, as well as animal meats and fats.[134]

The *Herbarius Manutius* (1484) by the publisher Peter Schöffer from Mainz (Johann Wonnecke's *Garden of Health* was printed on his press in 1485) appeared within a very short time in various new editions. Although the initiative originally came primarily from printers and publishers, soon botanists and doctors were reaching for their pens. They included, for example, the Basel town doctor Otto Brunfels (1488), whose herbal book was illustrated by Hans Weiditz, a pupil of Dürer, followed by Hieronymus Bock from Zweibrücken (1539), author of the *New Kreuterbuch*, and the physician and universal scholar Leonhard Fuchs (1543), whose *opus* was illustrated by artists from Holbein's sphere of influence.[135] The interest of laypersons in specialist medical questions was aroused everywhere; the erudite discipline of medicine became less elusive, and even popular. In 1544, Pier Andrea Mattioli, court physician to Ferdinand I and Maximilian II, produced a herbal book which ran to 32,000 copies!

The herbal books were soon as popular as the house books. In 1614, finally, the artistic culmination came in the form of the coloured *Hortus Eystettensis* by the Nuremberg apothecary Besler, a work that was even displayed in art chambers.[136] Under the influence of the herbal books, efforts were made to develop medieval plant symbolism, which had attained its most consummate form in religious painting, for example on the Ghent altar by the van Eyck brothers or in Botticelli's 'Primavera'.[137] Carnation, columbine, rose or whitethorn acquired new, primarily Mariological significance, and contributed to meditation and to a more profound piety. Religious plant symbolism drew on old folk traditions; however, it also increased the significance of the represented herbs, flowers, blossoms and leaves for folk medicine. The aforementioned mandrake, which was harvested at the risk of one's life, was considered a particularly valuable treasure. Some went as far as dressing it like a doll, conserving it in glass cases and even bathing it like a child.[138]

The Thirty Years' War entailed in Germany a distinct decline in scientific botany, in the art of gardening and in printing. The old copper plates of the herbal books were lost. In addition, superstition gained new ground; aphrodisiac herbs, poisonous potions and magic compounds became fashionable, particularly among the nobility. A failed new edition of Mattioli's book produced by the botanist and alchemist Johann Joachim Becher from Speyer was just as emblematic for the second half of the seventeenth century as the *Heilsame Dreckapotheke* by Christian Franz Paullini, medical attendant to the bishop of Münster (1696). The author believed he was able to cure 'almost everything, even the worst, most noxious illnesses and ensorcelled harms from the head to the feet'.[139] The herbal books that continued to be published were intended to satisfy the aesthetic desires of collectors rather than their scientific or therapeutic curiosity.[140]

Dietetics in daily life

The well-known discrepancy between theory and practice also applied in the Renaissance. However, Cornaro's tract, as well as the paterfamilias literature (*Hausväterliteratur*) or *secreta* literature prove that dietetics constituted an important part of the humanist 'ars vivendi', and in the sixteenth and seventeenth century even represented a sort of *everyday phenomenon*. Self-examinations, autobiographies and letters, in particular, bear witness to a new, highly subjective perception of the body. Physical exercises such as fencing, running and jumping accompanied the congenitally rather delicate mathematician and physician Girolamo Cardano (1501–1576) throughout his entire life.[141] It is striking how meticulously he records his private routine, including his daily exercise: 'I habitually spend ten hours a day in bed; of these I sleep eight hours when I am healthy and not disturbed, four or five when I am less well . . . In the second hour after sunrise I get up. If I am bothered by sleeplessness during the night, I get up, walk around my bed and count up to one thousand in my thoughts; then I also abstain from food and eat at least half less than usual.'[142] To eat very little in the mornings and reduce one's diet with increasing age were important rules for Cardano.

Like the layman Cornaro, Cardano composed an individual diet, with particular emphasis placed on tolerance and subjective preferences 'With my meal I enjoy a sweet . . . new wine, in a measure of approximately half a pound, along with a double measure or more of water. I particularly love the wings of very young chickens, the liver and all other blood-filled internal parts of chickens and turtle doves. I also like to eat crayfish.' Fruit, onions or rue acquired particular importance as a potential 'antidote, not merely a prophylaxis'.[143] In typical Renaissance style, Cardano strove for eternal, lasting fame, but simultaneously emphasized the inanity of life and social standing. He observes, not without irony, that even 'benevolent fortune' cannot disturb his equanimity. Cardano considers hobbies and intellectual interests to be just as important factors in the promotion of good health as the correct kind of clothing, piety, intellectual commerce and education.

Among the intellectuals and artists of the sixteenth century in particular, pedantic self-observation, often combined with hypochondria, was common. Vasari describes how the Florentine painter Pontormo had, like many of his colleagues, a tendency towards melancholy and combated illness and thoughts of death in a voluntary state of isolation. In his diary (*Il mio libro*), the artist gives details not only about his dietary plan, but also about indispositions of every kind:

> On Wednesday I did the rest of the putto, for which I had to bend the whole day in an extremely incommodious manner, so that I was afflicted by pain in the kidneys on Thursday . . . In the evening I ate nothing, and on the morning of the twenty-ninth day I painted the hand and half the arm of the large figure, and on the evening of this day I did not consume anything. I ate nothing at all until Saturday evening, then approximately one hundred grams of bread, two eggs and salad . . . At first I got up, but because it was cold and windy, went to bed again at six o'clock.[144]

Self-treatments of this kind, magic, prayers and confidence in the lower hierarchies of healers were doubtless of greater importance for the masses than the endeavours of *physicians* or complicated dietetic programmes. As there are fewer written attestations of practical dietetics than of its theoretical foundations, the question of what associations the term 'health' carried for the less privileged craftsmen, day labourers, farmers and even mercenaries must remain unanswered. Notwithstanding all controversies concerning definitions, there is every reason to assume that, here as well, the goal was a relative freedom from discomfort, social integration (even for beggars!), ability to work (often for children as well), positive expectations of the future (in whatever form) and the hope that one would not have to confront death in too short a period of time.[145] The neutral state between sickness and health defined by Galen was certainly not perceived as pathological.

The question of whether a dietetic approach which obviously differentiated between social classes is indicative of a certain relativity as regards the (admittedly purely physiological) concept of health, as argued by Jütte, must remain unanswered. In a large town such as Cologne, knowledge of hygiene and dietetics was widespread, even in theoretical form. It was clear to everyone that 'bad' air was unhealthy – who would have contradicted a rule that had endured over millennia? – and that, for example, animal faeces lying around on the streets could cause illnesses. The toilets of the Cologne hospital were situated so far away from the building that 'the stink can be kept out of the hospital'.[146]

The alderman Hermann Weinsberg, whose writings have survived, ate together with his family every day. If he felt weak, he contented himself with 'lighter' meals. In winter he wore warm clothes and stayed at home when it was cold. The avoidance of wine and beer and the consumption of mineral water were also considered beneficial to health. The medical attendant to the archbishop of Cologne, Petrus Holtzemius (1570–1651), recommended a course of Tönnisstein water, which was valued as a general prophylaxis as well as against stomach, kidney and bladder complaints. The amount of water consumed was to be increased carefully from 24 to 54 ounces, four times a day.[147] The health care of the early modern period was doubtless inhomogeneous and subjective, with traditions from the 'regimina', from house books and 'folk medicine' occurring in combination.

It is an interesting phenomenon that milk – with the exception of breast milk – was barely considered in the daily diet, even in the case of children. It was served, at best, in dishes containing milk. Only breast milk was regarded as indispensable in the diet of infants, and attention was paid to the health of the wet nurses. If they fell ill, the child that had been entrusted to them was taken away. An alternation between rest and movement, between recreation and work, was a matter of course – thanks, in the first instance, to the annual calendar. Working on holidays was forbidden by the churches and guilds alike. Like Cardano, the alderman of Cologne, Weinsberg, adhered to a strict daily rhythm: he got up between five and six o'clock in the morning and, after a fastidious daily routine, took to his bed at nine o'clock in the evening.[148]

Rest was rarely taken after meals, except in the case of the elderly. As the temperatures in the northern latitudes did not climb as high at midday as in the south, the 'siesta' was unknown in German towns. There were many remedies for sleep disorders; the elderly Weinsberg, however, suffered on account of pressure in his bladder and noise in the vicinity of his house. After getting up, he paid meticulous attention to his bowel actions. Everyone in his family slept in his or her own bed.[149]

In the course of the sixteenth century, 'hygiene' came increasingly to mean also 'social self-representation in cultural signs and symbols', that is to say, not only teachings on health. Expensive perfumes or elaborate clothes were worn from the seventeenth century for reasons of hygiene, but also to distinguish oneself from the 'dirty' lower classes. As there was reason to fear that one would open the pores of one's skin to, for example, 'plague vapours' by washing too frequently, powders or the application of perfumes were preferred over cleaning with water. The spread of syphilis, which had been prevalent in Europe since the end of the fifteenth century, was attributed to the bathhouses, which were therefore prohibited in the local communes from Hutten's day onwards.[150] Collective hardship necessitated the adoption of drastic measures to protect the health of the people, although utilitarian policies established themselves very quickly.

Despite the increase in specialist medical literature, self-prescribed medication or treatment by laypersons represented the norm in the sixteenth and seventeenth centuries. A trained physician was consulted only in emergencies; surgeons, barbers or skilled laypersons were sought out regularly, however. From a total of 153 cases of illness within the (wealthy) Cologne family Weinsberg, a 'medicus' was summoned in only thirty-four cases. The poorer classes probably abstained from calling for a trained physician as a matter of course. Trust was repeatedly placed in magic remedies or in the 'filth pharmacy'. As the scheme of the four humours was also easy to comprehend for a layperson, doctors and health prophylaxis bore little relation to one another for the greater part of the population, contrary to Galen's requirements.[151] It should not surprise us that many physicians referred to their lay colleagues as 'foolhardy vagrants', 'bladder prophets' or 'bunglers'; others, however, desired to enable the 'common man' – in rural areas, for example – to act as his own private physician.[152]

The complex matter of caring for one's own health is also attested in the writings of Michel Montaigne (1533–1592). In his journal of his therapeutic travels (1580), he keeps a detailed record of his physical complaints, which are due primarily to bladder stones. Even Montaigne, the critical author of the *Essais*, gratefully accepted a miracle cure from an old 'patriarch of Antioch':

> He gave me the remedy sealed in a small, earthen pot and assured me that I could keep it for ten or twenty years, and that it would be of so great benefit to me that I would be cured completely from my affliction after a single administration. So

that I am able to recover his instructions if I should lose them, I will repeat them here: after a light evening meal and before retiring, one must rub an amount the size of two peas between one's fingers and then dissolve it in warm water and take this five times, leaving out one day after every administration.

The traveller constantly had medication for all eventualities to hand. He paid careful attention to food and drink, convinced that certain wines and cloudy water assisted the formation of the stones. He noted enviously that the pope, who received him in Rome, had experienced 'neither gout nor colic nor stomach complaints'.

Even the highly educated believed in the sixteenth century in substances with magical powers, magical remedies and amulets, which Paracelsus also included in his courses of treatment. Medicinal herbs were often selected for their resemblance to body organs or their particular colour, which formed the basis for a highly differentiated *doctrine of signatures*.[153] The bathing culture also enjoyed a heyday; Montaigne reports from Plombières in the Vosges:

> It is a custom simply to bathe there, and, indeed, two or three times a day. Some take their meal during the bath itself, have themselves cupped in it and purged thoroughly before they get in. If they drink any water at all, then only one or two glasses . . . We saw people there who had been cured of abscesses, and others of a heat rash covering their entire body. The period from spring until May is most strongly recommended; after the month of August one should avoid bathing on account of the cold climate.

The famous traveller also witnesses therapies involving drinking *and* bathing in Bagni di Lucca, one of the most famous spas of the age.

It was recognized at an early stage that health was jeopardized in a very specific manner by certain professions. A book by Paracelsus on miners' phthisis and other miners' diseases appeared posthumously (1567), and the town physician and mayor of Chemnitz, Georg Agricola (1494–1555), made recommendations for the improvement of the air supply in mines, in his tract *De re metallica* (1556). Dust in the lungs (pneumoconiosis), asthma and bronchitis were to be combated *prophylactically* by improving the hygienic conditions of the workers. The author wished to deal with the topic of mining as Columella and Varro before him had dealt with farming. However, as respected an authority as Paracelsus still considered spirits to be at work in the dust in the mines.

6

Dietetics in the Seventeenth Century

Cartesianism and conservative tendencies

The early modern period was very ambivalent with regard to what constituted health and how it might be achieved. Initially, the traditions of 'regimens' were continued alongside the introduction of new developments. The *Gerocomica* by the Mantuan doctor Aurelio Anselmo (1606) represents an example of the 'conservative' literature of the day. 'Suitable not just for philosophers and doctors, but for everyone', the book warns against excessive consumption of wine, fits of rage, the uncontrolled use of medicines and other 'dangers in old age'. Like the herbals, such works were tremendously popular and must have influenced the composition of menus at court and among the nobility.

One year later saw the publication in London of *Differences of the Ages of Mans Life* by the Oxford doctor and humanist Henry Cuffe. Even though Paracelsus may have claimed to be able to advise anyone such that he might die at an old age free of illness, his own early death had demonstrated that longevity was also determined by a person's constitution.[1] This is subject to guidance and control, but within certain individual limitations; two people pursuing the same way of life will not necessarily live to the same age. God has the last word here, which is why not everything which determines life and death can be explained empirically and by reason. Nature – which embraced nature as a whole as well as individual disposition – was increasingly regarded as a health-sustaining force.

The moralizing work *Die Greuel der Verwüstung menschlichen Geschlechts . . . zu sondern Nutz, Glück, Heil, Wolfahrt, langen*

Gesondt, zeitlich und ewigen Leben [*The Horror of the Destruction of the Human Race . . . to the Furtherance of Particular Benefit, Happiness, Salvation, Welfare, Health and Long Life*] (Ingolstadt, 1610), by Hippolytus Guarinonius, the town doctor of Hall in the Tyrol, stood out among the century's dietetic treatises. It was aimed at the careless, unintentional destruction of health, maintaining that inadequate dietetics jeopardized the lifespan allotted by God, or rather by nature, of which he is the creator. Basic to a natural, healthy life was an orderly and carefully constructed daily routine. Just as with Cuffe, however, the final word on the state of one's health lay with God himself. It is God who heads the list of the 'six non-naturals' in a mnemonic, the initials of which spell out the archaic German word for healthy, 'gesondt': *G*ott, *E*ssen und trincken, *S*chlaffen und Wachen, *O*ede oder Ringerung deß Vberfluß, *N*utzen oder Vbung des *Leybs, *D*auglich Lufft, *T*rost des Gemüths [God, eating and drinking, sleeping and waking, abstemiousness, use and exercise of the body, pure air, comfort for the soul]. Society, man, culture and nature, according to Guarinonius, ail or prosper in a process of mutual interdependence.[2]

The English philosopher Francis Bacon (1560–1626), who, in upgrading observation and experimentation, laid the decisive foundations for a new empirical approach to research into natural history, also drew up a 'regimen'. It proposed that the pattern of life followed in youth determined health in old age, and stated that everyone should determine their optimum way of life by monitoring their weaknesses and strengths, bearing in mind that worries and dark thoughts would hasten death. 'To be free minded and cheerfully disposed, at Houres of Meat, and of Sleep, and of Exercise, is one of the best Precepts of long Lasting.'[3] Anger, anxiety, and 'Exhilarations in Excesse', as well as 'Sadnesse not Communicated', are considered dangerous. Sport and gymnastics should not be overdone, since their effectiveness will otherwise diminish 'when Sicknesse commeth'. Moderate physical exercise, on the other hand, toughens the body against illness. As Ficino before him, Bacon advocates an *intellectual* dietetics in the form of 'Studies that fill the Minde with Splendide and Illustrious Objects, as Histories, Fables, and Contemplations of Nature'.[4]

The increasingly rapid succession of new discoveries in the fields of anatomy and physiology in the seventeenth century undoubtedly led to an identity crisis among medical doctors. It was for this reason that the idea of self-control and treatment fell in many places on fertile ground.[5] The abbot of Choisy, for instance, swore by fruits which he ate in winter 'as a sound precaution', and Robert Hooke, who coined the term 'cell' in biology, noted in a diary entry for 2 September 1673 that he 'slept not soe well after eating Rice pudden'.[6] Such reflections are reminiscent of Cardano and Pontormo, and, indeed, individual preventive medicine in the seventeenth century followed humanistic traditions. Cardinal Mazarin sent his niece to recuperate in a nunnery since she had neglected the 'règles' of health and had fallen ill as a result. Madame Sévigné, on the other hand, swore by the health- and strength-giving meat of young lambs. Moreover, she urged her daughter to 'go for walks, do gymnastics, breathe good air, and do not remain the whole time in this gloomy palace or dungeon of a room.' Descartes, too, who in 1645 described the maintenance of health as the 'main aim of his studies', recommended that man live as healthily as the animals and – since God would hardly have given us senses in which we could not trust – always eat only what seemed easily digestible.[7] Little wonder that criticism was directed at courtly etiquette and the impositions of its table. Concerned doctors and onlookers at the court of Louis XIV such as Liselotte von der Pfalz were put in their place with the half-ironic, half-serious observation that it was the task of the cooks to fill the king, and of the doctors to empty him.[8] Nevertheless, the doctors in Versailles warned the corpulent monarch against excessively brisk movements.

As has already been seen in the *Hausväterliteratur* (paterfamilias literature – the term goes back to Luther) and in the *secreti*, a fundamental part of the 'oeconomia', the care and regulation of a household, was concern for the body and soul of its occupants. According to the Lower-Austrian country nobleman Helmhard von Hohberg, the *oeconomus prudens*, like the *paterfamilias* in former times, carried a special responsibility. Security, spiritual harmony, peace within the family, and piety, but also a healthy diet, were the guarantee that both body and soul would prosper. According to Johannes Colerus' *Oeconomia ruralis et domestica* (1609), too, a good head of the household must 'have knowledge of the law and of medicine'.[9]

Works offering aphoristic admonition or advice, such as the *Oráculo manual y arte de prudencia*, the 'pocket oracle' *Art of Worldly Wisdom* (which was admired by Friedrich Nietzsche and translated into German by Arthur Schopenhauer) by the Spanish Jesuit priest Baltasar Gracián (1601–1658), must have been influential in intellectual circles. Making provision for the health of body and soul was considered an indispensable part of the catalogue of human duties. 'The person who races through a life of vice comes to a doubly quick end. The one who races through virtue, never dies', it says on the macrobiotic topic of living long and well.[10] To remain healthy one must lead a peaceable life: 'Listen and see, but keep quiet. A day without contention means a night of rest. To live much and to take pleasure in life is to live twice: the fruit of peace.'[11] And, shortly after, one can read: 'Nothing is sillier than to take everything seriously.'[12] There is also an admonition to keep the emotions under control, an old legacy of the 'six non-naturals': 'The sudden movements of the passions throw prudence off balance, and here is where you can be lost.'[13]

Collections of sayings and aphorisms such as the *Art of Worldly Wisdom* were absolutely characteristic of the century. In the *Cherubinische Wandersmann* [*Cherubic Wayfarer*] of 1657 by the imperial court doctor Johannes Scheffler, later to become famous as Angelus Silesius, health is seen after the mystical tradition as reinvigoration of the soul and union with God. Body, soul and God are bound together in harmony: 'The soul is a crystal glittering with the godhead within it: the body which you inhabit is their shrine.' The *Sinngedichte* (epigrams) of the Silesian lawyer and court official Friedrich von Logau (1604–1655) touch on such matters as religion, love, politics, intellect and wellbeing. The old adage 'never to excess' is evoked, along with traditional advice such as: 'When you're hungry, when you're weary, spice the food, and be abed early.' How to care for one's health is also a topic: 'He who fish broth imbibes at table, will never the demon gout disable.' Notwithstanding indications of something similar in Aristotle, the counsel that 'In danger and great need, the middle way leads to death' is – in its contradiction of the ancient doctrine of balance and 'eukrasia' – as sensational from a health-philosophical as it is from a pedagogic viewpoint.[14]

An event of enormous consequence for European theories of health was the division by Descartes (1596–1650) of the human organism into a body which functioned as a machine and a soul which operated autonomously. This Cartesian dualism meant in fact the secularization of the body. Its functioning was no longer determined by *virtutes* or mysterious *vires*, but by technical concepts (motion, size, tubes, temperature, etc.). For many, this seemed to point the way towards a medicine 'without soul'.[15] However, the celebrated *cogito ergo sum* by the same author seemed to recall the dependence of this 'machine body' on the soul. Nevertheless, from now on physical and mechanical concepts were at the centre of theories of health.[16]

The corporeal world ('res extensa') was now being researched with the aid of mathematics and geometry, and of 'technology' in a wider sense. On the other hand, soul, consciousness and thinking ('res cogitans'), let alone God himself ('res infinita'), could not be understood through these methods. The feelings of the senses and passions rested for Descartes on an interplay between the body and the 'anima rationalis' via the pineal gland. Soul, will and reason, however, occasionally fly in the face of nature: 'And yet it is not unusual for us to go wrong', wrote Descartes, 'even in cases where nature does urge us towards something. Those who are ill, for example, may desire food or drink that will shortly afterwards turn out to be bad for them. Perhaps it may be said that they go wrong because their nature is disordered, but this does not remove the difficulty. A sick man is no less one of God's creatures than a healthy one, and it seems no less a contradiction to suppose that he has received from God a nature that deceives him.'[17]

A certain demythologization of the body presents itself in the following sentences:

> Yet a clock constructed with wheels and weights observes all the laws of its nature just as closely when it is badly made and tells the wrong time as when it completely fulfils the wishes of the clockmaker. In the same way, I might consider the body of a man as a kind of machine equipped with and made up of bones, nerves, muscles, veins, blood and skin in such a way that even if there were no mind in it, it would still perform all the same movements as it does now in those cases where movement is not under the control of the will or, consequently, of the mind.[18]

According to Descartes, the warmth which dwells within the heart and is transported by the blood empowers the body's movements.

Tommaso Campanella (1568–1639), author of *La citta del sole*, but also of a theoretical medical work, *Medicinalium iuxta propria principia libri VII*, which appeared in Lyon in 1653, took account of this development, but also saw – and this reveals the ambivalence of the baroque period – in magic, alchemy or other supernatural activities promising paths to healing.[19] Within this context, an important role also fell to Galileo (*d.* 1642), who, in his work *Le meccaniche*, defended the 'machine' as a scientific model and, with regard to physiology, earned the approval of many doctors with his concept for a *scienza del moto*.[20]

By measuring pulse rate, body temperature or perspiration, numerous *iatrophysicists* (Rothschuh) extended the Cartesian theories. Giovanni Borelli (1608–1679), a pupil of Campanella, explained in his book *De motu animalium* (1681) the interaction between bones, muscles and joints with the help of the laws of leverage, despite seeing himself as an opponent of the Frenchman. After William Harvey had, in 1928, expounded his theory of the circulation of the blood as a system of tubes, a physical explanation could be given for haemorrhaging, congestion, oedemas, thromboses and unexplained fatalities. Fevers, cramps and pains, but also contamination of the bodily fluids were, according to Borelli's pupil Lorenzo Bellini, the result of disrupted circulation.[21] Already in 1614 there had appeared in Venice *De medicina statica* by the Paduan professor and doctor Santorio Santorio (1561–1636), who constructed pulsometers and clinical thermometers which were probably modelled on one of the measuring instruments developed by Galileo.[22] Notwithstanding the fact that *iatrophysics* was in competition with the alchemy favoured by Paracelsus, people's health from the seventeenth century on was increasingly subject to measurement. The healthy body seemed to have no secrets to hide; the unknown was regarded as the *not yet known*!

Suffering was also demythologized. Pain was regarded as a necessary part of the body's warning or defence system. Devoid of every metaphysical function – in the *Idea medicinae philosophica* (1571) by the Danish doctor Petrus Severinus (1542–1602) it had been described as the inevitable consequence of the Fall of Man – it merely represented a 'reaction', or an 'affect'.[23] Health was threatened by technical disorders which revealed themselves in the body's regulatory mechanism.

In 1689 the Leiden medical professor Theodor Craanen (1620–1690) compared daily intake of food to the winding up of a clock.[24] In 1719 there appeared the *Elementa anthropologiae* by the Jena anatomist Hermann Friedrich Teichmeyer (1685–1746), in which 'all activities of the body' may be explained 'by the recent discoveries in anatomy, physics, chemistry and finally mechanics'. The automated figures so popular in the baroque period, dancers, musicians, etc., and even the training of animals, seemed to support the thesis that how man functioned was explicable in technical terms. As early as 1748 Julien de La Mettrie (1709–1751), in his celebrated book *L'Homme machine*, explained motion as a consequence of the vibrations of the fibres which made up the human body. He postulated that body, intellect and soul, man and beast, were all subject to the same mechanical rules, and was convinced that apes could be educated to be human beings. De La Mettrie talked of the human machine, 'which winds its main-springs up itself'. The English doctor Francis Glisson (1597–1677), on the other hand, saw in the mechanically excitable body fibres the sphere of activity of the health-giving *Robur insitum*.[25] Giorgio Baglivi (1668–1707) also attributed a health-maintaining *vis insita* to the fibres. If their tone was normal, and in balance with the bodily fluids, this was a sign of good health; if they were over tense or too slack, this signified illness.[26] Such models or definitions attempted to explain the phenomenon of sickness and health in a mechanistic-positivist way, and had little to do with subjective feeling or even individual pleasure at the smooth functioning of the body. In Germany the mathematician Johann Christoph Sturm (1635–1703) constructed remarkable models of the muscles, and the medical faculties of new universities such as Duisburg elevated Cartesianism to be the basis of their pathology, and indeed their whole teaching.[27]

However, in no sense did Cartesianism hold unlimited sway over the health doctrines of the seventeenth century. Even the revaluation of the importance of nature was not accepted by all doctors and naturalists. In his *Pensées*, Pascal (1623–1662) commented in lapidary fashion that 'all men hate one another instinctively',[28] and, in talking of fathers' 'natural love of their children', asks the question: 'What then is this nature which is likely to be obliterated? Habit is a second nature which destroys the first. But what is nature? Why is habit not natural? I am very much afraid that nature is only a first habit, as habit is a second nature.'[29] Elsewhere the important French philosopher and mathematician offered the criticism that 'the calculating machine produces results which come closer to thought than anything animals can do; but it does nothing which can make us say that it possesses will-power like animals.'[30] Pascal understood health not as the automaton-like functioning of the body, but as the religious security of the soul. It made no sense, therefore, 'to stop at nature'. With respect to theology, he added: 'The only form of knowledge which is opposed to common sense and nature is the only one which has always existed among men.'[31] In similar fashion the convert to Catholicism Niels Stenson (1638–1686), one of the leading anatomists of the seventeenth century, argues in a letter to Spinoza (1671) against the Cartesians: 'Because they know nothing but physical matter, they create God from the sum total of all material things and allow man all the pleasures of the senses, because there is no free will, because there is no sense in praying, and because death will be followed by neither punishment nor reward.'

Thus was the seventeenth century marked by increasing intellectual and ideological uncertainty, by religious doubts and a search for meaning. Many Romance countries saw the blossoming of a dark iconography; 'playing with horror' became fashionable.[32] In literature the 'memento mori' acquired – in the poetry of Andreas Gryphius, for instance – a new significance. In painting, Guercino's motif of the skull in an Arcadian landscape ('Et in Arcadia ego') set a whole new trend.[33] The emphasis in the cabinets of curiosities such as that assembled by Rudolf II in Prague was also on the macabre, the humorous, the strange and the alien. Art collections became peep shows, chambers of horror and mystery. Monsters, freaks, and images of strange diseases fascinated late baroque society in a Central Europe which had suffered the horrors of the Thirty Years' War. Automata and machines such as those it was believed Daedalus had once created exerted their magic.[34] As early as in Paolo Lomazzo's treatise *On the Art of Painting* (1584) artists were urged to make the transition from illusion to seemingly life-like movement.[35] Baroque gardens with their fountains and grottoes were meant to evoke associations with alchemists' caves or kitchens where, it was suspected, homunculi or monsters were being concocted. If the creation of human beings was seemingly feasible, then health too must be well within man's grasp.

As the writings of Johann Valentin Andreae or Heinrich Khunrath demonstrate, secret societies such as the Rosicrucians made provision for vaults and caves which stored the wherewithal deemed necessary for the creation of a healthy new world and society.[36] To be one of the initiated in the Cabbalists' 'hermetic museums' was already considered as being on the path to recovery. Implicit in the search for the *philosopher's stone* was also the search for happiness, fulfilment and physical wellbeing.[37] Robert Fludd (1574–1637), who also influenced Shakespeare, was, with his cosmological visions and speculative models, one of the most prominent representatives of this symbolical, theosophical world.[38]

Astrology too went from strength to strength, and a roaring trade was done in almanacs. In the example of one from Minden 'For the year of our Lord 1687', by Johann Heinrich Voigt, we find the following remarks on autumn: 'One will now see and hear many new mercurialists, not only good, but bad ones too. Those, however, who are very dedicated to their studies, and get weak heads from it, should be more moderate in their studying and speculating, lest a seizure bring them to an all too sudden end.' That a blood-letting calendar was included doubtless boosted the work's circulation. It also listed the days of the patron saints and the various illnesses from which they offered protection, as well as a 'Prognosticon astrologicum', a weather report. 'Dry air' and unhealthy weather were predicted for autumn. The summer would 'heat up many a soul and consume their life energy such that a host of young people as well as old would, after a brief illness, be carried off to the grave. Around St Michael's day, a spate of rapid deaths would bring down many of high estate.' Exotic elixirs concocted by alchemist apothecaries were regarded as a means of protection. In Paris in 1681 the praises were being sung of a preparation which opened the pores and released pathogenic fluids, and an allegedly 400-year-old Venetian by the name of Galdo seemed to be living proof of its efficacy.[39] The church, too, was not slow to disseminate pious works on healthy living. There appeared in Cologne in 1623 Benedictus de Bacquere's *Senum medicus*, which contained similar rules for clergymen. Not only are the health-giving effects of individual foods, fruits and drinks investigated, but also the consequences of anxiety, sadness or insomnia (the memory of the old clerical vice of 'acidia' had clearly not yet faded).[40] The pulse was already considered to be 'morbi et sanitas index'. Significantly, the work, which was basically a recapitulation of the 'six non-naturals', begins like the medieval Lorsch pharmacopoeia with a defence of medicine. It is made clear that doctors ultimately are not able to raise people from the dead, but can only exploit the natural resources at their disposal.

In the newly founded scientific academies, London (1662) or Paris (1666), for instance, collections of machine models and automata soon took on programmatic significance. Descartes, moreover, who by his own admission inclined to melancholy, was governed not only by the world of 'mechanistic' thought. His health-political motto, which took its cue from the principle of *vita solitaria*, was: 'Qui bene vixit, bene latuit'.[41] In Cesare Ripa's *Iconologia*, which was reprinted several times in the seventeenth century, health (*sanitas*) was still portrayed in heavily symbolical fashion as a mature woman with a rooster and a snake, with the rooster representing the patient's attention to dietetics, and the snake the wisdom of the doctor.

In the sixteenth and seventeenth centuries the extent to which 'love sickness' might be ruinous to health was still a serious topic of discussion. While the Basel town doctor Felix Platter had suggested treating the heartache of the love-sick according to Galen's principle of 'contraria contrariis', and advised them if possible to transform their love into hate in order to put an end to the 'arousal of the spirit and the juices', the deliberations of many scholars were directed to the danger of the love-spell (*philtron*), which was suspected to be at the root of many passionate love affairs.[42] On the other hand, according to the dissertation by the Wittenberg doctor Johannes Gröllmann (1683), the 'philtra vera' were absolutely necessary for the maintenance of human health. Not infrequently, the influence of witches and demons, too, was detected behind the dangerous love potions which robbed people of their reason. But if illnesses could be attributed to the influence of sorcery then, according to the Marburg iatrochemist Jakob Waldschmitt (1644–1689), it could also be used to remove them.[43]

From the end of the sixteenth century are found – in both Catholic and Protestant areas – increasing instances of trials for soothsaying, magic, sorcery and witchcraft. Undoubtedly, fear was growing about all manner of threats to health. Since, according to the thesis of Brian Levack, in an (early) Enlightenment society 'those who felt threatened by a suspected witch could no longer, at least in Protestant areas, make the sign of the cross, sprinkle holy water on their houses, hang up medals of the saints or perform many of the protective rituals that Europeans had traditionally employed when threatened with diabolical power', from 1600 witch hunts were often reinforced and complemented with 'rational' arguments.[44]

Van Helmont, Sylvius and other 'iatrochemists'

As already mentioned, not all doctors in the century ushered in by Galileo and Kepler were devotees of fashionable Cartesianism. However, Johann Baptist van Helmont (1577–1644), the founder of *iatrochemistry* (probably under the influence of Paracelsus), propagated the view in 1648 in his posthumously edited *Ortus medicinae* that the 'medieval' worship of Aristotle had blocked medical progress for long enough. Many believed that the time had come to 'decipher' the 'book of nature', and with it the secrets of the body.[45] Even if the new discoveries in physiology initially had hardly any dietetic consequences, most doctors, but also lawyers and philosophers, were fascinated by the *lex naturae* (Kepler).[46] Van Helmont distinguished between the *archaeus influus*, a force or soul which endowed the *whole* body with health, and an *archaeus insitus*, which gave the individual parts of the body their function and mobility.[47] The 'archaei' sustain life by inducing chemical processes. They are tools of nature which breathe life into all being, for instance, plants, baths, salts, water or medicaments. Health disorders may be attributable to disarray among the 'archaei' caused by the *hospes ignotus*, mysterious external influences.

Since the 'archaeus' comes from God, and is to be understood as a religious principle, healing must be a solely spiritual process.[48] Illnesses are no longer considered to be the result of imbalances but possess an *essentia* all of their own which is induced by a 'seed' and can be conquered by activating the 'archaeus'. Recovery is possible because the idea contained within the 'archaeus' fights against that within the illness, and that within the remedy – whether plant, drug, healing stones or magical means – supports the process of recovery.[49] Fever, cramps, trembling, cloudy urine, and so on, provide evidence of the reaction of the 'archaeus' and are therefore to be interpreted positively.[50] Van Helmont also accepted Paracelsus' idea of mercury, sulphur and salt as the three elements of life.[51] The *gas vitale* is the substance which nourishes the vital spirits, a kind of balsam which 'protects from decay'.

Recuperation thus appears to be a multifaceted process. For van Helmont it is above all the soul which is of central importance as the life-sustaining principle.[52] Its stability is therefore necessary, not least to secure health against the danger of 'imaginations': merely the fear of the plague can induce infection. Interesting, furthermore, is that, for the 'Faust of the seventeenth century', spirit (*mens*) is far superior to parasitic (!) reason (*ratio*): 'Reason is radically different from truth. It has merely brought the doctors to the point where they no longer heal, but merely talk.'[53]

The 'iatrochemist' François de la Boe (Sylvius) (1614–1672), on the other hand, defined health as the correct balance between alkalis and acids in the body, with mechanistic concepts also playing a part. The life function constitutes a chemical process ('fermentation'). Its physiological end products are acidic and alkaline substances which are a direct measure of health.[54] In order to avoid the dangerous *acrimoniae* which can damage the organs, acidity must be counteracted by alkaline solution, and alkaline solution by acidity. As the principle of life Sylvius postulates a 'vital fire', which can be regulated by breathing and be measured by the pulse.[55] Health was degraded to a matter of optimal acid base ratio, the soul dismissed from the care of the doctor.

The theory of the Wittenberg doctor Daniel Sennert (1572–1637) represented a bridge between iatrochemistry and humoral pathology. 'Medicine is the art', declared the author of *Institutiones medicinae*,

> of, if possible, preserving or restoring man's health . . . to be able to judge his condition, the doctor must first of all know what conforms to and what contradicts the laws of nature. The criterion for health cannot be sought in the soul, since it remains unchanged in sickness and in health. Only the condition of the organs and the bodily fluids as well as the functions of the body can indicate the state of health.

In this, controlling characteristics are attributed to the soul, over the influence of which, however, 'doctors are not at one with the philosophers'. The former 'characterize the soul in a general way', the latter 'attribute to it a vegetating, discerning, intellectual and activating capacity.' In the case of 'warm' illnesses Sennert recommends cooling foods such as mint, absinthe, red roses, nutmeg, aloe or sugar, and for memory disorders mixtures of wine in order to counteract the 'coolness and dryness of the head'. With both medicaments and food the old principle of 'contraria contrariis' comes into play.

It is hardly surprising that, in the seventeenth century, consideration was given for the first time to the idea of a state-organized health system. For one thing, mechanics, chemistry and reason formed a seductive invitation to redefine the idea of the perfect, 'healthy' body politic. Admittedly, ever since the Middle Ages – one thinks here of the medical ordinances of Friedrich II of Hohenstaufen (1231) or the numerous edicts issued in times of plague[56] – there had been repeated examples of official regulation. However, writings such as the *Politia medica* by the Frankfurt city doctor Ludwig Hörnigk (1600–1667) propagated the idea of a comprehensive municipal hygiene which – so ran his suggestion – was to be supported at 'all the courts of the land' by a sizeable administrative apparatus. In his *Teutscher Fürsten Staat [German Princes' State]* of 1665, which had as its theme the healthy growth of the population, Veit Ludwig von Seckendorff (1626–1692) argued a similar case, as did the doctor, alchemist and economist Johann Joachim Becher in his work of 1672 dedicated to Leopold I of Austria – *Politischer Discurs von den eigentlichen Ursachen des Auf- und Abnehmens der Städte, Länder und Republiken, in specie wie ein Land volckreich und nahrhafft zu machen, und in eine rechte soci- etatem civilem zu bringen [Political Discourse on the Real Causes of the Growth and Demise of the Towns, Lands and Republics, in specie how a Country may Successfully Nourish its Populace and be Brought to the Condition of a Civil Society].* Demands are made for a sub- stantial administration not only as protection against 'secret and public enemies', but also to maintain and promote the 'health of the subjects'.[57] In vague allusion to classical traditions – Plato or Pliny, for instance – the anatomy and mechanics of the body were considered to be models for the state system.

Around 1700 the name Galen had become a term of abuse for many doctors. The four-humour doctrine, *eucrasia*, the therapeutic effect of balance and harmony, as well as the culture of the 'six non-naturals', provoked little more than a contemptuous smile from most Cartesians. With reference to Hippocrates, however, Galenist practice continued for some time. It also played a role in herbals and other popular books on health. For want of satisfactory scientific explana- tions, and despite Logau's previously mentioned dictum, the concept of the golden mean continued to exert a secret fascination.

Doctrines of health in England – the dietetics of the state

A strong advocate of the 'organism of the state' was James Harrington (1611–1677), author of the utopian treatise dedicated to Oliver Cromwell entitled *The Commonwealth of Oceana* (1656), which argues a robust case for the old analogy between body and state. Unrest, turmoil, injustice are seen as disruptions to the health of the commonwealth, and the people at times must take revolutionary steps to heal themselves and 'become their own politicians, as certain beasts when they are sick become their own physicians and are carried by a natural instinct unto the desire of such herbs as are their proper cure.'[58] Harrington was also a convinced champion of state care and supervision in the field of health. Shortly after, William Petty (1623–1687) drew up health legislation along the lines of anatomy and mechanics. He reformed military and public hospitals, made proposals for a reorganization of the study of medicine, and argued that doctors – like judges or soldiers – should be employed by the state.[59] In the introduction to his monumental work on the circulation of the blood, *Exercitatio anatomica de motu cordis et sanguinis in animalibus* (1628), William Harvey, in order to emphasize the parallels between the body and the state, characteristically described the English king as the 'heart of the state'. It was above all the philosopher Thomas Hobbes (1588–1679), however, who derived his images of the state of the healthy community from anatomy: bodily health corresponded in the public realm to 'concord', sickness to 'sedition', while the death of the individual was equated with the repercussions of civil war. Political upheavals were reminiscent of a 'malaria sickness', tax debts evoked 'pleuritis' of the *res republica*. Hobbes was also the first to invest the word 'parasite' with a political meaning.[60] It was the age in which – following the example of the Italian art historian Francesco Scannelli of Forlí, in *Il microcosmo della pittura* (1657) – even famous painters, or styles, were associated with particular bodily organs: Raphael with the liver, Titian with the heart, Corregio with the brain. Even the study of art was pursued with physiological arguments.

Particularly in England, books on macrobiotics and maintaining good health enjoyed great popularity. Along with Henry Cuffe's *Differences* (1607), there appeared in London in 1620 the treatise *Via recta ad vitam longam* by the doctor Tobias Venner (1577–1660), which, as the author explained, contained 'a broad philosophical discourse on the nature, possibilities, consequences of all such things as nourishment and its influence on health, with its correct application for every age, every bodily constitution, and for every season.' Dietetics and lifestyle are central themes in the treatise since, Venner maintains, they are of the utmost importance to people who are 'by nature weakly and not of sound bodily disposition'.

The English (and European) doctrine of health took particular stimulus in the seventeenth century from Robert Burton (1577–1640), and his *The Anatomy of Melancholy* (1621). A scholar at Christ

Church College, Oxford, Burton attributed responsibility for the state of melancholy – as had Aristotle before him – to a wide variety of causes. Insofar as it was not a case of punishment inflicted by God, or the consequence of unfavourable astrological constellations, 'The heavens . . . with their comets, stars, planets',[61] factors such as age, heredity, poor nutrition, fear, envy, covetousness, ambition, love of learning, but also social reasons such as poverty, were seen as causes. An immaterial 'pathogenic matter' which 'works together, in a negative way', with the vital spirits is thought to increase 'black bile'. By means of its purifying effect, however, blood-letting, for example, of varicose veins or haemorrhoids, expels the melancholic ills. 'I write of melancholy, by being busy to avoid melancholy', the author confesses candidly.[62]

His verdict on intellectuals – scholars and students – was harsh: they are invariably plagued by melancholy: 'Tis a common moll unto them all, and almost in some measure an inseparable companion', he notes, using an observation of Marsilio Ficino here to describe their mental state, and recalling in the process Varro's description of philosophers as 'sad and austere'.[63] Studying, as Machiavelli had noted, 'weakens their bodies, dulls the spirits, abates their strength and courage.'[64] Burton gave further reasons why scholars were more subject to this malady than others. 'The one is, they live a sedentary, solitary life, *sibi et musis* [for themselves and their studies], free from bodily exercise, and those ordinary disports which other men use . . .; but the common cause is overmuch study.' In view of this, a certain Johannes Voschius 'would have good scholars to be highly rewarded, and had in some extraordinary respect above other men, to have greater privileges than the rest, that adventure themselves and abbreviate their lives for the public good.'[65]

In view of the fluid boundaries between sickness and health, the concept of 'normality' propagated by the iatromechanics seemed questionable to Burton. Furthermore, he did not exclude metaphysical causes for disruptions to health, whether of a psychological or a physical nature: 'General causes are either supernatural or natural. Supernatural are from God and His angels, or by God's permission from the devil and his ministers. That God Himself is a cause for the punishment of sin, and satisfaction of His justice, many examples and testimonies of holy Scriptures make evident unto us.'[66] Above all, it was their lifestyle which made Europeans sick: 'To see the [unhappy rivalry] of our times, a man bend all his forces, means, time, fortunes, to be a favourite's favourite's favourite, etc., a parasite's parasite's parasite, that may scorn the servile world as having enough already.'[67] Burton's social criticism was not free of intellectual arrogance, but it delivered an excellent psychograph of English society before the 'Glorious Revolution' (1648). Like Cornaro or Hutten before him, he was unsparing in his moral side-swipes. 'A true saying it is, *Plures crapula quam gladius*, this gluttony kills more than the sword, this *omnivorans et homicida gula*, this all-devouring and murdering gut.'[68]

Burton considered illness in terms of breakdown: 'For what is sickness, but as Gregory Tholosanus defines it, "a dissolution or perturbation of the bodily league, which health combines".'[69] History, he maintained, and all its heroes, bore testament to the eternal madness of human behaviour, which was why health and the renunciation of arrogant self-deception must almost inevitably remain an unattainable goal. He points to the observation of the sixteenth-century doctor and writer Paulus Jovius that the enormous consumption of meat in the northern countries was not a sign of generous hospitality, but of a 'riot in excess, gluttony and prodigality', which 'brings in . . . hereditary diseases, consumes their fortunes, and overthrows the good temperature of their bodies'.[70] Burton pleads nonetheless for a more just form of state, and more efficient government. As with Harrington and Petty, welfare and health became a political programme. A prerequisite of this was that people should marry and procreate, with the exception, however, of those who were 'dismembered, or grievously deformed, infirm, or visited with some enormous hereditary disease in body or mind'.[71] Marriage and procreation of the beautiful were more desirable, it would seem, than the propagation of the ugly.

Health, according to Burton, can also be determined by individual disposition.

> As Levinus Lemnius farther adds, old men beget most part wayward, peevish, sad, melancholy sons, and seldom merry. He that begets a child on a full stomach will either have a sick child or a crazed son (as Cardan thinks), or if the parents be sick, or have any great pain of the head, or megrim, headache . . ., or if a drunken man get a child, it will never likely have a good brain.

He recalls Plutarch's observation that 'one drunkard begets another', noting that 'foolish, drunken, or harebrain women most part bring forth children like unto themselves.'[72] *The Anatomy of Melancholy* offers a delightful picture of seventeenth-century English society. In targeting its eccentric and fashionable self-help therapies, Burton warns particularly against the damaging effects of 'artificial evacuations' and 'blood-letting, purging, unseasonably and immoderately used'. They have, he notes, the effect of hot-houses and baths and – quoting Montanus (the Paduan doctor Giovanni Battista del Monte) – 'they over-heat the liver'.[73]

The theory of health proposed by Thomas Willis (1621–1675), professor of natural philosophy at Oxford, was shaped by various 'iatrochemical' but also Paracelsian ideas. The royalist doctor regarded health as the consequence of optimal *fermentations*,[74] and was close to the 'Spagyrics', who based their beliefs on Paracelsus and used chemical instead of plant remedies. 'It pleases me', he notes, 'to give my sentence for the Chymists . . . affirming all bodies to consist of spirit, sulphur, salt, water and earth.'[75] Willis explains the old experience that climate, the seasons, constitution, or the composition of the air influence health by the fact that they change the chemical constitution of the blood and induce a sour or bitterly caustic mood.[76] He also attaches importance to 'Hippocratic' therapies or treatments such as emetics, laxatives, antipyretics, purgatives, blood-letting, and aids to digestion and sleep as ways of maintaining good health. They cleanse the blood of harmful substances, he explains, and prevent a surplus of the principal chemical elements. Precious stones are also thought to have a therapeutic use.

Willis recognized that scurvy was the result of a nutritional deficiency, without being able, however, to define the clinical picture. He discovered that the consumption of salted and smoked foods, meat, wine and brandy encouraged the disease, whereas people who lived off milk, unripe fruits and similar 'absurda' remained largely free of it.[77] Like Burton, he did not question the notion that illness came from the devil, and that exorcism was therefore an effective method of healing.[78] Willis ultimately came to the conclusion that excessive ambition and stress in his profession, as well as aggravation 'within his own Faculty', had undoubtedly shortened his life, and furthermore 'principally for the sake of Mammon'.[79]

Thomas Sydenham (1624–1689), who systematically put the new empiricism into medical practice, became even more famous. Like van Helmont before him, the London medical practitioner viewed disease as 'nothing else than the effort of Nature endeavouring with might and main the expulsion of the morbific matter for the health of the sick person.'[80] Above all, he regarded fever as an effective means whereby the body fights disease. Like Hippocrates (with whom he was soon being compared – he was described as the 'English Hippocrates'),[81] but also most of the Cartesians, he was a persistent advocate of nature as a curative force, urging doctor and patient alike to respect its healing potential. Trusting, or as Sydenham put it, 'joining hands with Nature', was a common denominator of many contemporary theories of health.[82] Even conservative authors such as John Twysden (*b.* 1607), who, despite his enthusiasm for 'mathematical' medicine, defended 'the old methods and rules', saw here a link between the various theories.[83]

Along with drugs such as quinine (whose therapeutic use he was one of the first to recognize), Sydenham did not hesitate to recommend to his sick and ailing contemporaries fresh air, gymnastics, a reduced food intake, mineral-water cures, and a balanced lifestyle. A policy of careful non-intervention always seemed to him more promising than aggressive treatments (in an age where the prescription of enormous amounts of medicines and miracle potions was coming into fashion, this wasn't always a self-evident approach).[84] He advised his friend the ailing philosopher John Locke to take easily digestible meals, give up wine, and adopt a natural way of life. Such advice depended on the individual condition of the patients, which he compared with the typical course and characteristics of the disease he had observed from experience.[85] Following the example of a treatise of 1650 by his fellow countryman Glisson on the *English disease*, rickets, Sydenham, too, described in the *chorea minor* of 1686 an illness which was the result of poverty and deprivation and could therefore be prevented.[86]

John Locke (1632–1704), tutor to the English philosopher Anthony Ashley Cooper, third earl of Shaftesbury (1671–1713), also devoted considerable attention to health provision in his *Some Thoughts Concerning Education* (1693). The best education, he maintained, had Juvenal's old ideal of 'mens sana in corpore sano' as its goal. A small number of people might achieve this 'sound mind in a sound body' thanks to their 'natural genius', but 'of all the men we meet with nine parts of ten are what they are . . . by their education.'[87] Locke explains what 'parents, without the help of physic, should do for the preservation and improvement of a healthy, or at least not sickly, constitution in their children.'[88] He thought it dangerous to soften and spoil them, for instance with too warm clothing or too little exercise. Fresh air, rustic habits, loose rather than the tightly laced-up clothing which was then fashionable for small children, a simple and reduced diet with sparing use of salt, sugar and seasoning, and eating only when hungry were the basis of an optimally healthy upbringing. Contrary to Hippocratic doctrine, Locke advocated irregular mealtimes in order to prevent the child's stomach from expecting 'victuals' at specific times.[89] Children should go to bed betimes and rise early so that they 'avoid the unhealthy and unsafe hours of debauchery, which are those of the evenings'.[90] He attaches particular importance to bowel regularity, and diarrhoea and constipation are equally harmful: 'Because, whenever Men have leisure to eat, they have leisure enough also to make so much court to Madam *Cloacina*, as would be necessary to our present purpose.' 'What concerns the body and health', he notes elsewhere, 'reduces itself to these few and easy observable rules: plenty of open air, exercise and sleep, plain diet, no wine or strong drink, and very little or no physic, not too warm and strait clothing, especially the head and feet kept cold, and the feet often used to cold water and exposed to wet.'[91]

Recreation, toughening the body, punishments and rewards, sport, intellectual work, pleasure in activity – all shape the fitness of the budding gentleman. As Locke put it: 'How necessary health is to our business and happiness, and how requisite a strong constitution, able to endure hardships and fatigue, is to one that will make any figure in the world, is too obvious to need any proof.'[92]

Despite all these enlightened trends, the phenomenon of sickness and the desire for health remained rooted more in theology and faith than is generally recognized. For the majority of scientists from Descartes to Haller it was beyond dispute that God could at any point disrupt the workings of the clock.[93] The Cartesian concept of nature was 'still imbued with a great religious impulse'; it was still believed that in the 'laws of nature' there could be found 'traces of godliness'. Ever more central in this respect was the issue of the soul, whose immortality was questioned by many interpreters of Descartes, albeit not by the master himself. This seems less surprising when one considers that van Helmont, for instance, supposed that it was located in the pylorus of the stomach.[94] An additional factor specific to England was that the Anglican church was opposed to traditional Catholic healing practices such as pilgrimages or the use of holy spring water, and condemned 'Catholic' as well as 'mechanistic' paths to health.[95]

Health through planning – the utopias

It cannot be stressed too often that the most diverse doctrines of health, of which Cartesianism was only one variant, were vying with each other in Europe around 1700.[96] Bernard Mandeville (1670–1733), social critic and doctor to the poor, expressed surprise at the rivalries and wide variety of paths to health and wellbeing propagated among and within the universities. In view of the backwardness of these institutions, he declared that health provision should be a task primarily for the state: 'Where things are well organized, hospitals are of equal benefit for the further development of students of the medical arts . . . as for the restoration of the health of the poor.'[97] In future, he maintained, the authorities should take responsibility for individual as well as general health care – a process which would find its provisional culmination (before 1817) in Johann Peter Frank's *Medizinische Polizey [Medical Police]*.[98]

The apologists for a 'mechanistic' view of society were faced particularly with the political and health consequences caused by the division of the healing profession into academic, increasingly Cartesian or 'iatrochemically' oriented doctors, whose clientele was to a greater extent limited to the upper class and the holders of public office, and practical, skilled empiricists whose 'target group' embraced all social groups. To this day, traces of this dichotomy between academic practitioners and down-to-earth doctors more in tune with the needs of the patient can be found in routine medical practice. Writers such as Molière (1622–1673), in his play *Le Malade imaginaire*, for instance, satirized in inimitable fashion the weaknesses, pomposity and affectation of many academic doctors.

In *Gulliver's Travels*, Jonathan Swift (1667–1745) depicted both the bright and the dark side of health, but also the necessity for provision and control. On the island of the Houyhnhnms, a race of rational, healthy, beautiful and well-bred horses rules over a degenerate people, the Yahoos. Gulliver, an enlightened doctor educated in Leiden, recognizes that the health of the Houyhnhnms is the result of an extensive policy of eugenics and education. No infringement of these principles is tolerated, and, correspondingly, everyone has a public duty to exercise self-control. People marry for convenience, not for love, and generally die – the positive consequence of a life governed by reason – of old age, not as a result of accidents.[99] The brutish Yahoos, on the other hand, lead unregulated lives in thrall to unbridled desires and passions. They are repulsive and prone to disease. Since, however, they are in tune with nature, they manage to survive, deriving a certain regenerative strength from this proximity to the natural world. It is at this point that Swift's criticism of civilization begins. Gulliver tells the leader of the Houyhnhnms how the Europeans eat without feeling hungry, drink without feeling thirsty, and, in order to numb their senses, consume drugs and spices, tea and coffee which are imported from distant lands under the most hazardous of circumstances, and how they love to intoxicate themselves with alcohol. In his home country there are, he says, 500 to 600 diseases which threaten all parts of the body, and there exists a strange class of healers who claim to have the remedies for a multitude of illnesses.

For Gulliver, health has nothing to do with a lost paradise or a gift from God. It is simply the fruit of well-considered effort and lifestyle, with nature serving as a catalyst.[100] Characteristic here are the eugenic principles of the Houyhnhnms: 'In their marriages they are exactly careful to choose such colours as will not make any disagreeable mixture in the breed. Strength is chiefly valued in the male, and comeliness in the female; not upon the account of love, but to preserve the race from degeneration.' But they also ensure that they produce only one of each sex 'to prevent the country from being overburthened with numbers'. The inferior Yahoos, however, are not restricted in this way: 'these are allowed to produce three of each sex, to be domestics in the noble families.'[101] The Houyhnhnms also take care,

> to train up their youth to strength, speed, and hardiness, by exercising them in running races up and down steep hills, and over hard stoney grounds; and when they are all in a sweat, they are ordered to leap over head and ears into a pond or river. Four times a year the youth of a certain district meet to show their proficiency in running and leaping, and other feats of strength and agility.[102]

Gulliver's Travels was part of a tradition, particularly in vogue in the seventeenth century, of utopian views of the state which gave broad scope for health planning. *Citta del sole*, by the previously mentioned Dominican monk Tommaso Campanella (1568–1639), which was written in prison in Naples in 1602 and published in Frankfurt in 1623, envisaged a philosopher king in the Platonic sense supported by a triumvirate of 'intellectual' princes who would make provision for civic health. As in Francis Bacon's *Nova Atlantis* (which appeared posthumously in 1627), and the Swabian rose breeder Johann Valentin Andreae's *Res publica Christianopolitana* (1619), which offers an outline for an ideal Christian state, optimal social and political conditions are the crucial prerequisites for civic health. Baths, hygienic living conditions, gardens and parks, artificial ventilation, water provision and heating all serve the 'salubritas publica', but the individual as well. In the work by Campanella, who, like Thomas More, sees private property as the cause of countless health and social problems and argues for its abolition ('Nihil usquam privati est'), we even find the description of a cleverly devised sewage treatment and disposal system.[103] Cattle are slaughtered outside the towns and are cleansed of blood and dirt by running water. Within the town walls medicinal herb gardens have been created. They give off a pleasant smell, and also serve to purify the air. For the same reason, cremation, which in the seventeenth century was rejected by the church and widely scorned, is in *Citta del sole* the norm.

For most Utopians, eugenics, the conscious planning, even organization, of healthy offspring, is viewed as a precondition of the public good. In Campanella's *Citta del sole* the authorities decide where and when who sleeps with whom.[104] Coitus, the time for which is determined by astrologists and doctors, is only allowed after an adequate period of digestion. 'It is customary to pray beforehand, and there are fine statues of famous men for the women to look at.' Shapely and beautiful girls are paired with 'great and diligent' men, obese ones on the other hand with thin men to produce a balance.[105] The woman has to be at least eighteen, the man twenty-one. Older women and a *maestro maggiore*, who is 'a great doctor and answerable to *Amor*', ensure that these regulations are observed. Civic morality, however, is of general concern; for reasons of propriety, only children are allowed to bathe in public!

Like Swift's Houyhnhnms, the inhabitants of the *Citta del sole* are scathing about other countries which devote great attention to the breeding of dogs and horses but neglect their own offspring. The head physician also issues the cooks with dietetic instructions, giving particular consideration to the needs of the sick or pregnant. Proper nourishment and an 'arcanum ad renovandam vitam' ensure that people live to be a hundred or even two hundred years old. If, as a result of their astrological constellation, certain people are threatened by illness, they are, for preventive purposes, locked in a white house full of pleasant odours, the surroundings of which are disinfected by fire.[106]

In Thomas More's celebrated *Utopia*, even euthanasia is practised:

But if, besides being incurable, the disease also causes excruciating pain, some priests and government officials visit the person concerned, and say something like this: 'Let's face it, you'll never be able to live a normal life. You're just a nuisance to other people and a burden to yourself – in fact you're really leading a sort of posthumous existence. So why go on feeding germs? Since your life's a misery to you, why hesitate to die? You're imprisoned in a torture chamber – why don't you break out and escape to a better world? Or say the word, and we'll arrange for your release.'[107]

In view of social pressure such as this which even encourages *active* euthanasia, it is hardly surprising that the utopians 'attach great value to special natural gifts such as beauty, strength, and agility.'[108] By way of contrast, the Pietist Andreae demanded that the community be charitable towards 'those to whom nature had been a stepmother'.[109] Bacon too described the necessity for hospitals and places of quarantine of sufficient capacity to deal with any catastrophic plague. The plethora of utopian works written in the wake of Thomas More demonstrates increasing dissatisfaction with outmoded social forms and values without, however, their having any chance of being realized *in toto*. The advantage of experience which we contemporary readers have over the utopians may cause us to shudder and to think more of Aldous Huxley and the abuses of the twentieth century than of liberation and enlightenment. In fact, More and Campanella gave us nothing less than the vision of an early surveillance state. To the utopians – as the Dominican Campanella emphasized – health seemed attainable by reason working in harmony with nature, which, nevertheless, did not exclude the existence of 'secret remedies for the preservation of vigour, health, and strength'.

The utopians promoted the notion that health could be regulated through reason. It was a smooth transition to the utilitarianism of a Jeremy Bentham (1748–1832) or a John Stuart Mill (1806–1873). The shadow could also be detected here of Jean-Baptiste Colbert (1619–1683), whose doctrine of *dirigiste* state control proposed that the idea of a community organized down to the last detail should apply equally to the health sector.[110] Bentham believed that the object of all legislation should be the 'greatest happiness of the greatest number'. Man's desire for happiness, health, and wellbeing was bound up ever more closely with the hedonistic striving of the community for 'welfare', a concept, however, which relegated those who were sickly or were, 'by nature', handicapped, to a prison-like 'Panopticon', which was privately run on commercial lines.[111] In his *Essai physique sur l'économie animale* (1747), François Quesnay (1694–1774), personal physician to Madame Pompadour, proposed that a free economic cycle was most conducive to the health of society, as well as to the optimal development of the individual, whose social value consisted mainly in his capacity for work, which was, in turn, dependent on his state of health. The *physiocrats* demanded that society be viewed in 'natural' rather than 'moral' terms. They therefore rejected state control and regulation along the lines of the utopians, and demanded, for instance, that the insane should be integrated into society (by means of organized, albeit reduced work), and evaluated sickness and health purely in terms of their effect on the general good of the community.[112]

The dietetics of the Enlightenment – philosophers, pedagogues, charlatans

Many seventeenth-century philosophers and doctors anticipated the theories of the Enlightenment. Suggestions for the state control of health, such as had been voiced by Burton, Hobbes and Locke, gained ever increasing currency. No less a figure than Leibniz (1646–1716), in his *Directiones ad rem medicam pertinentes* (1670), welcomed the new developments, which promised a complex improvement in individual as well as collective health. Leibniz demanded that every citizen should undergo a 'health confession' several times a year which would be modelled on the religious confession and come with a free choice of medical 'father confessor'. Instead of a penance, 'maxims for healthy living' would be imposed.[113] Taking account of each individual biography, special 'societies' would have to help people draw up a 'natural history' of their lives. Like Locke, Leibniz had in mind primarily the general good, which seemed to him to be the precondition for *individual* health. Like Swift he bemoaned the 'negligible attention that people give to health' and confronted the fatalistic attitude of the masses with the idea of a 'programme for life'. 'In many cases our sufferings could quite readily be eased if a physics or medicine – I make no mention here of other skills – of a preventive kind could be set up.' In all of this, it falls to the doctors to supervise how people lead their lives, to keep a check on foodstuffs, to record their experiences with respect to climate and certain other environmental factors, to conduct trials and mass screenings, and to advise governments. Leibniz also modifies Descartes' theory of the relationship between body and soul. The monad determining the individual is neither 'res cogitans', nor 'res extensa', but an *entelechy* freed of all materiality.[114] 'The body belonging to a Monad (which is its entelechy or its soul) constitutes along with the entelechy what may be called a living being, and along with the soul what is called an animal.'[115] The body, however, remains 'a kind of divine machine or natural automaton, which infinitely surpasses all artificial automata'.[116]

There is a discussion down to the last detail of the structures of a health police, whose medical members are never allowed to accept presents and – along the lines of an integral medicine – who have to provide for the welfare and health of the entire body politic together with all its citizens. With Leibniz and his pupil Christian Wolff (1679–1754), whose programmatic and pioneering work *Vernünftige Gedanken vom gesellschaftlichen Leben der Menschen und in Sonderheit dem gemeinen Wesen zur Beförderung der Glückseligkeit des menschlichen Geschlechtes* [*Sensible Thoughts on the Social Life of Man and in Particular on Furthering the Happiness of the Human Race*] was published in 1721, philosophy became a 'physical and psychological' doctrine which now applied itself to (previously disdained) practical matters such as baby care, nutrition, sexual practice, gymnastics, and other dietetic topics.[117]

Around 1700 a nature-oriented health education replaced the worldly and sensual lifestyle of the baroque princes. Even concerned peers reproached the nobility for its decadence, enfeeblement, profligacy, moral degeneracy and – depending on their ideological position – atheism. Jovellanos, minister of justice under Charles VI of Spain and member of the Council of Seville, describes a typical grandee as follows: 'He led a dissolute life, gambled, dissipating both his health and fortune. He was of barely forty summers when the hand of pleasure pushed him into the grave.' Ever more frequently, courtly fashions were subjected to ridicule, while the image of the peasant labouring at the heart of nature was juxtaposed with that of the sexually promiscuous nobleman riddled with venereal disease.[118] Montesquieu, who was also much concerned with physiological questions, was of the opinion that luxury was 'at odds with the spirit of self-discipline'.[119]

The Lippe-Detmold court doctor Johann Christian Scherf (1750–1818) propagated the idea of a public health education free of outmoded concepts and practices. In his *Beyträge zum Archiv der medizinischen Polizey und der Volksarzneykunde* [*Contributions to the Archive of the Medical Police and of Popular Pharmacology*] of 1790, he emphasized: 'Needless to say, I understand health to be not the absence of actual diseases, but a person's overall physical strength and capacities at their highest point of perfection.' To achieve this state Scherf demanded that 'popular pharmacology' should be made a required school subject. 'Every improvement of human kind' must, he maintained, 'begin with young people'. In accordance with the 'philanthropic' education plans typical of the time, young persons were instructed in 'what they themselves must do for their health, and without which even medical provision would be in vain. This can easily be brought under the two headings of: wise behaviour in healthy times to maintain one's health, and wise behaviour at times of sickness in order to restore it.' The strongest of warnings is delivered against quacks and 'the most dangerous consequences of their foolishness'. Twentieth-century commentators have identified a 'medicalization' of society in these developments.

As a consequence of the problematic variety of medical concepts and doctrines of health, everyday medical life around and after 1700 was determined by a multitude of different healers. Soothsayers, faith healers, miracle workers, spiritualists, exorcists or 'wise women', herbalists, sorcerers, and specialists in the occult such as Cagliostro held out the promise of good health, while Cabbalists, chemists, Paracelsians and Rosicrucians offered explanations which they kept deliberately obscure. The Mannheim doctor and Enlightenment philosopher Franz Anton Mai commented in mocking fashion on the situation around 1800:

> Forsooth, how droll and edifying in future must be the bedside consultations of these natural philosophers and neo-chemical doctors when they squabble à la Theophrastus Paracelsus over their life factors and polarities, their oxygen and nitrogen, their oxidizing and non-oxidizing and, with the scornful laughter of the immortal Molière ringing in their ears, finally transform the primeval factors of life in their sick patient into a well-spiced Egyptian mummy, or give them over to the process of putrefaction. Oh Enlightenment! Oh century of natural philosophy! Sacred Hippocrates and Boerhaave, have mercy on these the wretched sick.

The French Revolution too had to confront this problem. After the recruitment of many doctors through the *levée en masse* (1793), the Directory warned in 1795 against the residue of charlatans who remained: 'The public is the victim of a horde of barely trained individuals who have declared themselves masters of the art and who are distributing medicines at random and jeopardizing the lives of thousands of citizens.'[120]

Even before the revolution, many people's view of the world had been shaken by social changes. According to Ariès, the old family structure was collapsing; the child, for instance, was losing its traditional role as a 'little adult'. The 'invention of childhood' shattered the old living, working and learning community which was under the control of the father of the house, and whose members were distributed between the home, place of work, and school. It was now inevitable that various bodies would come to take responsibility for their wellbeing, and that the state itself should also become aware of its obligations.[121] The education of the young was no longer a matter for the family. In Mannheim the wife of the elector herself, in cooperation with doctors, organized 'pedagogic' children's festivals aimed not only at warning children but also at convincing parents of the need to carry out their pedagogic and hygienic obligations.[122]

In Stettin in 1647, the doctor Georg Kirstein was already giving lessons on hygiene in schools, and in Palatinate Bavaria in 1782 and Nuremberg in 1793 there appeared, respectively, the volumes *Gesundheitsregeln* [*Rules for Health*] and *Gesundheitslehre für Kinder* [*Hygiene for Children*]. Bernhard Christian Faust, court counsellor and physician in Schaumburg-Lippe, produced in 1794 a *Gesundheits-Katechismus zum Gebrauche in den Schulen und beym häuslichen Unterrichte* [*a Catechism of Health for Use in Schools and Instruction at Home*], which by 1802 had already gone to a ninth edition.[123] Man's most noble strivings serve his wellbeing, which is described as follows: 'The man who is healthy feels strong, full of life and energy; he enjoys his food and drink, and is impervious to wind and weather; exercise and work never pall, and he feels well in himself.' On a trip to Switzerland, Faust had got to know the Enlightenment thinker and Lausanne physician Tissot and, more importantly, Rousseau's philosophy of nature.[124] Since man was unable to restore his original state of nature, those conditions deleterious to health had to be counteracted by perfecting the art of living one's life.[125] Faust's *health compass* consisted of questions and answers, and claimed 'to show people the way to live'. The following is an extract from this didactic text, constructed in the form of a dialogue:

> Since staying healthy is the most precious thing in life, what obligations does man have with respect to his own good health? – He must seek to preserve it. – Is it sufficient for man to look to his own health? – No, it is also his duty to look to the life and health of his fellows. – Is it sufficient that you comprehend this lesson, and commit it to memory? – No, we must also follow it in our daily lives. – How long should man live? – Life is the good gift of God, and man should therefore live long, and to a great age. – How long should man remain healthy? – He should, if free of irksome illnesses, remain healthy and well throughout almost the whole of his life. – How must parents be constituted who wish to have virtuous and healthy children? – They must themselves be virtuous and healthy. – How could men once again become strong? – By a sensible education and way of life. – What must one know, therefore, to educate man in a sensible way? – The nature and order which God invested in man.

Whereas Kant, in 1784, had produced the formulation 'Enlightenment is man's release from his self-incurred tutelage',[126] Johann Karl Osterhausen's *Über medizinische Aufklärung* [*On Medical Enlightenment*], which appeared in Zurich in 1798, began with the sentence: '*Medical* enlightenment is man's release from his self-incurred tutelage in matters which concern his physical wellbeing.' The author recommended 'educated habits' with regard to eating and drinking, light and air, work and recreation, sleeping and waking, sex, passions and pleasures.[127] By implication, such demands were, without doubt, politically extremely explosive since, for many people, their realization was impossible.

Luther himself – and this was not without importance for Protestant, Enlightenment thinkers – had interpreted the 'daily bread' mentioned in the Lord's Prayer as embracing 'everything which belongs to the nourishment and necessities of life, such as eating, drinking, clothes, shoes, house, farm, fields, cattle, money, estate, pious spouse, children, servants, pious and faithful masters, sound rule, clement weather, peace, health, discipline, honour, good friends, good neighbours and the like.' In the seventeenth century health was regarded as an equally diverse matter. The Enlightenment thinkers were convinced that they could preserve it by solid persuasion and living a consciously sensible life. It was merely a matter of 'enlightening' people!

7

Doctrines of Health in the Eighteenth Century

Medical theories of health

In the eighteenth century the issue of health acquired new, previously unforeseen significance. 'Nulla datur in orbi sanitas generalis', acknowledged Albrecht von Haller (1708–1777). Galen's definition of the *Scopus et finis medicinae* emerged as an elegant paraphrase of innumerable variations on wellbeing.[1] Herman Boerhaave (1668–1738) had already recognized, in his *Aphorisms*, that 'every man [has] his particular health', which is threatened by an impairment of the 'actiones vitales, naturales atque animales'. Boerhaave alluded to Hippocrates, who, he claimed, gave a correct account of the influences on human health of the environment, the air, the ground, heat and cold. Mechanistic and hydraulic models now also permitted plausible explanations for *illnesses*. The free circulation of liquids as well as interaction between materials were believed to denote health and life; their stagnation, illness and death. Like his didactically coloured *Institutiones*, Boerhaave's aphorisms influenced generations of medical students. For the physician from Leiden, all measures leading to cures or improved health had to be inferred from the individual *medical history*. Boerhaave was an 'empiricist' and was less interested in the physiological or anatomical discoveries of his age.[2] He himself adhered to a strict regimen, took regular walks and gymnastic exercise, and, according to the testimony of his pupil Linnaeus, drank neither coffee nor tea.[3] He also recommended careful dietary selection to his patients, as well as sport and coach journeys, which in the eighteenth century amounted to gymnastic exercise.[4] Mineral water, wines from the Rhine and Moselle, poultry and various types of meat should, as stipulated in the chapter of the *Institutiones medicae* devoted to 'diaeta ad longaevitam', be consumed 'dietetically'. It is not difficult to see why, concerning the eternal battle for health, some contemporaries secretly agreed with La Rochefoucauld: 'It is a boring illness to wish to preserve this by means of a far too strict diet.'

Another excellent dietician was the Halle physician Friedrich Hoffmann (1660–1742), who was regarded as an 'iatromechanic', but whose works also feature theories by the iatrochemists and methodists, citations from Hippocrates and borrowings from Galen, and demonstrate a proximity to both Descartes and Leibniz.[5] It is not possible to detail his extensive conception of physiology here – for example, the dependence of the metabolism on the 'facultas naturalis'.[6] By modifying the various dispositions to illness according to age, sex, hereditary traits and the 'temperaments', he made an important contribution to the theory of prophylaxis, which consists primarily in observance of the 'six non-naturals', in physical exercise and work (the thesis that laziness, by contrast, merely makes one ill, which was also derived from dietetics, became a popular moral argument). In case of debility, the famous 'Hoffmann drops', which are still used today, were prescribed, whereas the no less famous Westphalian *pumpernickel* was praised as the ideal nutriment for those engaged in hard physical labour (*De pane grossiori Westphalorum vulgo Bonpournickel*, 1695).[7]

For Hoffmann, rest and sleep are indispensable for regeneration; however, too much 'repose' is damaging: the body gains weight, hysterical and hypochondriac afflictions are advanced. Even more dangerous, however, are anxiety, fear, dolefulness and terror.[8] By contrast, seven *rules* guide one towards a 'salutary way of life':

1   Avoid everything in excess, for that is contrary to nature!
2   Take care when changes take place, for usage is akin to our second nature!
3   Be cheerful and calm in spirit all the time – that is the best medication!
4   Stay out in the fresh, temperate air for as long as possible!
5   Furnish yourself with the best foodstuffs, which enter the body easily and swiftly pass out of it again!
6   Accurately measure and weigh all meals according to the movement of the body and its rest!

However, as the final point Hoffmann adds:

7   He who loves his health should flee the *medicos* and all medication!

In accordance with the old motto that 'the glutton destroys more than the sword', Hoffmann also considers moderation to be a *pedagogical* concern. The digestibility of food can be ascertained without difficulty: the more closely it resembles the blood (into which it is to be transformed by the digestive process), the 'healthier' it is; the greater the deviation from the composition of the blood, the more cautious one should be about its consumption.[9] Coffee, tea and herbal infusions dissolve mucous, tenacious and acid substances in the gut and are therefore considered conducive to health, as are spices, which assist the digestive process. Hoffmann's *Gründliche Anweisung, wie ein Mensch vor dem frühzeitigen Tod und allerhand Arten Kranckheiten durch ordentliche Lebensart sich verwahren könne* [*Thorough Directions on How a Person Can Protect Himself from Premature Death and all Kinds of Illness by Means of an Orderly Way of Life*] became a bestseller.[10] The work aimed, characteristically for the Pietistic author, to achieve a synthesis between an enlightened scientific confidence and a fundamental Christian faith: 'True felicitousness rests on three factors: that one is cheerful and calm of mind in God, that one possesses a healthy and well-cultivated reason, and that one also enjoys health of the body. The first is taught by true theology and morality, the second particularly by diligent practice in Mathesipura, and the third by thorough knowledge of the physical science.' It is striking in this connection that contemporary physicians such as Jan van Heurne or Pieter van Foreest barely touch on the topic of dietetics – this may be an indication that some iatrophysicists, with their engineer-like confidence in the rectifiable nature of all conceivable illnesses, paid less attention to prophylaxis.[11]

The most significant physiologist of the century was Boerhaave's Swiss pupil Albrecht von Haller. The conservation of health was a central concern of the universalist from Bern. Following on from Cartesianism, it was initially explained in physiological or 'material' terms.[12] Wellbeing is determined not by vitalist principles, but by the complex interaction of nerves and mechanics (Haller believed he had located the foundations of physiology in the 'sensibility of the nerves' and the 'irritability of the muscle tissues'), of nerve juices and electricity.[13] In practice this is assisted by a 'healthy' and moral way of living, which, in a godless world, 'where gnawing desire and false hope seethes', has become as rare as sensitivity to 'nature's splendour', which he celebrated in his poem *Die Alpen* [*The Alps*], much admired by Schiller and Goethe. The study of nature and of Christian dogma were by no means mutually exclusive for Haller.

De La Mettrie had also taken up the cudgels for dietetics in his *Lettres sur l'art de conserver la santé* (1738); however, he criticized the fact that physiologists such as Haller were only concerned with analysing the 'machine man' by means of dissection and vivisection. They were not fascinated by health itself, he claimed, but by the prospect of satisfying their anatomical and physiological curiosity – a reproach which, on the whole, was not without pertinence for the medicine of the Enlightenment![14] Many curious individuals and scholars, but also bored nobles, had indeed discovered dissection as a fashionable hobby: 'on the one hand I had my Burlamaqui, my Grotius and my Pufendorf', wrote the French count of Montlosier, 'on the other my anatomical dissection exercises, the foundations of surgery by La Faye and Winslow's anatomy.'

Haller's pupil Johann Georg Zimmermann (1728–1795) also deserves recognition for his services to the practice of dietetics. Like Haller, Zimmermann, who was municipal physician in Brugg and court *medicus* in Hannover, wrote poetry and, in his work *Über die Einsamkeit* [*On Solitude*] (1784–5) praised the benefits of solitude for body and soul (the work could have been directly descended from Petrarch).[15] As a *physician*, however, he called for a condition *between* the world and solitude, for then 'it is certain that neither will the frivolousness of those addicted to distractions lead us into folly, nor will the dour and gloomy seriousness of the hermit lead us into misanthropy.' In the fourth book of the work *Von der Erfahrung in der Arzneikunst* [*Of Experience in the Art of Medicine*] and in the tract *Von der Diät für die Seele* [*Of the Diet for the Soul*] (early version, 1764), Zimmermann concerned himself with health care. He first explains the obligatory 'six non-naturals', and in the second part recommends rules for the protection of the *soul*. For the Swiss physician, state of mind is dependent on the properties of the air, on the diet and on sufficient physical exercise. 'Just as wine is most suitable for poets, so coffee is most suitable for philosophers', we read elsewhere.[16] A kind of trimming instrument for the preservation of health, such as that invented by an English doctor, is, he claims, useful in hospitals, mental asylums and prisons, whose existence made an increasing impression on the consciousness of the general public in the eighteenth century.

As madness was considered a consequence of intellectual overexertion, Zimmermann warned against intellectual work without breaks for recovery.[17] Physical health, he argued, could only be attained with the assistance of the soul, with the consequence that anyone who attempted to help 'must be physician and philosopher at the same time'. The body, however, seemed 'to have greater influence on the soul than the latter on the body, if we observe the important changes, with manifold physical causes, that arise in the soul.' In view of these connections, the purely mechanistic approach of the Cartesians appears ridiculous to Zimmermann: 'Our entire way of thinking is so very subject to wind and weather, to an empty or a full or overfull stomach, so very subject to our drinks, to our entire way of living and to a thousand causes either external or lying within the body itself, that everything seems to be changed with regard to us, because these causes change with regard to everything.' Like Hoffmann, he invokes the old adage of 'moderatio': 'Moderation in all stages of human life has the most auspicious influence on the health of the soul.' It is considered an 'auxiliary to a longer life'.[18]

In his work *Ruhr unter dem Volke im Jahre 1765* [*On Dysentery among the People in the Year 1765*], Zimmermann called for the systematic cleaning of streets and towns, fresh air in sickrooms, the expedient disposal of faeces and the careful burial of the dead. The authorities must also radiate courage and optimism during an epidemic, he argues, for 'fear and sorrow together have wretched effects on the healthy and infinitely more so on the sick.' It was also necessary, he claimed, to reduce 'prejudices among the peasantry' against trained physicians. Even in epidemics, peasants preferred to consult 'execrable doctors and charlatans' rather than an established specialist. A Swiss law from 1765 even forbade 'village doctors', in other words, skilled barbers and military surgeons, from practising 'Arzneykunst' (the art of medicine). However, many officials were hesitant about implementing the law, fearing their revenge, perhaps in the form of witchcraft.[19]

The most consistent theory of a *vital force* which preserved health was devised by the Halle physician Georg Ernst Stahl (1659–1734). In the view of this Pietistic professor, an 'immaterial' soul guaranteed the unity of the body.[20] Peace of mind and health were mutually dependent: fear, in contrast, induced heart palpitations or diarrhoea, anxiety or sleeplessness. The court physician to Friedrich Wilhelm I of Prussia and president of the Collegium Medicum in Berlin attempted to save the Christian concept of the soul from the incipient Enlightenment. According to the 'animism' theory, the entire mechanical apparatus of the body, but also the intellect, is governed by the soul. Illnesses arise from processes of disintegration and decay, as soon as the controlling function of the *anima* (*vis medicatrix naturae*) is weakened. Stahl's psychodynamistic theory relativized the significance of the anatomical and physiological discoveries of the seventeenth and eighteenth centuries and instead, following Boerhaave's example, pushed clinical experience to the fore.[21]

Understandably, dogmatic Cartesians and dualists (Hoffmann, Stahl's colleague in the faculty, among them) rejected the close coherence between soul and body propagated by the 'animists'. Pietists such as Stahl contrasted pure iatromechanics with the religious aspect of sickness and health. Their ethical impetus, based on the commandment to love one's neighbour, led to the flourishing of *community* health-care provisions. The hygiene measures introduced by Christian Friedrich Richter (1676–1731), the resident physician at the orphanage in Halle, as well as the exemplary administration of the Franckesche Anstalten (Francke's institutes), also contributed considerably to the reputation of this movement.

The fact that the purely positivist world view of many physicians reduced medicine to a mere 'technical procedure' disturbed many contemporaries in the eighteenth century. In his *Anthropologie für Ärzte und Weltweise* [*Anthropology for Physicians and the Worldly-Wise*] (1772), the Leipzig doctor Ernst Platner wrote that 'this science [has] lost more from its growth than it has gained'. For man, he continued, was 'neither body nor soul alone; he is the harmony of both'. He complained about the pressure that the 'mechanics' and 'physicists' put on their colleagues: 'A doctor, who . . . concerns himself with ethical doctrine or with knowledge about the world' is considered a renegade. Platner offers an extensive definition of health; in animals it manifests itself in the 'satiation of hunger, thirst, of natural desires, in freedom, safety, a comfortable arrangement of the limbs and in the elimination of all sensory pain'. In human beings, 'in addition to the general animal qualities', it is manifested in 'a feeling of beauty, order, proportion, of newness', as well as 'abundance, excellence and the idea of all kinds of past and future riches'. Health is complemented and perfected by security, hope and even aesthetic pleasures.

Another major influence was the stimulus theory propounded by the Scottish physician John Brown (1735–1788). Brown considers 'excitability' to be a basic quality of life, and *moderate* stimulus a precondition for health. If no stronger stimuli are present, there is an increase of excitability (which is considered in entirely quantitative terms) in the organism (*sthenia*). This condition represents as great a threat to health as an excess of stimulus, which weakens the power of physical excitability (*asthenia*). There is therefore a reciprocal relationship between stimulus and excitability.[22] Brown differentiates between external stimuli (such as warmth, nutrition, climate, spices or the composition of the air) and internal stimuli (such as emotions, muscle contractions, passions and intellectual exertions). Between an excess and a deficiency of excitability there is an infinitely variable transitional stage; a strictly individual dietetic regime could bring about an increase or diminution of stimuli, as required. Brown's teacher and compatriot William Cullen (1712–1790) had conjectured before him that the principle of life was nothing other than the 'power of the nerves', and health was to be found in the midpoint between the conditions of 'spasm' and 'atony'.[23]

A theory of dietetics based on social and Christian principles, which was representative for a not insignificant number of physicians in the eighteenth century, can be found in *Dr Johann Samuel Carls Armenapotheke nach allen Grundtheilen und Sätzen der Medizin* [*Dr Johann Samuel Carl's Poor Man's Apothecary after all Basic Parts and Theories of Medicine*] (Frankfurt, 1789), a manual for laypersons and for all those 'who attend to them and yet have no knowledge of the art of medicine'. As early as the preface, Tissot's opinion is reiterated that better medical provision is made for the higher social classes than for the lower classes. The first chapter therefore advises everyone to put together a medicine chest 'of herbs, roots, flowers and seeds'. The manual goes on to explain that the majority of medicinal herbs can, thanks to the goodness of God, be found at no charge in nature, and names the example of the greater celandine.

> It begins to bloom in April and goes on into the summer. It prefers old walls, fences, hedges. It is of a drying, warming, purifying character. It opens up the liver and does much to cure jaundice and dropsy. It is praised particularly in the event of eye disorders, as a healing herb for scurf, old injuries and toothache. The dried, ground plant is sprinkled on old injuries and wounds. The yellow juice is applied to warts and corns. The herb, bound when fresh onto swollen feet, draws out wateriness. The distilled water, or the yellow juice from the plant, removes the hide-like and frail appearance from the face. The root, taken in powder, wine or beer, serves against the aforementioned internal conditions, as well as the plague.

According to Carl, health is threatened by two factors: by 'surplus bloods', in other words, a kind of disposition, but primarily 'externally, [by] all manner of aberrations in the health regime with regard to eating, drinking, air, and so on'.

A physician with a social conscience, Carl also designed a *summary plague table* (the Black Death represented a constant, latent threat following the epidemic in Marseilles in 1720), which gave information on 'preservation', medication and public measures during periods of epidemic. The author presents in twelve points the duties of society in an emergency. The authorities are charged with passing the necessary decrees; it is expected of the priests 'that they comfort the sick and healthy with divine mercy, strength, prayer and faith throughout the struggle', of the doctors 'that they watch over the patients and all those who have to deal with them', of the chemists 'that they provide themselves with appropriate medicines, and relinquish them in a well-prepared state and cheaply'. The surgeons are expected 'to refrain from other remedies than blood-letting, vomiting and purging' and the 'spice peddlers' are to buy the required wares in advance. He expects of the landlords 'that they maintain a supply of good old wine and unadulterated foods for refreshment', of the midwives and female attendants 'that they do not work against these treatments with tempestuous behaviour, coldness, wine-drinking and the like', of the bakers and butchers 'that they keep themselves supplied to excess at all times with good and fresh wares', of the carpenters 'that they maintain a good supply of boards, so as to be able to speed burial', of the farmers 'that they make possible the speedy supply of firewood and wood for smoking in addition to victuals and foodstuffs', and of the ordinary subjects 'that they acquire a good supply of victuals, foodstuffs and medicines, so that they and theirs are not lacking in anything.' However, every effort is in vain, concludes Carl, if God does not give his blessing and vouchsafe health. For this reason, the authorities should follow examples in the Old Testament and introduce a 'plague Sabbath'.

Works such as Carl's *Poor Man's Apothecary* were not, of course, taken very seriously by many 'enlightened' colleagues. However, they met a deep-rooted desire on the part of the devout public to secure good health by means of correct behaviour *and* God's assistance.

The French Enlightenment and Rousseau

A particularly significant influence on the intellectuals of the eighteenth century and, thus, also on medicine and the philosophy of health was exercised by the volumes of the *Encyclopédie* edited by Diderot and d'Alembert from 1751 onwards. The health controversy divided opinions increasingly, with faculties of medicine also becoming involved in the debate.[24] In addition to numerous other contributions on the art of healing, Boerhaave's pupil from Leiden, Louis de Jaucourt (1704–1780), wrote his article 'Santé' in 1765, in which he programmatically also took social and psychological needs into account:

> We are concerned with the most complete condition of life; it can therefore be defined as the proper arrangement [*disposition convénable*] of the parts of the vital body. It follows from this that all its functions permanently operate or are able to operate with ease, in freedom and adequate to all the possibilities and

capabilities of each organ – depending on its function [*dans toute l'étendue dont est susceptible chacun de ses organes*]; also with due consideration given to the current situation, to the different needs, to age, sex, to the temperament of the individual concerned who is in this condition, and to the climate in which this individual lives.

Life, function, sex, society, and climate are important keywords, while the diagnostic significance of age, constitution, humours, qualities, elements, degrees, idiosyncrasies, regimens and the 'non-naturals' is presented as secondary.

The critical spirit of the *Encyclopédie* becomes evident when we compare its definition of health with the description inserted into *Zedlers Universallexikon* from 1735, which restricts itself to a paraphrase of the 'six non-naturals': 'Healthy, *sanus*, is the man whose body and soul function correctly and in accordance with the motion of nature. The noblest indications of health are a brisk *ingenium*, cheerful mind, pure unspoiled speech, sharp vision and other, well-trained senses, tranquil sleep, a regular appetite, a good and correct digestion.' The definition given in the *Realen Staats-, Konversations- und Zeitungslexikon* [*Authoritative Lexicon for State, Public and Current Affairs*] by Johann Hübner (1727) must have appeared even more antiquated to proponents of the Enlightenment:

> Health (*sanitas*) is a natural constitution of the body which enables the latter to perform its functions in an orderly and proper manner. It consists in the harmony of the life spirits, in a correct temperament of dampness and correct interrelation of the solid parts; for this reason it is divided by some into solidam, humidam and spirituosam, and it is therefore considered an unmistakable sign if a person can perform his habitual actions well, retain well what he should keep to himself but be able to discharge what he should discharge. Healthy people can also be recognized by the fact that they do not experience any pain when there is a change in atmosphere and do not feel the effects of the moon; they see health as a noble treasure which must be preserved primarily by moderate eating and drinking and other exercises, but in particular by the subjugation of their desires and effects.

The *Dictionnaire portatif de santé* (1771) also restricts itself to a conservative description of health: 'This consists in a good disposition of all parts of the body, enabling it to function in an optimal fashion; a harmony and symmetry which characterizes the solid and fluid parts, resulting in a consonance of all bodily functions. It is a most precious gift, which we have received from the creator of nature and which we should therefore tend in the most careful manner.' The healthy individual is described as follows:

First and foremost, one must be well shaped, at least in the vitally important parts such as the head, the chest and the abdomen; one requires a good constitution, many muscles and little fat, large and strong bones, a broad and square ribcage, a large rather than a small head, a stomach that does not hang down too much. The appetite should be neither too great nor too small; one should have a regular daily bowel action, urinate and sweat out a good deal. After eating, the body should be light, the limbs supple and without tiredness. One should not feel any pain; sleep should be pleasant and peaceful.

Yet the extent to which the *Encylopédie* was influenced by Cartesianism is demonstrated by Jaucourt's article 'Life', which was also composed in 1765:

I define it as the continual motion of solid and fluid matter in . . . the body. From this double and reciprocal motion originate nourishment, growth, decomposition and death. It suffices to say that the distribution of the watery, mobile, fluid parts results from this motion. The [solidly formed] remainder is not able to move, but is rather a part of the pipe that it plugs [*et fait corps avec le tuyau qu'il bouche*]. The thickening of the juices and the ossification of the vessels are here lamentable but necessary consequences of life. Physiology shows us how the organism self-destructs gradually, without us being able to arrest it by means of any remedy.

The objective of the *encyclopédistes* was the systematization of human nature. D'Alembert himself, who aligns himself with Bacon in the introduction to the *Encyclopédie*, immediately broaches the topic of health: 'Of all the things that impress us by their presence, the existence of our own body attracts our attention the most . . . As it is subject to thousands of needs and reacts extremely sensitively to external things, it would quickly be ruined if we did not concern ourselves constantly with its conservation.' He rejects theological or philosophical relativizations of health in the manner of Pascal; the greatest fortune and goal are believed to consist in freedom from pain. 'Free from the prejudices of education and upbringing', the task of the intellectuals is to strive for this condition and to help others to do the same. In order to achieve this, comprehensive health planning is required, which encompasses social and political aspects: 'The necessity of protecting our body from pain and decay causes us to discover those things in the outside world which are beneficial and harmful to us, in order to seek out the former and avoid the latter.' We share this task with our fellow citizens: 'We should see the great benefit in seeking out that in nature which can sustain or can harm us . . . This is the origin of the formation of a society and, simultaneously, also the birth of language.'

'Free from the prejudices of education and upbringing' – in evidence here was the ghost of Jean-Jacques Rousseau (1712–1778), whose call to arms against 'civilization' inspired innumerable contemporaries. More radically than any author before him, Rousseau pointed to nature as the force that conserves health, but which has been corrupted by conventions and upbringing, by the state, law and religion. The veneration, and even deification, of nature quickly seized broad swathes of the intellectual sphere and brought with it a renaissance of ancient dietetic traditions. 'English' landscape gardens had also long been a feature in the parks of European castles, as had pavilions, which beckoned the individual to retreat from society. In Haller's poem *Die Alpen* [*The Alps*], we find a lyrical description of a landscape untouched by the blessings of civilization; this landscape is set up in opposition to the luxuriant lifestyle in the towns and courts, as well as to the intellectualism of the age: 'Far from the vain extravagance of wearisome affairs, here abides the soul's peace and flees the transience of the towns.'

In contrast to Haller, who saw the roots of all evil in distance from nature, but also from God, Rousseau demanded distance from the old religion as well. Civilization and Christianity hindered man's natural development.[25] In *Émile* (1762), the Enlightenment thinker gives a vision of the new, free, and healthy man: 'Hygiene is the only useful part of medicine, and hygiene is rather a virtue than a science. Temperance and industry are man's true remedies.'[26] Enthusiasm for the 'unspoiled', which is reminiscent of utopians such as Swift, leads to acerbic criticism of European lifestyles. The philosopher is convinced that the enfeeblement of civilized man has come about because 'virtue, the voice of nature', has been disregarded.[27] As a consequence, Rousseau has a very low opinion of medicines and medical aid: 'If common observation shows us that medicine neither increases health nor prolongs life, it follows that this useless art is worse than useless, since it wastes time, men, and things on what is pure loss.'[28]

The health of the man living in tune with nature is also threatened. However, unlike his 'civilized' contemporaries, he does not await death in fearful expectation, but dies in peace because he has not been influenced by doctors, philosophers and priests, 'who debase the heart and make us afraid to die'.[29] Rousseau demands that people become accustomed in childhood to the idea of hygiene and the possibility of sickness: 'This one art takes the place of every other, and is often more successful; it is the art of nature.'[30] Animals, he maintains, live more in tune with nature, and are therefore less subject to suffering than people.

He also advocates 'the value of manual labour and bodily exercise for strengthening the health and constitution'. Most examples of longevity 'are to be found among the men who have taken most exercise, who have endured fatigue and labour.'[31] Another of his maxims is that he (Émile) 'must work like a peasant and think like a philosopher', since 'the great secret of education is to use exercise of mind and body as relaxation one to the other.'[32] Rousseau's image of nature has little in common with the fulsome, romantic attitude to nature which became popular in Germany and England at the beginning of the nineteenth century; the idealization of physical labour was much more a degradation of every semblance of 'idleness' to a health-endangering violation of nature, reducing every 'good-for-nothing' to a parasitic sponger.

Rousseau moves from theory to practice. Clothing must never impede movement or growth: 'there should be nothing tight, nothing fitting closely to the body, no belts of any kind. The French style of dress, uncomfortable and unhealthy for a man, is especially bad for children.'[33] On how to live one's life, he notes:

> There are habits of body suited for an active life and others for a sedentary life. The latter leaves the humours an equable and uniform course, and the body should be protected from changes in temperature; the former is constantly passing from action to rest, from heat to cold, and the body should be inured to these changes. Those, however, who come and go in the sun, wind, and rain, who take much exercise, and spend most of their time outdoors, should always be lightly clad, so as to get used to the changes in the air and to every degree of temperature without suffering inconvenience.[34]

Rousseau was very sceptical about inoculation against smallpox, which was a topic of much discussion in the eighteenth century.[35] Sooner or later, he maintained, everyone would catch it, since it was one of those diseases which are 'part of man's very nature', and have to be distinguished from illnesses which are caused by aberrations in daily life – excesses, deprivations and exhaustion.[36] Intervening in the workings of nature by inoculating or attempting to treat children was senseless, since an individual's 'nature', or disposition, could not be outwitted. Undeniably, there were tiny patients who were in a wretched state. But, he argued, pampering them with too much care, and torturing them with various therapies, would only increase their misery.[37]

The great systematic botanist Carl von Linné (Linnaeus) (1707–1778) employed the old topos of man as a 'servant of nature',[38] arguing that it was only in this capacity that man could hope for health and social happiness. Georges Buffon (1707–1788), director of the Jardin des Plantes, advocated in his *Histoire naturelle générale et particulière* that nature be saved, the countryside cleared, swamps drained and canals built. Implicit in the admiration for such a 'constructed' nature was the challenge of correcting and optimizing it. In addition, the trial and execution of the king were justified as the return of the nation to the natural 'primitive state'. Robespierre noted ominously in 1794: 'Everything has changed in nature; everything will also change in morality and politics.' Society was diagnosed as suffering from a serious ailment which, it was thought, could only be cured by the elimination of everything artificial and unnatural. How could human life flourish peacefully if, as the English social scientist Thomas Malthus noted a short time later (1798), the food reserves increased in a linear manner, while the population grew exponentially?[39] Even nature, it was argued, could not be relied upon in this respect; it had to be improved by means of rational action, which at the same time legitimized active dietetics.

These meditations also engendered the concept of the modern *clinic*. The dissolution of the old poorhouses, which were regarded as the epitome of princely or, rather, royal mismanagement, was followed in France by the establishment of a new, modified institution (proto-clinic), which initiated a smooth transition to the modern institution serving the cure or alleviation of illnesses.[40] In Foucault's opinion, an 'entirely new medicine, based upon the clinic', ousted the idea, which dominated until 1793, of a medicine that was 'liberated' from the hospital, that accepted nature alone as its taskmistress. Parallel with prophylactic and dietetic aspects, scientific and administrative notions increasingly gained acceptance.[41] However, the objective in Paris both *before* and *after* the revolution was 'to prevent, in so far as it is possible, every illness'.

The dispute surrounding inoculation further illustrates the different conceptions of nature that were in existence. Those opposed to inoculation followed Rousseau's example, seizing the moment to condemn every manipulation of the body organized by the state. Following Lady Mary Wortley Montague's efforts to publicize active smallpox inoculation from 1717 onwards, books, educational tracts, pamphlets and newspapers in all European countries rounded on methods practised 'only by a few ignorant women within an uneducated populace'.[42] Many physicians were opposed to the new 'charlatanry', although they professed to defend enlightenment, science and reason. However, when the medic William Buchan defended inoculation on the basis of empiricism and observation in his work *Domestic Medicine, or, A Treatise on the Prevention and Cure of Diseases by Regimen and Simple Medicines*, published in 1772, he won approval. Yet it was doubtless akin to a revolution in 'individual prophylaxis against illness' when James Jurin proved, in the first well-known statistical evaluation in medical history (1724), that 'one-fourteenth of the human race is killed by smallpox', whereas, even according to the most pessimistic estimates, 'only one in fifty dies as a result of inoculation'.[43]

The chances and risks of survival had been expressed in percentages for the first time. Jurin's statistical examination advocated individual prophylaxis and, at the same time, made an impression on the authorities. The critics silenced, a state programme of aid developed slowly. Inoculation was carried out free of charge in Northampton in 1746. In 1756 Louis XVI of France was inoculated following the death of his predecessor, Louis XV, from the plague. The principle of inoculation triumphed, accompanied in secret by the utilitarian basic intention, which was underpinned by statistics: the individual must bear a certain risk in the name of the health of the general public.[44] As late as the eighteenth century, attempts were still being made in France to determine the life expectancy of individual age groups in respect of epidemics, endemic illnesses and other health-endangering factors.[45]

Tissot, Triller, Mai: health education at grassroots

Whereas Rousseau regarded criticism of civilization as a programmatic element of dietetics and abhorred paternalism on the part of the state, the Swiss physician and scholar Simon-André Tissot (1728–1797) underlined the responsibilities of the state with regard to public health. In the preface of the *Avis au peuple, sur sa santé* [*Advice to the People in General, with Regard to their Health*], which Rousseau also valued highly, health education is described as 'an important task of the administration' and is even opposed to tyranny, which is represented as conducive to the indisposition of the individual as well as the state.

Tissot is particularly concerned with *social* health risks. As the most important reason for illnesses among country-dwellers he identifies their strenuous working routine, which is no longer exalted, as it was by so many authors in the eighteenth century, Haller and Rousseau included. Quite the contrary, the conservation of health is interpreted as the avoidance of every 'excès de travail'. The social allusions cannot be missed: 'There is one further reason for exhaustion . . ., which is induced by extreme poverty, a lack of sufficient food, a poor diet, bad drinks.' The Swiss physician, who also taught in Pavia, suggested restorative soups and a little wine, admittedly difficult to put into execution in Switzerland, as an antidote 'for the moment'. However, he argues, it is primarily the want of a healthy way of life, whether caused by social circumstances or precipitated by negligence, 'which allows illnesses to become worse than necessary and constantly endangers people's health'. Tissot also composes a detailed regimen for the sick, in which he states, for example, that fresh air should be let into the sickroom every day (the pragmatic author recommends fastening the curtains between chairs or stools in order to avoid the dreaded draughts). He also prescribes that those afflicted with acute illnesses should not, for example, consume too solid meals, so as not to put a strain on their digestive organs.

'While we are attending to the *more renowned* part [of the population] in the towns, the *more useful* half perishes in wretched conditions in the countryside', the committed social critic laments, and dedicates his work 'to those whose great distance from physicians forces them to forego their assistance'. The *Avis* gives hints as to the nature of the rural population around 1779. While the 'calculated sentimentality of the Ancien Régime' (Hippolyte Taine) was fashionable within (and beyond) the French court, eighteenth-century peasants lived throughout Europe in extremely degrading conditions. Tissot hopes in particular that the clergy 'will exercise the greatest possible influence to bring about the desired improvement of medicine for the common man'. It is, he continues, 'their duty to combat harmful prejudices and superstition', and their 'compassionate heart' predisposes them to the task of educating the general populace.[46] Landowners should also, he believes, encourage the general population to lead a healthy life, as well as 'schoolmasters', who, like midwives and surgeons, should all read his book. The aforementioned Detmold physician Johann Christian Scherf, who wished to establish health education as a school subject, was just one of those who drew on these arguments.

In reality, the common man was, according to Tissot, entirely capable of following instructions to produce medicaments himself, although he conceded that it was necessary to proceed as severely against the 'market vendors and quack doctors' as against the extortionate prices of the apothecaries, who prevented the poor from purchasing herbs and essences. He advocated 'that all astrological rules relating to medicine should be banished from the calendars' and that hospitals should be established in the countryside to counteract the views of villagers that 'the doctors were experienced only with illnesses typical for the towns'. He did, however, see a possibility of linking urban and rural consciousness through the fashionable interest in rural life taken by the rich.

It was primarily lay healers who tended the peasants' health. They also drew, as in the sixteenth and seventeenth centuries, on house books or calendars. One such example was *Des Mährischen Albertus Magnus Andreas Glorez' Klostergeistlicher und Naturkundiger Eröffnetes Wunderbuch* [*The Moravian Albertus Magnus Andreas Glorez' Miracle Book from Monastic Clerics and Experts on Nature*] (1700), which, as is declared on the frontispiece, deals 'with weapon salve, magic illnesses, wonder cures as taught by the Holy Scriptures and using things of very little value, the magical power and signature of plants and herbs, Egyptian secrets, the transplantation of illnesses onto animals and trees, birch rods which point to metals hidden in the earth, sympathetic powders, the investigation of illnesses through urine, and other strange secrets from the manuscript treasures of monasteries'. The author assumes that divine or magic powers can be evoked by means of oath and even compelled to bestow health. 'The Lord Christ and his apostles made the faithful and the elect healthy not by means of natural medicaments, but supernaturally by means of the word of faith and the power of prayer; nonetheless, all natural remedies must be employed and blessed with word and prayer, if they are to be otherwise sacred and beneficial.' Faith in miracle healings was a matter of course for the majority of the sick in the eighteenth century.

Glorez also believes that it is possible to ensure by means of magical intervention that a new-born baby 'will, his life long, contract neither ailments after birth nor chickenpox nor minor woes or other illnesses, which originate from the decay of women's monthly bloods.' A piece of a skull was thought to protect against bloody stools, the tooth of a dead person against toothache, and a human cranium against infected wounds, whereas the menstruation blood of a virgin was thought to be effective against podagra. Like water, human urine, 'from which one can make many diagnoses', was believed to heal many afflictions. 'Salt, sulphur, mercury' were also considered useful. 'The chemists believe that all illnesses come from internal salt, brimstone and quicksilver, and must be dispelled by them again.' Also of interest is the advice, reminiscent of the archaic scapegoat theory, that arthritis should be transferred to animals. In general, 'the healthy also tend to lay such fat little dogs over their bodies on account of their weak stomach, of their dry nature or of their gaunt bodies.' The basic tone of the work is entirely aggressive, the diction reminiscent of that Paracelsus, and 'looks the people in the mouth'. The content is not always logical; Paracelsism, magic, popular piety and lay medicine rub shoulders with each other. According to Glorez, a 'universal medicine, by means of which one can cure the most dangerous illnesses and conserve one's life', would make all other remedies unnecessary; however, he argues, such a remedy is too expensive and is mixed using mysterious ingredients.

The work of 'the Moravian Albertus Magnus' was 'ideologically' opposed to Tissot's *Avis au peuple*. The *medical* educational tracts of the eighteenth century, by contrast, aimed to instil trust in conventional medicine among the general populace. Journals such as *Der patriotische Medicus* [*The Patriotic Medic*] (Hamburg, 1724), *Der aufrichtige Medicus* [*The Honest Medic*] (Regensburg and Nuremberg, 1726), *Der Arzt* [*The Doctor*] (Hamburg, 1760), *Artzeneien, eine physikalisch medicinische Monatsschrift* [*Medication, a Physical and Medical Monthly*] (Langensalza, 1766), *Der cursächsische Land-Physicus* [*The Saxon Country Physician*] (Naumburg, 1771), *Der praktische Landarzt* [*The Practical Country Doctor*] (Mitau, 1773) or the *Gazette de santé* [*Health Gazette*] (Zurich, 1782) were composed by physicians and addressed a diverse range of questions in the vernacular. The promotion of smallpox inoculation, the prevention of infanticide, the reduction of child mortality, the fight against quack doctors and diverse forms of medical superstition figured just as prominently as Boerhaave's or Sydenham's teachings on illness. Preventative measures against epidemics, the occupational image of the physician who has studied medicine, the recommendation of bathing and whey treatments, as well as medical matters arising at home and abroad constituted further thematic focal points.[47]

In addition to journals, educational books also became fashionable. Alongside Friedrich Hoffmann's *Anweisungen*, titles such as *Mitliediger Arzt* [*Compassionate Doctor*] (Gottfried Samuel Bäumler, Germersheim, 1736), *Ruhr unter dem Volke* [*Dysentery among the Populace*] (Johann Georg Zimmermann, Zurich, 1767), *Irrtümer, Warnungen und Lehren, welche das Publicum in Ansehung der praktischen Arzeneykunst betreffen* [*Misapprehensions, Warnings and Doctrines which Affect the General Public in Consideration of Practical Medicine*] (D. J. S. Kretschmar, Würzburg, Bamberg and Fulda, 1770) or *Zweite vorläufige Abhandlung von den wahren Mitteln ein hohen Alter zu erreichen* [*Second Provisional Treatise on the True Means of Reaching an Advanced Age*] (David Schulz, Mannheim, 1772) marked a new, pedagogical orientation, which was certainly not entirely self-serving. Health was, according to the basic tenor of these works, safeguarded primarily by the physician, who had studied medicine and who was therefore also responsible for supervising the private dietetic regime.[48] The common man was expected to understand that his life could be organized 'according to nature' and that the academically trained medic was his natural advisor. However, the opprobrium with which the non-academic healers were viewed demonstrates the extent to which the latter individuals enjoyed the confidence of the general populace.

Daniel Wilhelm Triller's verse composition *Diätetische Lebensregeln oder Belehrung, wie es anzufangen ein hohes Alter zu erlangen* [*Dietetic Maxims, or, Instruction on How to Approach Reaching an Advanced Age*] (Frankfurt, 1783) underlined once again the radical personal responsibility borne by the individual for his health. 'God indeed lengthens our life', the 83-year-old author, who is reminiscent of Cornaro, explains, 'yet the individual must also for his part endeavour to draw out the thread of his life.' He follows the Carthusian tradition, comparing the body with the workings of a clock: 'composure and diet alone have the effect that the clock always functions correctly and has done so continuously until now.' Healthy people should not take 'medicaments', as they will 'merely [destroy] the order of nature for nothing'. He warns in particular against popular miracle remedies, 'and the same is true of the panaceas of the alchemists'.

The conservative Triller abhors 'market vendors' as well as fashionable doctors. Revelry, opulent food, strong foreign wines, meals taken at night, exotic dishes, 'a full table and voluptuousness' all, he argued, shortened one's life, for 'if a lamp is to burn for a long time, it should be allowed only moderate amounts of oil.' That fasting sustains one's health is considered just as indisputable as the necessity of a lifelong dietetic regime. However, the author considers it ridiculous to measure meals and to eat according to weight and quantity, 'according to Sanctorius' directions'.[49] A balanced psychological constitution is also considered important for the conservation of health: 'For Solomon wrote long ago, and Sirach is also in agreement with him, that one should not be dejected at the table, but rather blithe and merry.' 'One should feed the body only moderately, so that it retains the same strength, and quieten the mind, so that it does not fall into agitation', he writes at the end of the short, populist tract, which anticipates Hufeland's *Makrobiotik* in many respects.

Like Tissot, the physician Gottfried Ernst Baldinger from Langensalza also pitted himself 'against medical prejudices', in other words, against quacks and superstitions. The indifference of people concerning their health robs the state of more individuals than the plague, he argues. The sick person has a civic duty to visit a physician, he continues, a matter of course for the modern reader, but a socially explosive topic for contemporaries in the eighteenth century.[50]

In the weekly tract *Der praktische Landarzt*, edited by Ernst Peter Wilde, it is argued that remedies are too expensive for many town-dwellers. The author concedes that medical provisions in the countryside are desperate; serfs do receive the traditional care from their masters, but this is administered 'not merely from a sense of moral duty, but rather out of self-interest'. The physician Gottfried Samuel

Bäumler had already presented similar arguments in his tract *Mitleidiger Arzt, überhaupt gegen alle Arme Krancke, insbesondere gegen die von den Medicus abgelegten Land-Leute ... [The Compassionate Doctor Treating all the Poor and Sick, in Particular the Rural Folk Remote from the Medicus]* (Strasbourg, 1736).[51] The needy should learn, he states 'to cure ... most illnesses of the body with common household remedies or less costly medicaments according to the simple method of nature.' Such concern for the rural population did not preclude, however, that the simple foods preferred by these people be considered 'natural' and 'sensible', and therefore beneficial to health, as is underlined by Johann Georg Reyher in his *Anleitung zur Erhaltung der Gesundheit für den Landmann [Directions on the Preservation of Health for the Country-Dweller]* (Schwerin, 1790). The domestic plants recommended there, such as onions, garlic, celery, radish, parsley, thyme and marjoram, were thought to quicken the healthy appetite and aid digestion.

In many places the geographical location dictated that clerics repeatedly assumed particular tasks within health organizations. *Pastoral medicine* used the church's infrastructure to impart both the Christian faith *and* health.[52] It goes without saying that health education was often embellished morally. In Sweden, the duties of the clergymen regarding this issue were laid down at a particularly early stage. Following the foundation of the Central Statistical Office in 1749, every parish clergyman was required, by means of an extremely detailed questionnaire which was evaluated by the government or the central state Collegium Medicum, to report births and deaths.[53] In addition, every bridal couple received an educational pamphlet on care for infants and parenting. Health care became a civic duty. 'Unreserved compliance with these duties is not only the Christian and natural task of the parents, it is also of great benefit to the entire empire', we read in paragraph 23 of the most popular Swedish educational brochure.

Marriage, sexual enlightenment and reproduction were particularly popular topics of medical instruction. In 1774, Theodor Gottlieb von Hippel's small volume *Über die Ehe [On Marriage]* was published in Germany. It deals, among other matters, with the question of the optimal age for marriage, which Hippel placed very early in life. Questions relating to eugenics and family planning also featured: 'The first children have, at any rate, always been the best; no wonder that illegitimate children are generally the brightest.' The author rejects the Catholic church's prescription of celibacy and innumerable 'unnatural' traditions. 'If a man is unfaithful, then it is wrong, but if a woman does the same, then it is unnatural and godless', he explains elsewhere. The work is also an apology for the marital privileges of the man, on which the bourgeois moral code of the fifteenth century placed even greater emphasis.

Seemingly more intimate in character is *Der Rathgeber vor bei und nach dem Beischlafe* [*Practice Guide for During and After Coitus*] by the Leipzig physician Gottfried Wilhelm Becker, which had already run to five editions by 1816. The 'understandable direction to practise intercourse in such a way that health suffers no detriment and that the propagation of the human race is advanced by the production of beautiful, healthy and strong children' favours a later marriage, contrary to Hippel's argument. Early maturity is apparently only possible 'at the cost of sickly offspring, who may have a moment of precipitation to thank for their miserable physical existence.' Becker also describes the advantages and disadvantages of diverse sexual practices for the health, although he, like Hippel, is of the opinion that all decisions in this respect fall only to the man. It is astonishing how many risks to the health of the offspring seemingly resulted from the sexual act alone!

Franz Anton Mai (1742–1814) made a special contribution to public health education. The Heidelberg professor and personal physician to the Palatine electress was a staunch devotee of Boerhaave,[54] whose empiricism he contrasted with the modern Brownianism. He also made a determined stand against the 'transcendental musings of natural philosophy, which puffs itself up self-importantly at the sickbed' and which captivated many German-speaking physicians around 1800. From 1873 onwards he gave public lectures in the Mannheim national theatre on 'dietetics for the body and soul', which were printed as *Medicinische Fastenpredigten* [*Medical Fasting Sermons*]. Mai referred to famous predecessors such as Tissot or Zimmermann and attacked in his foreword those colleagues who had, he claimed, been seized by the French 'freedom and equality humbug'. In opposition to such trends, the conservative dietetics expert presented his reader with 'the archetype of old German health and rectitude'. Detrimental to one's health were, he argued, an unhealthy way of life, separation from nature, the hustle and bustle of the town, but also the influence of states such as France, where 'the physical and moral health of the citizens is undermined by neglect of dietetics for the soul and body and the body of the state is rendered vulnerable to incurable contagions and the danger of a general disruption.' The 'in itself, dry subject matter of dietetics' is presented in a humorous manner, however, in order, as Mai emphasizes, to 'sweeten the pill and dispel boredom'.

The fasting sermons represented a kaleidoscope of dietetic ideas, but were pragmatic in tenor. 'Robust health in mind and body', we read in the first lecture, is undisputedly the noblest treasure, the greatest gift of the infinitely beneficent creator. Without the possession of this pleasant companion, our life is an enduring domestic scourge; we are incapable of enjoying admissible pleasures, unfit for studying and lost citizens of the world in social life. Fresh air, moderation in food and drink, in rest and exercise, the restraint of excessive passions, the banishment of damaging prejudices, an inclination towards rectitude are the means to acquire a contented, healthy and long life.

Mai was deeply sceptical of everything foreign. 'One should deprive a nation that tends towards mania', he postulates elsewhere, 'of the numerous meat dishes, the spices, the wine and all other liqueurs, and one will observe a miraculous cure of the entirely unadulterated national character.' The responsibility of society is particularly visible with regard to the consumption of alcohol and of 'hot drinks'. The tea kettle is similar to Pandora's box, he continues; it has already brought a good deal of misfortune to the Chinese and the Japanese. The 'harangues of virtuous physicians' may have had some effect there, but, 'in the meantime, the coffee epidemic has escalated in the same proportions and even more acutely among the Europeans.' It is not only tea and coffee that are elevated to national epidemics by the majority of educators; every luxury food or drink, every luxury of any form seemed to augur danger and illness.

The poet Christian Fürchtegott Gellert may have defended dietetics as well as 'control of the desires' in his *Moralischen Vorlesungen* [*Moral Lectures*] (1770); however, he also warned against taking such precepts to extremes. 'Love of life and health, if we do not moderate and govern it, will become a slavish diffidence, to our misfortune.' Moderation is, in Gellert's opinion, necessary in dietetics itself. Many a contemporary loved life so much, he continued, 'as if it were there merely in order never to be lost . . . He pays attention to every minor disorder of his body, to every distant enemy of his health with a childish caution. He hears news of a deceased friend and immediately turns pale. He sees a coffin, and is immediately transfixed.' Gellert even feared a new egomania among his contemporaries. Man can, he continues, 'cease to be efficient, compassionate and helpful . . . in order to preserve his greatest treasure, life and health', and therefore, in a higher sense, 'damage his health, enfeeble his body, weaken his vital spirits'.

Whereas Rousseau was emphatically opposed to state paternalism in pedagogy and health education, educators such as Tissot and Mai considered this to represent the only chance of success. In the olden days, Rousseau and his supporters claimed confidently, everyone had administered his own therapy; 'knowledge was passed on from the father to the children.' The decline in health, it was believed by at least those authors of the day who were opposed to medicine, began when the written word and secrecy were introduced and this knowledge was restricted to a privileged group of healers.[55] Whereas Hippocrates, it was argued, had completely mastered the medical art of observation, this art – and here the Foucault school was in agreement – had been abandoned in the course of the history of medicine in favour of methodology and dogmatism. This was a reproach that was not, by any means, applicable to all physicians of this age.

Public health care

The 'birth of the clinic' described by Foucault was – notwithstanding numerous precursors – the logical consequence of public health-care provisions. Around 1800, almost all Western European governments embraced this task. In 1827 in Berlin, the first state institution in Prussia for the care of the sick was opened in the form of the Charité, a military hospital that also comprised departments for midwifery and infection. The goal of Frederick William III was not so much the realization of the notion of caritas as the strengthening of the state's economy. Economic reasons were also given for the foundation of the general hospital in Vienna in 1784: 'The state loses nothing by making this expenditure. The small amount of money required for the running of the hospital is compensated plentifully by the preservation of many citizens who would otherwise perhaps be lost or would ail.' It should be mentioned peripherally that the effectiveness of the newly structured study of medicine (focusing particularly on tuition at the bedside of the sick) was soon inhibited by a previously unknown mass rush; in Paris, for example, only the *private tuition* offered by the luminaries was adequate to requirements.[56] Such aberrations were doubtless a bitter experience for the reformers of the health system.

Johann Peter Frank (1745–1821) played an exemplary role in demanding that the state assume responsibility in general questions of health; as a young physician he had already reformed the training of midwives and reduced infant mortality in the court towns of Bruchsal and Rastatt.[57] In 1778, the important organizer, who had taught in Vienna since 1780, published his most important work, the *System einer vollständigen politischen Polizey* [*System of a Complete Political Police*]. From 1790, together with Tissot, he was to build up a medical reform faculty in Pavia, which was then under Austrian administration. As early as 1764, the second edition of the *Gedanken von dem*

Nutzen und der Nothwendigkeit einer medicinischen Polizeyordnung in einem Staat [*Thoughts on the Benefits and the Necessity of a Medical Police in a State*] by the 'town and country physician' Wolfgang Thomas Rau appeared in Ulm; in it, the necessity of general health care was justified using 'utilitarian' arguments: 'The affairs of peacetime cannot be conducted by the sick; and strong and steady people are needed in order to wage war . . . In short, sick people are not capable, in any condition, of contributing to the good of the state.'

As early as the seventeenth and the early eighteenth centuries, English social reformers and national economists such as the physician and landowner William Petty (1623–1687) or the economist Nehemiah Grew (1641–1712) had developed similar arguments. Petty offered concrete suggestions for the improvement of sanitary conditions and spoke up for the construction of hospitals, better surveillance during epidemics and a more effective care for infants.[58] Tissot's influence in particular had, from Switzerland to Italy, raised awareness concerning such issues. The campaign against luxury food and drink became virtually programmatic. Just as Mai had fulminated against tea and coffee, the English, for example, denounced the consumption of gin.[59]

In 1776, the Société Royale de Médecine was established in France. Its main tasks were surveillance during epidemics, the chronicling of developments, and therapeutic measures, as well as the supervision of the physicians involved.[60] The most modern departures, such as direct cooperation with the 'epidemic physicians', circumventing the 'normal channels', broke down in the confusion of the revolution, but particularly as a result of the death of the most important medical member of the society, the anatomist Félix Vicq-d'Azur (1794). If one considers that, around 1790, 78 per cent of all French physicians still lived in the towns, it becomes obvious that the success of the Société cannot be overestimated.[61] However, the early establishment of the society, as well as the revaluation of surgery as an academic discipline, demonstrate that the reform of the French health system had already begun under the Ancien Régime. The Comité de la Salubrité, which was founded by the revolutionaries in 1790, was concerned, once again under the influence of Vicq-d'Azur, 'with the instruction and practice of medicine as well as with medical institutions in the town and the country'. Care for the sick was to be left to the families, with support from public institutions, while those without families were the responsibility of municipal clinics. In the country, district physicians were responsible for surveillance during epidemics, conducting vaccinations and caring for the sick and destitute.[62] The 'important place [accorded] to regimen and diet' necessitated the establishment of appropriate public bodies.[63]

Public health administrations were also called for in the German-speaking states. From 1725, the Ober-Collegium Medicum des Staates and the Provincial-Collegia Medica supervised the Prussian public health system, while the Collegium Sanitatis was in charge during epidemics.[64] Although statistical approaches are attested in the Prussian public health system from 1741 at the latest,[65] official public health statistics were not introduced until 1803. From this point onwards, all rural and urban physicians in the state were required to submit annual 'medical tables of persons' with detailed demographic and epidemiological statistics to the highest medical department.[66]

Whereas Rau's 'Policey' (police) idea aimed primarily to bring about an 'improvement in the quality' of the physicians and state control of public health, Frank devoted himself to a detailed plan for the *education of the general public* by the state. Like his compatriot Mai, but with immeasurably greater success, he put together a system of social medicine and hygiene which barely left a single practical question unanswered. He placed less trust in journals and sermons delivered from the pulpit, setting great store instead by the actions taken by the authorities and their laws. In Joseph II, the enlightened Austrian emperor, he found an open-minded patron. However, the reform of the health system should benefit not the monarch, but rather the citizen, as Frank openly admitted in his work *Servandis et augendis civibus*. His famous *Akademische Rede vom Volkselend als Mutter der Krankheiten* [*Academic Address on the Wretchedness of the Populace as the Mother of Disease*], given in Pavia, also contains some of Rousseau's ideas, even though the latter's disciples naturally rejected Frank's faith in the state authorities and their influence on the citizens.[67]

In 1786, the physician Zacharias Gottlieb Hußty openly described his *Diskurs über die medizinische Polizey* [*Discourse on the Medical Police*], published in Preßburg, as an excerpt from Frank's work, which 'is probably read less widely due to its high price'. According to Christian Friedrich Ludwig Wildberg (1765–1850), the author of such promising-sounding tracts as the *Hygiastik oder Kunst, die Gesundheit des Menschen zu erhalten* [*Hygiastics, or, The Art of Preserving Man's Health*] (Berlin, 1818), the citizen had the right to expect that the state should 'not only protect his life from public violence, but provide generally for his physical wellbeing'. It was not only in Frank's works, then, that humanity was linked to education and a centralist view of the state was associated with the right to individual freedom from harm. Nothing was frittered away as wastefully as the health of the citizens, Hußty complained, and therefore considered strict political legislation for its protection to be entirely justified:

Medical policing, like the entire study of governance [*Policeywissenschaft*], is therefore a defence art, a doctrine that can protect man and his animal helpmates against the harmful consequences of larger forms of collective habitation, but which, in particular, can advance their physical wellbeing in such a manner that they, without suffering many physical ills, may at the latest possible date succumb to the ultimate fate to which they are subject.

That not everyone was enthused by the increasingly paternalistic role assumed by such a 'Policey' vis-à-vis the population is illustrated by a passage from Goethe's famous letter to Charlotte von Stein of 8 June 1878: 'I must also say myself that I consider it true that humanity will ultimately be victorious; I fear only that, at the same time, the world will become a great hospital where everyone is everybody else's humane nurse.'

8

Around 1800

The notion of 'Lebenskraft' (vital force) – Hufeland and Kant

Rousseau's idea that nature – in contrast to civilization – bestows health in an extravagant manner reappeared in the *Makrobiotik* [*Macrobiotics*] of Christoph Wilhelm Hufeland (1762–1836), a nineteenth-century bestseller to which the author gave the programmatic subtitle 'The Art of Extending Human Life'. 'If one considers', he tells the reader in the fourth book, 'how little primitive men on the South Sea islands know of illnesses, and compares this to one of the European pathological compendia which march forth in regiments and companies and whose number now amounts to many thousands, one is dismayed by what has been made possible by luxury, moral corruption, an unnatural way of life and excesses. Many, in fact the majority, of these illnesses are our own fault.'[1] Hufeland considers himself responsible for enlightening others and condemns 'medieval' techniques for seeking health, such as 'sorcery, sympathy of bodies, philosophers' stones, secret forces, chiromancy, Kabbala, universal medicine, and so on', as well as astrology, alchemy and Paracelsism, and Cagliostro and the miracle healers of the eighteenth century (which proves once again that these methods were by no means out of date around 1800!). A prominent positive figure among many false counsels was the Venetian Cornaro, whose 'simplest and strictest' diet was admired greatly by the personal physicians to Goethe and to Queen Luise.[2] Like so many physicians in the eighteenth century, Hufeland postulates a *vital force* as the 'root cause of all life'. This represents, he explains, the 'finest, most pervasive, and most invisible activity of nature', as can be found in a grain of corn, which can contain a 'bound life' over many years. If it were to be withdrawn, the body would obey 'the laws and affinities of dead chemical nature', and would pass over into decay.[3] Every individual has a particular quantum of this force at his disposal, he continues, which is diminished by exertions or by an unhealthy way of life, which produce 'consumption'. Healthy life consists in the 'free, active state' of this force, and the 'agility and efficacy of the organs, which are inseparably connected to it'.[4]

As mentioned previously, the idea of the vital force did not originate with Hufeland. The term was probably used for the first time in Haller's tract *De partibus corporis humani sensibilibus et irritabilibus* (1753), although the author, for his part, attributes it to Francis Glisson.[5] As early as 1774, the Mannheim physician Friedrich Kasimir Medicus (1736–1808) had published a work with this title; terms such as 'vis vitalis', 'principe vital', 'function vitale', 'force vitale', 'vital power', 'living principle' or 'vitalia' were common in European medical literature around 1800.[6] It had been noticed that the 'mechanistic' theories that had prevailed since Descartes and de La Mettrie could not explain certain organic phenomena (for example, reproduction, regeneration and autokinesis). Critical voices therefore postulated an elementary force, 'which we have not as yet been able to account for by means of the laws of the physical force of unorganized nature which are known to us', as the Kiel professor Joachim Dietrich Brandis (1762–1845) phrased it, simultaneously modest and trusting in future developments. The natural scientist Johann Friedrich Blumenbach (1752–1840), who corresponded with Lichtenberg, Goethe and Kant, explained the regulation of the healthy, gradual development of embryos (epigenesis) with the aid of the term 'nisus formativus'; a pupil of his, the Swabian botanist and natural historian Carl Friedrich Kielmeyer (1765–1844), referred to 'organic forces', which he understood as a collective term for 'irritability, sensibility, the forces of reproduction, secretion and repulsion'.[7] The professor of medicine Paul Joseph Barthez (1734–1806), who taught in Montpellier, also publicized the notion of a 'principe de vie', which animated every part of the organism.[8] The Parisian pathologist François Xavier Bichat (1771–1802), however, located the vital force in the body tissue, which he considered to be the substratum of a healthy interplay of the forces in the organism. If one knew the vital principle, many physicians in the eighteenth century believed, health could be constructed.[9]

However, despite all theoretical conceptions, the vital force remained one of the most hotly discussed secrets of the age. The physiologist and psychiatrist Johann Christian Reil (1759–1813) admitted in 1796 'that we cannot say any more about it than is displayed by the characteristics of the organism'. 'The physical, chemical and mechanical forces of animals' bodies, it is said, are subject to the vital force, are bound by it, in a manner of speaking, and are only freed from this subordination and restored to their dominance by the death of the animal. Yet such a dominance and subordination cannot really be conceived of in nature.' The vital principle would, Reil continued, threaten to invalidate the laws of nature, for which reason he even feared that it would also suspend 'the law . . . in our reason'.[10]

Hufeland believed the 'fortification of the vital force' to represent the key to a long life, which was also determined by clothing, diet, way of life and climate. It was predominantly sleep, however, that delayed the 'consumption' of the force; old people, for example, sleep less 'because among them intensive living, consumption of life is weak, and requires less repose'.[11] Hufeland opposed the 'vital force' to 'vital weakness', a 'quite peculiar pathological condition, which is only possible at the beginning of life'.

Whereas the term 'vital force' quickly disappeared in the nineteenth century, together with the vitalistic doctrine, the notion of 'vital weakness' has persisted in paediatrics up to the present day. Around 1800, it directed the attention of physicians and society in general towards the child, which, beginning with Rousseau's *Émile*, was idealized as the bearer of hope in innumerable tracts on health education. Illnesses contracted at this age are considered examples of 'the product of the vital force, which is first excited by those stimuli and manifests itself in a particular manner'; however, if this force is impaired, then 'the dead mechanical and chemical forces [gain] the upper hand'.[12] Adherents of Brownianism also considered almost all children's illnesses to be the consequence of the 'weakening' of the organism specific to this age, which Hufeland distinguished from 'pathological vital weakness' and the French paediatrician Charles Michel Billard distinguished from 'debilité congénitale' (1828).[13]

In view of the poor air in the towns, where it was impossible 'that someone who lives in the centre can take a breath of air that was not shortly before in the lung of another',[14] Hufeland called for a public hygiene plan at municipal level. However, more important than any state organization, he insisted, was a responsible lifestyle. Immoderate eating habits were as damaging to health as 'elaborate cuisine': 'After such a meal one always has an artificial fever, and of such people is said correctly: consumendo consumimur.'[15] The consumption of liqueurs and 'digestiva' is condemned for the same reason. Idleness, inactivity, boredom, bad moods, timidity, immoderate passions, but also envy and resentment exhaust the vital forces and 'impede the important business of restoration'. A 'good physical pedigree' is, he continues, certainly advantageous as far as life expectancy is concerned; there are, after all, entire families 'in which growing old was a family privilege'. As we are 'made in our parents' mould', the selection of a partner and the act of procreation are to be approached particularly responsibly.[16]

Hufeland repeatedly praises the 'country and garden life', where everything contributes to the 'preservation of health and of life'.[17] It is true, he continues, that medicine attempts 'by fortification and other means to elevate *every* individual to the highest level of his physical perfection'; however, macrobiotics have demonstrated 'that [there is] also a limit here' and that 'a degree of strength that is taken too far can become a means of accelerating and therefore of shortening life.'

In a lecture given to the Royal Academy of Sciences (1812), Hufeland sketched a 'history of health'. In his opinion, the development of man, like nature in general, is teleological; the healthy and the good have always prevailed, despite opposition. He notes with concern that the increase in the sophistication of lifestyles in the eighteenth century has led to a heightened sensibility, as well as a 'mobility and convulsiveness of the nervous system'.[18] Henceforward, 'more intellectuality, but also less force' will be produced, for 'intellectual life does not increase the force of the intellect; it merely enhances its receptivity, its mobility, its pleasures, the dominance of the imagination rather than that of reason.'[19]

Immanuel Kant (1724–1804) also concerned himself with dietetic matters. In the *Grundlagen zur Metaphysik der Sitten* [*Fundamental Principles of the Metaphysics of Morals*] (1785) he defined 'our own perfection' and 'the happiness of others' as 'ends which are also duties'. However, health and welfare should also be considered as such, as their absence, for example, privation and pain, represents a great temptation to shirk one's duties. For this reason, contrary to common belief, health does not primarily serve to bring about happiness; rather, it fosters moral conduct. Kant believes the negative consequences of an unbalanced lifestyle, or, to be more precise, of a kind of self-anaesthetization resulting from immoderateness, to consist less in the reduction of one's own happiness (which is the initial effect of a decline in health) than in the fact that this reduction leads to a neglect of one's duties.

In a response to Hufeland's *Macrobiotics* (1797), the philosopher Kant addresses concrete aspects of dietetics, and accords particular significance to self-observation. He knows that it is possible to feel healthy without being healthy, but, on the other hand, that others 'of whom . . . it is said that they are forever ailing, can never become ill'.[20]

Longevity alone can never represent a purpose in life; health is more than merely the 'enjoyment of life'. Kant considers the view, held widely in the eighteenth century, 'that those who have lived to a very old age have, for the most part, been married people' to be questionable.[21] Of decisive importance for longevity, he argues, is primarily the nature of the individual. Philosophizing can prolong life, as can hobbies, such as collecting watches or keeping songbirds, whereby the individual enjoys 'the benefit of stimulating the forces in such a manner'. As a prophylactic, Kant also recommends regularity in one's way of life, for which he served as a proverbial example, with the consumption of food divided carefully into two meals in old age. He also considers it 'a fact confirmed by experience that those who are courageous, who are not easily frightened or disgusted, contract illnesses the most seldom'.[22] In addition, 'the class driven by privation or by the duty of labour [ail] more seldom . . . than the idle class' – a topos that recurs from Burton through to Rousseau and Hufeland.

Hegel, by contrast, considered health to be unstable and vulnerable, thanks to the integration of the organism in the cycle of growing and dying. Health was, he argued, only a *transitory* privilege, and this 'is the real sickness, not weakness or excessive strength'.[23] The philosopher considered health to consist 'in the evenly proportioned relation of the organic to the inorganic, so that there is no inorganic material for the organism that it cannot overcome', but not in the circumstance 'that a stimulus is too great or too small for the excitability'. The rejection of the doctrines of excitability and polarization devised by theorists such as Haller or Brown is unusual for an age when many were fascinated by the study of electricity.

The recurrent topic of a dietetic regime for intellectuals

As in earlier times – one need only remember Marsilio Ficino or Robert Burton – many theoreticians of the eighteenth century suspected that their own health was especially at risk. In particular, professors of medicine seemed to fall victim to a certain hypochondria. Hufeland surmised that this was due to the 'crooked sitting position and the air in the enclosed room'. He recommended changing one's posture while studying, 'lying or standing, or walking, or even riding on a wooden horse; furthermore, not always in small rooms, but also in the fresh air'.[24] He considered hypochondria and haemorrhoids to be symptoms of the 'scholars' disease' that had been unknown among the ancient philosophers, 'because they did not require coffee and tobacco as an accompaniment, and because they did not forget to exercise and cultivate their body'.

Kant saw thinking as a scholar's 'nourishment', 'without which he cannot live, when he is awake and alone'.[25] However, 'intentional thinking' was to be curbed at regular intervals by taking physical exercise such as walks and 'allowing the imagination to play freely'. It is well known that the philosopher attempted to stabilize his health, which was considered at risk, by means of iron discipline and a regimented, clockwork-like daily routine.

That Rousseau, who was hostile to civilization and intellectualization, adopted a sceptical attitude towards 'scholarliness' was discussed in the previous chapter. 'Science is good for nothing, and never does anything but harm, because it is by its very nature bad', he remarks in the preface to *Narcisse*. 'Only the learned are vicious, only a man who knows nothing is virtuous.' Fortunately, his advice 'to banish science and the learned forthwith, to burn our libraries, to close our Academies, our Colleges, our Universities, and to plunge back into the barbarism of the first centuries' was not followed.[26] Rousseau suspected that scholarliness was motivated primarily by ambition and by 'a craving for distinction', and offered this as an explanation for the diverse, and even 'absurd', disciplinary systems. In addition, he argued, 'a taste for letters, philosophy and the fine arts' damages the body and the soul. 'Work in the study makes men frail and weakens their temperament, and it is difficult for the soul to retain its vigour once the body has lost its vigour. Study wears out the machine.'[27] An author or a philosopher degenerates morally, in the first instance: 'Public applause is to be his alone: I would say that he does everything to obtain it, if he did not do even more to deprive his competitors of it.'[28]

Tissot had already published the tract *De la santé des gens de lettres* in 1766. The contents consisted of a paraphrase of a *Sermo inauguralis de valetudine litteratorum*, written shortly before, which had been translated into French and, for its part, was based on a tract entitled *Della preservazione della salute de' letterati*, printed in Venice (1762). The main causes of the 'scholars' disease' were, according to the author, 'the diligent activity of the mind and the constant repose of the body'. If the action of the soul is too great, he continued, it inflicts blows on the body 'which rob it of its strength', as Plato before him had recognized. The Swiss scholar cited van Swieten's report concerning one patient 'who entirely ruined his health with nightly study', and claimed that constant sitting leads among scholars to muscle atrophy, impairs the circulation, and induces dropsy, bladder disorders, haemorrhoids and insomnia. Even those who write about health suffer from such ailments, because their lifestyle is in opposition to nature. In addition, Tissot warned 'older' scholars against choosing new fields of research, as this puts a strain on their brain, 'in which this provokes a violent condition which weakens the nervous system'. Palsy affects clerics more frequently than those in other professions. Tissot reminds us that Hippocrates had good reason for prescribing a regimen for the scholar, according to which nutrition was to be in correct proportion to work. Field-workers are held up as an example, as, it is claimed, they are 'always in a condition of perfect health'. The writing profession and a natural lifestyle could not, in the view of the majority of contemporaries, be easily reconciled.

The dangers of intellectual work and a sedentary profession had already been discussed by Galen, Rufus of Ephesus, Aretaeus of Cappadocia and Plutarch. Marsilio Ficino, in *De vita triplici* (1489), had developed a concrete doctrine on healthy living for scholars. The Utrecht edition (1703) of the tract *De morbis artificum diatribe*, by the Paduan professor of medicine Bernardo Ramazzini (Modena, 1700), contains an additional chapter on the 'vita sedentaria', the 'sedentary lifestyle'.[29] Ramazzini admittedly ascribed the eccentric behaviour of many artists (which the latter liked to attribute to the sign of Saturn) simply to poisoning by the paint fumes breathed in while working; however, he continued, intellectuals, authors, aesthetes and philosophers frequently suffered from an abdominal weakness, as they 'redirected' the *spiritus* necessary for digestion to the brain. The consequences were flatulence, a pale complexion, weight loss and melancholy. In addition, the stomach and pancreas were compressed by a bent posture.[30] Preachers and teachers were prone to catarrh and tears in their veins; the burden of their office made lawyers, judges and servants of princes insomniac, hypochondriac and consumptive. Ramazzini credits doctors with a rather healthier way of life, which is characterized by mobility and reinforced by a cheerful disposition, 'when they return home, well paid'. Chocolate, he continues, has a positive effect on dispositions dominated by black bile, as does good wine.[31] The Göttingen physicist and social commentator Georg Christoph Lichtenberg (1742–1799) urged scholars in his aphorisms: 'Familiarize yourself with your body and whatever you can find out about your soul, accustom yourself to work and learn to overcome your comfort; accustom your mind to doubt and your heart to tolerance.' Moderation in particular represents a difficult task here, as it can only be accomplished with the aid of experience: 'Moderation presupposes enjoyment; abstinence does not.' However, Boerhaave considers hypochondria 'an ornament for the scholar, just as a scar is for the soldier'. Exaggerated concern with their health is entirely common among intellectuals, he states, citing the example of Cardano, who regularly inspected his health with the aid of a mirror.

Princes naturally had to keep to a different regime from that of clerics, philosophers or men of letters. According to Franz Anton Mai, actors also represented a particularly vulnerable occupational group.[32] In the Mannheim National Theatre, where he had witnessed the debut performance of Schiller's *Die Räuber* [*The Robbers*] as resident doctor, he observed 'that the Duke Albert, Kaspar Thoringer, the kidnapped, mistreated Agnes Bernauerin, the furious Medea, the despairing Ariadne on Naxos all suffered from heart tremors, a racing pulse, trembling in all body parts, after they had plundered nature of all its beguiling magic in a physical performance.' Mai, who also treated the most famous thespian of the day, August Wilhelm Iffland, believed that 'cold dissimulation' came naturally 'only to ice-cold and insensitive actors'. The best representatives of the trade, however, were 'slaves of our pleasure' and 'victims of their art', their nerves 'more sensitive than those of the most tender lady'. The performance of a drama such as *Die Räuber* meant a loss in nerve juices for the protagonists, leading to 'recurring fevers and enfeeblement'. Only a sophisticated dietetic regime could help them to 'preserve the health so necessary to the affairs of the soul'. Pure spring water, a little red wine, exercise, cold ablutions and good company are all recommended. The theatre should be closed two times a year, so that the ensemble can rest. Mai considered it a duty of the authorities to help the actors, as they themselves affected the 'health of the citizens . . . as they make vice appear ridiculous and virtue appealing'.

Alternative paths to health

In addition to the advice of the doctors, there were always directions for the conservation and restoration of health that did not correspond to the predominant medical paradigm. Nature was often invoked – a highly heterogeneous term, with which, for example, the Presocratics, the Hippocratics, the Stoics, medieval Galenics, Paracelsus, Rousseau, Pantheists and proponents of the Enlightenment associated diverse subject matter.[33] If one equates 'alternative' therapeutic forms primarily with 'naturopathy', one can subsume beneath this term many historical guidelines on health. It is not surprising that even Rousseau, who was so hostile to learning, referred on the title page of his educational work *Émile* to the Stoics, whose exhortation 'secundum naturam vivere' was recalled over thousands of years in European dietetic thought.[34] Like Rousseau, numerous ancient philosophers had condemned 'unnatural' modes of living; 'methodists' such as Nero's contemporary Thessalus of Tralles attempted to 'retune' the body by means of regima for the metabolism, fasting, special diets, baths, massages and compensational gymnastics. One can, of course, also class the cult of Aesculapius as an alternative form of therapy.

Even in the high Middle Ages, which were apparently dominated by scholastic medicine, there were 'irrational' backlashes. In the thirteenth century, for example, the aforementioned Dominican Nicholas of Montpellier took issue with the *ratio* demanded by university medicine, as well as with Aristotelianism and the *experimentum* advocated by, among others, Roger Bacon. Petrarch and Montaigne also came close to Rousseau's theses. For the fourteenth-century author Petrarch, there was 'nothing healthier' than allowing the body to repose in the 'natural reclusion' of Vaucluse or Arquà.[35] He had nothing but contempt for the humoral-pathological school of medicine, which considered itself responsible for the care only of the body, and not of the soul. For Montaigne, 'the mere thought of nature', which 'makes us spurn the lower and earthly things', was 'food for the mind'. Like Rousseau after him, the sixteenth-century essayist and traveller was inspired by the (recently discovered) 'savages' in America, who, it was believed by all, lived 'healthily'. Montaigne also invoked the times when people lived without physicians, and noted with pleasure that many of those in this profession became ill themselves. It should not surprise us that he also made ironic comments about 'book-learning'.[36]

Of the Renaissance physicians, Paracelsus was particularly attached to alternative therapeutic methods, in other words, methods that ran contrary to university doctrine. His hostility towards authority has been shared by numerous alternative therapists throughout history, while his 'chemical' medicaments were absorbed rapidly by broad swathes of the 'humoral school'. It was, however, the liberal use of Paracelsian remedies such as arsenic, antimony, bismuth and gold compounds by the adherents of humoral medicine that was criticized by the 'natural physicians' of the nineteenth century.[37] Yet Paracelsus also departed in other ways from traditional medicine. The notion of an 'archaeus' operating within the body was close to the 'natural healing force' of later natural physicians, and his faith in the effectiveness of therapeutic baths tied in with ancient hydrotherapeutic traditions. 'For you see outside in nature how some corrections must take place, so it is also here with baths.'[38] He investigated the effects of numerous springs in south-west Germany, Austria and Switzerland, while his contemporary Johannes Dryander was the first to analyse the salt content of mineral springs, in his tract *Vom Eymser Bad*, written in 1535.[39] The humanist and geologist Georg Agricola wrote a comprehensive work on this subject in 1535 (*De natura eorum quae effluent ex terra*), which was also of interest to the adherents of iatrochemistry.[40] A clear distinction could not always be drawn, however, between 'exact' science and alternative medicine.

Even in the fifteenth century, bathhouses were doubtless geared more towards pleasure than therapy; however, provision was also made for the health of the guests. The barber cut hair, shaved, washed heads, tended wounds, treated spots and swellings, performed cupping, rubbed the skin and performed massages. The distinction between the scope of his duties and those of surgeons and physicians was, in fact, unclear.[41] Around 1500, however, there was, for the first time since antiquity, a boom in the popularity of fashionable spas – for example, those in Switzerland, Bagni Vignoni and Abano in Italy, and Wildbad, Pyrmont, Liebenzell and Ems in Germany. Guests at spas expected relaxation, conviviality, health and beauty. The ancient idea of the fountain of youth,[42] which is attested as early as the twelfth century in Constantinople, or of the 'Altweibermühle' (old women's mill), a mill that was thought to turn old women into young women, was also a theme in literature and in the visual arts.[43] The therapeutic effectiveness of the spa had been asserted as early as 1300 by devotees of humoral medicine such as Pietro d'Abano, and was naturally also well known in Roman antiquity. It is a well-established fact that an outbreak of syphilis was to blame for a temporary disruption in the bathing culture in the fifteenth century.[44]

A dry morning toilet was advocated in the seventeenth century by Jean du Chesne in his hygiene tract *Le Portrait de santé* (1606). It was thought that water affected health negatively, by opening the pores of the skin and admitting air contaminated by miasma. Yet, according to humoral medicine, water could also exercise a therapeutic effect in the case of certain illnesses, such as kidney stones, or counteract a 'dry consistency'. This accounts for the practice in Strasbourg in 1627 of taking a hot steam bath against inflammations caused, it was thought, by cold and dryness.[45]

It is nonetheless true that many people considered lice and even worms to be natural inhabitants of the human skin. They were sometimes even seen as proof of a healthy physical condition. It was also a commonly held view among medical experts at the universities that vermin can crawl forth from the body. Lice and maggots were, according to the scholastic view, produced by putrid bodily juices (which was interpreted both as a sign of flourishing health and as a memento mori!).[46] As a consequence, the employment of water was frequently considered a revolutionary innovation in the early modern period. The bathing tracts of the sixteenth century announce a new trend towards balneotherapy; this was advanced by the heathen and Christian tradition of the 'healing spring' as a remedy for, for example, eye disorders, infertility or forms of palsy.[47] Many pilgrim sites where health was supposed to be bestowed featured spas and holy water.

Hydrotherapy underwent a significant increase in popularity in the nineteenth century. In 1738, the Schweidnitz physician Johann Sigmund Hahn composed a tract entitled *Die wunderbaren Heilkräfte des frischen Wassers bei dessen innerlichen und äußerlichen Gebrauche* [*The Wondrous Healing Powers of Cold Water when Used Internally and Externally*], in which cold baths and drinking regimens are prescribed for the most diverse illnesses.[48] He capitalized on the enthusiasm for nature which began with Rousseau and chimed with the political Zeitgeist. Soon, the nobility and the pre-revolutionary society of the eighteenth century were heading for the fashionable spas, which were also famed for their drinking regimens.

The construction of bathing pools, toilets and private baths demonstrates that the expectations were also beginning to change in respect of hygiene. Hydrotherapeutic remedies were prescribed with increasing frequency, as was the use of baths. Friedrich Hoffmann and Paul Noguez also praised the healing powers of pure water (1730). According to the Brownian doctrine of excitability, cold water represented a kind of antidote to 'asthenia'. 'All firm components of the body are contracted and thereby strengthened in this manner.'[49] Simplicity stood opposed to luxury, energy to decay, health to artificial affectations. Swimming also became fashionable; according to the *encyclopédistes*, it was preferable to taking normal baths, 'because the constant vigorous movements that one makes in order to overcome the resistance of the water facilitate its entrance into the body, make the muscular movements smoother in all parts of the body, assist beneficial secretions and excretions and, in a word, serve as a guarantee of the best possible health.'[50]

Great importance was also attached to the 'mobilization of bodily energies' *after* the revolution, although not everyone desired such a development within the health sector. Notions of hidden vital forces and essences continued to circulate. Alongside the religious tradition – and prayers for the conservation or restoration of health were a matter of course, particularly within the Catholic cultural sphere – notions of health-damaging 'Bergmännlein' (mountain sprites), witches, devilish forces and magic also played an important role.[51] The Jesuit father Joseph Gaßner expressed the opinion in 1775 that all illnesses are,

without exception, induced by the devil and his helpers. People were
freed from their sufferings in large-scale ritual exorcisms.[52]

Such mass movements also explain the success of the 'miracle
doctor' Franz Anton Mesmer (1734–1815), who won acclaim in
Vienna and Paris with his techniques of suggestion and hypnosis and
the aura of his personality, and who ridiculed Gaßner's methods.[53]
Mesmer was convinced that a magnetic fluid determines health and
sickness in the human and animal organism. He attempted, by means
of the supposedly magnetic force of his personality, to bring about
positive changes in the fluid of the patients. The success of this sug-
gestive method was impressive, and paved the way for the age of
Romantic medicine. From 1784, when Mesmer left Vienna following
a contested 'healing of the blind', his pupils were trained in the
'Societies of Harmony' in France, where even the royal court showed
interest in Mesmer. Under the influence of Romantic natural philosophy and the 'somnambulism' that was popular around 1800,
Mesmer's doctrine also anticipated the foundations of modern psychotherapy and depth psychology. Some, however, considered it
simply a form of charlatanism that had been adapted to chime with
the Zeitgeist.

Samuel Hahnemann (1745–1843) believed that he had discovered
a further effective method of healing ailments; his nosological and
therapeutic approach is the only method to have survived, to a considerable degree, up to the present day. Against the medicine of his
time, which was dominated by iatromechanics and iatrochemy, by sys-
tematism or religious speculation, he set 'immaterial' medical forces
based on the 'vital force' (autocracy) postulated by so many contemporary physicians. In his chief work, *Organon der rationellen
Heilkunde* [*Organon of Rational Medicine*], Hahnemann argued that
illnesses can be combated with the aid of remedies which cause an
affliction similar to that against which the vital force is fighting. 'Every
effective medicine provokes a kind of illness within the human body,
an illness which is all the more unique, exceptional and severe, the
more effective the medicine is.' The artificial ailment, which is caused
by a minimal dosage, is, like the original ailment, overcome by the
vital force according to the principle of *similia similibus*.[54] Baths,
coffee and massages were also held as 'homeopathic aids' to reinforce
the basic therapy. The *conservation* of health was considered possible
only by means of a superior 'life regime', which prevents the diminution of the vital force. Tea, spirits, smelling salts, perfumes, strong
spices, cakes and pastries, frozen foods, cheese and so on were all considered dangerous, as were excesses and the 'affects'; here Hahnemann
drew on traditional doctrines. Hahnemann had an uncompromis-

ing aversion to 'allopathy', although he was himself attacked by nineteenth-century 'natural physicians' hostile to homeopathy, such as Hufeland, for his use of foreign matter to trigger the substitute illness. By contrast, the aging Goethe wrote in 1820: 'I now believe more fervently than ever in the doctrine of the wondrous doctor, since I felt and continue to feel the effects of a tiny dose so intensely.'

In his work *Praktische Übersicht über die vorzüglichsten Heilquellen Deutschlands nach eigenen Erfahrungen* [*Practical Survey of the Most Excellent Spas in Germany, from my own Experience*] (Berlin, 1815), Hufeland also argued that every course of treatment at a spa represented an 'artificial illness', for which reason stimulating and debilitating activities should be avoided at health resorts. As a consequence, he advocated a strict *spa diet*. Eucharius Oertel (1765–1850), a grammar school teacher from Ansbach who, like many proponents of alternative medicine, lacked any training in medicine, also publicized treatments with water, alluding to the doctrine of the Silesian 'water doctor' Johann Siegmund Hahn (1696–1773). He composed many popular scientific tracts on this subject and, in 1832, founded the Hydropathic Health Association, which continued the tradition begun by Hahn.[55] Around 1800, the naturopathic movement was, as Rothschuh notes, 'full of dynamism, activeness and aggressiveness', and was carried by broad swathes of the population,[56] reaching its zenith in the nineteenth century.

Goethe

Goethe indisputably occupies a prominent position in the history of dietetics and the doctrine of health. For him, health was related to vital force and moderation, but also to happiness. It could not be attained easily without commitment to philosophical and moral issues or without practical 'worldly wisdom'. Its value is uncontested: 'I beg of you', he writes to a friend from his youth, Augustin Trapp, from Worms, 'care for this body with persistent faithfulness. The soul must see through these eyes, and when they are dim, there is rainy weather in the whole world.' In the *Farbenlehre* [*Theory of Colours*], similarly, we read: 'Health and capability occur together. We desire a healthy mind in a healthy body. And long life takes the place of immortality.' Physical wellbeing remains hidden to all intents and purposes, but the individual must fight for it all his life. 'What is virtue?' is a central question for Goethe; his answer is simply: 'A very beautiful name for the simplest of things: health.'

Education is therefore necessary in order to deal with health and sickness – 'the apprenticeship in the art of living', as Novalis referred to the positive side of the illnesses and misfortunes of human existence.[57] Contrary to the legend, Goethe by no means glowed with good health; he therefore considered dealing with old age, illnesses and ill humour to be an existential challenge. His health, and even his life, were greatly in danger not only after his separation from Ulrike von Levetzow (1823) and following the death of his son August (1830); as a nineteen-year-old student in Leipzig he only barely survived a stomach haemorrhage.[58] Suffering and illness were for him an 'immense hammer', which man admittedly needed 'to free his nature from the many waste products'.[59] Yet he was constantly dogged by the fear of physical and mental degeneration. Health, he wrote in 1823 to Lily Parthey, should always be valued most highly, particularly 'when one is still completely healthy'. His idea was that the gods should 'rather bring forward the end than allow me to crawl miserably the last stretch towards the destination'. This wish, expressed by the young Goethe in 1778 to Frau von Stein, is programmatic for his anxiety. Intellectual pursuits, music and art, but in particular the 'vis medicatrix naturae', help the individual to withstand illness and death. After the struggle 'with life and death', the journey to Italy in 1786, with all its stimuli, afforded 'a second day of birth, a true rebirth'.

For Goethe, body and soul could only attain health conjointly. The endeavour to reach this goal is of existential significance: 'If I wished to let myself go, unchecked, then I would probably find it in myself to run myself and my surroundings into the ground.' Influenced by Hippocrates, Boerhaave, Carus and Hufeland, he also believes in the powers of the body to heal itself. In 1782 he wrote to Johann Caspar Lavater: 'Nature deserves many thanks that she placed so much healing power in the existence of every living being that it can stitch itself back together when it has been ripped at one end or another. And what are the thousands of kinds of religion if not thousands of expressions of this healing power!' According to Goethe, a regular retreat from the community, as advocated by Petrarch and the humanists, also assists the process of reinvigoration and recovery. In 1821, the 72-year-old Goethe assured Alexander von Humboldt that he was, 'thanks to the most resolute solitude and dietetic caution, in a better condition this winter than for many years'.

Goethe joined the 'vitalists' in criticizing the techniques of measuring and counting emerging in medicine and warned resolutely against the 'Newtonian spirit': 'Measuring a thing is a crude act, which cannot be applied in any other way than extremely imperfectly to living bodies.' For him, health can 'only exist in the balance of opposing forces, just as the suspension of health appears and exists only as a result of the dominance of one over the others';[60] here his contact with the Romantics, but also his familiarity with classical dietetic traditions becomes clear.

For Goethe, nature reflects the harmony of the 'cosmos', which acts as a model for body and soul. The consolation and hope of mankind can be found in the 'orderliness' of existence, 'which includes dietetics and culture of living'. The physician becomes the servant of nature, the mouthpiece of its laws; preoccupation with natural sciences becomes in itself a part of medicine. He explains to Johann Peter Eckermann, on 18 May 1824, 'the observation of nature requires a certain calm purity within, which cannot be disturbed and preoccupied by anything at all.' As a student of law in Strasbourg, he is already interested in medical matters and envies those fellow students who study such subjects: 'The objects of their endeavours are the most sensual, and, simultaneously, the highest, the simplest and the most complicated. Medicine preoccupies the whole man, because it is preoccupied with the whole man.' He writes from Rome in 1788: 'The study of the human body now has me totally. Everything else is fading beside it.'

It was last but not least his physiological studies that instilled in Goethe the conviction that health is based on a constant process of reshaping. 'The theory of metamorphosis is the key to all signs of nature.' A constant transformation from simplicity to diversity, in the course of which 'something sublime [emerges] from something lowly, something strong from something weak, something beautiful from something inconspicuous', is the secret of evolution and explains the essence of health. Like illness, health here acquires a philosophical, even spiritual dimension; the conditions of the soul and of the body are inseparably connected.[61]

Goethe's pragmatism taught him at an early stage that health cannot be static, but consists rather in the pursuit of higher goals, of a better condition. It is precisely the feeling that one can advance further, further cultivate body and mind, that produces the positive prevailing moods which conserve health. 'It was pronounced long ago with good reason and importance: one cannot remain for long at the pinnacle of condition.' Thus the eternal fluctuations of the temperament and of physical states bring about repeated new attempts, even dynamic impulses, on the part of health, to reach the optimal state. The author is no doubt orientating himself to the ancient maxim 'Melius est ad summum quam in summo';[62] at the highest point, one can neither remain static nor climb further – anyone who is absolutely 'healthy' is almost necessarily under threat from illness and relapses.

The healthy life has an undulating course and has nothing to do with freedom from any complaints, nor with 'top form'.

Everyday life and everyday dietetics merge together for Goethe. The fact that the author ascribed particular importance to upbringing, like almost all intellectuals of the seventeenth and eighteenth centuries, should not surprise us; however, we may be startled by the implacability with which he adheres to the maxim used to preface *Dichtung und Wahrheit* [*Poetry and Truth*]: 'The man who is not mistreated is not educated.' However, an intelligent dietetic regime also includes avoiding despair during illness and even translating suffering into a beneficial experience. 'I have learned a good deal in illness that I could not have learned anywhere else in my life', he wrote as a student in 1768 to Käthchen Schönkopf, adding that he feels 'revitalized' after crises. This does not mean, however, that he overlooks the advantages brought by health.

His interest in the natural sciences and medicine are also linked to the significance that he ascribes to the issue of health. Goethe shrank back in horror from the existential threat connected with possible illness. In this respect, he regarded the medical professional as sinister, inhuman. 'Who would become a physician, if he were to see at once all the inconveniences that await him?' Would one not be driven to despair, 'knowing ills as a physician knows them'?

We should not neglect to mention that Goethe loved movement, sport, fresh air and the great outdoors above all else, and that it was his conviction that 'moderate exercise refreshes the mind and brings the body into an exquisite balance.' Hufeland confirmed that he was, all physical complaints notwithstanding, 'the first . . . in all forms of physical exercise: riding, fencing, vaulting, dancing'.[63] Juvenal's ideal goal of the 'mens sana in corpore sano' was to him a daily challenge.

Romantic medicine – Schelling, Carus, Novalis

The numerous theoretical models that were thought to explain the causes and secrets of sickness and health – for example, Brownianism or homeopathy – increasingly threw physicians and patients into confusion around 1800. In practice, Galenic humoral pathology was still employed in many places, although it was relativized by vitalistic theories.[64] A medical eclecticism became increasingly widespread; with the assistance of the newest doctrines people endeavoured to make sickness and, similarly, health comprehensible. Reil noted in 1799, in his work *Über die Erkenntnis und Chur der Fieber* [*On the Diagnosis and Cure of Fevers*]:

> I am writing in an age where nerve and humoral pathologists, Brownians and anti-Brownians, are at loggerheads with each other, where the common theories in medicine have been shaken . . . I have tested the doctrinal edifices of older and newer physicians, and have been an adherent now of this, now of another system. Yet, I confess sincerely, in none have I found the reassurance that I was seeking.

The time had come for the Romantics to fill this spiritual vacuum within medicine and to exploit currents of a Zeitgeist that had been devoted to Cartesianism only a few years previously. The growth of interest in 'Romantic medicine' in recent years can easily cause us to overlook the fact that, for example, as late as 1775, the physician (and, subsequently, revolutionary) Jean-Paul Marat, in his treatise *De l'homme, ou Des principes et des loix* [*On Man, or On Principles and Laws*], drew liberally on Descartes: 'The body is a real hydraulic machine that consists of an astounding number of vessels and different bodily juices . . . It is the interplay between the organs of the circulation that constitutes . . . life; its complete cessation constitutes death.'

The natural philosophy of Friedrich Wilhelm Josef Schelling (1775–1854) seems to have had a particularly liberating effect in this context.[65] The year 1797 saw the publication of the *Ideen zu einer Philosophie der Natur* [*Ideas for a Philosophy of Nature*], which heralded the age of Romantic medicine in a narrower sense.[66] In this work, Schelling described the 'structure of nature in steps', which he states is determined by the 'drive . . . which, struggling, so to speak, with the raw matter, now prevails, now succumbs'. This force, he continues, is perceptible from animate to inanimate nature, from 'net of moss' to 'refined form'.[67] Matter in its entirety is defined by 'polarity and duality', with forces of attraction and repulsion, positivity and negativity, irritability and sensibility, male and female principles, lightness and heaviness, necessity and freedom, oxygen and hydrogen, naturally also characterizing the condition of the human being.[68] 'Health must be understood as a state in which all polarities of the organs are in the correct relationship to each other and, taken altogether, harmonize with the external world.'[69] According to Schelling, nature is continuously subject to restraints in the course of evolution, whereby light, warmth, electricity and heaviness represent the graduations or concomitant phenomena. The actual 'purpose' of this process is the advancement of the genus; the development of a healthy organism, on the other hand, is merely a 'goal'. The sensibility of the body corresponds to the magnetic phenomena in nature, its irritability to electricity, and the formative drive ('nisus formativus'), he concludes boldly, to light.[70] Between 1805 and 1810, the majority of German physiologists were fascinated by Romantic natural philosophy. Later, Schelling took a speculative, religious line, whereby he made a distinction between the (divine) *soul* of the human being and his *mind*, which, alone, was prone to illnesses and melancholy. Health was therefore equated with the subjection of body and mind to the soul, which can never fall ill, as it has a 'rapport with God'.[71]

Although Goethe's statement that the classical is healthy and the Romantic sickly is still a prevalent assessment of the period,[72] it was not shared by the 'Romantic' Schelling and his circle, which was 'scientifically' active and measured health by reference to three organic activities: sensibility, irritability and reproductive powers.[73] The separation between philosophy and medicine which emerged in the eighteenth century was in opposition to the attempt to intermix philosophy and healing. The 'natural philosophical' channel favoured by Schelling can here be contrasted with a group of 'Romantic' physicians, who dealt in a particular way with the 'self', with the soul and the mind, with dreams, art and literature, with meditation and the unconscious.[74]

Non-physicians such as Novalis or Görres concerned themselves with medicine; physicians such as Carus and Justinus Kerner with painting or poetry. Their holistic world view was based on a spiritual and physical conception of health that was, admittedly, anything but uniform. Like Goethe, they saw health not as a measurable entity, but rather as a harmonious interdependence of forces, oscillations, tensions and sensations.

An important representative of Romantic medicine was the physician and painter Carl Gustav Carus (1789–1869). He required that every individual should devise a 'living work of art', that is to say, should develop their natural disposition to an optimum point with the assistance of an individual dietetic regime, whereby professional, social and political success were considered as beneficial as artistic sensibility and the performance of charitable activities. Carus, a close friend of Caspar David Friedrich, considered the visual arts an important self-help resource: 'Many a sombre cloud over the life of my soul dissipated when I was able to allow it to emerge freely in a painting, and anyone who was not able to reconcile the lugubrious mood of my paintings with the fresh activity of my life demonstrated to me thereupon how little he had understood about my inner life.' He also emphasized that disruptions to health were a part of life: 'Precisely a nature which is entirely healthy manifests itself in the fact that it is also, if one can put it like this, capable of healthy illnesses, that is to say that illnesses – physical or psychological – to which no mortal is entirely impervious, develop and pass over with a particular regular course and with forceful and complete arbitrariness.'

Carus, who was personal physician to the king of Saxony, was the first to coin the term 'unconscious', which, dependent on the interaction between physical and mental influences, can only too easily preserve, advance or destroy health.[75] In addition he argued that the history of an individual's illness and suffering, his constitution and his temperament, could be observed in his physical appearance; his mental disposition, on the other hand, was discernible only in the shape of his skull and his face.[76] He thus incorporated ideas from Lavater in the *Physiognomik* [*Physiognomics*], and modified the expression 'pathognomic'. He also considered language to be an expression of the physical and psychological state.[77]

Observation of nature, Carus claimed, gave people strength and metaphysical security; a fundamental pantheistic strand linked his philosophy with the world of Caspar David Friedrich.[78] Nature is presented as a force which heals, calms, comforts and delights. The observation of nature becomes religious contemplation, repose and the source of health.

Kant had already divided mankind into races; in his lecture on physical geography (1775), the philosopher professed to identify 'mankind in its greatest perfection in the race of the whites'. Carl von Linné, Johann Friedrich Blumenbach (1752–1840) and the naturalist Lorenz Oken (1779–1815) had also developed 'racial typologies';[79] for his part, Carus differentiated between 'night peoples', the 'eastern and western twilight peoples' and 'day peoples', who represented 'the real bloom of mankind'.[80] From this categorization, he deduced an inequality in terms of mental aptitude as well as of physical health and perfection, but also insisted on the obligation of the 'day peoples' to help those who were less gifted. The term 'health' was correlated in an entirely elitist manner with 'mental freedom' and 'beauty of the soul' and, to the approbation of a number of 'Bildungsbürger' (the educated middle classes), approximated to the Greek ideal of 'kalokagathia'.[81]

Johann Caspar Lavater's *Physiognomische Fragmente zur Beförderung der Menschenkenntnis und Menschenliebe* [*Physiognomic Fragments for the Advancement of the Knowledge and Love of Mankind*] appeared as early as 1775. In this work, he claimed that it was entirely possible 'to observe the blood composition, the constitution, the warmth, the coldness, the coarseness or refinement, the wetness, the dryness, the pliancy and irritability of an individual'. Lavater, a pastor from Zurich, for his part, drew on Christian Adam Peuschel's

Abhandlung der Physiognomie, Metoskopie und Chiromantie [*Treatise on Physiognomy, Metoscopy and Chiromancy*] (1769), and, with the assistance of Zimmermann, Merck, Herder, Geßner, Füßli and Sulzer, established 'medical physiognomy' as a 'discipline founded in nature', which dealt with the *Zeichen der Gesundheit und Krankheit* [*Signs of Health and Sickness*] (1775). Guessing the health and character of an individual based on the form of the head, as well as, frequently, the side profile, was a popular parlour game in Goethe's day.

Some contemporaries were aware of the dangers associated with physiognomics. While Carus put forward similar views in his work *Symbolik der menschlichen Gestalt – Ein Handbuch zur Menschenkenntnis* [*Symbolism of the Human Form – A Handbook on Human Nature*] (1852), Lichtenberg wrote as early as 1778: 'If physiognomics becomes what Lavater expects it to become, children will be hanged before they commit crimes worthy of hanging.' The 'public hygiene' approaches of numerous physicians from the eighteenth century reinforced his scepticism 'that . . . powerful, popular and, simultaneously, active dilettantes could become dangerous in their company.' Lichtenberg was to be proved right: the tradition of 'measuring' the human being, from the phrenology of the nineteenth century through to the criminal experiments of Nazi physicians, had its origins in physiognomics.

The imperilled existence described by the Romantics became a biographical topos, particularly popular with artists and authors. Friedrich Schlegel (1772–1829), Franz Xaver von Baader (1765–1841), Gotthilf Heinrich Schubert (1780–1860), Karl Josef Hieronymus Windischmann (1775–1839) and Carus all describe their psychological hardships with a previously unknown openness. Johann Nepomuk Ringseis, personal physician and travel companion to the Bavarian king with a predilection for art, postulated a close connection between healing and religious experience, which, he believed, manifested itself in 'real art'. Health, he claimed, was present, 'where . . . there is neither a lack nor anything alien present in the body, soul and mind, and therefore all actions pass off with ease and comfort.'[82] According to Ringseis, *relative* health is the state 'in which the harmony of the present mental, physical and corporeal qualities is not noticeably disrupted', whereas the signs of 'normal' health are as follows: 'the mind unfettered in all its channels; all organs, in particular those related to sensory and motor functions, developed in harmony and working with ease; the blood in a medium amount, pleasantly red and of moderate thickness, the warmth of the skin pleasant, the pulse regular and strong.' The way that such definitions linked together psychological and physiological descriptions is remarkable.

There can be no doubt that many Romantic physicians were in possession of a particular charisma. Their presence alone instilled a subjective sense of health, not only in weak patients. The Swabian physician Justinus Kerner, for example, was treated when still a child by the pioneer of magnet treatment, Gmelin; he lost consciousness at the mere touch of the famous physician (this phenomenon is also described by the patients of Franz Anton Mesmer).[83] The holistic world view of such doctors also fascinated many people. 'The fact that he has drawn from the whole and the complete', wrote a pupil of Ringseis, 'that he has never detached his scholarship from the entire scientific truth, from that which endures in the history of the world and of man, from the initiator of all things' – this was primarily what fascinated people, 'although (admittedly) others reproach him primarily for this.'

Kerner (1786–1862) himself was not untypical of this period. He was, on the one hand, the discoverer of botulism (and, as a consequence, a forerunner of scientific medicine), but he also became a fervent supporter of a medical mysticism which sought to heal by means of empathy, hypnosis, prayer and magic.[84] According to the *Naturlehre* [*Doctrine on Nature*] written by the Bamberg clinician Andreas Röschlaub (1768–1835), to which Kerner referred, human existential orientation vacillates between 'illness' and 'wellness', whereby the latter refers to the 'consonance of the vital activities of the complete organic structure of an individual, to the end of attaining all of his aims'.[85] Quantitative changes in the vital activities only lead to illness, he claims, when all parts of the organism are suffering as a result. The *constitution*, which is defined as a mixture of protective energy and receptive force, plays an important part in this process.[86]

A further important advocate of Romantic medicine was the author Friedrich von Hardenberg (1772–1801), who, from 1798 onwards, adopted the name Novalis. He claimed that 'the sensation of health, of wellbeing, of contentedness' was unique for every individual; it was 'entirely personal', the law student and director of a Saxon salt mine emphasized. A 'basic trust' gained from the experience of nature afforded some protection from ailments, but further protection resulted from the recognition that 'illnesses also gain positive value, . . . [represent] an apprenticeship in the art of living and the cultivation of the mind', and bear within themselves the inclination towards spiritual and anthropological recovery. As a prophylactic, Novalis called for a comprehensive 'culture of life', which elevated the individual above everyday routine: 'The more that one learns to live, not only for the moment, but for years, and so on, the nobler one becomes. The hasty agitation, the petty ado of the mind gives way to great, calm, simple and expansive activity, and excellent patience appears.'[87]

For Novalis, health and sickness have a spiritual dimension, and cannot easily be measured according to subjective criteria. 'An uncritical perception of oneself as healthy, as well as an uncritical perception of oneself as ill, both are erroneous and – sickness.'[88] A new, and certainly bold, 'similia similibus' principle – although, admittedly, not in the pharmacological or homeopathic sense – is invoked for the preservation and attainment of health: illness is 'to be cured through illness'. From a kind of spiritual, holistic perspective, the experience of suffering benefits the soul, and therefore also the body. At the same time, the author considers medicine to be at the forefront of scholarship. The coveted state of health is attained with its assistance, although not without reflection:

> The more that medicine becomes an elementary science of every individual, the greater the progress made by physics in its entirety and the more this is used by medicine, the more fervently all the disciplines convene in order to advance their communal interest and the good of mankind, and take philosophy as the governess and directress of their decisions, the lighter the heart of the human race.[89]

Novalis also devised a concrete everyday dietetic regime. 'All sensitive people should receive a small and very diluted amount of mental (narcotic) substances. Coarse food, physical exercise, regular cerebral pursuits, diversion and observation of the sensory world . . ., these are the main features of their healing method.' The suggested invigorating activities range from 'the use of warm provisions, for example, milk, meat broth, eggs, wine, china, and so on', through to hill-climbing, brisk walking and riding, which is 'certainly very beneficial to weak lungs'. Novalis criticized Brownianism, in which he admired only the confidence 'with which Brown presents his system as generally valid'. The author adds ironically: 'The greater the magus, the more arbitrary his practices, his dicta, his instruments.'[90]

Novalis considered the 'doctrine of the art of living', which is related to wisdom concerning lifestyle and philosophy, but also to social integration and the love of art, to be of fundamental importance. The following sentence is reminiscent of Goethe's conception of health: 'There is no real unhappiness in the world at all. Happiness and unhappiness are in a relationship of eternal balance. Every instance of unhappiness is a kind of obstacle to a current, which breaks through all the more powerfully after the obstacle has been overcome.'[91] Traditional dietetic patterns might be adopted, but a prophylactic was ultimately possible only with the assistance of the community. It included the communal meal, which represents a daily repetition of the assimilation processes of our life.[92] 'It is with intellectual enjoyment as with the physical consumption of food', he writes elsewhere. 'A good deal is dependent on stomach, health, age, time, habit.'[93]

Novalis, but also Carus, advocated a holistic system of health care, which was characterized by a close interweaving of the art of living and health, by an elevation of the status of the layperson, and by individual responsibility for one's physical and mental state, as well as by a relativization of the physician's role in dietetics.

9

The Nineteenth Century

Trends in the nineteenth century

In the course of the nineteenth century, the traditional regimens, as well as Romantic concepts of health, were increasingly replaced by a 'highly specialized hygiene'.[1] It seemed as if universally valid 'regimina' had lost almost all currency. By the end of the century, hygiene had been reduced to a technique, dietetics to a matter of diet. Even more difficult was the reconciliation of the moral and philosophical, pedagogic, and spiritual aspects of health with the scientific paradigms which were becoming fashionable. Factors such as lifestyle, environment, profession and age seemed to call for special forms of dietetics. In other words, health became a matter of social policy. Public welfare was seen as under threat from 'natural' diseases – plagues, for instance – for which no individual blame could be attributed, but also from diseases of people's own making.[2] Although this was in no way new – the significance of 'nature', or 'disposition', had been a topic of discussion from the Hippocratics to the Romantics – in the nineteenth century the question of social responsibility became a central tenet of health doctrine.[3] State planning, which had derived considerable impetus from Johann Peter Frank's *System einer medicinischen Polizey* [*System of Medical Police*] of 1779,[4] seemed the prerequisite for the health of the people. The necessity for it was seldom questioned.

Nevertheless, in the rational and positivist environment into which the avant-garde of traditional medicine was increasingly moving, the voice of Romantic doctrines could still be heard. Carus published some of his most important works in the 1840s, and the Viennese doctor and poet Ernst von Feuchtersleben (1806–1849), in books such as *Diätetik der Seele* [*Dietetics of the Soul*] (1838), *Die Gewißheit und Würde der Heilkunst* [*The Certainty and Dignity of the Art of Medicine*] (1839), or *Beiträge zur Literatur, Kunst und Lebenstheorie* [*Contributions to Literature, Art, and the Theory of Life*] (1837), propagated once again the concept of 'life as a work of art', which culminated in 'Kalobiotics', 'the art of beautiful living'.[5] Under the influence of Kant's *Von der Macht des Gemüths, durch den bloßen Vorsatz, krankhafter Gefühle Meister zu sein* (translated by John C. Colquhoun in 1806 as *Kant on the Art of Preventing Diseases*), the goal of the not uncontroversial Doctor Feuchtersleben, who today is considered to be a pioneer of psychosomatic medicine,[6] was to create 'a prophylaxis of physical diseases by psychic means'. He distinguished an entire 'hierarchy of healths' – from the 'rude', to the 'consonated', to the 'educated' – and called for an integrated 'spiritual renewal' of man.[7]

This would not be the place to outline the changes in the concepts and methods of psychiatry since the eighteenth century, particularly since – under the influence of Foucault and Canguilhem – an almost limitless amount of literature has been devoted to this topic in recent years. The same could be said of physiology in general, which in many places, in France for instance, is still dominated by Brown's theory of stimulation.[8] Worthy of mention among those health doctrines propagated at the beginning of the nineteenth century is the *Grundriß der Theorie der Medizin* [*Outline of the Theory of Medicine*] by the Swiss physician Ignaz Paul Vitalis Troxler (1780–1866), who adopted Schelling's idea of a step-by-step development of the individual as well as the dietetic effect of philosophy. Health for him was maintaining a 'balance between the mixture of internal and external forces which determine human life'.[9] Competing with the ideas of Hufeland, the Berlin professor of medicine Carl Heinrich Schultz propagated in his book *Über die Verjüngung des menschlichen Lebens* [*On the Rejuvenation of Human Life*] of 1842 the notion that human life was determined by a process of 'upsurge and decline'. The precondition for recovery from illness, as well as for longevity, was 'regeneration [of the blood]', which interrupted the process of decline. 'Recovery is an upsurge of vitality in the mortal process of sickness', which is to be seen as 'an overcoming of the normal decline in individual organs'. 'In the steadiness of health the residues of the regeneration process gather themselves gradually and imperceptibly in the body.'

One of the consequences of Romanticism was that sickness long remained fashionable in artistic and intellectual circles. On 27 July 1820 Shelley wrote to Keats that he had learned 'that you continue to wear a consumptive appearance'.[10] It was not only in Bohemian circles that suffering was seen as the proof of higher creativity, of sensibility, or even of a superior existence. Until well into the second half of the century, health in the sense of dynamic vitality and the ideal cultivated from Petrarch to Rousseau of a robust and simple way of life were considered by 'snobs and parvenus' to be unacceptable, obsolete and tasteless. Above all, tuberculosis was viewed as proof that one was refined, gentle and sensitive. Thus Théophile Gautier, in his youth, 'could not have accepted as a lyrical poet anyone weighing more than ninety-nine pounds.'[11] This fashion would certainly have been restricted to a somewhat bored and not entirely poverty-stricken upper class as well as to artistic circles. Here, consumption was held to be *the* distinguishing sickness, which was 'a disease particularly fond of people who write such good verses as you have done', as Shelley put it while consoling the dying Keats in Rome.[12] Many of the Romantic painters and artists from the north who went to Italy, to Rome, Florence and Venice, used illness as a 'pretext for leisure, and for dismissing bourgeois obligations in order to live only for . . . art'.[13] Consumption was considered to be a hereditary disease which smote mainly the rich, the young, women, and fragile and sensitive creatures, and was associated with weariness of life and 'existential affliction'. It was considered a thing of 'aethereal beauty', pandering to its victim's vanity.[14] Tuberculosis could encourage a life of luxury and idleness, and as late as 1920 Kafka wrote to Milena Fischerova that it was an illness in which there was 'much sweetness'.[15]

Among ordinary people, however, there was little trace of this elitist, Romantic yearning for sickness. It was specifically the 'social' dimension which made tuberculosis, particularly in France and Russia, a theme of literature. Victor Hugo's *Les Misérables* or the Goncourt brothers' *Madame Gervaise* are typical examples of this.[16] No sensible doctor, no intellectual in the early nineteenth century doubted that health meant something more than standard physiological values, the first important advocate of which in this period, Johannes Müller (1801–1858), stressed, in his inaugural lecture in Bonn, their 'intimate connection with philosophy'.[17] Sociology, politics, science, reason and progress seemed here to be locked together in singularly remarkable fashion.

Rudolf Virchow and the dietetics of reason

The scientific paradigm change in medicine in the middle of the nineteenth century is associated primarily with the name Rudolf Virchow

(1821–1902). As early as his first important speech – *Über das Bedürfnis und die Richtigkeit einer Medizin vom mechanischen Standpunkt* [*On the Need for, and Correctness of, a Medicine from the Mechanical Point of View*] in 1845 – he mounted an attack on the 'Romantic spirit'.[18] For Virchow, health and sickness revealed themselves in the condition of the body cells, whose interdependence, he was convinced, could also serve as a model for the community.[19] In his *Handbuch der speziellen Pathologie und Therapie* [*Handbook of Special Pathology and Therapy*] (1854), he described the intact cell formation as a physiological substratum of bodily harmony. Healing meant the 'regulation of disrupted conditions' at the level of the (then) smallest known constituent parts of the body. A remark in the preface to the lectures on cellular pathology published in 1858 makes it clear that Virchow's concept of harmony also took its cue from historical models: 'Indeed, I find not merely in antiquity and the Middle Ages that the opinions of doctors are not universally in thrall to traditional prejudices, but even more that good common sense among the populace has clung to certain truths despite the fact that learned criticism has declared them outmoded.'

Although a purely scientific definition of health seemed to him problematic since, in his opinion, this excluded the 'transcendent' aspects, Virchow associated the concept of health closely with standard values. Following from this, the Belgian physician L. A. Quetelet wrote in 1869: 'An individual who, at a particular time, would unite within him all the qualities of the average person would be the representative of everything great, good and beautiful; all immoderate deviation from his circumstances or his existence would be malformation and sickness.'[20] It seemed impossible 'to judge the condition of an individual without comparing it to that of a fictitious being whom one considers to be in a state of normality.' The consequence of this thesis was the definition of health as 'all individual parameters being located in the statistical mean'. The diagnostics of measurement was institutionalized primarily by Carl Reinhold Wunderlich's introduction of the temperature chart in Leipzig in 1859.

Taking care of health, according to Virchow, was one of the most important tasks of medicine, which he regarded as the 'mother of the social sciences'.[21] He recognized very early on that the inhuman working conditions in early capitalism presented a challenge for doctors and government: 'People are viewed merely as hands! Is that supposed to be the meaning of machines in the cultural history of the peoples? Are the triumphs of human genius to serve no other purpose than to bring misery to the human race?' The journal *Die medizinische Reform* [*Medical Reform*], founded in 1848, the year of revolution, had therefore as its theme changes in science *and* society. Its tenor was simultaneously conservative and progressive: 'Man should work only as much as is necessary to wrest enough from the soil, and from raw material, as to ensure the comfortable existence of the whole race, but he should not waste his best efforts to make capital.' Virchow justified his optimism, which was shared by almost all the representatives of scientific medicine, with historical arguments: having overcome the religious as well as the philosophical age, mankind had now entered the stage of positive knowledge. Doctors now had to take on the role of leaders, to advise politicians, and also to make provision for individual as well as state and collective wellbeing.[22] Enlightened thinkers such as Virchow were distinguished by their pseudo-religious elevation of the power of science, but also by the conviction that they might relieve in the shortest possible time the manifold sufferings of mankind.

The social situation throughout the states of Europe had indeed become serious. In England, out of every thousand workers, one hundred died as a result of 'factory work, their living conditions, and the immoderation which was bound up with this state and these conditions'.[23] It was clear not only to Virchow that reforms were imperative. Welfare associations arose; industrial workers and artisans fought for light, hygiene and health. Edwin Chadwick's *Report on the Sanitary Condition of the Labouring Class* (1842) or the *Tableau de l'état physique et moral des ouvriers employés dans les manufactures de coton, de laine et de soie* [*Picture of the Physical and Moral State of Workers Employed in the Manufacture of Cotton, Linen and Silk*] (1840) by the physician Louis-René Villermé took on programmatic significance. And thus, even before Bismarck's social legislation, efforts were being made in Europe to improve the lot of industrial workers.[24] Herbert Spencer (1861) declared it a moral duty for both state *and* the individual to take responsibility for health: 'Perhaps nothing will bring about more quickly the time when adequate provision will be made for both the body and the spirit than when the conviction is spread that the maintenance of health is a duty. Few people seem aware that there is such a thing as a physical morality.' Maxims such as this were crucially influential.

In 1877 the Danish physician Julius Petersen announced that medicine would largely abandon its emphasis on curing, in order to 'further the happiness of mankind' by means of health provision.[25] Most of these theoreticians represent an eminently utilitarian standpoint. Not least because of the influence of Darwin, they were convinced that the wellbeing of the community took precedence over individual interests. Auguste Comte (1798–1857) emphasized, however, the connection between scientific progress and a growing humanity; 'sociology' and 'social physics' gained increasing influence. Comte considered the individual to be a pre-scientific abstraction; only the collective seemed real and positive. The authorities, for the good of the community as a whole, were given the right to intervene in public as well as private life. All forms of sickness should be administered, all forms of health be planned for.[26]

In his Stettin lecture *Über den Einfluß der Medizin auf das materielle Wohl der Völker* [*On the Influence of Medicine on the Material Wellbeing of the Peoples*] of 1863, the physician Karl Heinrich Schultz-Schultzenstein declared: 'Almost all questions regarding material wellbeing are already included in the great sphere of medical policing, since, in addition to the maintenance of good health, it is also concerned with the provision of healthy nourishment, healthy air and water, healthy dwellings, clothes and location.' The 'arrangements for the correct use of foodstuffs' is also a 'matter for medicine'. Dietetics is held to be the 'playground on which the different views on material wellbeing desport themselves'.[27]

In 1886 Werner von Siemens made the optimistic announcement 'We recognize that, in the age of the dominance of the natural sciences, men are being relieved more and more of the burden of physical labour by the growing use of the powers of nature in the execution of mechanical work.' The inventor and industrialist was convinced that the 'intellectual pleasures of life' would 'lead to the healthier development of future generations'.[28] At a natural history research conference in Frankfurt in 1867, Max von Pettenkofer (1818–1901), too, propagated the importance of public health care. The hygienist emphasized that 'no one is absolutely healthy, and no one is absolutely ill; everyone has organs and parts of the body which are more or less one or the other. In general, health is the sum of organic functions whose harmonious interaction makes it easy for us to pursue the purpose of life.' He then went on to underline the new, protective task of his chosen science: 'the task of health care, and hygiene in its widest sense, is to develop and strengthen individual functions, and to keep at bay everything which destroys the harmony of the whole.' Good health, he maintains, raises the people's capacity for work, which is why since time immemorial hygienic arrangements have played a special role in religion, legislation, and the lives of outstanding personalities.[29] His writings *Boden und Grundwasser in ihren Beziehungen zu Cholera und Typhus* [*Soil and Groundwater in their Relationship to Cholera and Typhoid*] of 1869 and *Über den Werth der Gesundheit für eine Stadt* [*On the Value of Health for a Town*] of 1873 made Pettenkofer world famous. Basing his ideas on those of the political economist Friedrich List (1789–1846), who regarded the intelligence and morality of a people as dependent on wealth, Pettenkofer understood hygiene as the *Wirtschaftslehre von der Gesundheit* [*Economic Doctrine of Health*]. In an essay of 1875 he added: 'Just as with political economy it is the pursuit of higher gains and not merely the fear of losses which is the driving force, so it must be with the theory of hygiene as an economic doctrine.' In consequence of the threat from cholera, a health police was already established in Berlin in the 1830s.[30]

If, as was believed, feeling, instincts and common sense all had a role to play in the old dietetics, Pettenkofer now saw the age of 'scientific hygiene' as having arrived: 'It is not only a matter of the physiology of the body; we now need – insofar as the extent of its health is influenced by it – a physiology of its environment. We need knowledge of the air, of the soil, of nourishment, of the house, of clothes, of the bed; we need a physiology which continues beyond the organism.'[31] According to the physician Eduard Reich, hygiene embraces 'the entire physical and moral world and communicates with all the sciences whose subject is the observation of man and the world which surrounds him.'[32] Health care, medicine and politics were all held to be interrelated. Pettenkofer complained that knowledge about hygiene had barely progressed since ancient times: 'Most people today still maintain the same position as Hippocrates, and are still not inclined to concede more than a completely vague and general connection between these matters and our health.'[33] It had escaped him that the old Hippocratic paradigm had, in this, his very own epoch, undergone a decisive change.

Nietzsche, Schopenhauer and the philosophical critique of positivism

It is scarcely surprising that the gigantic step from Romantic to scientific medicine should provoke criticism, and that it should give rise to profound reflection about sickness and health. In the second half of the century, the contradictory theories of doctors, the opposition between traditionalism and belief in progress, once again saw the philosophers called into action. There was again the recognition that there were mental dimensions to health and sickness which – notwithstanding all the enthusiasm for the Enlightenment and Comte – had been neglected since Virchow. In the preface to *Die fröhliche Wissenschaft* [*The Joyful Wisdom*] (1886), Nietzsche invokes the philosopher physician, 'who applies himself to the problem of the

collective health of peoples, periods, races, and mankind generally.'
Ultimately, it has not been a question in all philosophising of truth,
but of therapy, 'namely, of health, futurity, growth, power, life . . .'.[34]
In his discussion of Socrates in *The Birth of Tragedy* (1872), Nietzsche
mounts a vigorous polemic against faith in 'the fathomableness of
nature and in the universal healing power of knowledge'. He is certain
that 'the spirit of science is being pushed to its limits'. Whereas
Virchow and Helmholtz, Bernard and Pavlov considered health and
politics to be closely connected, but believed that health and mind had
little to do with one another, Nietzsche alluded directly to existential
experiences which could only be understood with prior experience of
illness: 'A philosopher who has passed and continues to pass through
many states of health has also passed through so many philosophies.'
A huge gulf separated the philosophers from the medical positivists,
who measured health as physical variants and negated spiritual influences: 'It is not for us philosophers to separate between soul and body;
even less is it for us to separate between soul and mind. We are not
thinking frogs, not apparatuses of objectification and registration,
with vitiated intestines!' Nietzsche sees suffering and illness as
unavoidable experiences in life, although he does not present them in
a positive light in the medieval, ascetic sense. Like Goethe, he takes a
polemic stance against the notion of the 'measurability' of life. The
physiologists, he claims, were preoccupied by the normative variants
of 'animal health', when 'great health' defied such norms.[35]

According to Nietzsche, real health is only possible when one has
overcome illnesses mentally; on the other hand, however, the body
should also not be neglected as a consequence of intellectual arrogance. The philosopher's prescriptions sound familiar: 'Against every
kind of tribulation and affliction of the soul one should at first try a
change of diet and hard physical work.'[36] According to Nietzsche,
health represented the positive end of a process of purification: 'It is a
far distance from the desert of such years of trial to that tremendous
and surging security and health, which illness itself cannot do
without.'[37] The route to 'great health' also necessitates for him a
departure from the 'error of the self', which does not, however, suggest
an intellectual affinity with Comte and the positivist political philosophers. 'Beyond myself and yourself! Feel cosmically!' is his demand. If
all these conditions are fulfilled, help comes automatically and 'all
things want to be your physicians'.[38]

Nietzsche, who had read Schelling, Bichat, Carus, Johannes Müller
and Virchow, was planning to write a dissertation on the subject 'The
Concept of Organization in Kant'. He would have been happy to take
up the medical profession and attended in an entirely practical way,

although admittedly in his own manner, to the 'great health'. His 'ignorance in physiologicis' seemed to him to be the 'real calamity in my life'.[39] Despite all philosophical exaltation – and no one felt this more acutely than Nietzsche – it was, he realized, precisely physical comfort which mattered in hours of despair. He wrote to Erwin Rohde in 1871: 'Alas, how I long for health! One merely intends to do something that will take somewhat longer than one will endure oneself – then one is thankful for every good night, for every warm ray of sun, and even for every regular digestion!'[40] In the preface to *Zarathustra*, he also states, somewhat cryptically: 'One has one's little pleasures for the day and little pleasures for the night, but one honours health.'

The secularization of society in the nineteenth century made health education, as it had done in the seventeenth and eighteenth centuries, an act of reason. In his *Aphorismen zur Lebensweisheit* [*Aphorisms on the Wisdom of Life*], Schopenhauer wrote: 'It follows from all this that the greatest of follies is to sacrifice health for any other kind of happiness whatever it may be, for gain, advancement, learning or fame, let alone, then, for fleeting sensual pleasures. Everything else should rather be postponed to it.' And, additionally, 'nine-tenths of our happiness depend upon health alone.'[41] Health seems to be so important that 'a healthy beggar is happier than an ailing king'.[42] Schopenhauer, too, emphasizes that health cannot be equated with being free of ailments.

> But however much health may contribute to the flow of good spirits which is so essential to our happiness, good spirits do not entirely depend upon health; for a man may be perfectly sound in his physique and still possess a melancholy temperament and be generally given up to sad thoughts. The ultimate cause of this is undoubtedly to be found as innate, and therefore unalterable, physical constitution.

He admits that 'a man's sensitiveness to his muscular and vital energy' varies from individual to individual, thereby revealing himself as a follower of Haller, or the vitalists.[43] Health contributes to the 'cheerfulness of the senses', and is thus quintessential to the bourgeois dream: 'A quiet and cheerful temperament, happy in the enjoyment of a perfectly sound physique, an intellect clear, lively, penetrating and seeing things as they are, a moderate and gentle will, and therefore a good conscience – these are privileges which no rank or wealth can make up for or replace.'[44] Despite his extreme respect for good health, Schopenhauer also stands for stoical principles: 'For what a man is in himself, what accompanies him when he is alone, what no one can give or take away, is obviously more essential to him than everything he has in the way of possessions, or even what he may be in the eyes of the world.'[45]

In the nineteenth century, the philosophical, theological, and cultural aspects of health were all subordinated to the dictate of reason. Karl Marx regarded the essence of work as the 'dialectical process of man's creation of himself'; there was a clear correlation between capacity for work and health. Work, for Marx, is the decisive testing ground where 'both man and Nature participate, and in which man of his own accord starts, regulates, and controls the material reactions between himself and Nature . . . setting in motion arms and legs, head and hands, the natural forces of his body, in order to appropriate Nature's productions in a form adapted to his own wants.'[46] Health and use to the community characterize the 'new' man.

The revolution in nutrition and alternative paths to health

The class-specific differences in the field of nutrition changed in the nineteenth century. Among the bourgeoisie, the slim and productive body became the model which seemed to sacrifice itself – puritanism and certain traditions of the Christian ideal of penance were certainly the influence here – for the production of goods, wealth and social responsibility.[47] On the other hand, the masses, but also those who were afraid of downward social mobility, displayed increasingly consumerist behaviour. The habit traditionally associated with the upper classes of eating a lot, and also being ostentatious about it, now became a feature of the general populace, although not of those who were upwardly mobile. One consequence of this was the appearance in Milan around the middle of the century of Giovanni Raiberti's *The Art of Inviting for the People*, aimed at popular instruction in eating and drinking. Criticism was directed at the fact that 'invitations to lunch were of an intolerable length, and that the quantity of dishes served up seemed designed to still the appetites of elephants and whales.'[48] Clearly, the calls for moderation which had appeared so frequently in the eighteenth century had seldom reached the ordinary people to whom Tissot, for instance, had expressly addressed himself. Meat became an increasingly abundant feature of the nineteenth-century dinner table, and fat was generally regarded as an energy-giving and 'healthy' source of nutrition. Wine, and not least imported wine, was highly esteemed by the new upper class, whereas beer and other drinks rich in calories were less well-favoured. Admittedly, the tradition of serving food and drink from other countries had already been fashionable in the sixteenth century,[49] but it took on fresh significance from around 1850 on. Without doubt, this caused people to lose their 'natural' relationship to food. In bourgeois circles, but also among city dwellers in general, the toil and difficulties involved in agricultural work, in growing, harvesting and processing food, were forgotten. For only a small group – the readers of Hufeland's *Makrobiotik*, for instance – were the health aspects of food a matter of prime concern. Widespread upheaval and insecurity, migration of population, and deplorable social conditions caused many to think more of sheer survival than of living healthily and 'according to the theory', which was in any case regarded as the privilege of the wealthy.

For this very reason, Karl Friedrich von Rumohr (1785–1843) directed his little book *Geist der Kochkunst* [*The Art of Cookery*] at the broad mass of the population.[50] The central theme of the book is the battle against the 'dispiriting cookery books' of the past; cuisine is now to be national and free of imports, and not to indulge in aping of what foreign gourmandism had dictated – with the exception, of course, of English roast beef and strong French broth. Just as the art historian sought to cure the Romantic artists of their 'Italophilia', so Rumohr proclaimed the kitchen to be the centre of a Germanic world shaped by German tradition. It was taken as read that the choice of food must have an effect on the character, intelligence and health of a nation:

> Nations given to vacant brooding are like animals for fattening who love to stuff themselves constantly with food which is hard to digest. Nations of wit and sparkle love food which tingles the taste-buds without overburdening the stomach. Profound, thinking nations have a preference for indifferent food-stuffs such as make not too much claim on the attention, either by their over-bearing flavour or their indigestibility.[51]

There is no lack of reference to ancient models such as Coelius Appius or Cato, although the difficulty of direct imitation is acknowledged on 'the grounds of our ignorance'.[52] Famous Renaissance cookery books are also consulted, but it is hard to ignore Rumohr's aversion to everything which is 'mannered', or his preference for what may appeal to popular taste.[53] Lord Byron, who travelled through Italy with a doctor who, in minute detail, prescribed for him rest periods and what he should eat, regarded the fact that he lost 24 kilos in 1807 by fasting and starving himself as proof of his good health.[54] Vegetables, biscuits, tea and mineral water were the main constituents of his diet. The connection between slimness and health seems to be documented for the first time in the case of the English poet. 'Nothing could give him more pleasure than to tell him that he had lost weight.'

In 1879 the first food legislation to stipulate bacteriological controls was introduced in Germany. Rickets and other illnesses caused by vitamin deficiencies very soon came to be linked with poverty and poor hygiene, as was tuberculosis. The clinician Bouchardat even believed he had found a connection between diabetes and pauperism. He called for a new nutritional policy in France in which cod-liver oil was recommended in the fight against tuberculosis. This led, in the second half of the century, to its increased production in Norway.[55] Around 1850 the suspicion arose that the military superiority of the English rested on '660 grams of meat a day'. Calories began to be counted and a comparison was made of different foodstuffs. Some doctors believed that going without meat would lead to degeneration, especially since the poor sought to substitute alcohol for the missing calories in their diet.[56] Meat became an important part of the daily fare, above all in the hospitals.

There were repeated attempts in the nineteenth century, with Darwin and Haeckel, to find reasons for the decadence which had been so feared since Edward Gibbon's *History of the Decline and Fall of the Roman Empire* (1776–88). The Stuttgart physician C. Stark saw the 'degeneration' of the French as the reason for their defeat in 1871, something taken very seriously by the scientific magazine *L'Année scientifique* in Paris.[57] France was also alarmed by an (apparently statistically demonstrable) increase in the number of the insane or deformed, while between 1800 and 1860 the fertility of married couples declined by a quarter.[58] Fear of hereditary disease initiated a battle against alcoholism. The 'fléaux dégéneratives' were to be countered by a 'morale préventive'. In this spirit, health education in almost all Western countries gained renewed importance.

Fear of medicaments prescribed by doctors convinced a good many people that chronic illnesses were the result of pharmaceutical poisoning. This anxiety was of particular benefit to 'hydrotherapy'. It was also discovered that clean water was just as important in the preparation of food as it was for personal hygiene.[59] The hygienic and pleasurable aspects of its use became increasingly intermingled in everyday life. Even before 1800, in cities such as Berlin, 'hydrotherapy' was enjoying a new lease of life.[60] Disillusioned by, and wary of, university medicine – Joseph Dietl's 'therapeutic nihilism' must have seemed like a declaration of medical bankruptcy – many people at the beginning of the new century turned to naturopathy, with Prießnitz's water treatment enjoying particular popularity.[61]

In 1840, the hydrotherapist Bernhard Hirschel wrote: 'Widespread is the inclination of the people to cure themselves, or to employ the services of those who claim to do away with all illnesses by universal remedies.'[62] On the Gräfenberg mountain in Silesia, the young auto-didact Vinzenz Prießnitz (1799–1851) had set up an important spa. In 1837, 500, and, by 1839, 1700 people, including 120 doctors, had taken a course of therapy here. Prießnitz expanded the cold-water applications described by the 'Schweidnitz water taps', and above all by Johann Sigmund Hahn, with shower and dipping baths, as well as drinking cures, into a comprehensive hydrotherapeutic programme which also included air- and sunbathing, drenchings, going barefoot, leg compresses, and massages.[63] In nearby Lindewiese, Johannes Schroth (1798–1856), a former cart driver, set up a sanatorium in which the programme of therapy was based mainly on fasting, as well as a 'purgative diet', the so-called Schroth cure. In 1855 Arnold Rikli (1823–1906), a Swiss dyeworks owner in Veldes (Krain), founded a sunbathing institution which became very fashionable among ele-vated society in the Danube monarchy in Switzerland and Germany. Walking, going barefoot, gymnastics, sunbathing and cold baths ensured the necessary 'thermodietetics'.[64]

With the foundation in 1867 of Eduard Baltzer's 'Society for Healthy Living', the nineteenth-century German alternative movement, whose diverse nuances cannot be dealt with here, was approaching the 'life-reform' movement.[65] Theodor Hahn (1824–1883) propagated around 1850 a vegetarian diet supplemented by wholemeal bread, milk and uncooked vegetables. In 1865 his bestseller *Das Paradies der Gesundheit, das verlorene und das wiedergefundene* [*The Paradise of Health, the Lost One, and the One Regained*] was published. In the second half of the century, the author became the leading propagandist for the 'natural' life. His vegetarian campaign, with its not infrequent anti-Semitic undertones, was supported by many leading figures of the day, including Richard Wagner. Finally, mention must be made here too of Sebastian Kneipp (1821–1897), who is the best-known representa-tive today of nineteenth-century 'nature therapy'.[66] Following the direc-tions of Johann Sigmund Hahn, he treated his patients with washes in cold water, rubs down, baths and showers. His adherents admittedly also looked to Kneipp underwear, Kneipp sandals, Kneipp medication, Kneipp malt coffee, and not least Kneipp associations and the Kneipp doctors' union, for their health. Kneipp's modest dictum is reminiscent of Paracelsus: 'I have learned most from the school of experience, and very little from books, since I have read no books other than the little pamphlet mentioned above.'

Only ideological pigheadedness, on the other hand, could seek to diminish the achievements of medical and scientific research in this epoch. In the second half of the century, doctors and researchers set about conquering the 'scourges of mankind'. In Europe, malaria alone still took an immense toll.[67] The use of quinine, which had already been known in Europe since the seventeenth century, led to the first effective measures. In midwifery and surgery, the health of countless people was preserved by the introduction of aseptic treatment, as well as efforts to eliminate all harmful bacteria from wounds and the body. Werner von Siemens calculated that, in view of advances being made in the chemical industry, famines would finally be a thing of the past: 'We can see that, with proper agricultural use of science and technology, the soil can be made to yield a significantly greater amount of food than ever before . . .; indeed, it seems very probable that chemistry, in league with electrotechnology, will one day be able to produce nourishment itself from the inexhaustible amounts of the elements of food which are everywhere available.'[68] On the threshold of the twentieth century, the outlook of most doctors was one of boundless optimism . . .

Afterword

A review of the history of European dietetics up to the end of the nineteenth century gives an impressive demonstration of the intimate connection between doctrines of health, culture, religion and philosophy. Notwithstanding some evidence of it in Cartesianism, it is not until the nineteenth century that the concept of health comes down to a matter of what is *measurable*. For most doctors, healing became a technical process, while sickness meant a deviation from the *norm*. However diverse the theories of health and sickness may have been in the various epochs, however much philosophical, religious or social factors were bound up with these concepts, the *subjective* conception of good health, apart from minor details, in essence remained astonishingly homogeneous throughout the ages. Even the ascetic tendencies of the Cynics and Stoics, and of the anchorites of early Christendom or the medieval mystics, and even the yearning for illness displayed by some artists and literary figures in the nineteenth century, did not exclude the notion of a freedom and capacity for hope, albeit with individual variations, which was ultimately directed towards the same goal. It was those very doctrines that were hostile to the body and favoured spiritual healing which held out the promise of intellectual health and freedom.

Now, at the beginning of the third millennium, it is well worth recalling what a varied and precious body of wisdom and experience is contained within Western doctrines of health, and can be passed on. Meditation, the interpretation of dreams, relaxation exercises, alternation between rest and exertion, aesthetic recreation or religious reverie as they are propagated today, for the most part by apologists for Asiatic doctrines of salvation and redemption, are self-evidently just as much a part of our cultural and intellectual history as the 'rational' paths of therapy and prophylaxis which have been dominant since Virchow. But what is also significant, and a source of food for thought, is that every predominant paradigm of health doctrine, indeed of medicine as a whole up to now, has been replaced by something different, and which has often been its opposite.

Notwithstanding the admiration for the achievements of scientific medicine – one has only to think of the impressive rise in average life expectancy in the last hundred years, something of which the macrobioticians and theoreticians of the past could only dream – it is sobering, depressing even, to observe how the simplest dietetic principles such as moderation, seeking harmony, relaxation or regularity in the structure of one's life have – to the considerable detriment of society – all been forgotten. At the same time, the question remains unanswered as to whether the scientifically biased medicine taught in Western universities today will be able to maintain its paradigmatic pre-eminence. The experience of history points to change, while a rational view suggests continuity. More than ever before, however, the question of cost will have a part to play in the coming century.

The spectre of genetics determining life today seems to be turning the old wisdoms to dross. The experience of self-control and taking responsibility for one's own health, of moderation and internal order, which, until the middle of the nineteenth century, had been progressively gained and extended, was, until a few years ago, displaced by 'measuring' medicine. If economic reasons are apparently to blame for this change, the hope nevertheless remains that the achievements of scientific medicine can be reconciled with the wisdom gained through a thousand years of Western cultural history.

Notes

Introduction

1 See Prologue.
2 On the discourse debate, see in particular the contribution of Roger Chartier in the collection of texts edited by Conrad and Kessel (1994), pp. 83–97; see also the various contributions in Paul and Schlich (1998).
3 Spiegel (1994), p. 179.
4 See von Staden (1989), p. 407.
5 Schnitzler (1967), p. 188.
6 Generally speaking, and not only in the ancient world, health was valued particularly highly when the image of death and the hereafter was gloomy. This was the case in Mesopotamia, for instance, and the experiences recorded in the Gilgamesh epic. See also Heiler (1982), p. 126.
7 Gadamer (1996).
8 The expression 'silence of the organs' comes from René Leriche; see Canguilhem (1989).
9 Gadamer (1996).
10 C. M. Wieland, *Fragmente von Beyträgen* (1778).
11 Rothschuh (1965), pp. 127–30.
12 Jaspers (1997).
13 Labisch (1992a).
14 Chartier (1992).
15 Ludwig Börne, *Dramaturgische Blätter*, *Aphorismen 2*.
16 Rothschuh (1965), p. 41.
17 In Kleist's essay of 1810, the puppet is capable of uninhibited movement 'from the point of balance', whereas any shift away from this is disruptive. See Kleist (1993), pp. 84–92.
18 Schipperges (1976), pp. 17–21.
19 It was particularly Bismarck's social legislation which – quite apart from its undisputed political and social consequences – encouraged this mentality. See Sigerist (1960), pp. 120–38.

20 Schipperges (1996), p. 80.
21 On this aspect, see Goethe's *Gesundheitslehre*.
22 Canguilhem (1989).
23 See the literary examples in Sandblom (1990).
24 Rothschuh (1978).
25 Schott (1998).
26 See, for instance, Rothschuh (1965), Schipperges (1985a, 1985b), Wöhrle (1990), Canguilhem (1989), Labisch (1992a).
27 On Alcmaeon, see pp. 19ff. Also Kudlien (1967), pp. 55–62.
28 Canguilhem (1989).
29 On Hufeland, see pp. 251ff; on Carus, see Genschorek (1989), p. 224.
30 See Foucault (2006), Laing and Esterson (1964), Dörner (1969), Szasz (1982), Michale and Porter (1994), and Berrios and Porter (1995).

Prologue

1   Sigerist (1967), pp. 267–9, and Canguilhem (1989).
2   Herodotus, *Histories* II, 5.
3   Schipperges (1985b), p. 58.
4   However, Herodotus describes the working and living conditions of the Egyptians as being particularly favourable. See Herodotus, *Histories* II, 14.
5   Assmann (1996), pp. 154–61.
6   As will be demonstrated in subsequent chapters, similar parallels can be found in Solon, Plato, Aristotle, Cicero, Livy, St Paul, Hobbes, Harrington, Virchow and others.
7   See Westendorf (1992), pp. 42–6, 87–91. The final version of the Smith Papyrus, which is an entreaty to the dead consisting of everyday wishes, was produced in the New Kingdom.
8   Schipperges (1985b), p. 61.
9   Westendorf (1992), pp. 19ff.
10 Herodotus, *Histories* II, 37.
11 Sigerist (1963a), pp. 31f.
12 Ibid., p. 28.
13 Herodotus, *Histories* II, 95.
14 On the tasks and competence of the healing gods, see Sigerist (1963a), pp. 48–51. On prayers to Isis, Thoth and Osiris, see Erman (1923), p. 377; and on Imhotep, see Hurry (1928).
15 On Hermes Trismegistus, see Heiler (1982), pp. 337f.
16 Origen, *Contra celsum* VIII.
17 Schipperges (1985b), p. 81.
18 Ibid., p. 70. Also Assmann (1996), pp. 196–210.
19 Schipperges (1985b), p. 64.
20 Maul (1996), pp. 34–9.

21 See, for instance, the collection of ancient Babylonian stories and myths entitled the *Epic of Gilgamesh*.
22 Sigerist (1963b), p. 55.
23 On Nergal, see Schretter (1974), pp. 88f.
24 Sigerist (1963b), p. 63.
25 Maul (1996), pp. 34ff.
26 Ibid., p. 35.
27 Sigerist (1963b), pp. 73–5. On hepatoscopy, see Mani (1959), p. 19.
28 Sigerist (1963b), p. 49.
29 The letter to Asarhaddon is reproduced ibid., p. 54.
30 On Ahura Mazda, see Heiler (1982), p. 268; on Ahriman, see Brandenburg (1969), pp. 12–17.
31 Heiler (1982), p. 271.
32 Brandenburg (1969), p. 14.
33 Ibid., p. 16.
34 There were doctors who healed with the 'sacred right', with the 'law', with the 'knife', with 'plants' and with 'consultations'. See ibid., p. 18.
35 Hampel (1982), p. 21.
36 The term *Asha-haftigkeit* (translated here as 'Asha-centredness') has established itself in German specialist literature and is considered to be untranslatable.
37 Brandenburg (1969), p. 15

I Greece

The ideal of health in ancient Greece

1 Examples of the gods sending sickness are found in *Iliad* I and *Odyssey* IX. For health-endangering daemons, see *Odyssey* V.
2 Kudlien (1967), p. 19.
3 See Krug (1993), pp. 159–63; also Schnalke and Selheim (1990), pp. 18f., and Koelbing (1977), pp. 59–64.
4 Kudlien (1967), p. 32.
5 Sobel (1990), pp. 5–8.
6 Decker (1995), pp. 46–8. Much the same was true of the Pythian, Isthmian and Nemean games.
7 See also Sigerist (1963b), pp. 49f.
8 For more detail on this aspect, see Kudlien (1967), pp. 48–52.
9 Among the public physicians were figures such as Democedes of Croton; see Herodotus III, 131. On Alcmaeon of Croton's dietetics, see pp. 19f.
10 Kudlien (1967), pp. 15–30.
11 Ibid., p. 23.
12 *Odyssey* XV.

13 Hesiod, *Erga* 112–15; trans. Evelyn-White (1914), p. 11.
14 See the fate of Thersites, the ugliest of the Greeks at Troy (*Iliad* II, 270), whom Odysseus kills in bloody fashion to the accompaniment of laughter from the Achaeans.
15 For example, in the case of the satyr depicted in Plato's *Symposium*, where the outward ugliness (of Socrates) is contrasted with his inner beauty. *Symposium* 215a–218c.
16 Particularly the young Ephebi. See Aelian, *Variae historiae* 14, 7; trans. Wilson (1997), p. 457.
17 Plato, *Politea* 410a.
18 Plutarch, *Lives*, trans. Perrin (1968), vol. 1, p. 255 [Lykurgos].
19 Scheffer (1935)
20 Ibid.
21 See also Assmann (1997), pp. 107ff.
22 See Solon's 'Eunomia'; on Plato, *Philebus* 16, 29b, *Timaeus* 42e, *Phaedrus* 270b, *Charmides* 156d–157a. For a general account, see Schumacher (1963), pp. 220–2; on Aristotle, see *Politics* IV, 1, 1288b (19–24) and VII, 13, 1331b (24–6).
23 Decker (1995), pp. 39–59.
24 Herodotus does not exclude the possibility that Cambyses, king of Persia from 530 to 522 BC, was mentally unstable because of a serious physical illness with which he had been afflicted since birth. See Herodotus III, 33.
25 Isocrates, *Orations* 12, 7; trans. Norlin (1962), vol. II, p. 377.
26 Plato, *Phaedo* 82e–84b.
27 Philolaos of Croton: 'The soul loves the body, because she cannot use it without the senses.'
28 Hippocrates, *Peri diaítes* 4, 86.
29 See *Iliad* I, 45–53.
30 *Odyssey* V, 395–7.
31 Kudlien (1967), pp. 48–55.
32 Celsus, *De medicina*, *Prooemium* 3; trans. Spenser, vol. 1 (1971), pp. 2f.
33 In reality, this development took place only in the seventh century. See Kudlien (1967), pp. 15–18 and 31–4.
34 The two concepts of health are only in contradiction when considered superficially. In reality, both are anticipated by Hippocratic precepts.
35 Hesiod, *Erga* 102; trans. Evelyn-White (1964), p. 9: 'Of themselves illnesses come upon men continually by day and by night, bringing mischief to mortals silently.'
36 Kudlien (1967), pp. 51f.
37 Edelstein (1966), p. 162.

The Presocratics

38 On Alcmaeon, see Schumacher (1963), pp. 66–73.
39 Canguilhem (1989).
40 Diogenes Laertius VIII, 70.
41 Xenophon, *Cyropaedia* I, 6, 16; trans. Miller (1955), p. 103.
42 Ibid., I, 6, 17.
43 One example is the aforementioned Diogenes Laertius, whose reliability is much disputed.
44 Gadamer (1998).
45 See chapter 8.
46 Gadamer (1998).
47 Schumacher (1963), pp. 105–25.
48 Empedocles, *Aetius* V, 22, 1; Schumacher (1963), p. 111.
49 Empedocles' doctrine assumed that illnesses were caused by the wrong mixture of humours.
50 Doubts concerning the chronological sequence of dates for these figures, which was produced by Apollodorus in the second century BC, could change the perspective on these developments. See Gadamer (1998).
51 Schumacher (1963), p. 166.
52 Diogenes, Fragment 2.
53 On this aspect, see Schumacher (1963), pp. 167–71.
54 The source is Diogenes Laertius (IX, 9f.).
55 Schumacher (1963), pp. 93f.
56 Ibid., p. 152.
57 Ibid., p. 146.
58 Kudlien (1968), p. 4.
59 Schumacher (1963), pp. 97–9. With the creation of Eros, Aphrodite first created 'the mixture and also the becoming of things'.
60 Sigerist (1961), pp. 89–91.
61 Gadamer (1998).
62 Schumacher (1963), p. 64; on Pythagorean medicine in general, see ibid., pp. 34–66.
63 Wöhrle (1990), pp. 35–49.
64 Iamblichus, *Vita Pythagorae* 218.
65 Plato, *Republic* 600b, 1ff.
66 Wöhrle (1990), p. 43.
67 Diodorus Siculus 10, 7, 1–2; trans. Oldfather (1961), vol. 4, p. 63.

The Hippocratic corpus

68 There is an inexhaustible secondary literature on Hippocratic medicine. On this, see the bibliography compiled by Leven in Diller (1994), pp. 243–57.

69 Hippocrates, *Aphorisms*; trans. Jones (1959), vol. IV, p. 98.
70 On the holistic mode of thought that provided the basis for this individual nosology, see Schumacher (1963), pp. 183–6.
71 See, among other sources, the tract *Peri diaítes* [*Regimen*]; Jones (1959), vol. IV, pp. 224–447; on the *Corpus Hippocraticum*, see Wöhrle (1990), pp. 60–98.
72 Plato, *Phaedrus* 270c; trans. Hackforth (1961), p. 516. On this aspect, see also *Charmides* 156b, c, where Socrates states that it is impossible for a doctor to treat the eyes without taking the head, and even the entire body, into consideration.
73 Schumacher (1963), pp. 220–2.
74 For a detailed study of humoral pathology, see Schöner (1964).
75 Ibid., pp. 17–21.
76 *De natura hominis* II, 16ff.; trans. Jones (1959), vol. IV, p. 7. See also Schöner (1964), p. 18.
77 *De natura hominis* IV, 1ff.; trans. Jones, vol. IV, p. 11. See also Schöner (1964), p. 18.
78 Trans. Jones, vol. IV, pp. 19f. For background information see Schöner, (1964), p. 19.
79 See Plato, *Timaeus* 90d.
80 *Peri diaítes* I, 10f.; trans. Jones (1959), vol. IV, p. 225 ('As a matter of fact, while many have already written on this subject, nobody yet has rightly understood how he ought to treat it.') In reality, the author is a true eclectic; see Schöner (1964), p. 39.
81 *Peri diaítes* I, 2, 21ff.; trans. Jones, vol. IV, p. 229.
82 Ibid., IV, 89–90, 9f.; trans. Jones, vol. IV, pp. 427–47.
83 Wöhrle (1990), p. 86.
84 *Peri diaítes hygieines* I, 1ff.; trans. Jones, vol. IV, pp. 44–59.
85 *Peri diaítes* II, 42–53; trans. Jones, pp. 315–29.
86 Galen, *In Hippocratis librum De victu acutorum commentarius* I, 1117, 11–13; see also Grensemann (1975), p. 25. It is questionable whether this division was as sharp as Galen claims; see Schöner (1964), p. 35.
87 Edelstein (1966), p. 163.
88 *Peri diaítes* I, 2, 45–55; trans. Jones, vol. IV, pp. 227–9. On this danger to health, see Diller (1973), p. 73.
89 *Peri diaítes* I, 2; trans. Jones, vol. IV, p. 227.
90 Schumacher (1963), pp. 209–11.
91 Ibid., p. 210.
92 Trans. Jones (1959), vol. II, p. 147. This is representative of the tenor of the famous tract *The Sacred Disease*.
93 Schumacher (1963), p. 199.
94 *The Sacred Disease* I–II; trans. Jones, vol. II, pp. 138–45.
95 Ibid., IV, 34f.; trans. Jones, vol. II, p. 149.
96 Ibid., II, 1–4; trans. Jones, vol. II, p. 141.

97 Ibid., III, 9f.; trans. Jones, vol. II, p. 145.
98 *Prognostikon* I, 20; trans. Jones, vol. II, pp. 8f.; the reading of '*tò theion*' is controversial.
99 *Peri, aeron, hydaton, topon* [*Airs, Waters, and Places*] I, 12ff.; trans. Jones, vol. I, pp. 71–3.
100 Trans. Jones, vol. I, pp. 70–137.
101 The town of Thasos is situated on the Thracian island in the Aegean of the same name.
102 *Epidimiai* I, 11; trans. Jones (1962), vol. I, p. 165.
103 *Peri trophes* [*Nutriment*]; trans. Jones (1962), vol. I, pp. 342–61.
104 Trans. Jones (1962), vol. I, p. 337.
105 Plato, *Phaedrus* 270c, *Protagoros* 311b. Aristotle also mentions Hippocrates; see *Politics* 1326.
106 Schöner (1963), pp. 46–58.
107 Assmann (1997), pp. 108f.
108 Scheffer (1935).

Diocles of Carystus, a fourth-century health pedagogue

109 Schöner (1964), p. 72.
110 For further details on Diocles, see Wöhrle (1990), pp. 173–83.
111 Pliny, *Historia naturalis* 26, 10.
112 See Jaeger (1963); for a critique of Jaeger, see Kudlien (1963) and van der Eijk (1996), pp. 251–5.
113 On this aspect, see Kudlien (1963), pp. 461ff.
114 Ten stages correspond to approximately 20 minutes; see Wöhrle (1990), p. 184, n. 71.
115 On '*kairós*', see the famous first aphorism by Hippocrates; trans. Jones (1959), vol. IV, pp. 98f.
116 See Jaeger (1963), pp. 51–4.
117 Jaeger considered the letter authentic to Diocles; ibid., pp. 70–8. He was first disproved by Heinimann in 1955; see Kudlien (1963), p. 458. For more detail on this issue, see Fischer and von Staden (1996).
118 See Jaeger (1963), particularly pp. 81–6.
119 Ibid., pp. 90–3.
120 This expression can be traced back to the doctor Philistion, who came from Sicily and studied at the academy in Athens. See Jaeger (1963), pp. 211ff.
121 These include, for example, Acron, Philistion and Diocles; see Kudlien (1963), p. 456.
122 On this issue, see, for example, Kudlien (1963) and van der Eijk (1996), who includes an extensive bibliography.
123 See Wöhrle (1990), p. 179.
124 This derives from a later transmission by Stephanus of Athens; see ibid., p. 162.

125 The fact that the individual authors place emphases on different elements does not detract from this aspect.

'Knidic' dietetics

126 Galen, *De methodo medendi*.
127 On the close relations between the two centres during Hippocrates' lifetime, see Kollesch (1989).
128 Galen, *In Hippocratis De victu acutorum commentarius* I, 17.
129 Kollesch is fiercely critical of the assumption that Herodicus was educated in Knidos; see Kollesch (1989), pp. 19f.
130 *Anonymous Londinensis* IV, 31–V, 35.
131 Wöhrle (1990), p. 54.
132 Plato, *Republic* III, 406a–b; trans. Shorey (1961), p. 650.
133 Ibid., 406c; trans. Shorey, pp. 650–1.
134 Aristotle, *Rhetoric* I, V, 10; Pliny, *Historia naturalis* XXIX, 4.
135 The term *paidotribes* comes from Plato, *Protagoras* 316d; see also Hippocrates, *Epidem* VI, 3, 18.
136 Galen, *In Hippocratis Epidemiarum librum VI commentarius*.
137 Aristophanes, *The Clouds*; trans. Bickley Rogers (1967), vol. I, p. 357.
138 Aristophanes, *The Frogs*; trans. Bickley Rogers (1967), vol. II, p. 399.
139 On the problem of Herodicus' identity, see Kollesch (1989), pp. 19f.; on Ikkus, see Schumacher (1963), pp. 83f.
140 Plato, *Nomoi* 839e–840b.
141 Grensemann (1975), p. 14.
142 Ibid., p. 217.
143 Ibid., pp. 121f., lists the occurrences of the word '*diaita*'.
144 Pliny, *Historia naturalis* 20, 9.
145 Pollak (1969), p. 139.
146 Wöhrle (1990), p. 90.
147 Ibid.

Health in Plato and Aristotle

148 Plato, *Timaeus* 87c–90d.
149 Ibid., 88c; trans. Jowett (1961), p. 1208.
150 Ibid., 89b; trans. Jowett, p. 1208.
151 Ibid., 87d; trans. Jowett, p. 1207.
152 Ibid., 82a; trans. Jowett, pp. 1202f.
153 Ibid., 90c–d.
154 Ibid., 72e–73a.
155 Plato, *Laws* VI, 773a, b, d, e; see also Aristotle, *Politics* 1334b, 29ff.
156 Plato, *Republic* 461c.
157 Plato, *Laws* 775d; trans. Taylor (1961), p. 1352.
158 Schumacher (1963), pp. 225–8.

159 Plato, *Philebus* 25e; trans. Hackforth (1961), p. 1102.
160 Plato, *Republic* IV, 444d; trans. Shorey (1961), p. 687.
161 Plato, *Timaeus* 88b; trans. Jowett (1961), p. 1208.
162 Plato, *Sophist* 228.
163 Schumacher (1963), p. 231.
164 Plato, *Symposium* 221c–222a; on the *soma–sema* concept, see *Phaedo* 82e–84b.
165 Plato, *Charmides* 156b, c; trans. Jowett (1961), p. 102.
166 Plato, *Phaedrus* 270c.
167 Plato, *Republic* 426a; trans. Shorey (1961), p. 667.
168 Ibid.; trans. Shorey, p. 668.
169 Plato, *Phaedrus* 270b; trans. Hackforth (1961), p. 515.
170 Plato, *Republic* 405d.
171 Ibid., 406d.
172 Hippocrates, *Peri diaítes*, and Diocles' dietetics.
173 The letter in question is Plato's 'seventh letter', which was composed after the death of Dion (354).
174 Plato, *Letters* 330c–d; trans. Post (1961), p. 1579.
175 On the relationship between Aristotle and the Hippocratics, see Jaeger (1963) – despite the refutation by Kudlien; also Jouanna (1996); Pellegrin (1996); López-Salvá (1996).
176 This was naturally due in part to the exceptional status of Aristotle in the Middle Ages. He became the primary authority both in the Islamic sphere (Averroës) and in the West (Thomas Aquinas).
177 Aristotle, *De generatione et corruptione* [*Generation and Corruption*] II, 3; see also Schöner (1964), p. 67.
178 Aristotle, *De partibus animalium* [*Parts of Animals*] II, 2, 648b, 4–10; trans. Peck (1961), p. 123. See also Schöner (1964), p. 67.
179 Aristotle, *Historia animalium* [*The History of Animals*] III, 2, 511b, 9–10. Admittedly, only phlegm and yellow and black bile are mentioned. See also Schöner (1964), p. 68.
180 Aristotle, *Meterologica*, I, 12 (348b).
181 Kalthoff (1938), pp. 34ff.
182 Ibid., p. 36.
183 Aristotle, *Politics*, VII, 1336a; trans. Rackham (1959), p. 627. See also Kalthoff (1938), p. 37.
184 Aristotle, *Nicomachean Ethics* III, v, 15–16; trans. Rackham (1962), p. 149.
185 Ibid.
186 Aristotle, *Magna moralia* 1187b.
187 Kalthoff (1938), pp. 39f.
188 Aristotle, *Nicomachean Ethics* X, ix, 15; trans. Rackham (1962), p. 637.
189 Aristotle, *Eudemian Ethics* II, 1, 24 (1220a).
190 For further details on this aspect, see Kalthoff (1938), pp. 34–51.

191 See Klibansky, Panofsky and Saxl (1964).
192 Aristotle, *Problemata* XXX, 1, 954a; trans. Hett (1957), vol. 2, pp. 161–3.
193 The term derives from the ancient notion that black bile is produced in the spleen.
194 Aristotle, *Problemata* XXX, 1954a, b; see also Klibansky, Panofsky and Saxl (1964).
195 Aristotle, *Eudemian Ethics* II, 3, 1221b, 16.
196 Aristotle, *Ars rhetorica* I, 6, 1362b, 15f.
197 Aristotle, *De cura rei familiaris*; see Kalthoff (1938), p. 43.
198 Aristotle, *Problemata* XII, 881b.
199 Aristotle, *Politics* VIII, 1339a; trans. Rackham (1959), p. 649.
200 Ibid.
201 *Politics*, 1288b, 10ff.
202 Kalthoff (1938), pp. 51–5.
203 Ibid., pp. 34–51.
204 Aristotle, *Politics* 1330b, VII, 11–17.
205 Ibid., VII, 1335a, b; trans. Rackham (1959), pp. 621–3.
206 Aristotle, *Metaphysics* 983a, 25ff.

Dietetics in Alexandria

207 Herophilus was the pupil of Chrysippos of Knidos as well as Praxagoras of Kos.
208 Von Staden (1989), p. 397.
209 Plutarch, *Quaestio symposiaca* 4, 1, 3; also von Staden (1989), p. 417.
210 See von Staden (1989), p. 406.
211 Ibid., p. 407.
212 See Galen, *De emperica subfiguratione* 5; von Staden (1989), p. 110: 'medicativam dicens scientiam esse sanorum et neutrorum et egrorum.'
213 Kümmel (1977), p. 24.
214 See von Staden (1989), pp. 46f.
215 See the examples given ibid., pp. 321–3.
216 See Celsus, *De medicina* I, *Prooemium* 23–7; trans. Spencer (1960), vol. 1, pp. 14f.
217 Edelstein (1966), p. 166.
218 Galen, *De sanitate tuenda* VI, 388k; see also Wöhrle (1990), p. 204.
219 The town experienced a further period of florescence in late antiquity. In AD 389, the Serapeion was closed and the famous library was plundered.

Cures and miracles, Aesculapius and Hygieia

220 Trans. Jones (1959), vol. II, p. 203.
221 *Edwin Smith Surgical Papyrus* (1930), illnesses 6 and 8.

222 Krug (1993), p. 122.
223 Strabo, *Geography* IX, 5.
224 Krug (1993), p. 121.
225 Ibid., p. 129.
226 Pausanias II, 27, 6; trans. Jones (1966), vol. I, pp. 394f.
227 Porphyrius, *De abstinentia* II, 19.
228 Pausanius II, 27, 6; trans. Jones (1966), vol. I, p. 395.
229 Aristophanes, *Plutus*, trans. Bickley Rogers (1967), vol. III, pp. 425–9.
230 Diogenes Laertius, *Lives of Eminent Philosophers* VI, 59.
231 The relief is in the Luku monastery in the Peloponnese. See Schnalke and Selheim (1990), p. 55; and Krug (1993), p. 123.
232 Krug (1993), pp. 126f.
233 Ibid., p. 148.
234 Schnalke and Selheim (1990), p. 19.
235 Livy X, 47, 7; Ovid, *Metamorphoses* XV, 622ff.
236 *Iliad* V, 401 and 899f.
237 A detailed account is given by Weinreich (1909).
238 Ibid., p. 171. Apollonius even woke the dead, although this is a spin-off of New Testament narratives.
239 Ibid., pp. 67–75.
240 Krug (1993), pp. 134–41.
241 Ibid., pp. 138f.
242 Lain Entralgo (n.d.), pp. 48–71.
243 Ibid., pp. 53ff.
244 Plato, *Charmides* 157e; trans. Jowett (1961), p. 103.
245 Ibid., 157a.
246 Sophocles, *Ajax*; trans. Storr (1967), vol. II, p. 51.
247 Plato, *Republic* 426.
248 Plato, *Laches* 188d.
249 On this aspect, see Kümmel (1977), pp. 91f.; also Plato, *Phaedo* 86b–c.
250 Plato, *Cratylus* 405a–b; trans. Jowett (1961), p. 442.
251 Kümmel (1977), p. 92.
252 Ibid., p. 158.

Public health care and sport

253 Herodotus, *Histories* III, 129–38; also Kudlien (1967), p. 18.
254 Krug (1993), p. 201.
255 Cohn-Haft (1956).
256 Koelbing (1977), pp. 138–41.
257 Kudlien (1979), pp. 53–6.
258 Koelbing (1977), p. 140.
259 Plato, *Gorgias* 456b–c.
260 Kudlien (1979), pp. 10f.
261 Ibid., pp. 11f.

262 Plato, *Republic* 405a; trans. Shorey (1961), p. 650.
263 Sophocles, *Fragments* 354.
264 Diodorus Siculus III, 12/13.
265 Kudlien (1979), p. 15.
266 Plato, *Logoi* 763d, 758e; Aristotle, *Politics* 1330b.
267 Plato, *Politics* 459cff., and Aristotle 1334b, 29ff.
268 Plato, *Republic* 407b; trans. Shorey (1961), p. 651.
269 Decker (1995), pp. 39ff.
270 Ibid., pp. 131–6.
271 Ibid., p. 146.

Early Stoics and Cynics

272 See Kudlien (1968), pp. 4–8.
273 Aristotle, *Eudemian Ethics* 1249a.
274 Epicurus, *Letter to Menoeceus* 128.
275 Ibid. 131.
276 Diogenes Laertius 7, 87.
277 Ibid.
278 Ibid. 7, 108.
279 Pollak (1969), p. 176.
280 Ibid.
281 Kulf (1970), pp. 48–50.
282 Ibid., pp. 88–91.
283 Ibid., pp. 118f.
284 Ibid., pp. 141f.
285 See Hossenfelder (1996), pp. 66f.
286 For Andronicus' definitions, see ibid., pp. 88–91.
287 Kudlien (1968), p. 5.
288 Stobaeus 2, 213f.
289 Stobaeus 3, 293f.
290 Dio Chrysostomus 10, 9, 14.
291 Diogenes Laertius IV, 9, 105.
292 See Schöner (1964), p. 83.

2 Rome

People and literati: dietetics in ancient Rome

1 Livy IV, 25, 29.
2 See Pollak (1969), p. 166.
3 Pliny XXIX, 8, 15–17.
4 Plutarch, *Marcus Cato* IV, 1f.; trans. Perrin (1968), vol. 2, pp. 313–15.
5 Ovid, *Metamorphoses* 15, 718–22.

6 Miracle healings did not occur on the Tiber island until after the birth of Christ.
7 Livy XL, 37, 2.
8 Cicero, *De divinatione* 2, 123.
9 I am grateful to Barbara and Jürgen Krieghoff, Rome, for alerting me to this site.
10 Cicero, *De divinatione* 2, 85.
11 Pliny, *Historia naturalis* [*Natural History*] XXIX, 11; trans. Jones (1968), vol. 8, pp. 191–3.
12 Plutarch, *Marcus Cato* 23, 3; trans. Perrin, p. 373. See also Pliny XXIX, 16 ('rem non antiqui damnabant, sed artes').
13 See Martial V, 9.
14 Vitruvius Pollio I, 4, 1f.; trans. Granger (1962), vol. 1, pp. 35–7.
15 Ibid. I, 6, 3; trans. Granger, p. 55.
16 Columella I, 2, and I, 4.
17 Virgil, *Georgics* II, 532–40; trans. Rushton Fairclough (1967), p. 153.
18 Tacitus, *Germania* [*Germany and its Tribes*] 20; trans. Church and Brodribb (1942).
19 Cicero, *De natura deorum* II, 164.
20 Cicero, *Cato Maior, De senectute* [*On Old Age*] 11; trans. Falconer (1964), pp. 43–5.
21 Ibid.; trans. Falconer, p. 45.
22 Ibid.
23 Ibid., 6; trans. Falconer, p. 27.
24 Livy, *Ab urbe condita* [*The History of Rome*] XXXIX, 40; trans. Roberts (1905).
25 Terence, *Phormio* IV, 19.
26 Virgil, *Bucolics* I, 46; trans. Greenough (1900). In general see also Cicero, *Cato Maior*.
27 Cicero, *Tusculanae* III, 6, and IV, 31; trans. King (1966), pp. 351, 231 and 361.
28 Lucretius, *De rerum natura* III, 510.
29 Ibid., III, 463, 474; trans. Rouse (1966), p. 211.
30 See Hossenfelder (1996), pp. 219–54.
31 Plinius Secundus [Pliny the Younger] *Epistles* III, 5, 11ff.; trans. Radice (1969), vol. 1, p. 177.
32 Ibid., III, 14.
33 Seneca, *De tranquillitate animi* [*On Tranquility of Mind*] II, 11; trans. Basore (1970), vol. 2, p. 221.
34 Lucretius, *De rerum natura* III, 1068.
35 Suetonius, *The Lives of the Caesars*, Life of Augustus 82–4; trans. Rolfe (1971), pp. 249–51.
36 Ibid., 83; trans. Rolfe, p. 251.
37 Suetonius, *The Lives of the Caesars*, from the chapter on Gaius Caligula; trans. Rolfe, p. 481.

38 Ibid., Life of Claudius 32; trans. Rolfe, vol. 2, p. 63.
39 Ibid., Life of Vespasian 20f.
40 For examples of this topos, see Xenophon, *Memorabilia* 2, 3, 18; Aesop 197; I Corinthians 12, 12–27.
41 Livy II, 32.
42 See Ziethen (1994), pp. 181–6.
43 Tacitus, *Historia* [*Histories*] 4, 81–4; Suetonius, *The Lives of the Caesars*, Life of Vespasian 7; also Cassius Dio 66, 8, 1.
44 Suetonius, Life of Vespasian 7; trans. Rolfe, vol. 2, p. 299.
45 Pliny, *Panegyricus* 6, 1; see Ziethen (1994), p. 186.
46 Seneca, *De brevitate vitae, De Otio.*
47 Virgil, *Aeneid* XII, 849; trans. Rushton Fairclough (1967), vol. 2, p. 357.
48 Ibid., IX, 603–15, X, 272–5; trans. Rushton Fairclough, p. 189.
49 Ovid, *Metamorphoses* XV, 320, and XV, 713; trans. Miller (1966), p. 387. *Fasti* IV, 363; trans. Frazer (1967), p. 215.
50 Ovid, *Epistulae ex Ponto* III, 2, 13; trans. Wheeler (1965), p. 385.
51 Ovid, *Tristia* III, 8, 25; trans. Wheeler (1965), p. 133.
52 See the examples in Weeber (1995), p. 156.
53 Pliny, *Historia naturalis* XXVIII, 183ff.; in general XX–XXXII.
54 Lucian, *Amores* 39.
55 Propertius I, 2; see Weeber (1995), p. 242.
56 Cicero, *Epistulae* XII, 20; Cato, *Agricultura* 83; Plautus, *Persa* [*The Persian*] V, 2, 36.
57 Caesar, *De bello Gallico* II, 14, 1; III, 9, 6. For further literary references, see Weeber (1995), p. 257.
58 Varro, *De re rustica* I, 2, 5.
59 Gellius XII, II, 6.
60 Ovid, *Ars amandi* [*The Art of Love*] I, 50; trans. Mozley (1969), p. 49.
61 Lucretius, *De rerum natura* IV, 633f.
62 Pliny, *Historia naturalis* XI, 118. Also Plautus, *Mostellaria* [*The Haunted House*] III, 2, 8; trans. Nixon (1963), p. 361.
63 Tacitus, *Annales* [*Annals*] VI, 46; trans. Moore (1963), p. 237.
64 See Weeber (1995), pp. 228f. (table).
65 See Horace, *Satyrarum libri* II, 6, 16ff.
66 Seneca, *Moral Epistles* 71, 2; trans. Gummere (1967) {vol. 2}. Also Juvenal XI, 16.
67 Horace, *Epistles* II, 2, 65–7; trans. Rushton Fairclough (1970), pp. 429–31.
68 See Highet (1957), pp. 169–87.

New doctors, new theories

69 Pliny XXIX, 12.
70 Health therefore corresponds logically to a well-balanced state of tension within the body. On Themison, see Moog (1994).
71 See Pollak (1969), p. 172.
72 Ibid., pp. 172-5.
73 See Wellmann (1895), pp. 11-17.
74 Ibid., pp. 210f.
75 See Schanz and Hosius (1935), pp. 395f.; on theriac, see also Pollak (1969), p. 180.
76 See Ruffato (1996).
77 Pliny, *Historia naturalis* XIV, 28; trans. Rackham (1960), vol. IV, p. 277.
78 On Scribonius Largus, see Schanz and Hosius (1935), pp. 793f.
79 Celsus, *De medicina* I, 1f.; trans. Spencer (1961), vol. I, p. 43.
80 Ibid., I, 2f.; trans. Spencer, p. 43.
81 Ibid., I, 4; trans. Spencer, pp. 43f.
82 Ibid., I, 4 – II, 2; trans. Spencer, p. 45.
83 Ibid., II, 2f.
84 Ibid., II, III.
85 Ibid., II, 2; trans. Spencer, p. 47.
86 See Pollak (1969), p. 192.
87 Celsus, *De medicina*.
88 Hippocrates, *Aphorisms* II, 49.
89 Celsus, *De medicina*.
90 For further details, see also Baader (1960).

Sport and baths

91 Seneca, *Epistles* 15, 3; trans. Gummere (1967), vol. 1, p. 57.
92 See Weeber (1995), pp. 102-4.
93 Vitruvius V, 10.
94 Cicero, *Laelius* 36.
95 See Weber (1996), p. 21.
96 Martial III, 87, and VII, 35.
97 Seneca, *Epistles* 56, 1f.; trans. Gummere (1967), vol. 1, pp. 373-5. See also Weber (1996), pp. 61f.
98 See Weeber (1995), pp. 40-2.
99 Suetonius, *Probi vita* 2, 1.
100 See Weber (1996), p. 62.
101 Martial, *Epigrams* 3, 44.

The sacred tales of Publius Aelius Aristides

102 Aristides, *Hierói lógoi* I, 8.
103 Ibid., I, 55f.
104 Ibid., I, 60.
105 Ibid., I, 65.
106 Ibid., II, 26ff.
107 Ibid., II, 47.
108 Only Montaigne comes to mind. See pp. 197f.

The Roman Stoics: Plutarch, Seneca, Marcus Aurelius, Epictetus

109 Seneca *De tranquillitate animi* [*On Tranquility of the Mind*] II, 4; trans. Basore (1970), vol. 2, p. 215.
110 Ibid., XV, 6.
111 Seneca, *Moral Epistles* 31, 8; trans. Gummere (1967), vol. 1, p. 227.
112 Seneca, *De providentia* [*On Providence*] VI, 6; trans. Basore (1970), vol. 1, p. 45.
113 Seneca, *Moral Epistles* 95, 15; trans. Gummere (1967), vol. 3, p. 67.
114 Ibid., 78, 5; trans. Gummere, vol. 2, pp. 183–5.
115 Ibid., 95, 20, 32; trans. Gummere, vol. 3, pp. 71, 79.
116 Seneca, *De ira* [*On Anger*] I, vii, 2; trans. Basore (1970), vol. 1, p. 125.
117 Marcus Aurelius, *Communings with Himself* IX, 41; trans. Haines (1961), pp. 255–7.
118 Ibid., IX, 37; trans. Haines, p. 253.
119 Ibid., II, 17; trans. Haines, p. 41.
120 Marcus Aurelius, *Communings with Himself* IV, 5; trans. Haines, p. 73.
121 Epictetus, *Manual* 9; trans. Oldfather (1966), vol. 2, p. 491.
122 Epictetus, *Discourses* 20.
123 Ibid., 3, 20.
124 Ibid., 3.
125 Aulus Gellius, *Attic Nights* 17, 19, 6.

Galen

126 For more detail on this aspect, see Schöner (1964), pp. 86–95.
127 Galen, *De sanitate tuenda* I, 1.
128 Galen, *De arte medica* I, 1.
129 Ibid., I, 21.
130 Ibid., XXIII.
131 On this aspect, see also Wöhrle (1990), p. 66.
132 See Schmitt (1979), pp. 21f.
133 See Schipperges (1978), p. 241.
134 Galen, *Ad Thrasybulum liber* 46.

135 Dieckhöfer (1990), p. 53.
136 See Wöhrle (1990), p. 213.
137 Galen, *De sanitate tuenda* I, 1. See also Wöhrle (1990), p. 216.
138 Galen, *De optima nostri corporis constitutiones* III.
139 Galen, *De temperamentis* II, 4.
140 Galen, *De sanitate tuenda* I, 5.
141 Ibid.
142 On this aspect, see Wöhrle (1990), p. 219.
143 See Wöhrle (1990), pp. 223–5.
144 Galen, *Liber, quod animi mores corporis temperamenta sequantur* I.
145 Galen, *De sanitate tuenda* I, 8.
146 Ibid., I, 6.
147 Ibid., I, 9.
148 See Rothschuh (1978), p. 190.
149 See Schipperges (1978), p. 242.
150 Galen, *De bono habitu* I.
151 Galen, *De usu partium* XIV, 3.
152 Fire, for example, is warmth 'in actu'; pepper is warmth 'in potentia'; see Rothschuh (1978), p. 191.
153 Rothschuh relativizes the role of nature in Galen's works; see ibid., p. 194.
154 Galen, *De usu partium*.
155 See Schipperges (1978), p. 242.
156 Virgil, *Aeneid* IX, 603–15; X, 273.
157 See Wöhrle (1990), p. 223.

3 Jewish and Early Christian Traditions

Jewish doctrines of health

 1 See 1 Samuel 16: 18.
 2 Daniel 1: 4.
 3 Jesus Sirach 30: 14–16 and 22 (revised standard edition).
 4 Leviticus 13 and 15; Numbers 19 and 11.
 5 Daniel 1: 8–16.
 6 Deuteronomy 21: 20; Proverbs 20.
 7 See Preuss (1911), p. 594.
 8 Deuteronomy 32: 39.
 9 Exodus 15: 2.
10 See Niehr (1991), pp. 10f.
11 Ibid., pp. 4f.
12 Rothschuh (1978), pp. 47f.
13 Mark 7: 3. Preuss (1911), pp. 617–23, gives a more detailed account of the cleansing rituals.
14 See Trusen (1853), p. 24.

15 Preuss (1911), p. 646.
16 Ibid., pp. 652–87.
17 Leviticus 16: 29; also Preuss (1911), p. 681.
18 See Preuss (1911), pp. 653–84.
19 Gittin 70a.
20 See von Harnack (1892), pp. 56f.

Christus medicus

21 See Sauser (1966); Grabar (1967); Sauser (1992), pp. 101f.
22 Sauser (1992), p. 105.
23 Fichtner (1982), p. 7.
24 Sauser (1992), p. 105.
25 Eusebius, *Vita Constantini* III, 56; trans. in Wace, vol. 1 (1890).
26 Epistle of Ignatius to the Ephesians VII; trans. in Roberts and Donaldson, vol. 1 (1979).
27 Clement of Alexandria, *Paedagogus* [*The Instructor*] I, XII; trans. in Roberts and Donaldson, vol. 2 (1979).
28 See Augustine, *Sermones* [*Sermons*] 155, 10.
29 Sauser (1992), p. 110.
30 Fichtner (1982), pp. 11f.
31 Eusebius, *Historia ecclesiastica* VII, 22, 710.
32 See, for example, Augustine, *De civitate dei*, 22, 8.
33 See Arbesmann (1954), pp. 3–5.

Early Christian doctrines of health

34 See Ohlmeyer (1989), p. 48 (on the author of the Lorsch pharmacopoeia); also Keil (1991b) and von Harnack (1892), pp. 57f.
35 Von Harnack (1892), p. 57.
36 Temkin (1991), pp. 152f.
37 St Ambrose, *De officiis* I, 67; trans. in Wace, vol. 10 (1955).
38 See von Harnack (1892), p. 40.
39 On the contested passage, which survives only in Arabic, see ibid., p. 42.
40 Ibid., pp. 42–8.
41 See Justin, *Apologies* I, 18–20.
42 Tatian, *Address to the Greeks*, trans. in Roberts and Donaldson, vol. 2 (1978).
43 Von Harnack (1892), pp. 63f.
44 Boethius, trans. Cooper (1902), p. 24.
45 Clement of Alexandria, *Paedagogus* [*The Instructor*] II, 2; trans. in Roberts and Donaldson, vol. 2 (1979).
46 Novatian, 'On the Jewish Meats' VI; trans. in Roberts and Donaldson, vol. 5 (1979).

47 Tertullian, *Apologies* 42.
48 Von Harnack (1892), pp. 57f.
49 Clement of Alexandria, *Paedagogus* [*The Instructor*] II, 1; trans. in Roberts and Donaldson, vol. 2 (1979).
50 Von Harnack (1892), pp. 59–61.
51 Ibid., p. 61.
52 Schneider (1957), pp. 313f.
53 Meyer-Steineg (1916), p. 90.
54 Caelius I, 83–99.
55 Meyer-Steineg (1916), p. 90.
56 See Caelius V, 132–4.
57 Theoderich was the son of Clovis.
58 See Epistula Anthimi I.
59 Ibid.

4 Medieval Traditions in the East and West

Healing and health in early monasticism

1 See Frank (1975), vol. 1, pp. 7–37.
2 Ibid., pp. 107–93.
3 Figala and Pfohl (1987), p. 239.
4 Benedict (1949).
5 Ibid., p. 241. Children were also brought up in the monasteries.
6 See Matthew 25: 35–45.
7 Seidler (1981), p. 21.
8 Ibid., p. 23.
9 Ibid., p. 24.
10 Figala and Pfohl (1987), p. 248.
11 Cassiodorus, *Institutiones* 32, 4: see Frank (1975), vol. 1, p. 279.
12 Frank (1975), vol. 1, pp. 107–93.
13 Frank (1975), vol. 2, pp. 41–106.
14 On this subject, see Bergdolt (1992a), p. 83.
15 See Evagrius Ponticus, *Logismoi* XII, 14.
16 Ibid., XII, 24.
17 Caesarius IV, 16f.; see Herles (1992), pp. 134f.

The first German pharmacopoeia

18 See Angenendt (1995), pp. 156–8.
19 Einhard, *Vita Caroli Magni* 22; trans. Turner (1880).
20 Ibid., pp. 22–5.
21 On the Lorsch pharmacopoeia, see Keil and Schnitzer (1991).
22 See Stoll (1991), p. 67.
23 Ibid., p. 78.

24 Péréz de Urbel (1945); Schipperges (1985a), pp. 173f.

25 See Isidor, *Etymologiae* IV: 'Nomen autem Medicinae a modo, id est a temperamento, inpositum aestimatur . . .'

26 Ohlmeyer (1989), p. 63.

27 Ibid., p. 58.

Dietetics in Islam

28 It is, incidentally, a remarkable phenomenon that, in spite of differences in milieu, the term 'health' carried similarly positive, if differently accentuated, associations of corporeal integrity, freedom from pain, and optimism regarding the future for monks, soldiers or heads of households alike.

29 See Schipperges (1990), p. 218.

30 Nabavi (1967), p. 30.

31 Surah II, 61; trans. Yusuf Ali (1987).

32 Surah V, 91.

33 Raslan (1975), p. 21.

34 Ibid., p. 22.

35 On the doctrine of degrees and complexions, see Harig (1974).

36 The model was probably Paul of Aegina.

37 See Whipple (1979), pp. 25–30; general information on the Academy of Gondishapur is provided by Schöffler (1979).

38 See Schipperges (1976), pp. 52f.

39 Ibid., pp. 139f.

40 Ullmann (1970), p. 201.

41 Ibid., pp. 199–203.

42 Schipperges (1976), pp. 58f.

43 Schipperges (1990), p. 59.

44 Biedermann (1972), pp. 92f.

45 Schipperges (1976), p. 15.

46 For a detailed account of Salernitan medicine, see Schipperges (1976).

47 See Schipperges (1990), pp. 52f.

48 See Schipperges (1976), p. 79.

49 Ibid., pp. 62f.

50 Ibid., pp. 104f.; Ullmann (1970), pp. 152f. and 200f.

51 An indication of the *Canon*'s influence is that the work still featured in the medical curriculum at the University of Jena as late as the eighteenth century. (Ullmann (1970), p. 155).

52 See Schipperges (1987), p. 34.

53 Ibid., p. 14.

54 See Schipperges (1976), p. 16.

55 Ibid., pp. 12f.

56 *Holy Qur'an*, trans. Yusuf Ali (1987).

Medieval doctrines of health in the West

57 See Schmitt (1973), pp. 31f. and 49f.

58 Ibid., pp. 58–78.

59 See Abbas, *Liber Pantegni*, Theorema IV, 20: 'Corpus enim illud est sanum, quod temperatum est in complexione membrorum similium et in compositione aequale est, sicut convenit esse.'

60 See Schipperges (1976), pp. 12–16 and 87ff.

61 A particularly important part was played by the school of translation in Toledo, which produced translations of hygienic–dietetic tracts by Ibn-Butlan, Avenzoar and Albucasis as well as the *Secretum secretorum*, which later won particular renown.

62 Thomas Aquinas, *Summa theologica* II, I, 96, 2; trans. Fathers of the English Dominican Province (1947).

63 *Summa theologica* II, I, 96, 2c; see Ridder (1996), pp. 63f.

64 See Schipperges (1985a), p. 242.

65 Petrarch also expounds an 'ars vivendi'; see Bergdolt (1992a), pp. 50–6 and 77–82.

66 See Schmitt (1973), pp. 10f.

67 When the Holy Roman Emperor Frederick II Hohenstaufen requested guidelines on health from the Salernitan doctors around 1240, he received only the aforementioned apocryphal letter to Alexander from Aristotle, which suggests that the famous *Regimen Salernitatem* did not yet exist.

68 Following Arnold of Villanova's numbering of the rules.

69 See Bergdolt (1992a), p. 13.

70 Hartmann von Aue, *The Unfortunate Lord Henry*, trans. Tobin (1983); see also Haage (1992), p. 139. On *The Unfortunate Lord Henry* see also p. 134.

71 See Schmitt (1973), pp. 11–19.

72 See Riha (1996), pp. 130f.

73 On the *consilia*, see the comprehensive survey by Schmitt (1973), p. 9.

74 Hagenmeyer (1995), pp. 122f.; also Riha (1985), p. 10.

75 Hagenmeyer (1995), p. 19.

76 On the 'accidentia animae', see Schmitt (1973), p. 87.

77 On these translations, see Bergdolt (1989b).

78 Hagenmeyer (1995), pp. 27f.

79 See Koch (1969), pp. 10f.

80 Ibid., pp. 17, 19 and 37.

81 See Schmitt (1973), p. 26.

82 On Gentile da Foligno, see Bergdolt (1989a), pp. 151–5.

83 See Riha (1985), p. 12.

84 Keil (1968); Riha (1985).

85 On Nicholas of Poland, see Eamon and Keil (1986); also Bergdolt (1992a), pp. 180–2.

Asceticism and mysticism – feasts and beauty care

86 See García-Ballester (1996).
87 The soul was believed to a be product of divine emanation.
88 Lasson (1868), p. 154.
89 Ibid., p. 255.
90 Ibid., p. 258.
91 Ibid., p. 265.
92 See Beyer (1996), pp. 127–37.
93 Ibid., pp. 139–45.
94 Ibid., pp. 145–50.
95 See Angenendt (1997), pp. 66f.
96 Schipperges (1994b), pp. 16–19.
97 *The Little Flowers of St. Francis of Assisi* XXV; trans. Hudleston (1965).
98 Ibid., XIX.
99 Borst (1973), p. 190.
100 See Schipperges (1994b), pp. 163f.
101 Ibid., pp. 164f.
102 See Sigerist (1952), pp. 22f.
103 See Nauwerck (1998), pp. 3–9.
104 See Bitsch (1991), p. 131.
105 See Keil (1991a).

Western and Eastern clerical scholars

106 See Schipperges (1995b), pp. 28f.
107 Ibid., p. 61; Maimonides therefore adopts the theory of 'ne-utrum' supported by Galen and Erasistratos.
108 Sterpellone and Elsheikh (1995), p. 163.
109 Ibid., p. 71.
110 See Bitsch (1991), p. 133.
111 See Schipperges (1994a), p. 111.
112 Ibid., p. 14.
113 Ibid., pp. 26–31.
114 Ibid., pp. 95–8.
115 Ibid., pp. 98–101.
116 According to Galenic doctrine, particular illnesses and old age lead to a decrease in the quality of 'warmth' and an increase in 'coldness'; see Schöner (1964).
117 Schipperges (1994a), pp. 112f.
118 See Schipperges (1994a), p. 103.
119 See Paravicini Bagliani (1997), pp. 21ff.
120 Ibid., pp. 192f.
121 For the 'Letter of Prester John', see Legner (1985), pp. 83–97.
122 Ibid., pp. 194f.

123 Paravicini Bagliani (1997), p. 197.
124 Little and Withington (1928), p. 120.
125 Ibid., p. 121.
126 Ibid., p. 128.
127 Ibid., p. 137.
128 See, for example, ibid., p. 139.
129 Ibid., p. 121.
130 Ibid., pp. 133–7.
131 Ibid., pp. 96f.
132 Schöner (1964), p. 91.
133 See Little and Withington (1928), p. 2.
134 Schipperges (1990), pp. 83f.
135 See Siraisi (1981), p. 292.
136 Kaufmann et al. (1904), p. 15.
137 Ibid., pp. 46f.
138 See Molenaer (1966), pp. 34–237.
139 Ibid., p. 22.
140 See Gabriel (1967), pp. 72f.

Hildegard of Bingen

141 The influence of Arab-Aristotelian medicine on Hildegard of Bingen was recognized only recently.
142 See Beyer (1996), pp. 20f.
143 See Schipperges (1995a), p. 43.
144 Ibid., p. 65.
145 See Müller (1997), p. 65.
146 *Scivias* I, 3.

Saints and miracle workers

147 See Sigerist (1927), pp. 314–17.
148 Ibid.
149 For further information, see Boskovits (1979); the arrows are not attested as an attribute of the saint before the tenth century.
150 On the later iconography of St Sebastian, see Ronen (1988).
151 Gurevic (1997), pp. 236f.
152 Ibid., p. 235.
153 See Angenendt (1997), pp. 72f.
154 See Folz (1984), pp. 117–35.
155 See Angenendt (1997), p. 125.
156 Ibid., pp. 132f.
157 Ibid., p. 135.
158 Rothschuh (1978), p. 54f.

The power of the stars

159 See Bergdolt (1992a), p. 29.

160 Ibid.

161 See Siraisi (1973), p. 91. The *Alphonsine Tables* enjoyed considerable renown in the Middle Ages.

162 See Garin (1983).

163 Ibid.

164 On Petrarch, see Bergdolt (1992a), pp. 29–32; on the stance of Pico della Mirandola, see his *Oration on the Dignity of Man*.

165 On Mesocco, see Engelmann (1977).

166 Lindberg (1992).

167 Garin (1983).

168 See Zimmermann (1986).

169 There is an extensive secondary literature on the *Lunare*; see, for example, Riha (1992), pp. 40–65.

170 See Lindberg (1992).

171 See Rothschuh (1978), p. 82.

5 Doctrines of Health in the Renaissance

Petrarch's concept of health

1 See Bergdolt (1992a), p. 1.

2 Garin (1961), p. 260.

3 The view that the sciences were suppressed in the Middle Ages and then prospered under the aegis of the burgeoning Renaissance has persevered since the Enlightenment. In fact, at first the very opposite was the case. See Bergdolt (1992a), pp. 1–4.

4 Ibid., pp. 1–32.

5 Ibid., pp. 27f.

6 Ibid., pp. 34f.

7 See Bergdolt (1994), pp. 221–9.

8 Bergdolt (1992a), p. 51.

9 Ibid., pp. 55f.

10 See Wiebel (1988), pp. 78f.

11 Ibid., p. 82.

12 See Siraisi (1973).

13 Bergdolt (1992a), p. 91.

14 Bergdolt (1997).

Alberti and other intellectuals around 1500

15 Heller (1978).

16 See Hardt (1996), p. 212.

17 Rodenwaldt (1968), pp. 32–7, 51.
18 Hardt (1996), p. 220.
19 Rodenwaldt (1968), p. 45.
20 Ibid., pp. 31f.
21 See Bergdolt (1992b), p. 29.
22 Kümmel (1987), pp. 53f.
23 Ibid., pp. 54f.
24 Ibid., p. 56.
25 Hardt (1996), pp. 224f.
26 Kümmel (1987), pp. 56f.
27 See Burke (1996), p. 20. On the *Cyropaedia*, see above, p. 20.
28 Burke (1996), pp. 20–61.
29 See Castiglione, *The Book of the Courtier*; trans. Hoby (1966), p. 10.
30 On the Palazzo Vecchio, see Muccini and Cecchi (1991), pp. 52f.
31 For further details on Rabelais, see Rommel (1997), pp. 100–7.
32 Hardt (1996), pp. 267f.
33 Ibid., pp. 265–7.
34 Kinkeldey (1966).
35 See Ridder (1996), pp. 99f.
36 See Körbs (1988), p. 53.
37 Ibid., pp. 14f.
38 Ibid., p. 51.
39 Bergdolt (1994), p. 25.
40 Dominici (1860), p. 147.
41 See Körbs (1988), p. 116.

House books and manuals – health and literature

42 See Schipperges (1990), pp. 82f.
43 See Kümmel (1977), p. 105.
44 Keil (1994).
45 Cf. Schipperges (1993b), p. 40; on the Lutheran interpretation of this aspect, see Labisch (1992a), pp. 63f.
46 See Schipperges (1990), pp. 84–6.
47 Lemmer (1991), pp. 181f.
48 Keil (1991a), p. 225; on dietetics relating to sleeping patterns, see Lauer (1998).
49 Mayer (1997), p. 5.
50 Ibid., p. 9.
51 On this aspect, see Gadebusch Bondio (1996), p. 59.
52 Alessio Piemontese is a pseudonym used by Gerolamo Ruscelli.
53 Gadebusch Bondio (1996), pp. 60f.
54 Ibid., p. 68.

55 Ibid., p. 71.
56 See Ariosto, *Orlando Furioso* XIX, 24.

Further humanists – Platina, More, Luther

57 Celsus I, 2–7.
58 See Ridder (1996), p. 101.
59 More, *Utopia*; trans. Richards (1965), p. 173.
60 Ibid., p. 175ff.
61 Ibid., p. 177.
62 See Aikema and Meijers (1989), pp. 131–48.
63 Luther, *Table Talk* DCLI; trans. Hazlitt (1995).
64 See Linder (1934), p. 721.
65 Ibid.
66 Luther, *Table Talk* DCCXXXIX; trans. Hazlitt (1995).
67 Linder (1934), p. 721.
68 Labisch (1992a), pp. 67f.
69 See Rommel (1997), p. 104.
70 Ibid., pp. 102–8.
71 On this aspect, see also Rommel (1997), pp. 104–7.
72 On the notion of a 'demystification' of death, see Labisch (1992b), p. 87.
73 See Bousquet (1985), pp. 9–12.
74 Ibid., pp. 125–254.

Philosophy of health and prophylaxis in Venice

75 See Bergdolt (1992b), p. 27.
76 Oswald (1989).
77 Bergdolt (1992b), p. 27.
78 Ibid., pp. 27f.
79 See Bentmann and Müller (1981), pp. 22–4.
80 Ciriacono (1980), pp. 497f.
81 Bergdolt (1992b), pp. 28f.
82 Ibid., p. 29.
83 Ibid., p. 33.
84 See Molmenti (1906), pp. 382–6.
85 Bergdolt (1992b), p. 34.
86 See Weddigen (1997), pp. 113f.
87 Ibid., p. 116.
88 Ibid.
89 On this aspect, see also Jütte (1992), p. 27.
90 Bergdolt (1991a), pp. 19–21.
91 Bergdolt (1992b), p. 30.
92 Ibid., pp. 23f.

93 Ibid., p. 74.
94 Ibid., p. 30.
95 Ibid., p. 31.

Gabriele Zerbi and the *Gerontocomia*

96 Zerbi, *Gerontocomia*; trans. Lind (1988), p. 17.
97 Pliny, *Historia naturalis* 28, 2, 9.
98 Zerbi, *Gerontocomia*; trans. Lind (1988), p. 20.
99 This is a testament to the author's universal education.
100 Zerbi, *Gerontocomia*; trans. Lind (1988), p. 71.
101 Ibid., pp. 87–9.
102 See Burckhardt (1976), pp. 348f.

Paracelsus' teachings on health

103 *Opus Paramirum*, in Paracelsus, *Werke* (1965), vol. 2, p. 2.
104 See Schipperges (1983), pp. 49f.
105 Jacobi (1991), p. 128.
106 Paracelsus, *Werke* (1965), vol. 2, p. 463.
107 See Schipperges (1993a), pp. 247f.
108 *Herbarius*, in Paracelsus, *Werke* (1965), vol. 1, p. 248.
109 Ibid.; here we are reminded of Poggio Bracciolini's reports concerning the books he found in monasteries in the vicinity of Lake Constance or of Vasari's account of the origins of the 'Gothic' style in architecture.
110 *Archidoxon*, in Paracelsus, *Werke* (1965), vol. 1, pp. 433ff.
111 See Schipperges (1993a), pp. 41f.
112 *Paragranum*, in Paracelsus, *Werke* (1965), vol. 1, p. 504.
113 See Schipperges (1993a), p. 44.
114 *Liber de longa vita*, in Paracelsus, *Werke* (1965), vol. 1, p. 471.
115 Ibid., pp. 477f.
116 See Schipperges (1993a), p. 46.
117 Pagel (1993), p. 27.
118 See Schipperges (1993a), p. 249.
119 Ibid., pp. 252f.
120 *Liber de longa vita*, in Paracelsus, *Werke* (1965), vol. 1, p. 483.
121 See Schipperges (1993a), pp. 252ff.
122 See Benzenhöfer (1993), p. 14; on the *entia*, see *Opus paramirum*, in *Werke* (1965), vol. 2, pp. 183ff.
123 See Benzenhöfer (1993), pp. 14f.
124 Jacobi (1991), p. 128.

Herbal books

125 See Stoffler (1996), pp. 7f. and 21ff.
126 On Hildegard of Bingen, see Fehringer (1994).
127 Bergdolt (1992c), pp. 203f.
128 Ackerknecht (1973).
129 Ibid., pp. 62f.
130 See Müller (1988).
131 Bergdolt (1992c).
132 See Heilmann (1973), p. 15; also von Engelhardt (1995).
133 Müller (1988), p. 27.
134 Ibid., p. 28.
135 See Heilmann (1973), p. 31; on herbal books, see also Müller-Jahncke and Friedrich (1996), p. 50.
136 Heilmann (1973), p. 37.
137 Levi d'Ancona (1983).
138 Heilmann (1973), p. 307.
139 Müller-Jahncke and Friedrich (1996), pp. 60f.
140 Heilmann (1973), p. 307.

Dietetics in daily life

141 Cardano (1969), pp. 30f.
142 Ibid., p. 31.
143 Ibid., p. 32.
144 Pontormo (1984).
145 On this aspect, see Jütte (1991), p. 90.
146 See Jütte (1991), p. 91.
147 Ibid., p. 60.
148 Ibid., p. 62f.
149 Ibid., p. 64.
150 See Hahn and Schönfels (1986), pp. 74ff.
151 Jütte (1991), pp. 76ff.
152 Telle (1988), pp. 44f.
153 Müller-Jahncke and Friedrich (1996), p. 58.

6 Dietetics in the Seventeenth Century

Cartesianism and conservative tendencies

1 Cuffe (1607), p. 71.
2 Wimmer (1991), pp. 22f.
3 See Bacon (1871), p. 132.
4 Ibid.
5 Müller (1988), p. 39.

6 Hooke (1968), p. 58.
7 Vigarello (1993), pp. 91f.
8 Ibid., p. 92.
9 See Schipperges (1993b), p. 48f.
10 Gracián (1993), p. 51.
11 Ibid., pp. 108–9.
12 Ibid., p. 109.
13 Ibid., p. 117.
14 See Aristotle, *Nicomachean Ethics* 1106b.
15 See Trevisani (1982), p. 202; Jütte (1997), p. 43.
16 See Labisch (1992b), pp. 89f.
17 Descartes (1988), pp. 118–19.
18 Ibid., p. 119.
19 Pagel (1986), pp. 489f.
20 Premuda (1996), pp. 134f.
21 See Berghoff (1947), p. 66.
22 On Santorio, who also demonstrated the 'perspiratio insensibilis', see Castiglioni (1920).
23 Toellner (1971), particularly pp. 38–43.
24 See Hartmann (1973), pp. 86f.
25 Ibid., p. 91.
26 Berghoff (1947), p. 66; Hartmann (1973), p. 91.
27 Trevisani (1992) deals with this in great detail.
28 Pascal (1962), p. 225.
29 Ibid., p. 166.
30 Ibid., p. 164.
31 Ibid., p. 211.
32 Bousquet (1985), pp. 210ff.
33 See Ebert-Schifferer (1992), pp. 156–9.
34 See Bredekamp (1993), p. 50.
35 Ibid.
36 Yates (1972).
37 Peuckert (1973).
38 See Roob (1996), pp. 8ff.
39 Vigarello (1993), p. 103.
40 On 'acidia', see p. 113.
41 Gaukroger (1995), pp. 16–19.
42 See Birchler (1975), p. 80.
43 Ibid., pp. 50f.
44 Levack (1987), p. 102.

Ven Helmont, Sylvius and other 'iatrochemists'

45 See Rossi (1997), p. 272.
46 See Berghoff (1947), p. 62.

47 Pagel (1982), pp. 96–103; Hartmann (1973), p. 90.
48 Berghoff (1947), pp. 63f.
49 Pagel (1982), p. 195.
50 Berghoff (1947), p. 63.
51 On gas, see van Helmont, *Ortus medicinae* (1648), pp. 73–81; on sulphur, mercury etc., ibid., pp. 70f.
52 Pagel (1986), pp. 46f.
53 Pagel (1982), pp. 20f.
54 See Berghoff (1947), pp. 64f.
55 King (1970), pp. 104f.
56 See Bergdolt (1994).
57 Wimmer (1991), pp. 22–4.

Doctrines of health in England – the dietetics of the state

58 Harrington (1992), p. 161.
59 See Hartmann (1973), p. 166f.
60 See Wahrig-Schmitt (1996).
61 Burton (1932), vol. 1, p. 134.
62 Ibid., vol. 1, p. 20.
63 Ibid., vol. 1, p. 301.
64 Ibid.
65 Ibid., vol. 1, p. 305.
66 Ibid., vol. 1, p. 178.
67 Ibid., vol. 1, p. 67.
68 Ibid., vol. 1, p. 225.
69 Ibid., vol. 1, p. 40.
70 Ibid., vol. 1, p. 108.
71 Ibid., vol. 1, p. 105.
72 Ibid., vol. 1, p. 213.
73 Ibid., vol. 1, p. 236.
74 See Isler (1968).
75 French and Wear (1989), p. 296.
76 Isler (1968).
77 Ibid.
78 See Harley (1989), p. 121.
79 Isler (1968).
80 Cunningham's translation of Sydenham's Latin text. See Cunningham (1989), p. 178.
81 Ibid., p. 164.
82 Ibid., p. 179.
83 See King (1970), pp. 145–60.
84 Dewhurst (1966), p. 59.
85 Ibid., p. 168.
86 Hartmann (1973), pp. 164f.

87 Locke (1964), p. 25.
88 Ibid., p. 29.
89 Ibid., p. 31.
90 Ibid., p. 36.
91 Ibid., p. 28.
92 Ibid., p. 29.
93 Toellner (1967), p. 131.
94 Henry (1989), pp. 101–3.
95 Harley (1989), pp. 116f.

Health through planning – the utopias

96 One thinks here of the criticisms of Pascal or Stensen.
97 See Hartmann (1973) pp. 178f.
98 On Frank, see pp. 247f. It should be noted that *Polizey* and its English cognate 'police' were in former times much closer in meaning to their Greek root 'politeia', and were used to refer to all matters relating to the internal governance of a state and the wellbeing of its citizens.
99 See Forster (1995), pp. 70–3.
100 Ibid.
101 Swift (1994), p. 297.
102 Ibid., p. 298.
103 For a detailed account of this, see Siefert (1970), pp. 24–41.
104 Ibid., p. 33.
105 See Campanella (1981).
106 See Bergdolt (1994), pp. 21–6. The ancient miasmata theory still held good in the seventeenth century.
107 More (2003), p. 83.
108 Ibid., p. 79.
109 Andreae, *Christianopolis*, ch. 98.
110 See Kohler (1979); on Colbert, see Friedell (1965), pp. 513–15.
111 See Kohler (1979).
112 See Hartmann (1973), pp. 186f.

The dietetics of the Enlightenment – philosophers, pedagogues, charlatans

113 See Hartmann (1973), pp. 167f.
114 See Leibniz, *Monadology*, ch. 18.
115 Ibid., ch. 63.
116 Ibid., ch. 64.
117 See Seidler (1975), p. 13.
118 Serna (1996), p. 87.
119 Montesquieu, *The Spirit of the Laws*.
120 See Foucault (1994), p. 80.

121 Ariès (1996).
122 Seidler (1975), p. 101.
123 Westphal (1964), p. 31.
124 On Faust, see ibid., p. 32.
125 See Rudolf (1969), p. 48.
126 See Kant (1963), p. 3.
127 See Schipperges (1994b), pp. 61f.

7 Doctrines of Health in the Eighteenth Century

Medical theories of health

1 See Rudolf (1995), pp. 117f.
2 See Boschung (1996).
3 See Lindeboom (1968), pp. 73, 250.
4 Ibid., p. 298.
5 See Müller (1991), p. 29.
6 Ibid., pp. 108f.
7 See Wahrig-Schmidt (1991).
8 See Müller (1991), pp. 178–88.
9 Ibid., p. 260.
10 See Glauer (1976), p. 17.
11 See Müller (1991), p. 256.
12 See Hartmann (1973), p. 92.
13 See Boschung (1996), p. 241.
14 See Jauch Staffelbach (1995); on the quarrel between Haller and La
   Mettrie, see Toellner (1967).
15 See Benzenhöfer and vom Bruch (1995), p. 18.
16 Ibid., p. 32.
17 Ibid., pp. 144–8.
18 Ibid., p. 92.
19 See Glauer (1976), p. 114.
20 Hartmann (1973), p. 91.
21 See Rothschuh (1978), pp. 294–8; for background information on Stahl,
   see Geyer-Kordesch (1987).
22 See van Spijk (1991), pp. 38f.; Hartmann (1973), p. 95.
23 Hartmann (1973), p. 95.

The French Enlightenment and Rousseau

24 See Rudolf (1995).
25 Hartmann (1973), pp. 113ff.
26 Rousseau (1966), p. 23.
27 Rudolf (1969), p. 35.
28 Rousseau (1966), p. 23.

29 Ibid, p. 22.
30 Ibid.
31 Ibid., p. 23.
32 Ibid., p. 165.
33 Ibid., p. 91. Rousseau is referring here to Montaigne.
34 Ibid., p. 92.
35 Ibid., p. 97.
36 Rudolf (1969), pp. 36f.
37 Ibid., p. 37.
38 See Lepenies (1989), pp. 8, 16.
39 On Malthus, see Glass (1953).
40 Foucault (1994), pp. 68f.
41 Ibid., p. 69.
42 See Vigarello (1993), pp. 145f.
43 Ibid., p. 146.
44 Ibid., pp. 142–8.
45 See Wimmer (1991), p. 17.

Tissot, Triller, Mai: health education at grassroots

46 See Glauer (1976), pp. 131f.
47 See Marti (1993), pp. 108–10; Glauer (1976), pp. 17f.
48 Glauer (1976), p. 18.
49 'Sanctorius' is Santorio, who discovered the 'perspiratio insensibilis'.
50 Glauer (1976), pp. 54–9.
51 Ibid., p. 108.
52 See Labisch (1992a), pp. 92f.
53 See Imhof (1990), pp. 92f.
54 See Seidler (1975), pp. 33–62.
55 See Foucault (1994), pp. 54–62.

Public health care

56 See Karenberg (1998), pp. 9f.
57 Hartmann (1973), p. 121.
58 Wimmer (1991), p. 15.
59 Ibid., p. 16.
60 See Foucault (1994), pp. 26f.
61 See Wimmer (1991), p. 19.
62 Ibid., p. 20.
63 Foucault (1994), p. 35.
64 Wimmer (1991), pp. 25–7.
65 See Süßmilch (1741).
66 Wimmer (1991), p. 26.
67 Hartmann (1973), p. 184.

8 Around 1800

The notion of 'Lebenskraft (vital force) – Hufeland and Kant

1   See Hufeland (1984), p. 126.
2   Ibid., pp. 20–4.
3   Ibid., pp. 34–41.
4   Ibid., p. 46.
5   See von Engelhardt (1997), p. 161.
6   Ibid., pp. 160f.
7   See Kielmeyer (1993).
8   See Rothschuh (1978), pp. 323–30.
9   See Hartmann (1973), p. 93.
10   Zaunick (1960), p. 17.
11   Hufeland (1984), p. 52n.
12   Seidler (1968), p. 36.
13   Ibid., p. 37.
14   Hufeland (1984), pp. 130f.
15   Ibid., p. 133.
16   On this issue, see also van Spijk (1991), p. 44.
17   Hufeland (1984), p. 181.
18   Hufeland (1812), p. 20.
19   Ibid., p. 21.
20   Kant, cited in Hufeland (1984), pp. 232f.
21   Ibid., pp. 236f.
22   Ibid., pp. 243–5.
23   See Hegel, 'Der animalische Prozeß' in *Jenaer Realphilosophie* (1805).

The recurrent topic of a dietetic regime for intellectuals

24   Hufeland (1984), p. 126.
25   Ibid., p. 246.
26   Rousseau (1997), p. 96.
27   Ibid., pp. 97f.
28   Ibid., pp. 99f.
29   Kümmel (1987), pp. 58f.
30   Ibid.
31   Ibid.
32   See Seidler (1975), pp. 67–77.

Alternative paths to health

33   Rothschuh attempted to introduce the term 'naturism' for the attempts to imitate a life lived in accordance with nature; see Rothschuh (1983), pp. 9–15.

34 Ibid., pp. 42f.
35 See Petrarch, *De vita solitaria* I; also Bergdolt (1992a), p. 52.
36 See Rothschuh (1986), pp. 48f.
37 Ibid., p. 50.
38 Ibid., p. 51.
39 See Hahn and Schönfels (1986), pp. 82f.
40 Ibid.
41 Ibid., p. 59.
42 Ibid., pp. 78f.
43 For example, Hans Sachs's 'Junkprunn'.
44 See Hahn and Schönfels (1986).
45 See Vigarello (1992), p. 33.
46 Ibid., pp. 56f.
47 See Rothschuh (1983), pp. 54f.
48 See Keil (1988), p. 253.
49 Vigarello (1992), p. 141.
50 Louis-Charles-Henri Macquart, *Manuel sur les propriétés de l'eau* (Paris, 1783).
51 On this point, see Schott (1998), pp. 296–328.
52 Ibid., p. 303.
53 Ibid., p. 309.
54 See Dieckhöfer (1985), p. 37.
55 Dieckhöfer (1985), p. 39.
56 Rothschuh (1983), p. 60.

Goethe

57 See Novalis (1929), p. 345.
58 See Nager (1990), pp. 24–39.
59 On this aspect, see Schipperges (1996), p. 23.
60 Letter to Friedrich Wilhelm Riemer of 6 December 1807.
61 See Schipperges (1996), p. 74.
62 Ibid., p. 80.
63 See Nager (1990), p. 107.

Romantic medicine – Schelling, Carus, Novalis

64 See Gerabek (1995), p. 45.
65 For general information on this aspect, see Toellner (1981).
66 See Rothschuh (1978), p. 243.
67 See Gerabek (1995), pp. 64–7 and 74–7.
68 See Rothschuh (1978), p. 392.
69 See van Spijk (1991), pp. 49f.
70 See Grüsser (1987), pp. 185ff.
71 Ibid., p. 188.

72 See Goethe, *Maximen und Reflexionen* 863.
73 See Rothschuh (1978), p. 393.
74 Ibid., pp. 386f.
75 Carus (1846), p. 1.
76 This topic is dealt with in detail in the 'Symbolik der menschlichen Gestalt' (1852).
77 See Hartmann (1973), p. 69.
78 See Huch (1951), p. 602.
79 See Stubbe (1989–90), p. 45.
80 Ibid., p. 46.
81 The Heidelberg anatomist Friedrich Tiedemann, however, disputed that 'there is an essential difference between negroes and Europeans' (1837); see ibid., p. 47.
82 See van Spijk (1991), p. 50.
83 See Huch (1951), pp. 590f.
84 For more details on this aspect, see Grüsser (1987).
85 See Lammel (1990), p. 73.
86 Ibid.
87 Novalis (1996), Vol. II, pp. 197f. (Fragment 190).
88 Novalis (1929), p. 349.
89 Ibid., p. 354.
90 Ibid., p. 359.
91 Ibid., p. 461.
92 See Schipperges (1985b), p. 202.
93 Novalis (1929), p. 426.

9 The Nineteenth Century

Trends in the nineteenth century

1 See Schipperges (1993b), pp. 67ff.
2 Labisch (1992b), pp. 93ff.
3 On the Hippocratics, see Schöner (1964), pp. 29ff.
4 Seidler (1996), pp. 260ff.
5 See Lesky (1965), pp. 178–86.
6 Ibid., p. 179.
7 Schipperges (1993b), p. 71.
8 See Rothschuh (1978), p. 399.
9 Rothschuh (1978), p. 402.
10 See Sontag (1991), p. 29.
11 Ibid., p. 30.
12 Ibid., p. 33.
13 Ibid., p. 34.
14 See Herzlich and Pierret (1987).
15 Kafka (1953).

16 Herzlich and Pierret (1987).
17 Schipperges (1970), p. 241.

Rudolf Virchow and the dietetics of reason

18 See Andree (1996), pp. 341ff.
19 Ibid., p. 345.
20 Van Spijk (1991), p. 53.
21 Schipperges (1993b), p. 72.
22 For a detailed account, see Schipperges (1985b), pp. 172–9.
23 Sigerist (1952), p. 49.
24 Ibid., pp. 51–3.
25 Ibid., p. 60.
26 See Schipperges (1968), pp. 74ff.
27 Schultz-Schultzenstein (1997), p. 61.
28 Von Siemens (1997), pp. 170–1.
29 Von Pettenkofer (1997), p. 77.
30 Münch (1995), pp. 133–40.
31 Schipperges (1993b), pp. 76ff.
32 Ibid.
33 Ibid., p. 81.

Nietzsche, Schopenhauer and the philosophical critique of positivism

34 Nietzsche (1910), pp. 5–6.
35 See Hick (1998), pp. 2f.
36 Nietzsche (1980).
37 Nietzsche (1996).
38 Hick (1998), pp. 2–3.
39 Nietzsche (1979).
40 Letter to Erwin Rohde from 29 March 1871.
41 Schopenhauer (1895), p. 19.
42 Ibid., p. 8.
43 Ibid., pp. 19–20.
44 Ibid., p. 8.
45 Ibid., pp. 8–9.
46 Marx, *Capital*, vol. 1; quoted here from Fischer (1973), p. 33.

The revolution in nutrition and alternative paths to health

47 See Montanari (1994).
48 Ibid.
49 See, for example, the criticism in Hutten (1911), p. 199.
50 Von Rumohr (1994).
51 Ibid., p. 19.

52 Ibid., pp. 26f.
53 Ibid., pp. 30f.
54 See Vigarello (1993), p. 216.
55 Ibid., p. 234.
56 Ibid., p. 236.
57 Ibid., p. 220.
58 Ibid., p. 221.
59 Münch (1995), pp. 206f.
60 Ibid., p. 209.
61 See Rothschuh (1983), pp. 20f., and Jütte (1996), esp. pp. 117–25.
62 See Rothschuh (1983), p. 62.
63 On this aspect, see Rothschuh (1983), pp. 70–3.
64 For a full history of naturopathy, see ibid. and Dieckhofer (1985).
65 See Rothschuh (1983), pp. 73–5.
66 Ibid., pp. 79–89.
67 On the voluminous amount of literature on this topic, see Winkle (1997), pp. 764–81.
68 Von Siemens (1997), p. 170.

References

Ackerknecht, Erwin H. (1973) *Therapeutics from the Primitives to the 20th Century*. With an appendix: *History of Dietetics*. New York: Hafner Press.

Aelian (1997) *Historical Miscellany* [*Variae historiae*], ed. and trans. H. G. Wilson. Cambridge, MA, and London: Harvard University Press.

Aeschylus (1901) *Tragedies and Fragments*, trans. E. H. Plumptre. London: Isbister.

Aikema, Bernard, and Meijers, Dulcia (1989) 'Gli incurabili', in *Nel regno dei poveri: Arte e storia dei grandi ospedali Veneziani in età moderna, 1474–1797*, ed. B. Aikema and D. Meijers. Venice: Arsenale.

Andree, Christian (1996) 'Die "Zellular-Pathologie" als Basis der modernen Medizin: Rudolf Virchow – Leitfigur einer Epoche', in *Meilensteine der Medizin*, ed. Heinz Schott. Dortmund: Harenberg, pp. 340–6.

Angenendt, Arnold (1995) *Das Frühmittelalter: Die abendlandische Christenheit von 400 bis 900*. 2nd edn, Stuttgart: Kohlhammer.

Angenendt, Arnold (1997) *Heilige und Reliquien: Die Geschichte ihres Kultes vom frühen Christentum bis zur Gegenwart*. Munich: Beck.

Aquinas, Thomas, St (1947) *Summa theologica*, trans. Fathers of the English Dominican Province. New York: Benzinger.

Arbesmann, Rudolph (1954) 'The Concept of Christus Medicus in St Augustine', *Traditio* X (1954), pp. 1–28.

Ariès, Philippe (1996) *Centuries of Childhood*, trans. Robert Baldick. London: Pimlico.

Ariosto, Ludovico (1823–9) *The Orlando Furioso of Ludovico Ariosto*, trans. William Stewart Rose. London: John Murray.

Aristophanes (1967) *The Plays of Aristophanes*, trans. B. Bickley Rogers, 3 vols. London: Heinemann; Cambridge, MA: Harvard University Press.

Aristotle (1959a) *Politics*, trans. H. Rackham, 4 vols. London: Heinemann; Cambridge, MA: Harvard University Press.

Aristotle (1959b) *Problemata*, trans. W. S. Hett, 4 vols. London: Heinemann; Cambridge, MA: Harvard University Press.

Aristotle (1961) *De partibus animalium*, trans. A. L. Peck, 4 vols. London: Heinemann; Cambridge, MA: Harvard University Press.

Aristotle (1962) *Nichomachean Ethics*, trans. H. Rackham, 4 vols. London: Heinemann; Cambridge, MA: Harvard University Press.

Assmann, Jan (1996) *Agypten: Eine Sinngeschichte*. Munich: Hanser.

Assman, Jan (1997) *Das kulturelle Gedächtnis: Schrift, Erinnerung und politische Identität in frühen Hochkulturen*, Munich: Beck.

Aue, Hartmann von (1983) 'The Unfortunate Lord Henry', trans. F. Tobin, in *German Medieval Tales*, ed. F. Gentry. New York: Continuum.

Augustine (1991) *Confessions*. Oxford: Oxford University Press.

Baader, Gerhard (1960) 'Überlieferungsprobleme des Aulus Cornelius Celsus', *Forschung und Fortschritte* 34, pp. 215ff.

Bacon, Francis (1871) 'Of Regiment of Health', in *Bacon's Essays and Colours of Good and Evil*, ed. W. Aldis Wright. London: Macmillan, pp. 131–3.

Bacon, Francis (1996) *Francis Bacon: The Major Works*, ed. Brian Vickers. Oxford: Oxford University Press.

Benedict, St (1949) *The Holy Rule of St Benedict*, trans. B. Verheyen. Atchison, KS.

Bentmann, Reinhard, and Müller, Michael (1981) *Die Villa als Herrschaftsarchitektur: Versuch einer kunst- und sozialgeschichtlichen Analyse*. 2nd edn, Frankfurt am Main: Syndikat.

Benzenhöfer, Udo (ed.) (1993) *Paracelsus*. Darmstadt: Wissenschaftliche Buchgesellschaft.

Benzenhöfer, Udo, and vom Bruch, Gisela (eds) (1995) *Johann Georg Zimmermann: Von der Diät für die Seele*. Hannover: Laurentius.

Bergdolt, Klaus (ed.) (1989a) *Die Pest 1348 in Italien: Fünfzig zeitgenössische Quellen*. Heidelberg: Manutius.

Bergdolt, Klaus (1989b) 'Scholastische Medizin und Naturwissenschaft an der päpstlichen Kurie im ausgehenden 13. Jahrhundert', *Würzburger Medizinhistorische Mitteilungen*, pp. 155–68.

Bergdolt, Klaus (ed.) (1991) *Alvise Cornaro: Vom maßvollen Leben*. Heidelberg.

Bergdolt, Klaus (1992a) *Arzt, Krankheit und Therapie bei Petrarca: Die Kritik an Medizin und Naturwissenschaft im italienischen Frühhumanismus*. Weinheim: VCH, Acta Humaniora.

Bergdolt, Klaus (1992b) 'La vita sobria: Gesundheitsphilosophie und Krankheitsprophylaxe im Venedig des 16. Jahrhunderts', *Medizin, Gesellschaft und Geschichte* 2, pp. 25–42.

Bergdolt, Klaus (1992c) 'Jacobus Theodorus Tabernaemontanus: Ein Arzt und Botaniker des frühen 16. Jahrhunderts', *Würzburger Medizinhistorische Mitteilungen* 1, pp. 201–23.

Bergdolt, Klaus (1994) *Der schwarze Tod in Europa: Die große Pest und das Ende des Mittelalters*. Munich: Beck.

Bergdolt, Klaus (1997) 'Freud im 14. Jahrhundert? Die Gesprächstherapie als literarisches Motiv bei Petrarca', *Schriftenreihe der Deutschen Gesellschaft für Geschichte der Nervenheilkunde* 2, pp. 35–43.

Berghoff, Emanuel (1947) *Entwicklungsgeschichte des Krankheitsbegriffs.* 2nd edn, Vienna.

Berrios, German E., and Porter, Roy (eds) (1995) *A History of Clinical Psychiatry: The Origin and History of Psychiatric Disorders.* London: Athlone.

Beyer, Rolf (1996) *Die andere Offenbarung: Mystikerinnen des Mittelalters.* Wiesbaden: Fourier.

Biedermann, Hans (1972) *Medicina Magica: Metaphysische Heilmethoden in spätantiken und mittelalterlichen Handschriften.* Graz: Akademische Druck- und Verlagsanstalt.

Birchler, Urs Benno (1975) *Der Liebeszauber (Philtrum) und sein Zusammenhang mit der Liebeskrankheit in der Medizin besonders des 16.–18. Jahrhunderts.* Zurich: Juris.

Bitsch, Irmgard (1991) 'Ernährungsempfehlungen in mittelalterlichen Quellen und ihre Beurteilung aus heutiger Sicht', in *Haushalt und Familie in Mittelalter und früher Neuzeit*, ed. Trude Ehlert. Sigmaringen: Thorbecke.

Boethius (1902) *Consolations of Philosophy*, trans. W. V. Cooper. London.

Borst, Arno (1973) *Lebensformen im Mittelalter.* Berlin: Propyläen.

Boschung, Urs (1996) 'Der klinische Unterricht am Krankenbett: Hermann Boerhaave in Leiden', in *Meilensteine der Medizin*, ed. Heinz Schott. Dortmund: Harenberg.

Boskovits, Miklos (1979) 'Gli affreschi del duomo di Anagni', *Paragone Arte* 28.

Bousquet, Jacques (1985) *Malerei des Manierismus: Die Kunst Europas von 1520 bis 1620*, rev. and with a contribution by Curt Grützmacher. Munich: Bruckmann.

Brandenburg, Dietrich (1969) *Priesterärzte und Heilkunst im alten Persien: Medizinisches bei Zarathustra und im Königsbuch des Firdausi.* Stuttgart.

Bredekamp, Horst (1993) *Antikensehnsucht und Maschinenglauben: Die Geschichte der Kunstkammer und die Zukunft der Kunstgeschichte.* Berlin: Wagenbach.

Burckhardt, Jakob (1976) *Die Kultur der Renaissance in Italien: Ein Versuch.* Stuttgart.

Burke, Peter (1996) *The Fortunes of the Courtier: The European Reception of Castiglione's Cortegiano.* University Park: Pennsylvania State University Press.

Burton, Robert (1932) *The Anatomy of Melancholy*, 3 vols. London: J. M. Dent.

Campanella, Tommaso (1981) *The City of the Sun*, trans. A. M. Elliott and R. Millner. London: Journeyman.

Canguilhem, Georges (1989) *The Normal and the Pathological.* New York: Zone Books.

Cardano, Girolamo (1969) *Lebensbeschreibung*. Munich.

Carus, Carl Gustav (1846) *Psyche*. Pforzheim.

Cassian, John (1999) *The Monastic Institutes*, trans. Jerome Bertram. London: St Austin Press.

Castiglioni, Arturo (1920) *La vita e l'opera di Santorio Santorio Capodistriano*. Bologna and Trieste.

Castiglione, Baldassare (1996) *The Book of the Courtier*, trans. T. Hoby, with an introduction by W. H. D. Rouse. London and New York: Dent.

Celsus (1971–94) *On Medicine I–VIII*, ed. W. G. Spencer, 3 vols. Cambridge, MA.

Chartier, Roger (1992) *L'uomo dell'illuminismo*. Rome and Bari.

Chartier, Roger (1994) 'Zeit der Zweifel: Zum Verstandnis gegenwartiger Geschichtsschreibung', in *Geschichte schreiben in der Postmoderne: Beiträge zur aktuellen Diskussion*, ed. Christoph Konrad and Martina Kessel. Stuttgart: Reclam, pp. 83–97.

Cicero (1964) *Cato Maior de senectute*, trans. W. A. Falconer. London: Heinemann; Cambridge, MA: Harvard University Press.

Cicero (1966) *Tusculan Disputations*, trans. J. E. King. London: Heinemann; Cambridge, MA: Harvard University Press.

Ciriacono, Salvatore (1980) 'Scrittori d'idraulica e politica delle acque', in *Storia della cultura veneta*, vol. 3, pt II: *Dal primo quattrocento al consilio di Trento*. Vicenza: N. Pozza, pp. 490–512.

Cohn-Haft, L. (1956) *The Public Physicians of Ancient Greece*. Northampton, MA: Smith College.

Cuffe, Henry (1607) *The Differences of the Ages of Mans Life: Together with the Originall Causes, Progresse, and End Therof*. London.

Cunningham, Andrew (1989) 'Thomas Sydenham: Epidemics, Experiment and the "Good Old Cause"', in *The Medical Revolution of the Seventeenth Century*, ed. Roger French and Andrew Wear. Cambridge: Cambridge University Press.

Decker, Wolfgang (1995) *Sport in der griechischen Antike: Vom minoischen Wettkampf bis zu den Olympischen Spielen*. Munich: Beck.

Descartes, René (1988) *Selected Philosophical Writings*, trans. John Cottingham, Robert Stoothoff and Dugald Murdoch. Cambridge: Cambridge University Press.

Dewhurst, Kenneth (1966) *Dr. Thomas Sydenham (1624–1689): His Life and Original Writings*. London: Wellcome Historical Medical Library.

Dieckhofer, Klemens (1982–3) 'Zur Rolle einer Psychohygiene im Griechenland des 5. vorchristlichen Jahrhunderts bis zur Zeitenwende', *Clio Medica* 17, pp. 81–94.

Dieckhofer, Klemens (1985) *Kleine Geschichte der Naturheilkunde*. Stuttgart.

Dieckhofer, Klemens (1990) 'Grundzüge der Geschichte der Naturheilkunde und Naturheilverfahren', in *Lehrbuch der Naturheilverfahren I*, ed. Klaus-Christof Schimmel. 2nd edn, Stuttgart: Hippokrates Verlag, pp. 46–94.

Diller, Hans (1973) *Kleine Schriften zur antiken Medizin*, ed. Gerhard Baader and Hermann Grensemann. Berlin and New York.

Diller, Hans (1994) *Hippokrates: Ausgewahlte Schriften*, with a bibliographical appendix by K. H. Leven. Stuttgart.

Diodorus Siculus (1961), *The Library of History Books*, trans. C. H. Oldfather, 4 vols. London: Heinemann; Cambridge, MA: Harvard University Press.

Diogenes Laertius (1995) *Lives of Eminent Philosophers*, trans. R. D. Hicks, 2 vols. London: Heinemann; Cambridge, MA: Harvard University Press.

Dominici, Giovanni (1860) *Regola del governo di cura familiare*. Florence.

Dörner, Klaus (1969) *Bürger und Irre: Zur Sozialgeschichte und Wissenschaftssoziologie der Psychiatrie*. Frankfurt am Main.

Eamon, William, and Keil, Gundolf (1986) 'Plebs amat empirica: Nicholas of Poland and his Critique of the Medieval Medical Establishment', *Sudhoffs Archiv* 70, pp. 180–96.

Ebert-Schifferer, Sybille (1991) *Il Guercino 1591–1666: Ausstellungskatalog (Bologna–Frankfurt)*. Bologna.

Edelstein, Ludwig (1966) 'Antike Diätetik', *Medizinhistorisches Journal* 1 (1966), pp. 162–74.

The Edwin Smith Surgical Papyrus (1930), trans. James Henry Breasted, 2 vols. Chicago: University of Chicago Oriental Institute.

Einhard (1880) *The Life of Charlemagne*, trans. S. E. Turner. New York: Harper.

Engelhardt, Dietrich von (1995) 'Luca Ghini (um 1490–1556) und die Botanik des 16. Jahrhunderts: Leben, Initiativen, Kontakte, Resonanzen', *Medizinhistorisches Journal* 30, pp. 3–49.

Engelhardt, Dietrich von (1997) 'Vitalism between Science and Philosophy in Germany around 1800', *Biblioteca di physis* 5, pp. 157–74.

Engelmann, Ursmar (1977) *Die Monatsbilder von S. Maria del Castello in Mesocco*. Freiburg.

The Epic of Gilgamesh: The Babylonian Epic Poem and other Texts in Akkadian and Sumerian (1999), trans. Andrew George. London: Allen Lane.

Epictetus (1966) *Discourses, Manual, Fragments*, trans. W. A. Oldfather. London: Heinemann; Cambridge, MA: Harvard University Press.

Erman, A. (1923) *Die Literatur der Ägypter*. Leipzig.

Fehringer, Barbara (1994) *Das Speyrer Kräuterbuch mit den Heilpflanzen Hildegards von Bingen: Eine Studie zur mittelhochdeutschen Physica: Rezeption mit kritischer Ausgabe des Textes*. Würzburg: Königshausen & Neumann.

Fichtner, Gerhard (1982) 'Christus als Arzt: Ursprünge und Wirkungen eines Motivs', in *Frühmittelalterliche Studien: Jahrbuch des Instituts für Frühmittelalterforschung der Universität Munster* 16, pp. 1–18.

Ficino, Marsilio (1978) *De vita libri tres*, ed. Felix Klein-Franke. Hildesheim and New York.

Figala, Karin, and Pfohl, Gerhard (1987) 'Benediktinische Medizin', *Studien und Mitteilungen zur Geschichte des Benediktiner-Ordens und seiner Zweige 98*, pp. 239–56.

Fischer, Ernst (1973) *Marx in his own Words*, trans. Anna Bostock. Harmondsworth: Penguin.

Folz, Robert (1984) *Les Saints rois du moyen age en Occident*. Brussels.

Forster, Jean-Paul (1995) 'Santé et maladie: Instruments de la satire de Jonathan Swift', in *Gesundheit und Krankheit im 18. Jahrhundert*, ed. Helmut Holzhey and Urs Boschung. Amsterdam: Rodopi.

Foucault, Michel (1994) *The Birth of the Clinic: An Archaeology of Medical Perception*, trans. A. M. Sheridan Smith. New York: Random House.

Foucault, Michel (2006) *History of Madness*, trans. Jonathan Murphy. London: Routledge.

Francis, of Assisi, St (1965) *The Little Flowers of St Francis of Assisi*, ed. and trans. R. Hudleston. New York: Heritage Press.

Frank, Karl Suso (1975) *Frühes Mönchstum im Abendland*, 2 vols. Zurich and Munich.

French, Roger, and Wear, Andrew (eds) (1989) *The Medical Revolution of the Seventeenth Century*. Cambridge: Cambridge University Press.

Friedell, Egon (1965) *Kulturgeschichte der Neuzeit: Die Krisis der europäischen Seele von der Schwarzen Pest bis zum Ersten Weltkrieg*. Munich.

Gabriel, Astrik L. (1967) *Vinzenz von Beauvais*. Frankfurt am Main.

Gadamer, Hans-Georg (1996) *The Enigma of Health: The Art of Healing in a Scientific Age*, trans. Jason Gaiger and Nicholas Walker. Cambridge: Polity.

Gadamer, Hans-Georg (1998) *The Beginning of Philosophy*, trans. Rod Coltman. New York: Continuum.

Gadebusch Bondio, Mariacarla (1996) 'Heilung des Körpers und Pflege der Schönheit anhand eines venezianischen Rezeptars des 16. Jahrhunderts', in *Kranksein in der Zeit*, ed. H. U. Lammel. Rostock: Institut für Gesundheitswiss, pp. 57–78.

García-Ballester, Luis (1996) *Improving Health: A Challenge to European Medieval Galenism*. Sheffield: European Association for the History of Medicine and Health.

Garin, Eugenio (1961) 'Gli umanisti e la scienza', *Rivista di filosofia 52*, pp. 259–78.

Garin, Eugenio (1983) *Astrology in the Renaissance*, trans. Carolyn Jackson and June Allen, rev. Clare Robertson. London: Routledge & Kegan Paul.

Gaukroger, Stephen (1995) *Descartes: An Intellectual Biography*. Oxford: Clarendon Press.

Genschorek, Wolfgang (1989) *Carl Gustav Carus: Arzt, Kunstler, Naturforscher*. Frankfurt am Main: Wötzel.

Gerabek, Werner E. (1995) *Friedrich Wilhelm Joseph Schelling und die Medizin der Romantik: Studien zu Schellings Würzburger Periode*. Frankfurt am Main: Lang.

Geyer-Kordesch, Johanna (1987) 'Georg Ernst Stahl: Pietismus, Medizin und Aufklärung in Preußen im 18. Jahrhundert'. Dissertation, Münster.

Glass, David V. (ed.) (1953) *Introduction to Malthus*. London: Watts & Co.

Glauer, Reiner (1976) 'Gesundheitserziehung durch Ärzte als naturrechtlich begründetes Programm aufgeklärter Medizin im 18. Jahrhundert'. Dissertation, Hannover.

Grabar, Andre (1967) *Die Kunst des frühen Christentums von den ersten Zeugnissen christlicher Kunst bis zur Zeit Theodosius 1*. Munich.

Gracián, Baltasar (1993) *The Art of Worldly Wisdom: A Pocket Oracle*, trans. Christopher Maurer. London: Heinemann.

Grensemann, Hermann (1975) *Knidische Medizin*, Teil 1: *Die Testimonien zur ältesten knidischen Lehre und Analysen knidischer Schriften im Corpus Hippocraticum*. Berlin and New York.

Grüsser, Otto-Joachim, *Justinus Kerner 1786–1862: Arzt, Poet, Geisterseher*. Berlin, Heidelberg and New York: Springer.

Gurevic, A. J. (1997) *Stumme Zeugen des Mittelalters: Weltbild und Kultur der einfachen Menschen*. Weimar, Cologne and Vienna: Böhlau.

Haage, Bernhard D. (1992) *Studien zur Heilkunde im 'Parzival' Wolframs von Eschenbach*. Göppingen: Kümmerle.

Hagenmeyer, Christa (1995) *Das Regimen Sanitatis Konrads von Eichstatt: Quellen, Texte, Wirkungsgeschichte*. Stuttgart: Steiner.

Hahn, Gernot von, and Schönfels, Hans-Kaspar von (1986) *Von der Heilkraft des Wassers: Eine Kulturgeschichte der Brunnen und Bäder*. Augsburg.

Hampel, Jürgen (1982) *Medizin der Zoroastrier im vorislamischen*. Husum.

Hardt, Manfred (1996) *Geschichte der italienischen Literatur: Von den Anfängen bis zur Gegenwart*. Darmstadt.

Harig, Georg (1974) *Bestimmung der Intensität im medizinischen System Galens: Ein Beitrag zur theoretischen Pharmakologie, Nosologie und Therapie in der Galenischen Medizin*. Berlin.

Harley, David (1989) 'Mental Illness, Magical Medicine and the Devil in Northern England 1650–1700', in *The Medical Revolution of the Seventeenth Century*, ed. Roger French and Andrew Wear. Cambridge: Cambridge University Press, pp. 114–44.

Harnack, Adolf von (1892) *Medizinisches aus der ältesten Kirchengeschichte*. Leipzig, pp. 37–152.

Harrington, James (1992) *The Commonwealth of Oceana and A System of Politics*, ed. J. G. A. Pocock. Cambridge: Cambridge University Press.

Hartmann, Fritz (1973) *Ärztliche Anthropologie: Das Problem des Menschen in der Medizin der Neuzeit*. Bremen.

Heiler, Friedrich (1982) *Die Religionen der Menschheit*, ed. Kurt Goldammer. Stuttgart.

Heilmann, Karl Eugen (1973) *Kräuterbücher in Bild und Geschichte*. 2nd edn, Munich.

Heller, Agnes (1978) *Renaissance Man*, trans. Richard E. Allen. London: Routledge & Kegan Paul.

Helmont, Johannes Baptist van (1948) *Ortus medicinae id est initia physicae inaudita: Progressus medicinae novus in morborum ultionem ad vitam longam*. Amsterdam.

Henry, John (1989) 'The Matter of Souls: Medical Theory and Theology in Seventeenth-Century England', in *The Medical Revolution of the Seventeenth Century*, ed. Roger French and Andrew Wear. Cambridge: Cambridge University Press, pp. 87–113.

Herles, Helmut (1992) *Von Geheimnissen und Wundern des Caesarius von Heisterbach*. 3rd edn, Bonn: Bouvier.

Herodotus (1996), *Histories*, trans. George Rawlinson. Ware, Hertfordshire: Wordsworth Classics.

Herzlich, Claudine, and Pierret, Janine (1987) *Illness and Self in Society*, trans. Elborg Forster. Baltimore and London: Johns Hopkins University Press.

Hesiod (1964) *The Homeric Hymns and Homerica*, trans. Hugh G. Evelyn-White. London and Cambridge, MA.

Hick, Christian (1998) 'Denken als Symptom – Symptome als Gedanken: Zur Kreisgestalt von Nietzsches "großer Gesundheit" ', *Nietzsche-Forschung 5*.

Highet, Gilbert (1957) *Römisches Arkadien: Dichter und ihre Landschaft: Catull–Vergil–Properz–Horaz–Tibull–Ovid–Juvenal*. Munich.

Hippocrates (1962–97) *Hippocrates*, trans. W. H. S. Jones (I, II, IV), E. T. Withington (III), W. D. Smith (VII), 7 vols. London and Cambridge, MA.

Hobbes, Thomas (1996) *Leviathan*, ed. Richard Tuck. Cambridge and New York: Cambridge University Press.

The Holy Qur'an: Text, Translation and Commentary (1987), trans. A. Yusuf Ali. Elmhurst, NY: Tahrike Tarsile Qur'an.

Hooke, Robert (1968) *The Diary of Robert Hooke M.A., M.D., F.R.S., 1672–1680*, ed. Henry W. Robinson and Walter Adams. London: Wykeham.

Horace (1970) *Satires, Epistles, Ars Poetica*, trans. H. Rushton Fairclough. London: Heinemann; Cambridge, MA: Harvard University Press.

Hossenfelder, Malte (1996) *Antike Glückslehren*. Stuttgart: Kröner.

Huch, Ricarda (1951) *Die Romantik: Blütezeit, Ausbreitung und Verfall*. Tübingen.

Hufeland, Christoph Wilhelm (1812) *Geschichte der Gesundheit nebst einer physischen Charakteristik des jetzigen Zeitalters*. Berlin.

Hufeland, Christoph Wilhelm (1984) *Makrobiotik, oder Die Kunst, das menschliche Leben zu verlängern. Mit einem Brief Immanuel Kants an den Autor*. Frankfurt am Main.

Hurry, Jamieson B. (1928) *Imhotep the Vizier and Physician of King Zozer and afterwards the Egyptian God of Medicine*. Oxford.

Hutten, Ulrich von (1911) 'Über die wunderbare Heilkraft des Guajak-Holzes und die Heilung der Franzosenkrankheit', in Hutten, *Die Schule des Tyrannen: Lateinische Schriften*, ed. Martin Treu. Leipzig, pp. 207–95.

Imhof, Arthur E. (1990) *Geschichte sehen: Fünf Erzahlungen nach historischen Bildern*. Munich: Beck.

Isler, Hansruedi (1968) *Thomas Willis, 1621–1675, Doctor and Scientist*. New York and London: Hafner.

Isocrates (1962) *Orations*, trans. G. Norlin. London: Heinemann; Cambridge, MA: Harvard University Press.

Jacobi, Jolande (1991) *Paracelsus: Arzt und Gottsucher an der Zeitenwende*. Olten: Walter.

Jaeger, Werner (1963) *Diokles von Karystos: Die griechische Medizin und die Schule des Aristoteles*. 2nd edn, Berlin.

Jaspers, Karl (1997) *General Psychopathology*, trans. J. Hoenig and M. W. Hamilton, 2 vols. Baltimore: Johns Hopkins University Press.

Jauch Staffelbach, Ursula Pia (1995) 'Krankheit als Metapher: Neue Überlegungen zu einer alten Querelle: Julien Offray de La Mettrie und Albrecht von Haller', in *Gesundheit und Krankheit im 18. Jahrhundert*, ed. Helmut Holzhey and Urs Boschung. Amsterdam: Rodopi, pp. 141–56.

Jouanna, Jacques (1996) 'Hippocrate et les Problemata d'Aristote: Essai de comparaison entre Airs, Eaux, Lieux, c. 10; Aphorismes III, 11–14 et Problemata I, 8–12 et 19–20', in *Hippokratische Medizin und antike Philosophie*, ed. Renate Wittern and Pierre Pellegrin. Hildesheim: Olms-Weidmann, pp. 273–93.

Jütte, Robert (1991) *Ärzte, Heiler und Patienten: Medizinischer Alltag in der frühen Neuzeit*. Munich: Artemis & Winkler.

Jütte, Robert (1992) 'The Social Construction of Illness in the Early Modern Period', in *The Social Construction of Illness*, ed. Jens Lachmund and Gunnar Stollberg. Stuttgart: F. Steiner, pp. 23–38.

Jütte, Robert (1996) *Geschichte der Alternativen Medizin: Von der Volksmedizin zu den unkonventionellen Therapien von heute*. Munich: Beck.

Jütte, Robert (1997) 'Therapie im Wandel: Krankheit und Gesundheit im interkulturellen Kontext', *Neue Rundschau* 108, pp. 37–50.

Kafka, Franz (1953) *Letters to Milena*, ed. Willi Haas, trans. Tania Stern and James Stern. London: Secker & Warburg.

Kalthoff, Paul (1938) *Das Gesundheitssystem bei Aristoteles*. Berlin and Bonn.

Kant, Immanel (1963) *On History*, ed. and trans. Lewis White Beck. Indianapolis: Bobbs-Merrill.

Kaufmann, Michael, Kunz, Franz Xaver, Keiser, Heinrich, and Kopp, Karl Alois (eds) (1904) *Ägidius Romanus' de Colonna, Johannes Gersons, Dionys' des Kartäusers und Jakob Sadolets Pädagogische Schriften*. Freiburg.

Keil, Gundolf (1968) 'Die Grazer frühmittelhochdeutschen Monatsregeln und ihre Quellen', in *Fachliteratur des Mittelalters: Festschrift für Gerhard Eis*, ed. G. Keil et al. Stuttgart, pp. 131–46.

Keil, Gundolf (1988) 'Medizinische Bildung und Alternativmedizin', in *Nicht Vielwissen sättigt die Seele: Wissen, Erkennen, Bildung, Ausbildung heute*, ed. Winfried Bohm and Martin Lindauer. Stuttgart.

Keil, Gundolf (1991a) 'Der Hausvater als Arzt', in *Haushalt und Familie in Mittelalter und früher Neuzeit*, ed. Trude Ehlert. Sigmaringen: Thorbecke.

Keil, Gundolf (1991b) 'Möglichkeiten und Grenzen frühmittelalterlicher Medizin', in *Das Lorscher Arzneibuch und die frühmittelalterliche Medizin: Verhandlungen des medizinischen Symposiums im September 1989 in Lorsch*, ed. G. Keil and P. Schnitzer. Lorsch: Laurissa.

Keil, Gundolf (1994) 'Das medizinische Weltbild des Nicolaus Copernicus', in *Nicolaus Copernicus (1473–1543): Revolutionär wider Willen*, ed. Gudrun Wolfschmidt. Stuttgart: Verlag für Geschichte der Naturwissenschaft und der Technik, pp. 139–51.

Keil, Gundolf, and Schnitzer, Paul (eds) (1991) *Das Lorscher Arzneibuch und die frühmittelalterliche Medizin: Verhandlungen des medizinhistorischen Symposiums im September 1989 in Lorsch*. Lorsch: Laurissa.

Kielmeyer, Carl Friedrich von (1993) *Über die Verhältniße der organischen Kräfte unter einander in der Reihe der verschiedenen Organisationen*. Marburg: Basilisken Presse.

King, Lester S. (1970) *The Road to Medical Enlightenment, 1650–1695*. London: Macdonald.

Kinkeldey, Otto (1966) *A Jewish Dancing Master of the Renaissance: Guglielmo Ebreo*. New York: Dance Horizons.

Kleist, Heinrich von (1993) *Das Marionettentheater*. Stuttgart: Reclam.

Klibansky, Raymond, Panofsky, Erwin, and Saxl, Fritz (1964) *Saturn and Melancholy: Studies in the History of Natural Philosophy, Religion and Art*. London: Nelson.

Koch, Manfred Peter (1969) 'Das "Erfurter Kartäuserregimen"': Studien zur diätetischen Literatur des Mittelalters'. Dissertation, Bonn.

Koelbing, Huldrych M. (1977) *Arzt und Patient in der antiken Welt*. Zurich and Munich.

Kohler, Wolfgang (1979) *Zur Geschichte und Struktur der utilitaristischen Ethik*. Frankfurt am Main.

Kollesch, Jutta (1989) 'Knidos als Zentrum der frühen wissenschaftlichen Medizin im antiken Griechenland', *Gesnerus* 46, pp. 11–28.

Korbs, Werner (1988) *Vom Sinn der Leibesübungen zur Zeit der italienischen Renaissance*. 2nd edn, Berlin.

Krug, Antje (1993) *Heilkunst und Heilkult: Medizin in der Antike*. 2nd edn, Munich: Beck.

Kudlien, Fridolf (1963) 'Probleme um Diokles von Karystos', *Sudhoffs Archiv* 47, pp. 456–64.

Kudlien, Fridolf (1967) *Der Beginn des medizinischen Denkens bei den Griechen: Von Homer bis Hippokrates*, ed. Olof Gigon. Zurich and Stuttgart.

Kudlien, Fridolf (1968) 'Der Arzt des Körpers und der Arzt der Seele', *Clio Medica* 3, pp. 1–20.

Kudlien, Fridolf (1979) *Der griechische Arzt im Zeitalter des Hellenismus: Seine Stellung in Staat und Gesellschaft*. Mainz.

Kulf, Eberhard (1970) 'Untersuchungen zu Athenaios von Attaleia: Ein Beitrag zur antiken Diätetik'. Dissertation, Göttingen.

Kümmel, Werner Friedrich (1977) *Musik und Medizin: Ihre Wechselbeziehungen in Theorie und Praxis von 800 bis 1800*. Freiburg and Munich.

Kümmel, Werner Friedrich (1987) 'Kopfarbeit und Sitzberuf: Das früheste Paradigma der Arbeitsmedizin', *Jahrbuch des Instituts für Geschichte der Medizin der Robert-Bosch-Stiftung* 6 (1987), pp. 53–70.

Labisch, Alfons (1992a) *Homo hygienicus: Gesundheit und Medizin in der Neuzeit*. Frankfurt am Main: Campus Verlag.

Labisch, Alfons (1992b) 'The Social Construction of Health', in *The Social Construction of Illness*, ed. Jens Lachmund and Gunnar Stollberg. Stuttgart: F. Steiner, pp. 85–101.

Lain Entralgo, Pedro (n.d.) *Heilkunde in geschichtlicher Entscheidung: Einfuhrung in die psychosomatische Pathologie*. Salzburg.

Laing, R. D., and Esterson A. (1964) *Sanity, Madness, and the Family*. London: Tavistock.

Lammel, Hans-Uwe (1990) *Nosologische und therapeutische Konzeptionen in der romantischen Medizin*. Husum: Matthiesen.

Lasson, Adolf (1868) *Meister Eckhart als Mystiker: Eine Darstellung des bedeutenden Mystikers mit einer Einführung in die mittelalterliche Mystik*. Berlin.

Lauer, Hans Hugo (1998) 'Schlafdiätetik im Mittelalter', *Somnologie* 2, pp. 151–62.

Legner, Anton (ed.) (1985) *Ornamenta ecclesiae: Kunst und Künstler der Romanik: Katalog des Schnütgen-Museums*, Vol. 1. Cologne.

Leibniz, Gottfried Wilhelm (1898) *The Monadology and Other Philosophical Writings*, trans. Robert Latta. Oxford: Clarendon Press.

Lemmer, Manfred (1991) 'Haushalt und Familie aus der Sicht der Hausväterliteratur', in *Haushalt und Familie in Mittelalter und früher Neuzeit*, ed. Trude Ehlert. Sigmaringen: Thorbecke.

Lepenies, Wolf (1989) *Gefährliche Wahlverwandtschaften: Essays zur Wissenschaftsgeschichte*. Stuttgart.

Lesky, Erna (1965) *Die Wiener Medizinische Schule im 19. Jahrhundert*, Graz and Cologne.

Levack, Brian P. (1987) *The Witch-Hunt in Early Modern Europe*. London: Longman.

Levi d'Ancona, Mirella (1983) *Botticelli's Primavera: A Botanical Interpretation including Anthropology, Alchemy and the Medici*. Florence: Olschki.

Lindberg, David C. (1992) *The Beginnings of Western Science: The European Scientific Tradition in Philosophical, Religious, and Institutional Context, 600 B.C. to A.D. 1450*. Chicago: University of Chicago Press.

Lindeboom, G. A. (1968) *Herman Boerhaave: The Man and his Work*. London: Methuen.

Linder, Richard (1934) 'Über Aerzte und Aerztliches aus Luthers Tischreden', *Münchner Medizinische Wochenschrift* 81, pp. 719–21.

Little, A. G., and Withington, E. (eds) (1928) *De retardatione: Accidentium senectutis cum aliis opusculis de rebus medicinalibus*. Oxford: Clarendon Press.

Livy (1905) *The History of Rome*, trans. W. M. Roberts. London: Dent.

Locke, John (1964) *Some Thoughts Concerning Education*. London: Heinemann.

López-Salvá, Mercedes (1996) 'Hippokratische Philosophie und aristotelische Handlungsphilosophie: Analogien und Parallelismen', in *Hippokratische Medizin und antike Philosophie*, ed. Renate Wittern und Pierre Pellegrin. Hildesheim: Olms-Weidmann, pp. 203–15.

Lucretius (1966) *De rerum natura* [*On the Nature of Things*], trans. W. H. D. Rouse. London: Heinemann; Cambridge, MA: Harvard University Press.

Luther, Martin (1995) *Table Talk*, ed. Thomas L. Kepler, trans. William Hazlitt. Grand Rapids, MI: Eerdmans.

Macquart, Louis-Charles-Henri (1783) *Manuel sur les propriétés de l'eau*. Paris.

Mai, Franz Anton (1793) *Medicinische Fastenpredigten, oder Vorlesungen über Körper und Seelendiätetik zur Verbesserung der Gesundheit und Sitten*. Mannheim.

Mani, Nikolaus (1959) 'Die Vorstellungen über Anatomie, Physiologie und Pathologie der Leber in der Antike'. Dissertation, Basel.

Marcus Aurelius (1961) *The Communings with Himself*, trans. C. R. Haines. London: Heinemann; Cambridge, MA: Harvard University Press.

Marti, Hanspeter (1995) 'Eine medizinische Schweizer Zeitschrift im Dienst der Aufklärung: Johann Heinrich Rahns Gazette de Santé', in *Gesundheit und Krankheit im 18. Jahrhundert*, ed. Helmut Holzhey and Urs Boschung. Amsterdam: Rodopi, pp. 107–16.

Maul, Stefan M. (1936) 'Medizinische Keilschrifttexte auf Tontafeln', in *Meilensteine der Medizin*, ed. Heinz Schott. Dortmund: Harenberg, pp. 32–9.

Mayer, Bernd M. (1997) 'Das Mittelalterliche Hausbuch: Ein spätmittelalterliches Kleinod auf Schloß Wolfsegg', *Im Oberland* 2, pp. 3–15.

Meyer-Steineg, Theodor (1916) *Das medizinische System der Methodiker: Eine Vorstudie zu Caelius Aurelianus 'De morbis acutis et chronicis'*. Jena.

Michale, Mark S., and Porter, Roy (eds) (1994) *Discovering the History of Psychiatry*. Oxford and New York: Oxford University Press.

Molenaer, Samuel Paul (ed.) (1966) *Li Livres du gouvernement des rois: A XIIIth Century French Version of Egidio Colonna's Treatise De regimine principium*. New York.

Molmenti, Pompeo (1906) *La storia di Venezia nella vita privata, dalle origini alla caduta della repubblica*. 4th edn, 2 vols, Bergamo.

Montanari, Massimo (1994) *The Culture of Food*, trans. Carl Ipsen. Oxford: Blackwell.

Moog, Ferdinand Peter (1994) 'Die Fragmente des Themison von Laodikeia'. Dissertation, Gießen.

More, Thomas (1965) *The Complete Works of St Thomas More*, trans. G. C. Richards, ed. E. Surtz and J. H. Hexter, Vol. 4. New Haven, CT, and London: Yale University Press.

More, Thomas (2003) *Utopia*, trans. Paul Turner. London: Penguin.

Muccini, Ugo, and Cecchi, Alessandro (1991) *Le stanze del principe in Palazzo Vecchio*. Florence.

Müller, Ingo Wilhelm (1991) *Iatromechanische Theorie und ärztliche Praxis im Vergleich zur galenistischen Medizin (Friedrich Hoffmann – Pieter van Foreest – Jan van Heurne)*. Stuttgart: Steiner.

Müller, Irmgard (1988) 'Arzneien für den "gemeinen Mann": Zur Vorstellung materieller und immaterieller Wirkungen stofflicher Substrate in der Medizin des 16. und 17. Jahrhunderts?', in *Pharmazie und der gemeine Mann: Hausarznei und Apotheke in der frühen Neuzeit*, ed. J. Telle. 2nd edn, Weinheim.

Müller, Irmgard (1997) *Die pflanzlichen Heilmittel bei Hildegard von Bingen: Heilwissen aus der Klostermedizin*. Freiburg: Herder.

Müller-Jahncke, Wolf-Dieter, and Friedrich, Christoph (1996) *Geschichte der Arzneimitteltherapie*. Stuttgart: Dt. Apotheker Verlag.

Münch, Ragnhild (1995) *Gesundheitswesen im 18. und 19. Jahrhundert: Das Berliner Beispiel*. Berlin: Akad. Verlag.

Nabavi, Mir-Hossein (1967) *Hygiene und Medizin im Koran*. Stuttgart.

Nager, Frank (1990) *Der heilkundige Dichter: Goethe und die Medizin*. Zurich and Munich: Artemis.

Nauwerck, Arnold (ed.) (1998) *Speisen wie die Äbte und essen wie die Mönche: Ein Mondseer Kochbuch aus dem 15. Jahrhundert und andere Zeugnisse der Küchenkultur des Klosters Mondsee in älteren Zeiten*. Mondsee: privately pubd.

Niehr, Herbert (1991) 'JHWH als Arzt', *Biblische Zeitschrift* new series 35, pp. 3–17.

Nietzsche, Friedrich (1979) *Ecce Homo*. Harmondsworth: Penguin.

Nietzsche, Friedrich (1980) *Morgenröte*. Munich: Goldmann.

Nietzsche, Friedrich (1996) *Human, all too Human*. New York and London: Routledge.

Nietzsche, Friedrich (2000) *The Birth of Tragedy*, trans. and ed. Douglas Smith. Oxford: Oxford University Press.

Novalis (1929) *Fragmente*, ed. Ernst Kamnitzer. Dresden.

Novalis (1996) *Werke*, 2 vols. Cologne.

Ohlmeyer, Albert (1989) 'Die Rechtfertigung der Heilkunde', in *Das Lorscher Arzneibuch: Klostermedizin in der Karolingerzeit*. Lorsch: Laurissa, pp. 48–60.

Oswald, Stefan (1989) *Die Inquisition, die Lebenden und die Toten: Venedigs deutsche Protestanten*. Sigmaringen: Thorbecke.

Ovid (1965) *Ex Ponto; Tristia*, trans. A. L. Wheeler. London: Heinemann; Cambridge, MA: Harvard University Press.

Ovid (1966) *Metamorphoses*, trans. F. J. Miller. London: Heinemann; Cambridge, MA: Harvard University Press.

Ovid (1967) *Fasti*, trans. J. G. Frazer. London: Heinemann; Cambridge, MA: Harvard University Press.

Ovid (1969) *The Art of Love*, trans. J. H. Mozley. London: Heinemann; Cambridge, MA: Harvard University Press.

Pagel, Walter (1982) *Joan Baptista van Helmont: Reformer of Science and Medicine*. Cambridge: Cambridge University Press.

Pagel, Walter (1986) *From Paracelsus to Van Helmont: Studies in Renaissance Medicine and Science*, ed. Marianne Winder. London: Variorum Reprints.

Pagel, Walter (1993) 'Paracelsus als "Naturmystiker"', in *Paracelsus*, ed. Udo Benzenhöfer. Darmstadt: Wissenschaftliche Buchgesellschaft.

Paracelsus [Theophrastus Bombastus von Hohenheim] (1965) *Werke: Medizinische Schriften*, ed. Will-Erich Peuckert, 2 vols. Stuttgart.

Paravicini Bagliani, Agostino (1997) *Der Leib des Papstes: Eine Theologie der Hinfälligkeit*. Munich: Beck.

Pascal, Blaise (1962) *Pensées*, trans. Martin Turnell. London: Harvill Press.

Paul, Norbert, and Schlich, Thomas (eds) (1998) *Medizingeschichte: Aufgaben, Probleme, Perspektiven*. Frankfurt am Main and New York: Campus Verlag.

Pausanias (1966) *Description of Greece*, trans. H. S. Jones, 4 vols. London: Heinemann; Cambridge, MA: Harvard University Press.

Pellegrin, Pierre (1996) 'Aristote, Hippocrate, Oedipe', in *Hippokratische Medizin und antike Philosophie*, ed. Renate Wittern and Pierre Pellegrin. Hildesheim: Olms-Weidmann, pp. 183–98.

Péréz de Urbel, J. (1945) *San Isidoro de Sevilla*. Barcelona.

Pettenkofer, Max von (1997) 'Öffentliche Gesundheitspflege', in *Forschung und Fortschritt: Festschrift zum 175jährigen Jubiläum der Gesellschaft Deutscher Naturforscher und Ärzte*, ed. D. von Engelhardt. Stuttgart: Wiss. Verl.-Ges., pp. 77-91.

Peuckert, Will-Erich (1973) *Das Rosenkreuz*. 2nd edn, Berlin.

Pico della Mirandola, Giovanni, 'Oration on the Dignity of Man', trans. Elizabeth Livermore Forbes, in *The Renaissance Philosophy of Man*, ed. Ernst Cassirer, Paul Oskar Kristeller and John Herman Randall, Jr. Chicago: University of Chicago Press.

Plato (1961) *The Collected Dialogues of Plato*, ed. E. Hamilton. Princeton: Princeton University Press.

Plautus (1963) *Mostellaria* [*The Haunted House*], trans. P. Nixon. London: Heinemann; Cambridge, MA: Harvard University Press.

Pliny (1960–8), *Natural History*, vol. IV, trans. H. Rackham, vol. VIII, trans. W. H. S. Jones. London: Heinemann; Cambridge, MA: Harvard University Press.

Pliny (1969) *Letters and Panegyricus*, trans. B. Radice. London: Heinemann; Cambridge, MA: Harvard University Press.

Plutarch (1968), *Lives*, trans. B Perrin. London: Heinemann; Cambridge, MA: Harvard University Press.

Pollak, Kurt (1969) *Die Heilkunde der Antike: Griechenland–Rom–Byzanz: Die Medizin in Bibel und Talmud*. Wiesbaden.

Pontormo (1984) *Il mio libro*, ed. Salvatore S. Nigro and Enrico Baj. Genoa.

Premuda, Loris (1996) *Da Fracastoro al novecento: Mezzo millenio di medicina a Padova, Trieste e Vienna*. Padua.

Preuss, Julius (1911) *Biblisch-Talmudische Medizin: Beiträge zur Geschichte der Heilkunde und der Kultur überhaupt*. Berlin: Karger.

Rangone, Tommaso (1550) *Thomae philologi Ravennatis medici clarissimi De vita hominis ultra CXX annos protrahenda*. Venice.

Raslan, Usama (1975) 'Über die Erhaltung der Gesundheit: Ein Hygienetraktat von Ali Ibn Sahl Rabban at-Tabari'. Dissertation, Bonn.

Ridder, Paul (1996) *Schön und gesund: Das Bild des Körpers in der Geschichte*. Kassel.

Riha, Ortrun (1985) *Meister Alexanders Monatsregeln: Untersuchungen zu einem spätmittelalterlichen Regimen duodecim mensium mit kritischer Textausgabe*, ed. Gundolf Keil. Pattensen.

Riha, Ortrun (1992) *Wissensorganisation in medizinischen Sammelhandschriften: Klassifikationskriterien und Kombinationsprinzipien bei Texten ohne Werkcharakter*. Wiesbaden: Reichert.

Riha, Ortrun (1996) 'Subjektivität und Objektivität, Semiotik und Diagnostik: Eine Annäherung an den mittelalterlichen Krankheitsbegriff', *Sudhoffs Archiv* 80, pp. 129–49.

Roberts, A., and Donaldson, J. (eds) (1979) *Ante-Nicene Fathers*, vols. 1–5. Grand Rapids, MI: Eerdmans.

Rodenwaldt, Ernst (1968) *Leon Battista Alberti – ein Hygieniker der Renaissance*. Heidelberg.

Rommel, Bettina (1997) *Rabelais zwischen Mündlichkeit und Schriftlichkeit: Gargantua – Literatur als Lebensführung*. Tübingen: Niemeyer.

Ronen, Avraham (1988) 'Gozzoli's St Sebastian Altarpiece in San Gimignano', *Mitteilungen des Kunsthistorischen Instituts in Florenz* 32, pp. 77–126.

Roob, Alexander (1996) *Alchemie und Mystik: Das hermetische Museum*. Cologne: Taschen.

Rossi, Paolo (1997) 'Der Wissenschaftler', in *Der Mensch des Barock*, ed. Rosario Villari. Frankfurt am Main and New York: Campus Verlag.

Rothschuh, Karl Eduard (1965) *Prinzipien der Medizin: Ein Wegweiser durch die Medizin*. Munich and Berlin.

Rothschuh, Karl Eduard (1978) *Konzepte der Medizin in Vergangenheit und Gegenwart*. Stuttgart.

Rothschuh, Karl Eduard (1983) *Naturheilbewegung, Reformbewegung, Alternativbewegungen*. Stuttgart.

Rousseau, Jean-Jacques (1966) *Émile*, trans. Barbara Foxley. London and New York.

Rousseau, Jean-Jacques (1997) 'Preface to *Narcissus*', in *The Discourses and Other Early Political Writings*, ed. and trans. V. Gourevitch. Cambridge: Cambridge University Press.

Rudolf, Gerhard (1969) 'Jean-Jacques Rousseau (1712–1778) und die Medizin', *Sudhoffs Archiv* 53, pp. 30–67.

Rudolf, Gerhard (1995) 'La santé dans l'Encyclopédie de Diderot', in *Gesundheit und Krankheit im 18. Jahrhundert*, ed. Helmut Holzhey and Urs Boschung. Amsterdam: Rodopi, pp. 117–40.

Ruffato, Cesare (ed.) (1996) *La medicina in Roma antica: Il Liber medicinalis di Quinto Sereno Sammonico*. Turin.

Rumohr, Karl Friedrich von (1994) *Geist der Kochkunst*. Heidelberg: Manutius Verlag.

Sandblom, Philip (1990) *Kreativität und Krankheit: Vom Einfluß körperlicher und seelischer Leiden auf Literatur, Kunst und Musik*. Berlin: Springer.

Sauser, Ekkart (1966) *Frühchristliche Kunst: Sinnbild und Glaubensaussage*. Innsbruck, Vienna and Munich.

Sauser, Ekkart (1992) 'Christus Medicus: Christus als Arzt und seine Nachfolger im frühen Christentum', *Trierer theologische Zeitschrift – Pastor Bonus* 101, pp. 101–23.

Schanz, Martin, and Hosius, Carl (1935) *Geschichte der römischen Literatur bis zum Gesetzgebungswerk des Kaisers Justinian*, II: *Die römische Literatur in der Zeit der Monarchie bis auf Hadrian*. 4th edn, Munich.

Scheffer, Thassilo von (1935) *Die Kultur der Griechen*. Vienna and Leipzig.

Schelling, F. W. J. (1988) *Ideas for a Philosophy of Nature*, trans. Errol E. Harris and Peter Heath. Cambridge: Cambridge University Press.

Schipperges, Heinrich (1968) *Utopien der Medizin: Geschichte und Kritik der ärztlichen Ideologie des 19. Jahrhunderts*. Salzburg: O. Müller.

Schipperges, Heinrich (1970) *Moderne Medizin im Spiegel der Geschichte*. Stuttgart: Thieme.

Schipperges, Heinrich (1976) *Arabische Medizin im lateinischen Mittelalter*. Berlin, Heidelberg and New York: Springer.

Schipperges, Heinrich (1978) 'Antike und Mittelalter', in *Krankheit, Heilkunst, Heilung*, ed. H. Schipperges, E. Seidler and Paul U. Unschuld. Freiburg am Breisgau and Munich: Alber.

Schipperges, Heinrich (1983) *Paracelsus: Das Abenteuer einer sokratischen Existenz*. Freiburg am Breisgau: Aurum.

Schipperges, Heinrich (1985a) *Der Garten der Gesundheit: Medizin im Mittelalter*. Munich and Zurich: Artemis.

Schipperges, Heinrich (1985b) *Homo patiens: Zur Geschichte des kranken Menschen*. Munich: Piper.

Schipperges, Heinrich (1987) *Eine 'Summa medicinae' bei Avicenna*. Berlin: Springer.

Schipperges, Heinrich (1990) *Heilkunst als Lebenskunde oder die Kunst, vernünftig zu leben: Zur Theorie der Lebensordnung und Praxis der Lebensführung.* Freudenstadt: VUD.

Schipperges, Heinrich (1993a) 'Die therapeutischen Systeme', in Udo Benzenhöfer (ed.), *Paracelsus.* Darmstadt: Wissenschaftliche Buchgesellschaft.

Schipperges, Heinrich (1993b) *Heilkunde als Gesundheitslehre: Der geisteswissenschaftliche Hintergrund.* Heidelberg: Verlag für Medizin Fischer.

Schipperges, Heinrich (1994a) *Arzt im Purpur: Grundzüge einer Krankheitslehre bei Petrus Hispanus (ca. 1210–1277).* Berlin: Springer.

Schipperges, Heinrich (1994b) *Gute Besserung: Ein Lesebuch über Gesundheit und Heilkunst.* Munich: Beck.

Schipperges, Heinrich (1995a) *Hildegard von Bingen: Healing and the Nature of the Cosmos*, trans. John A. Broadwin. Princeton, NJ: Wiener.

Schipperges, Heinrich (1995b) *Krankheit und Gesundheit bei Moses Maimonides (1138–1204).* Berlin, Heidelberg and New York: Springer.

Schipperges, Heinrich (1996) *Goethe – seine Kunst zu leben.* Frankfurt am Main: Knecht.

Schmitt, Wolfram (1973) 'Theorie der Gesundheit und "Regimen sanitatis" im Mittelalter'. Dissertation, Heidelberg.

Schmitt, Wolfram (1979) 'Gesundheitstheorien in Antike und Mittelalter', in *Medizinische Ökologie*, ed. Maria Blohmke, Heinrich Schipperges and Gustav Wagner. Heidelberg, pp. 19–35.

Schnalke, Thomas, and Selheim, Claudia (1990) *Asklepios: Heilgott und Heilkult.* Erlangen-Nürnberg: Universitätsbibliothek.

Schneider, R. (1957) 'Was hat uns Augustins "Theologia medicinalis" heute zu sagen?' *Kerygma und Dogma* 3, pp. 307–15.

Schnitzler, Arthur (1967) *Ohne Maske: Aphorismen und Notate*, ed. Manfred Diersch. Frankfurt am Main.

Schöffler, Heinz Herbert (1979) *Die Akademie von Gondischapur: Aristoteles auf dem Wege in den Orient.* Stuttgart.

Schöner, Erich (1964) *Das Viererschema in der antiken Humoralpathologie.* Wiesbaden.

Schopenhauer, Arthur (1895) *The Wisdom of Life: Being the first part of Arthur Schopenhauer's 'Aphorismen zur Lebensweisheit'*, trans. T. Bailey Saunders. London.

Schott, Heinz (ed.) (1998) *Der sympathetische Arzt: Texte zur Medizin im 18. Jahrhundert.* Munich: Beck.

Schretter, Manfred K. (1974) *Alter Orient und Hellas: Fragen der Beeinflussungen griechischen Gedankenguts aus altorientalischen Quellen, dargestellt an den Göttern Nergal, Rescheph, Apollon.* Innsbruck.

Schultz-Schultzenstein, Karl Heinrich (1997) 'Über den Einfluß der Medizin auf das materielle Wohl der Völker', in *Forschung und Fortschritt: Festschrift zum 175jährigen Jubiläum der Gesellschaft Deutscher Naturforscher und Ärzte*, ed. D. von Engelhardt. Stuttgart: Wiss. Verl.-Ges.

Schumacher, Joseph (1963) *Antike Medizin: Die naturphilosophischen Grundlagen der Medizin in der griechischen Antike*. 2nd rev. edn, Berlin.

Seidler, Eduard (1975) *Lebensplan und Gesundheitsführung: Franz Anton Mai und die medizinische Aufklärung in Mannheim*. Mannheim.

Seidler, Eduard (1981) 'Heilkunst und Lebensordnung: Die Medizin in der benediktinischen Tradition', *Erbe und Auftrag: Benediktinische Monatsschrift* 57, pp. 18–27.

Seidler, Eduard (1996) 'Anfänge einer sozialen Medizin: Johann Peter Frank und sein "System einer vollständigen medicinischen Policey" ', in Heinz Schott (ed.), *Meilensteine der Medizin*. Dortmund: Harenberg, pp. 258–64.

Seidler, Eduard, and Hilpert, H. (1968) 'Zur Begriffsgeschichte der "Lebensschwache" ', *Fortschritte der Medizin* 86, pp. 35–8.

Seneca (1967) *Moral Epistles*, trans. R. M. Gummere, 3 vols. London: Heinemann; Cambridge, MA: Harvard University Press.

Seneca (1970) *Moral Essays*, trans. J. W. Basore, 3 vols. London: Heinemann; Cambridge, MA: Harvard University Press.

Serna, Pierre (1996) 'Der Adlige', in *Der Mensch der Aufklärung*, ed. Michel Vovelle. Frankfurt am Main and New York: Campus Verlag.

Siefert, Helmut (1970) 'Hygiene in utopischen Entwürfen des 16. und 17. Jahrhunderts', *Medizinhistorisches Journal* 5, pp. 24–41.

Siemens, Werner von (1997) 'Das naturwissenschaftliche Zeitalter', in *Forschung und Fortschritt: Festschrift zum 175jährigen Jubiläum der Gesellschaft Deutscher Naturforscher und Ärzte*, ed. Dietrich von Engelhardt. Stuttgart: Wiss. Verl.-Ges.

Sigerist, Henry (1927) 'Sebastian-Apollo', *Archiv für Geschichte der Medizin* 19, pp. 301–17.

Sigerist, Henry (1952) *Mens sana in corpore sano: Das Gesundheitsideal im Wandel der Jahrhunderte*. Stuttgart.

Sigerist, Henry E. (1960) *On the Sociology of Medicine*, ed. Milton I. Roemer New York: MD Publications.

Sigerist, Henry (1961) *A History of Medicine*, II: *Early Greek, Hindu, and Persian Medicine*. Oxford: Oxford University Press.

Sigerist, Henry E. (1963a) *Der Arzt in der Ägyptischen Kultur*. Zurich.

Sigerist, Henry E. (1963b) *Der Arzt in der Mesopotamischen Kultur*. Zurich.

Sigerist, Henry E. (1967) *A History of Medicine*, I: *Primitive and Archaic Medicine*. Oxford and New York: Oxford University Press.

Siraisi, Nancy G. (1973) *Arts and Sciences at Padua: The Studium at Padua before 1350*. Toronto: Pontifical Institute of Medieval Studies.

Siraisi, Nancy G. (1981) *Taddeo Alderotti and his Pupils: Two Generations of Medical Learning*. Princeton, NJ: Princeton University Press.

Sobel, Hildegard (1990) *Hygieia: Die Göttin der Gesundheit*. Darmstadt: Wissenschaftliche Buchgesellschaft.

Sontag, Susan (1991) *Illness as Metaphor; and AIDS and its Metaphors*. Harmondsworth: Penguin.

Sophocles (1967) *Ajax*, trans. F. Storr, 4 vols. London: Heinemann; Cambridge, MA: Harvard University Press.

Spiegel, Gabrielle M. (1994) 'Geschichte, Historizität und soziale Logik', in *Geschichte schreiben in der Postmoderne: Beiträge zur aktuellen Diskussion*, ed. Christoph Conrad and Martina Kessel. Stuttgart: Reclam, pp. 161–202.

Spijk, Piet van (1991) *Definition und Beschreibung der Gesundheit: Ein medizinhistorischer Überblick*. Muri: Sekretariat SGGP.

Sterpellone, Luciano, and Elsheikh, Mahmoud Salem (1995) *La medicina Araba: L'arte medica nei Califfati d'Oriente e d'Occidente*. Milan: Ciba Edizioni.

Stoffler, Hans-Dieter (1996) *Der Hortulus des Walahfried Strabo: Aus dem Kräutergarten des Klosters Reichenau*. Sigmaringen: Thorbecke.

Stoll, Ulrich (1991) 'Ein Überblick über Herkunft, Inhalt und Anspruch des älteste Arzneibuchs deutscher Provenienz', in *Das Lorscher Arzneibuch*, ed. G. Keil and P. Schnitzer. Lorsch: Laurissa.

Stubbe, Hannes (1989–90) 'Hatten die Germanen graue Augen? Rassenpsychologisches bei Carl Gustav Carns (1789–1869)', *Psychologie und Geschichte* 1, 3, pp. 44–50.

Suetonius (1971), *The Lives of the Caesars*, trans. J. C. Rolfe. London: Heinemann; Cambridge, MA: Harvard University Press.

Süßmilch, Johann Peter (1741) *Die göttliche Ordnung in den Veränderungen des menschlichen Geschlechtes, aus der Geburt, Tod, und Fortpflanzung desselben erwiesen*. Berlin.

Swift, Jonathan (1994) *Gulliver's Travels*. Harmondsworth: Penguin.

Szasz, T. (1982) *Der Mythos der Psychotherapie*. Vienna: Europaverlag.

Tacitus (1942) *Complete Works of Tacitus*, trans. A. J. Church and W. J. Brodribb. New York: Random House.

Tacitus (1963) *Annals*, trans. C. H. Moore. London: Heinemann; Cambridge, MA: Harvard University Press.

Telle, Joachim (1988) 'Arzneikunst und der "gemeine Mann": Zum deutschlateinischen Sprachenstreit in der frühneuzeitlichen Medizin', in *Pharmazie und der gemeine Mann: Hausarznei und Apotheke in der frühen Neuzeit*, ed J. Telle. 2nd edn, Weinheim.

Temkin, Owsei (1991) *Hippocrates in a World of Pagans and Christians*. Baltimore: Johns Hopkins University Press.

Toellner, Richard (1967) 'Anima et irritabilitas: Hailers Abwehr von Animismus und Materialismus', *Sudhoffs Archiv*, pp. 130–44.

Toellner, Richard (1971) 'Die Umbewertung des Schmerzes im 17. Jahrhundert in ihren Voraussetzungen und Folgen', *Medizinhistorisches Journal* 6, pp. 36–44.

Toellner, Richard (1981) 'Schellings Konzeption der Medizin als Wissenschaft', in *Schelling: Seine Bedeutung für eine Philosophie der Natur und Geschichte: Referate und Kolloquien der Internationalen*

Schelling-Tagung Zürich 1979, ed. Ludwig Hasler. Stuttgart: Frommann-Holzboog, pp. 117–28.

Trevisani, Francesco (1982) 'Medizin und Cartesianismus in Deutschland am Ende des 17. und zu Beginn des 18. Jahrhunderts', in *Heilberufe und Kranke im 17. und 18. Jahrhundert*, ed. W. Eckart and J. Geyer-Kordesch. Münster.

Trevisani, Francesco (1992) *Descartes in Germania: La ricezione del cartesianesimo nella Facoltà filosofica e medica di Duisburg (1652–1703)*. Milan.

Trusen, J. P. (1853) *Die Sitten, Gebräuche und Krankheiten der alten Hebräer*. 2nd edn, Breslau.

Ullmann, Manfred (1970) *Die Medizin im Islam*. Leiden and Cologne.

van der Eijk, Philip J. (1996) 'Diodes and the Hippocratic Writings on the Methods of Dietetics and the Limits of Causal Explanation', in *Hippokratische Medizin und antike Philosophie*, ed. Renate Wittern and P. Pellegrin. Hildesheim: Olms-Weidmann, pp. 229–57.

Vigarello, Georges (1992) *Wasser und Seife, Puder und Parfum: Geschichte der Körperhygiene seit dem Mittelalter*. Frankfurt am Main and New York: Campus Verlag.

Vigarello, Georges (1993) *Le Sain et le malsain: Santé et mieux-être depuis le Moyen-Age*. Paris: Seuil.

Virgil (1910) *Aeneid*, trans. T. C. Williams. Boston: Houghton Mifflin.

Vitruvius (1962), *On Architecture*, trans. F. Granger. London: Heinemann; Cambridge, MA: Harvard University Press.

Von Staden, Heinrich (1989) *Herophilus: The Art of Medicine in Early Alexandria*. Cambridge: Cambrige University Press.

Wace, H. (ed.) (1890–) *Nicene and Post-Nicene Fathers*, 2nd ser., 14 vols. Edinburgh: T. & T. Clark; repr. Grand Rapids, MI: Eerdmans.

Wahrig-Schmitt, Bettina (1991) 'Der aufgeklarte Pumpernickel: Friedrich Hoffmann und das Vollkornbrot', in *Philosophischer Taschenkalender: Jahrbuch zum Streit der Fakultäten*, ed. Rudiger Schmidt und Bettina Wahrig-Schmitt. Lübeck: Luciferlag, pp. 73–85.

Wahrig-Schmitt, Bettina (1996) 'Der Staat als Mensch-Maschine'. Dissertation, Lübeck.

Weber, Marga (1996) *Antike Badekultur*. Munich: Beck.

Weddigen, Erasmus (1997) 'Tommaso Rangone "monologus" oder die Profanata Conversazione', in *Kunst und ihre Auftraggeber im 16. Jahrhundert: Venedig und Augsburg im Vergleich*, ed. Klaus Bergdolt and Jochen Brüning. Berlin: Akademie Verlag, pp. 113–32.

Weeber, Karl-Wilhelm (1995) *Alltag im Alten Rom*. Zurich: Artemis.

Weinreich, Otto (1909) *Antike Heilungswunder: Untersuchungen zum Wunderglauben der Griechen und Römer*. Gießen.

Wellmann, Max (1895) *Die pneumatische Schule bis auf Archigenes in ihrer Entwicklung dargestellt*. Berlin.

Westendorf, Wolfhart (1992) *Erwachen der Heilkunst: Die Medizin im Alten Ägypten*. Zurich: Artemis & Winkler.

Westphal, Paul-Gerhard (1964) 'Ärztliche Gesundheitsbelehrung im ausgehenden 18. Jahrhundert'. Dissertation, Heidelberg.

Whipple, Allen O. (1979) *The Role of the Nestorians and Muslims in the History of Medicine*. Princeton: Princeton University Press.

Wiebel, Christiane (1988) *Askese und Endlichkeitsdemut in der italienischen Renaissance: Ikonologische Studien zum Bild des heiligen Hieronymus*. Weinheim.

Wimmer, Johannes (1991) *Gesundheit, Krankheit und Tod im Zeitalter der Aufklärung: Fallstudien aus den habsburgischen Erbländern*. Vienna: Böhlau.

Winkle, Stefan (1997) *Geißeln der Menschheit: Kulturgeschichte der Seuchen*. Düsseldorf: Artemis & Winkler.

Wöhrle, Georg (1990) *Studien zur Theorie der antiken Gesundheitslehre*. Stuttgart: Steiner.

Xenophon (1914) *Cyropaedia*, trans. Walter Miller. Cambridge, MA: Harvard University Press.

Yates, Frances (1972) *The Rosicrucian Enlightenment*. London: Routledge & Kegan Paul.

Zaunick, Rudolph (ed.) (1960) *Johann Christian Reil 1759–1813: Vier auf der Reil-Feier in Halle am 25. Februar 1959 gehaltene Vorträge*. Leipzig.

Zerbi, Gabriele (1988) *Gerontocomia: On the Care of the Aged and Maximianus, Elegies on Old Age and Love*, ed. and trans. L. R. Lind. Philadelphia: American Philosophical Society.

Ziethen, Gabriele (1994) 'Heilung und römischer Kaiserkult', *Sudhoffs Archiv* 78, pp. 171–91.

Zimmermann, Volker (1986) *Rezeption und Rolle der Heilkunde in landessprachigen handschriftlichen Kompendien des Spätmittelalters*. Wiesbaden.

Index